DUMBARTON OAKS STUDIES

⊰ III ⊱

THE HOMILIES OF PHOTIUS
PATRIARCH
OF CONSTANTINOPLE

THE HOMILIES OF PHOTIUS
PATRIARCH
OF CONSTANTINOPLE

*English Translation, Introduction
and Commentary
by*

CYRIL MANGO

WIPF & STOCK · Eugene, Oregon

Wipf and Stock Publishers
199 W 8th Ave, Suite 3
Eugene, OR 97401

The Homilies of Photius, Patriarch of Constantinople
Translation and Commentary
By Mango, Cyril
ISBN 13: 978-1-5326-4138-1
Publication date 9/26/2017
Previously published by Harvard University Press, 1958

The present volume offers an English translation of the Homilies of Photius, Patriarch of Constantinople (856–867, 877–886). The translation of sixteen of the Homilies is based on the edition by Aristarches; that of the remaining two on the edition by G. P. Kournoutos and B. Laourdas. The work is a partial result of a more comprehensive project on Photius' writings initiated by the late Professor A. M. Friend, Jr., former Director of Studies at Dumbarton Oaks. It has not proved feasible to publish a critical edition of the Greek text at this time. Care has been taken, however, by Dr. Mango to check all of Aristarches' emendations, as well as other doubtful passages in his text, against the available manuscripts; wherever the translation here offered departs from the text in the above-mentioned editions, justification is supplied in the footnotes.

THE COMMITTEE ON PUBLICATIONS

Preface

The middle of the ninth century was a particularly momentous period in the history of the Byzantine Empire. It was then that the Iconoclast movement, which had divided Eastern Christendom for over a century, was finally liquidated; that the Slavs were converted to Christianity, thus immeasurably enlarging the orbit of Byzantine cultural influence, and that a renewed interest in classical literature and learning assured the preservation of the ancient Greek heritage. It was also at that time that the growing hostility between the Eastern and Western Churches erupted in the first great schism.

The study of these significant events has made considerable progress in the last two or three decades. Thanks to the work of such outstanding scholars as Henri Grégoire and Francis Dvornik, both the political and the ecclesiastical history of the ninth century now appear in a new light. It has been shown, for example, that the achievements of the Amorian dynasty, and in particular those of its last member, Michael III (842–867), have been deliberately belittled in the interests of subsequent imperial policy; and, to take another instance, that the schism between the Churches calls for a new appraisal if it is to be seen in the light of contemporary conditions at Constantinople, instead of being regarded mainly as an episode in Papal history. Such advances in historical interpretation have not, however, been accompanied by any comparable activity in the textual field. It is true that, as a result of the publication of some hagiographic material and especially of the Arab historians, the available sources for the ninth century are more numerous now than they were in the time of Cardinal Hergenröther. Yet the principal Greek sources still have to be consulted in the same faulty editions in which they were used a hundred years ago, and much important material remains unpublished. New editions and translations of Byzantine texts are needed, therefore, as a basis for a fuller understanding of the history of this period.

Among the literary documents of the ninth century an important place is held by the Homilies of the Patriarch Photius, unquestionably the greatest figure of his time. In view of the enormous and

PREFACE

constantly growing literature about him, it is surprising that many of his works should have received relatively little attention. His voluminous correspondence is still in need of comment and elucidation. His scholia on the New Testament have never been edited in their entirety. Complex problems of authenticity are still posed by his *Contra Manichaeos*. Even his *Bibliotheca*, a well-known quarry for classical scholars, can still shed much light on the intellectual history of the time. His Homilies in particular have remained almost unread by modern historians, although they were published over fifty years ago. There are probably two reasons for this neglect: the scarcity of the Greek edition and the difficulty of Photius' style. Because of them, it has appeared desirable to present the Homilies in an English version, and thus make more generally available this primary source for the intellectual, religious and political history of the ninth century.

A few words should be said about the principle of this translation. A faithful rendering of a rhetorical Byzantine text into English (or, for that matter, into any western European language) is virtually impossible. The stilted conventions of Byzantine style, the elaborate antitheses and chiastic structure, the puns and assonances, the obscure literary allusions, the empty dialectic learned in the schools of rhetoric—all these are alien not only to our taste, but also to our ways of expression. In fairness to Photius, it must be said that he did not share all the literary vices of his contemporaries. His prose is usually clear and often moving. It is even stimulating by comparison with the turgid efforts of, for example, the emperor Leo VI, or Arethas of Caesarea. Nevertheless, Photius conformed to the rhetorical style of his time, and he is not easy reading. Since these Homilies are more likely to be used as historical documents than as specimens of literary composition, my aim has been to follow the original as closely as possible, in spite of the great difficulties inherent in making such a literal translation. Consequently, my rendering may at times be found harsh and unnatural. Of this fault I am fully aware, but it could hardly have been avoided without incurring a more serious loss of verbal accuracy. For a fuller account of the method adopted the reader is referred to pages 36–37.

PREFACE

It remains for me to express my gratitude to all the scholars who have generously given me their help and advice, in particular to the late Professor A. M. Friend, Jr. who initiated this work. His intention, which was to bring out a much more comprehensive publication of the Homilies, including the Greek text and a fuller commentary, has not been entirely realized here; nevertheless, I hope that he would not have been too disappointed by this more meagre offering. I am also greatly indebted to Professors R. J. H. Jenkins and Francis Dvornik for a large number of corrections and suggestions. The whole manuscript has been read by Mr. John P. Cavarnos, and part of it by Professor Paul J. Alexander, both of whom have made many useful contributions. Finally, I should like to thank my colleagues, both past and present, at Dumbarton Oaks.

Dumbarton Oaks   CYRIL MANGO
Washington, D.C.
June, 1957.

CONTENTS

Introduction 3
    Chronology of the Homilies 18
    Manuscript 24
    Lost Manuscript 32
    Editions and Translations 34
    Method of the Present Publication 36

Note on Homilies I and II 38
    Homily I. The Beginning of Lent 41
    Homily II. Good Friday 55
Note on Homilies III and IV 74
    Homily III. The Russian Attack 82
    Homily IV. The Departure of the Russians 95
Note on Homily V 111
    Homily V. The Annunciation 112
Note on Homily VI 123
    Homily VI. Good Friday 124
Note on Homily VII 138
    Homily VII. The Annunciation 139
Note on Homily VIII 150
    Homily VIII. Palm Sunday 153
Note on Homily IX 161
    Homily IX. The Birth of the Virgin 164
Note on Homily X 177
    Homily X. The Inauguration of a Church in the Palace . 184
Note on Homilies XI and XII 191
    Homily XI. Holy Saturday 193
    Homily XII. Holy Saturday 212
Note on Homilies XIII and XIV 220
    Homily XIII. Tyrophagy Week 223
    Homily XIV. Tyrophagy Week 230
Note on Homilies XV and XVI 236
    Homily XV. The Arian Heresy 244
    Homily XVI. The Arian Heresy 260

CONTENTS

Note on Homily XVII 279
    Homily XVII. The Image of the Virgin in St. Sophia ... 286
Note on Homily XVIII 297
    Homily XVIII. The Council of 867 306
Addendum.. 316
Abbreviations 318
Index 319

THE HOMILIES OF PHOTIUS

INTRODUCTION

Eighteen Homilies of Photius, Patriarch of Constantinople (858–867 and 877–886), have been preserved. All of them, as will be shown below, are probably to be dated in the period of his first patriarchate, a time of momentous developments in the political and ecclesiastical life of the Byzantine Empire. The historical role of Photius has, all too often, been viewed only as it concerned the rift between the Western and Eastern Churches. He has been regarded either as the "Father of the Schism" or as the staunch defender of Greek Orthodoxy against the encroachments of Rome. It is hoped that by presenting the Homilies of Photius in English translation these one-sided views may to some extent be corrected. For, surprising though it may appear, we shall not find in the Homilies a single reference to the Papacy. When they are not purely didactic, the Homilies are dominated by such topics as the suppression of the Iconoclast movement, the re-establishment of sacred painting, the propagation of the true faith among heretics, and the quelling of internal division in the Church of Constantinople. Although their purpose is naturally edifying rather than polemical, these Homilies constitute nevertheless an important historical document, and help us towards a better understanding of the patriarch's personality and activities.

The life of Photius is too well known to need re-telling.[1] It will be sufficient for the comprehension of the Homilies to recall the main landmarks of his first incumbency of the patriarchal throne. Canonically appointed (December 858) after the enforced abdication of the Patriarch Ignatius, Photius had to contend continually with the opposition of the more stubborn of Ignatius' supporters. The

---

[1] See esp. Francis Dvornik, *The Photian Schism*, Cambridge, 1948, where a full bibliography of previous literature is given. A good, less extensive account is E. Amann's article "Photius" in *Dict. de théol. cath.*, XII 2 (1935), cols. 1536–1604. Among older works the fullest are J. Hergenröther, *Photius, Patriarch von Constantinopel*, 3 vols., Regensburg, 1867–69, and F. Rossejkin, Первое патріаршество патріарха Фотія, Sergiev Posad, 1915 (also separately in the periodical Богословскій Вѣстникъ).

extent of the opposition has often been exaggerated, but it was nevertheless loud, and there are several references to it in the Homilies. It was indeed the Ignatians who started the conflict by gathering in the church of St. Irene and excommunicating the new patriarch. Photius retaliated by holding a synod at the church of the Holy Apostles (summer 859), at which Ignatius and his principal followers were deposed. In June 860, while the Emperor Michael III had gone off to campaign against the Arabs, Constantinople was suddenly attacked by a Russian flotilla. The invaders soon withdrew, but for a short time the inhabitants of the capital stood on the brink of total annihilation (Homilies III and IV). In the spring of 861, a Council was held at Constantinople in the presence of the papal legates Radoald and Zachary. The deposition of Ignatius was confirmed, and Photius was acknowledged to be the legitimate Patriarch. While Pope Nicholas I repudiated his own legates and fulminated against Photius at the Roman Council of April 863, the Patriarch's position, supported by the imperial government, remained unshaken. Besides, the Eastern Church was being remarkably successful in its proselytizing activities, such as the mission of SS. Constantine and Methodius to Moravia. Soon after their piratical raid, the Russians too came to ask for a bishop, while in 864 King Boris of Bulgaria was converted to Christianity. It was not until 866 that the tide began to turn. On April 21st of that year, Photius' chief supporter and patron, the Caesar Bardas, was murdered. On the 26th of May, Basil the Macedonian, whose relations with Photius were somewhat cool, was crowned Co-Emperor. In August King Boris, frustrated in his desire of obtaining his own archbishop from Constantinople, turned to Rome, and for a while the Greek missionaries were driven out of Bulgaria. Photius was not slow in preparing a rejoinder. A local synod held at Constantinople in the early part of 867 condemned the Latin missionaries in Bulgaria and in particular the dogma of the double procession of the Holy Ghost which they were disseminating. Photius followed this up by an Encyclical Letter to the three Oriental Patriarchs, whom he invited to send legates to a general Council that was to assemble in Constantinople. The Council met in August–September 867 and appears to have excommunicated

INTRODUCTION

Pope Nicholas. It also condemned Iconoclasm anew, as well as all the other heresies (Homily XVIII). Shortly after, on September 24th, Michael III was murdered by Basil's associates. On the latter's accession, Photius was immediately driven out and Ignatius reinstated as patriarch.

Such are the main events that form the background to the Homilies of Photius. The collection of eighteen sermons which has come down to us represents, of course, only a small part of the patriarch's entire homiletical output. Of his lost sermons—and there is every reason to believe that Photius was a prolific orator—we are able to name a few. For example, in a manuscript which perished in the Escorial fire of 1671 there existed a Homily on the Ascension now lost.[2] The two sermons on the Arian heresy (nos. XV and XVI) were preceded by at least one other and followed by probably two more on the same subject.[3] A chronicler reports that following a violent earthquake,[4] Photius mounted the ambo and told his congregation that earthquakes were caused not by the multitude of our sins, but by the abundance of water, and furthermore that each man had two souls of which one sinned and the other did not.[5] While this report is certainly malicious, and nothing could

---

[2] See below, pp. 32–33.
[3] See below, p. 236.
[4] This probably refers to the series of earthquakes that shook Constantinople in August and September 862 (*Vita Ignatii*, PG 105, col. 525 A–B). For the date, see Bury, *History of the Eastern Roman Empire*, London, 1912, p. 198, n. 4 and p. 445, n. 1; Vasiliev, *The Russian Attack on Constantinople in 860*, Cambridge, Mass., 1946, pp. 224–25. The earthquake was ascribed by the populace to the unjust treatment of Ignatius; and if Photius made some remark in his sermon to dispel that superstitious belief, it is easy to see how the story in Pseudo-Symeon arose. In addition to the earthquake of 862, there was at least one, and possibly two more in the reign of Michael: one occurred on Ascension day (Theoph. Cont., p. 196_{22}; *Vita Ignatii*, col. 529 C–D; Cedrenus, II, p. 173_{15}); the other (if it is not the same) threw down a statue in a quarter called Deuteron, and was interpreted by Leo the Mathematician as foreshadowing the death of Bardas, the second man (*deuteros*) after the emperor (Theoph. Cont., p. 197; Pseudo-Symeon, p. 677; Genesius, p. 105; Georgius Hamartolus, ed. Istrin [Хроника Георгія Амартола, II, Petrograd, 1922], p. 12). Theoph. Cont. (*loc.cit.*) implies two distinct earthquakes, while Cedrenus lumps them into one; if they were one and the same, the date must have been May 31, 865.
[5] Anastasius (Mansi XVI, col. 6 A) alleges that Photius propounded this doctrine as a deliberate sham to confuse Ignatius. It is also ascribed to Photius in a very biased resumé of the Council of 869–70 (*ibid.*, col. 456 A). This teaching was, in fact, condemned by the Council (*ibid.*, col. 404, can. X, and col. 166, can. XI), but without any reference to Photius. Cf. Dvornik,

have been further from the spirit of Photius than to have stated that natural calamities had no connection with our sins, there is no reason to doubt that Photius preached a sermon after an earthquake and that he was intentionally misinterpreted.

In 1900 there appeared at Constantinople an edition of no fewer than eighty-three "Speeches and Homilies" of the Patriarch Photius, published by S. Aristarches (or d'Aristarchi, as he styles himself), Great Logothete of the Oecumenical Patriarchate.[6] Of the eighty-three, only sixteen are genuine Homilies, one is a rhetorical encomium,[7] while the rest were ingeniously reconstructed by the editor to the deception of many an unheeding scholar. Starting with the assumption that fragments of Homilies have been incorporated into other works of Photius, Aristarches proceeded to extract those supposed fragments from the *Amphilochia*, the *Contra Manichaeos*, the *Bibliotheca*, the Letters, etc., and then arranged them in a fictitious chronological order. While there is no justification for the method adopted by Aristarches, his basic assumption is not altogether wrong, since parts of Homilies V and XI have in fact been included in a *catena* on St. Luke, and, just as there is considerable overlapping between the Letters and the *Amphilochia*, so passages from Homilies may have been incorporated into other works. It must be made clear, however, that we are concerned here only with actual sermons that have come down to us in a complete form. Possible fragments of other sermons, such as the one on the Last Judgment, published by Cramer[8] and Hergenröther,[9] have therefore been excluded. Anyone who wishes to extract supposed homiletical fragments from other works of Photius will almost always be forced,

---

The Photian Schism, pp. 33-4. There is, of course no trace of such heresy in the writings of Photius, beyond the statement that the soul contains two elements, τὸ λογικόν and τὸ ζωτικόν (cf. *Amphilochia*, quaest. 253, PG 101, col. 1061).

[6] Τοῦ ἐν ἁγίοις πατρὸς ἡμῶν Φωτίου, πατριάρχου Κωνσταντινουπόλεως, λόγοι καὶ ὁμιλίαι ὀγδοήκοντα τρεῖς, Constantinople, 1900, 2 vols.

[7] The encomium of St. Thekla, published by Aristarches, II, pp. 252-267, and more correctly by Oscar von Gebhardt, *Die lateinischen Übersetzungen der Acta Pauli et Theclae* (= *Texte u. Untersuchungen*, N.F. VII 2, 1902), pp. 176-182. There is no evidence that this encomium was intended for delivery as a sermon.

[8] *Anecdota graeca e codd. mss. bibl. Oxon.*, IV, Oxford, 1837, pp. 168-169.

[9] *Monumenta graeca ad Photium ... pertinentia*, Ratisbonae, 1869, pp. 18-19.

INTRODUCTION

like Aristarches, to rely on subjective criteria, since it is extremely difficult to distinguish stylistically between passages that were actually spoken from the pulpit and those that were never intended for oral delivery. To take one instance, it is not impossible that Books II and III of the *Contra Manichaeos* represent a series of sermons in compressed form;[10] but even if that were known to be so, how would one proceed to carve out the original sermons? A far more difficult situation is presented by Photius' commentaries on the Bible, since they are to a large extent unpublished.[11] Besides, the whole study of *catenae* is a notoriously complex subject, and one must proceed with the greatest caution in determining the authorship of individual scholia. Thus, in 1892 Papadopoulos-Kerameus published a *catena* on Matthew from the Sabait. 232 under the title Φωτίου σχόλιά τε καί τεμάχια ὁμιλιῶν (*Photius' Scholia and Fragments of Homilies*).[12] In actual fact, this *catena* is for the most part not by Photius: it is the anonymous *catena* attributed to Peter of Laodicea with Photian additions.[13] It would be of the

---

[10] This view was put forward by Aristarches, I, pp. 333 sq. It is accepted as plausible by Amann, "Photius," *Dict de théol. cath.*, XII 2 (1935), col. 1542. The authenticity of Books II and III of the *Contra Manichaeos* has not been seriously questioned, whereas that of Book I has been the subject of some debate. See. H. Grégoire, "Les sources de l'histoire des Pauliciens," Acad. royale de Belgique, *Bull. de la Classe des Lettres*, 5ᵉ sér., t. 22 (1936), pp. 95–114; *id.*, "Sur l'histoire des Pauliciens," *ibid.*, pp. 224–226; F. Scheidweiler, "Paulikianerprobleme," *BZ*, XLIII (1950), pp. 29 sq.; J. Scharf, "Zur Echtheitsfrage der Manichäerbücher des Photios," *BZ*, XLIV (1951), pp. 487–494; M. Loos, "Deux contributions à l'histoire des Pauliciens," *Byzantinoslavica*, XVII 1 (1956), pp. 48–56.

[11] Photius is credited with commentaries on the Psalms, the four Gospels (those on Matthew being, apparently, the most extensive) and the Pauline epistles. See, amongst others, R. Devreesse, "Chaînes exégétiques grecques," *Dictionnaire de la Bible*, Suppl. I (1928), cols. 1139, 1166–67, 1174–75, 1181–82, 1193–94, 1204, 1212, 1224; C. H. Turner, "Greek Patristic Commentaries on the Pauline Epistles" in Hastings' *Dictionary of the Bible*, Extra vol. (1904), pp. 519–20; L. Thomas, *Les collections anonymes de scolies grecques aux évangiles*, 2 vols. (lithographed), Rome, 1912; K. Staab, *Pauluskommentare aus der griech. Kirche* (*Neutestamentliche Abhandlungen*, X, 1933), pp. xl–xlvii and 470–652; J. Reuss, *Matthäus-, Markus- und Johannes-Katenen* (*Neutestamentliche Abh.*, XVIII, 1941); *id.*, "Die Matthäus-Erklärung des Photius von Konstantinopel," *Ostkirchliche Studien*, I (1952), pp. 132–34 (announcing the discovery of over a hundred Photian scholia on Matthew, which the author believes to be derived from Homilies).

[12] Православный Палестинскій Сборникъ, XI 1, St. Petersburg, 1892, pp. vii–ix and 53–140.

[13] See Devreesse, *op. cit.*, cols. 1166, 1174–75; Reuss, *Matthäus-, Markus- und Johannes-Katenen*, p. 94.

greatest value to have a reliable edition of all of Photius' commentaries on the Bible; such an edition, when it comes out, will certainly contribute to the study of the Homilies. Furthermore, there always remains the possibility that Homilies of Photius may be lying concealed under another author's name. The corpus of Photian Homilies, which only four years ago was enriched by two new items,[14] is not therefore a closed one.

The eighteen Homilies presented here form a collection which probably originated at a time and in a circle not far removed from the Patriarch. Our three principal manuscripts give the Homilies in the same order,[15] and, as will be shown below, there is some reason to think that the order is chronological. If this is true, we must assume that the original collection was made by a person fairly close to the Patriarch. The same conclusion is suggested by the *tituli*, which show a detailed knowledge of the circumstances in which several Homilies were delivered. Since, however, three of the *tituli* are probably incorrect (nos. I, XIII, XIV),[16] we may conclude that their author was either a somewhat absent-minded member of the Patriarch's entourage, or, more likely, one of his younger disciples.

Once the unified nature of the collection is granted, we are one step nearer to understanding its origin. Another interesting fact is the extreme paucity of the manuscript tradition. The tedious sermons of George of Nicomedia or of Leo VI are extant in a great many manuscripts. One might have expected an orator of Photius' stature and fame to have been widely read and appreciated, yet the opposite is true, as a glance at the list of manuscripts will show (see below, pp. 24 sq.). We are, therefore, justified in looking for a reason other than the usual accidents of manuscript preservation.

Unfortunately, we do not know how the sermons of Photius were first published. In the case of the Patriarch Tarasius (784–806), it is reported that his sermons were taken down stenographically[17]

---

[14] Nos. XII and XIII, published by G. Kournoutos and B. Laourdas in Θεολογία, XXV (1954) pp. 188–198.
[15] Except the lost Escorial MS. See below, pp. 33–34.
[16] See below, pp. 39–40, 220–21.
[17] On Byzantine tachygraphy, see amongst others, R. Devreesse, *Introduction à l'étude des manuscrits grecs*, Paris, 1954, pp. 36–39.

INTRODUCTION

and then conveyed for copying to the best calligraphers.[18] The Patriarch Euthymius (907–912), on the other hand, himself copied out his sermons for the first week of Lent, and presented them to his monastery.[19] Whichever method was adopted by Photius, it is, in any case, quite possible that individual Homilies were put into circulation, and have thus found their way singly into mixed homiletical collections, such as the Coislin. 107, the Monac. 443, the Chalc. 1, and others. As for the corpus of Photian Homilies, now represented by our three principal manuscripts, it must have originated as a special collection. Particularly significant is the fact that the last Homily (no. XVIII) was delivered not more than three weeks before Photius' downfall, and celebrates the Council of 867. It gives praise to the Emperors Michael and Basil, to the senatorial class and the clergy for having taken part in the Council. We know, however, that Basil's government immediately repudiated the embarrassing Council—in fact sought to prove that it had never taken place, that Basil had not signed its Acts, and that most of the other signatures had been forged by Photius. The official copies of the Acts were burnt, while anyone who kept and refused to surrender documents pertaining to the condemned Council was threatened with excommunication. Photius' own archives were impounded. Seven bags sealed with lead, so the story goes, were concealed by Photius in a plot overgrown with reeds, but the Emperor's emissaries discovered and confiscated them. Among the papers found, were the synodal condemnation of Ignatius as well as that of Pope Nicholas I.[20] In such circumstances it is obvious that Homily XVIII, even if it had been "released" in the short interval between the end of the Council and the murder of Michael III, must have been immediately banned from circulation. Its preservation is probably due to some devoted member of Photius' group. Nor is it likely that other Homilies eulogizing Michael III (especially nos. X and XVII) would have been particularly welcome under the first Macedonian emperors. It may therefore be inferred that the corpus of Photian Homilies was compiled and preserved in secret

[18] *Vita Tarasii*, ed. I. A. Heikel (*Acta Soc. Scient. Fennicae*, XVII, 1891), p. 423.
[19] *Vita Euthymii*, ed. De Boor, Berlin, 1888, p. 30$_{24}$.
[20] *Vita Ignatii*, PG 105, cols. 540–41.

THE HOMILIES OF PHOTIUS

by the Patriarch's friends and disciples, which fact may also account for the paucity of the manuscript tradition.

Another factor which points to Photius' entourage is the character of our principal manuscript, the Iviron 684. This codex, late though it is, provides such a good text, that its archetype must have been of very high quality. Apart from the Homilies, it also includes the Letters of Photius, in the same order and with the same marginal scholia as in the Barocc. gr. 217 (early tenth century), but has some additional letters not found in the latter.[21] Since the Barocc. gr. 217 is itself a copy, and presumably unfinished, it is likely that its archetype is also that of the Iviron 684 (as regards the Letters). Thus, we are brought to the generation of Photius' younger contemporaries and disciples. Now, the scholia to the Letters are written in a spirit of great admiration for Photius and may (though this is not established) be by the famous Arethas of Caesarea.[22] The scribe of the Iviron 684 was, therefore, in the case of the Letters, copying a text which emanated directly, or nearly so, from the circle of Photius' friends. In his text of the Homilies there is only one extensive scholion,[23] yet both in spirit and in phraseology, it is akin to the scholia on the Letters. It is not, therefore, unlikely that the collection of Homilies in the Iviron 684, like that of the Letters, is traceable to that group of intellectuals, formed under the tutelage of Photius, among whom Arethas was the most outstanding figure.

The fate of the Homilies during the Middle Ages is practically unknown to us. A few passages were excerpted from them, probably in the fourteenth century, and included in anthologies,[24] while nos. III and IV provided material for an address by the metropolitan Dorotheus of Mitylene during the siege of Constantinople in 1422 (see below, p. 82); on the whole, however, the Homilies do not appear

---

[21] Twenty-one previously unknown letters were published after this MS by Papadopoulos-Kerameus, Святѣйшаго патріарха Фотія ... XLV неизданныхъ писемъ, St. Petersburg, 1896.

[22] Cf. B. Laourdas, Τὰ εἰς τὰς ἐπιστολὰς τοῦ Φωτίου σχόλια τοῦ κώδικος Barocc. gr. 217, Ἀθηνᾶ, LV (1951) pp. 125-54, and esp. p. 130, n. 1.

[23] See below, p. 232, n. 8. There are besides the usual marginal notes ση(μείωσαι), ὡρ(αῖον), and γνώ(μη), on which cf. Nestle in BZ, XVII (1908), pp. 479-80. See below, p. 27.

[24] See below, pp. 29-30, Cod. Palat. 129 and Chalc. 64.

INTRODUCTION

to have been widely read. It is only with the Renaissance that we can pick up their story again. In a synodal decree issued *ca.* 1478 under the Patriarch Maximus IV, there is a vague allusion to "one of the speeches" of Photius (ἕν τινι τῶν αὐτοῦ λόγων) on the subject of ecclesiastical dissension,[25] a topic that does indeed hold a prominent place in the Homilies. If Papadopoulos-Kerameus was right in holding that both of our principal manuscripts, the Iviron 684 and the Metochion Panagiou Taphou 529, were written by Alexander Hierax, Great Logothete of the Oecumenical Patriarchate,[26] it would indicate that towards the close of the sixteenth century there existed at Constantinople at least two ancient copies of the Homilies and that there was some interest in reproducing them. It is, of course, well known that Constantinople still possessed at the time a great wealth of ancient manuscripts, many of which were being acquired by visiting scholars and diplomats such as Dousa and Busbecq.[27] In the *milieu* of Alexander Hierax an interest in Photius would have been very natural. His father, Constantine Hierax, likewise Great Logothete, was a man of letters who entertained friendly relations with Martin Crusius and Stephan Gerlach.[28] Alexander himself is known as the scribe of several manuscripts, mostly of religious content. Four of these are dated between 1593 and 1603, the year of Alexander's death.[29] It does not fall within the limits of this enquiry to ascertain whether our two chief manuscripts of the Homilies are indeed in the hand of Alexander Hierax.

[25] Quoted by Aristarches, I, p. 213.
[26] See below, pp. 25-26.
[27] There exist several catalogues of manuscripts preserved at Constantinople and Rhaedestus in the 16th century, totalling about 630 titles. The Homilies of Photius are not, however, among them. See Richard Foerster, *De antiquitatibus et libris manuscriptis Constantinopolitanis commentatio*, Rostock, 1877.
[28] Cf. Martin Crusius, *Turcograeciae libri octo*, Basel, 1584, pp. 204, 332. On Constantine and Alexander Hierax see K. N. Sathas, Νεοελληνικὴ φιλολογία, Athens, 1868, p. 202; *id.*, Μεσαιωνικὴ βιβλιοθήκη, I, Venice, 1872, pp. ρλε'-ρλζ'.
[29] Cf. Vogel and Gardthausen, *Die griechischen Schreiber des Mittelalters und der Renaissance*, Leipzig, 1909, pp. 12-13. The MSS written by Alexander Hierax appear to be the following: Athos, Esphigmenou 2277. 264 (Feb. 1593); Metochion 520 (Dec. 1595: not mentioned by Vogel and Gardthausen); Metochion 363 (1596); Bruxell. 19 (Sept. 1603: see following note); Athen. 1474 (apparently undated: see Papadopoulos-Kerameus in Φιλολ. Σύλλογος Παρνασσός, Ἐπετηρίς, VIII [1904], pp. 24 sq). Papadopoulos-Kerameus also attributes to Alexander Hierax Metochion 339 (after 1588) and 415 (undated).

THE HOMILIES OF PHOTIUS

A comparison with Cod. 19 (14870) of the Bibliothèque Royale of Brussels, an autograph of Alexander Hierax,[30] has failed to show any striking similarity of handwriting. In any case, it is most likely that the two manuscripts were written by the same person, and if that is so, one may wonder what prompted that person to transcribe two slightly divergent texts of the Homilies, and whether it was not with an eye to their publication.[31]

In 1600 a reference to Photius' *discours d'apparat* (οἱ πανηγυρικοὶ τῶν λόγων) is made by Maximos Margounios, bishop of Cythera, who helped David Hoeschel with the *editio princeps* of the *Bibliotheca*.[32] The publication of Byzantine texts was beginning to gather momentum. It was in the fine folios of the mid-seventeenth century that two of our Homilies were first published: no. IX by François Combefis (1648) and no. X by Peter Lambeck (1655).[33]

The next incident in the story of the Homilies is of some importance, and centres round the curious figure of Paisios (Pantaleon) Ligarides, metropolitan of Gaza (1610?–1678). For an understanding

[30] See Omont, *Catalogue des mss grecs de la Bibl. Royale de Belgique*, Gand, 1885, pp. 12–13; J. Van den Gheyn, *Catalogue des mss de la Bibl. Royale de Belgique*, II, Brussels, 1902, p. 33. The title-page and colophon are not given correctly either by Omont or by Van den Gheyn. They read as follows: (fol. 2, in a later hand) Τὸ παρὸν βιβλίον, ὃ περιέχει λόγους τοῦ Νύσσης Γρηγορίου, ἐγράφη διὰ χειρὸς τοῦ ποτὲ λογοθέτου Ἀλεξάνδρου, υἱοῦ δηλαδὴ Ἱέρακος τοῦ μεγάλου λογοθέτου, τοῦ κατὰ τὸ ζπ^{ον} ἀδαμιαῖον ἔτος (= 1572) ἐν τῷ πατριαρχικῷ οἰκουμενικῷ θρόνῳ τῆς Κωνσταντινουπόλεως ἀκμάσαντος, οὗ καὶ ἡ ἐν τῷ τέλει τοῦ βιβλίου ἐσχάτη σελὶς ἰδιόχειρος ὑπάρχει, ἀναπληρώσαντος τὸ ἐλλεῖπον, διὰ τὸ τελευτῆσαι τὸν ῥηθέντα υἱὸν αὐτοῦ πρὸ τοῦ λαβεῖν πέρας τὸ βιβλίον, καθὰ κἀκεῖνος ἐκεῖσε σημειοῖ ἰδίᾳ χειρί. (Fol. 68^v, in the hand of the elder Hierax) τελευτήσαντος φεῦ τοῦ υἱοῦ μου τοῦ λογοθέτου, ἀνεπλήρωσα ἐγὼ τὸ ἐλλεῖπον τοῦτο τοῦ ζρια^{ου} τρέχοντος ἔτους, ἐν μηνὶ σεπτεμβρίῳ, ἰνδικτιῶνος β^{ας}. It follows that the volume, except for the last page, was written by Alexander Hierax, and upon his death, completed by his father in Sept. 1603 (not 1593, as Omont and after him Van den Gheyn as well as Vogel and Gardthausen have it).

[31] Thus Cod. Par. suppl. gr. 471 is a copy of Photius' *Bibliotheca* made by Maximos Margounios (on whom see the following note) expressly for Hoeschel's edition. The Nürnberg manuscript of Cedrenus (without a number) was likewise copied for a printed edition, presumably that by G. Xylander (Basel, 1566). The latter manuscript, according to Vogel and Gardthausen (*op. cit.*, p. 12), was written by the elder Hierax in 1556. Its colophon (fol. 463), however, is signed ἐν ἱεροδιακόνοις ἐλάχιστος Ἀλέξανδρος, ὁ μέγας χαρτοφύλαξ τῆς μεγάλης ἐκκλησίας ὁ ἀποτυρᾶς (?).

[32] See Margounios' letter printed at the head of Hoeschel's ed., Augsburg, 1601, p. 3; reprinted in PG 103, cols. 13–14. Cf. B. Laourdas, Μάξιμος Μαργούνιος καὶ Φώτιος, Ὀρθοδοξία, XXVI (1951), pp. 311–18.

[33] See below, p. 34.

INTRODUCTION

of his role in the manuscript tradition of the Homilies a brief account of his life is necessary.[34] A native of the island of Chios, Ligarides was educated at the Greek College of Rome and was ordained Catholic priest in 1639. In 1642 he was sent to Constantinople with a view to disseminating Roman propaganda, but met with little success there. In 1647 we find him in Wallachia as court confessor to the Prince and teacher at the school of Jassy. His scholarly advice was sought in connection with the Roumanian edition of the *Nomocanon*. He came in contact with visiting dignitaries, among them the famous Russian monk Arsenij Suchanov and Paisios, Patriarch of Jerusalem. In 1651 Ligarides accompanied his new friend, the Patriarch, to Jerusalem, whither Suchanov was also bound. There, on the 16th of November 1651, he was made a monk under the name of Paisios, and placed under Suchanov's spiritual supervision.[35] While in the Holy Land, he wrote a *History of the Patriarchs of Jerusalem*, in which he is said to have revealed his Catholic bias and, ironically enough, his hostility towards Photius.[36] Notwithstanding the condemnation of his work, he was promoted metropolitan of Gaza, although it is doubtful if he ever visited his diocese. By 1656 we find him back in the more congenial clime of

---

[34] On the life of Paisios Ligarides, see esp. E. Legrand, *Bibliographie hellénique*, IV, Paris, 1896, pp. 8–61; (A. V. Gorskij), "Нѣсколько свѣдѣній о Паисіи Лигаридѣ до прибытія его въ Россію," Прибавленія къ твореніямъ св. Отцевъ, XXI, Moscow, 1862, pp. 133–148; L. Lavrovskij, "Нѣсколько свѣдѣній для біографіи Паисія Лигарида," Христіанское Чтеніе, Nov.-Dec. 1889, pp. 672–736. The fullest account of his activities in Russia, excluding Nikon's trial, is by N. F. Kapterev, Характеръ отношеній Россіи къ Православному Востоку, 2nd ed., Sergiev Posad, 1914, pp. 182–208. Cf. also Grumel, art. "Ligaridès, Paisios" in *Dict. de théol. cath.*, IX 1 (1926), cols. 749–57; R. Salomon, "Paisius Ligarides," *Zeitschr. für Osteuropäische Geschichte*, V (1931), pp. 37–65; K. Amantos, Παΐσιος Λιγαρίδης, Ἐπετηρὶς Ἑταιρ. Βυζαντ. Σπουδῶν, XIII (1937), pp. 224–29; E. Šmurlo, "Паисій Лигаридъ въ Римѣ и на греческомъ Востокѣ," Труды V-го Съѣзда Русскихъ Акад. Организацій за Границей, I, Sofia, 1932, pp. 531–588; Chrysostomos Papadopoulos, Οἱ πατριάρχαι Ἱεροσολύμων ὡς πνευματικοὶ χειραγωγοὶ τῆς Ῥωσίας κατὰ τὸν ιζ' αἰῶνα, Νέα Σιών, III (1906), pp. 592–601; IV (1906), pp. 3–31, 177–196, 314–329, 413–428; B. Laourdas, Παΐσιος Λιγαρίδης καὶ Φώτιος, Ὀρθοδοξία, XXVI (1951), pp. 467–73 (putting forward the untenable suggestion that Ligarides' manuscript of the Homilies may have been the Metochion 529).

[35] On the relations between Paisios and Suchanov, see S. Belokurov, Арсеній Сухановъ (Чтенія въ Имп. Общ. Ист. и Древн. Росс. при Моск. Унив., 1891, 2), pp. 215 sq.

[36] Dositheus (Patriarch of Jerusalem), Ἱστορία περὶ τῶν ἐν Ἱεροσολύμοις πατριαρχευσάντων, Bucharest, 1715, p. 1180.

THE HOMILIES OF PHOTIUS

Wallachia, where he met Macarius, Patriarch of Antioch, then homeward bound from Moscow.[37] The scholarly reputation of Ligarides reached the Russian Patriarch Nikon, who was especially anxious to secure the services of Greek scholars for the revision of church books. In 1657, therefore, Nikon extended a pressing invitation to Ligarides to come to Moscow, but the latter tarried in Wallachia for another five years. When he finally reached Moscow (February 12, 1662), the situation had entirely changed, for Nikon had incurred the Czar's displeasure and was in disgrace. With his usual opportunism, Ligarides lost no time in espousing the side of the Czar against that of the Patriarch. His infamous role in Nikon's trial and condemnation need not concern us here.[38]

From Nikon's trial Ligarides emerged as one of the Czar's most trusted counsellors on Church affairs. This position, which he exploited to the fullest to promote his own financial interests, Ligarides maintained until 1672. In 1668, it is true, the new Patriarch of Jerusalem, Nectarius, exposed in a letter to the Czar the shameful career of the so-called metropolitan of Gaza; unwilling, however, to repudiate his counsellor, the Czar succeeded in having Ligarides absolved. Nevertheless, the cunning Chiote must have realized at that time that his influential position was seriously threatened.

In October 1669 there arrived in Moscow on a diplomatic mission the Dutch scholar and poet Nicholas Heinsius.[39] In a letter dated in Moscow December 1st, 1669, he wrote his friend, the famous Utrecht scholar Joh. Graevius, that he had met Paisios Ligarides and been shown by him two manuscripts, one containing some works of St. John Chrysostom, the other the Homilies and Letters of Photius. Knowing that the Letters had appeared in London,[40] but that the Homilies were still unpublished, Heinsius entertained some hope of obtaining the manuscript itself with a view to having them

---

[37] Paul of Aleppo, *The Travels of Macarius*, trans. F. C. Belfour, II, London, 1834, pp. 342–44.

[38] See William Palmer, *The Patriarch and the Czar*, III, London, 1873.

[39] On his previous career, see F. F. Blok, *Nicolaas Heinsius, in Dienst van Christina van Zweden*, Delft, 1949. The negotiations between Heinsius and Paisios have been analysed by Kunik, "О трехъ спискахъ Фотіевыхъ бесѣдъ," *Mém. de l'Acad. Imp. des Sciences de St. Pét.*, VIIIe sér., Cl. hist.-phil., VII, no. 8 (1906), pp. 49–83.

[40] *Photii ... Epistolae*, ed. R. Montacutius, London, 1651.

INTRODUCTION

printed.[41] Graevius, in a letter of April 13th, 1670, replied that he would be willing to undertake the task himself. Obstacles, however, immediately arose: in the first place, the Russian authorities, who kept all foreigners under constant police supervision, forbade further meetings between Heinsius and Paisios; nor was the latter willing to surrender the manuscript, since he was hoping to publish the Homilies himself, and dedicate them to the rulers of the Netherlands in return for a financial remuneration. Negotiations thus came to a standstill. Heinsius left Moscow in August 1670, but not before receiving from Paisios, by way of token, some extracts from the Homilies together with their titles. On his return to Stockholm, Heinsius allowed the matter to lapse, although he received a further reminder from Ligarides, dated March 7th, 1671, in which the Chiote hinted that other interested parties were willing to pay him 1000 gold pieces for the manuscript of Photius.

Ligarides' position in Moscow was meanwhile deteriorating and he announced his intention of visiting Palestine. On May 4th, 1672 he was granted permission to leave by way of Kiev. He was given a retinue and funds for the journey, but his house and books in the Simonovskij monastery were to remain in the keeping of the dragoman Nicholas Spatharios. Ligarides did not leave until February 1673 and having reached Kiev, he decided not to proceed to Palestine. He tarried in Kiev for two years engaging in various machinations. In August 1675 he was ordered back to Moscow, where he found his position even more awkward than before, especially on the death of the Czar Alexis (1676). In September 1676 he was again allowed to depart for Palestine, and again he did not go beyond Kiev. There he died on August 24th, 1678 and was buried in the monastery of the Brotherhood. All his belongings were assigned by the Czar's command to the same monastery.

We have given these biographical data in the hope of throwing some light on the question that concerns us: what manuscript of the Homilies did Ligarides have, and what has happened to it? The extracts which Ligarides made for Heinsius have come down to us,

---

[41] Letter to Graevius (Kunik, *op. cit.*, p. 56, n. 11): "Si sit apud vos, qui harum editionem moliri velit, ipsum volumen impetrari posse ab homine non agresti aut inhumano, qualem mihi se praebet hactenus, spes adfulget."

and prove beyond doubt that their model was extremely close to the Iviron 684, but was probably not identical with the latter. It was in fact somewhat better than the Iviron 684.[42] Moreover, inasmuch as manuscripts of the Homilies were few and far between, it is not unlikely that the codex of Ligarides was the archetype of the Iviron 684. Where Ligarides acquired it is a question we are unable to answer: it could have been in Constantinople, Jerusalem or Wallachia. We know that in Wallachia he had access to the library of Constantine Cantacuzenus which contained a unique *Exposition of the Psalms*,[43] and that Ligarides was a connoisseur of rare books. It has even been suggested that the manuscript of Photius may not have been the property of Paisios at all, but belonged to one of the libraries of Moscow.[44] We know, of course, that in 1654 Arsenij Suchanov was sent to Mount Athos and came back with 498 manuscripts, of which the greatest share (158 items) was from the Iviron monastery. The Homilies of Photius do not, however, figure in the list of those manuscripts, although the list we have is admittedly not altogether complete.[45] It is true that in 1663 Ligarides petitioned the Czar to be granted free access to the Greek and Latin books kept in the various libraries of Moscow;[46] and that in 1671 he was given a manuscript of Photius by the Voskresenskij monastery.[47] Nevertheless, unless Ligarides practised wholesale deception in his relations with Heinsius, we must suppose that the manuscript was his own and not one he had borrowed from a public library. It is also most likely that the manuscript never left Russia again. We have seen that when Paisios departed from Moscow in 1673 on what was to be a temporary trip, his books were placed in the keeping of the dragoman Spatharios. Besides, Paisios had no serious intention of going away from Russia, as indicated by his protracted sojourns at Kiev, so that he had no reason to smuggle the manuscript out of the country. We must therefore conclude that the *Codex Mosquensis* either re-

[42] See below pp. 28–29.
[43] Paul of Aleppo, *The Travels of Macarius*, loc. cit.
[44] Jernstedt in *Mém. de l'Acad. Imp.*, VIIIe sér., Cl. hist.-phil., VII, no. 8, p. 04.
[45] Given by Belokurov, *op. cit.*, pp. 354–406.
[46] W. Palmer, *op. cit.*, III, p. 317.
[47] Jernstedt, *loc. cit.*

INTRODUCTION

mained in the Simonovskij monastery or accrued to the monastery of the Brotherhood at Kiev, and that it has since been lost.

The extracts from the Homilies which Paisios Ligarides made for Heinsius have had a chequered history of their own. Heinsius, who considered them unfit for publication,[48] deposited them with the publishing house of Elzevier, from whom they were received by Emeric Bigot in 1671. The latter communicated the titles of the Homilies to Combefis, who printed them in his *Bibliothecae graecorum Patrum auctarium novissimum* in 1672.[49] Bigot died in 1689, and the extracts of Paisios came into the possession of Montfaucon († 1741) who published a succinct description of them in his famous *Bibliotheca bibliothecarum manuscriptorum nova* (1739).[50] The library of Saint-Germain-des-Prés, where Montfaucon lived and worked, was dispersed during the French Revolution.

In 1845 the Russian historian A. A. Kunik began a systematic search for the two Homilies "on the attack of the Rhos," which he knew to be the earliest Greek source concerning the Russian people. Having drawn a blank in the Synodal Library of Moscow and in other Russian collections, he turned his attention to Paris, but was informed by C. B. Hase and E. Miller that there was no trace of Paisios' manuscript at the Bibliothèque Nationale. Kunik then shifted his quest to Spain, but there too his efforts ended in failure.[51] By what means the extracts of Paisios, which could not be located in 1845, found their way into the Bibliothèque Nationale, where they are still preserved, has never been explained.

The final scene in this lengthy search took place on December 28th, 1858 in the Iviron monastery of Mt. Athos. There the notorious

---

[48] In a letter to Graevius of October 1670, he calls them "abrupta et decurtata admodum, ac quae proinde editioni moliendae minime respondeant." Quoted by Kunik, *op. cit.*, p. 58, n. 13.

[49] *Pars altera*, pp. 299–302, placed after p. 548 of the first part.

[50] II, pp. 1156–57. The headings and incipits of the Homilies, after Combefis, were reprinted a number of times: Oudin, *Commentarius de scriptoribus ecclesiae antiquis*, II, Leipzig, 1722, pp. 209–14; Fabricius, *Bibl. graeca*, IX, Hamburg, 1737, pp. 563–65; Fabricius—Harles, XI, 1808, pp. 30–31; Φωτίου ... ἐπιστολαί, ed. J. N. Valettas, London, 1864, pp. 93–96; PG 102, cols. 541–45.

[51] See Kunik, "Que sont devenues les deux homélies εἰς τὴν ἔφοδον τῶν ʽΡῶς, découvertes à Moscou par Païsi Ligaridès et mentionnées pour la dernière fois par Montfaucon?" *Bull. de la Cl. des Sciences hist., philol. et pol. de l'Acad. Imp. des Sciences de St.-Pét.*, VI, nos. 23–24 (1849), cols. 373–379.

THE HOMILIES OF PHOTIUS

archimandrite (later bishop) Porphirij Uspenskij, whose unscrupulous practices have depleted many an Oriental library, found to his great amazement a complete text of the Homilies in the Iviron 684. This is how he describes his own discovery: "The Homilies of Photius occupied my whole attention as being unheard of rarities. Eagerly I read the first two of them, but when I saw the titles of the third and fourth—First sermon on the invasion of the Russians, Second sermon on the same occasion—I became so overjoyed that my whole being was transported with happiness. There was indeed something to be happy about! Since I, who was seeking precious pearls in the Orient, had chanced on two diamonds, of which few people knew, while many, very many, had not even heard of them, and which I was yearning to find, and yearning so much, that after their discovery I could not have wished for better luck."[52] Uspenskij's own edition of Homilies III, IV, XVII and XVIII, which appeared in 1864, was incomplete, incorrect and accompanied by a commentary which can only be described as fantastic. The manuscript text of Homilies III and IV was, however, photographed in 1859 by Sevast'janov, thus making possible the accurate edition of these invaluable documents by A. Nauck.[53]

On the basis of the Iviron 684 all the Homilies (with the exception of nos. XII and XIII) were published by S. Aristarches, first in the periodical Ἐκκλησιαστικὴ ἀλήθεια and later as a separate edition.[54] It is on the latter that the present English translation is founded.

CHRONOLOGY OF THE HOMILIES

The order in which the Homilies are given here is based on the lost Moscow MS, the Iviron 684 and the Metochion Panagiou Taphou 529, all of which, however, omit our nos. XII and XIII. The latter are preserved only in the Athen. 2756, where they appear after our no. XI. That is where we have also placed them.

Inasmuch as the order of the Homilies does not conform to the liturgical calendar, we may enquire whether the arrangement of the

---

[52] Четыре бесѣды Фотія, St. Petersburg, 1864, p. 52.
[53] *Lexicon Vindobonense*, St. Petersburg, 1867, pp. 201-232.
[54] See bibliographical indications below, p. 35.

INTRODUCTION

collection does not depend on some other principle. Of the eighteen Homilies, only five can be dated with any accuracy. These are:

no. III — Shortly after June 18, 860, perhaps on the 23rd, which was a Sunday.
no. IV — Probably beginning of July 860.
no. X — After April 12, 864, and presumably before the end of the year.
no. XVII — March 29, 867.
no. XVIII — September 867.

As can be seen, the order of these five Homilies is chronological. The question, therefore, arises whether the remaining thirteen are likewise arranged in chronological order of their delivery. Of these, six (nos. II, V, VI, VII, XI and XII) conclude with a prayer for a single Emperor, and there can be no doubt that this Emperor was Michael III, since there was no time during Photius' second incumbency (877–886) when Basil I was, officially at least, sole ruler.[55] Thus, these six Homilies must be dated between 859 (since Photius did not become Patriarch until late December 858) and 867. We now have to see whether the thirteen Homilies of uncertain date yield any indication that might confirm or invalidate the chronological arrangement of the whole collection.

No. I, as we shall see, was delivered not on Good Friday, as stated in the title, but at the beginning of Lent. This Homily contains, moreover, a reference to Sodom which seems to be picked up in no. III,[56] thus indicating that no. I is probably earlier than June 860. It could, therefore, be dated with some likelihood to Lent in either 859 or 860.

No. VI was delivered on Good Friday (ὁμιλία τρίτη λεχθεῖσα ... τῇ ἁγίᾳ παρασκευῇ, i. e. third *after* nos. I and II, on the mistaken assumption that no. I belonged to Good Friday). Its confident claim that the Ignatian opposition is a mere handful[57] can best be placed after the Synod of 861 which ratified the deposition of Ignatius and curbed the power of his monkish supporters. This

---
[55] See below, p. 179.
[56] See below, p. 40.
[57] P. 135 below = Ar II. 198.

THE HOMILIES OF PHOTIUS

Synod ended some time after Easter 861.[58] Thus no. VI could be datable to Friday April 17, 862, or later.

Nos. XV and XVI, which evidently followed each other at no more than a week's interval, present a more difficult problem. Aristarches[59] dated them to 859 because the passage in which Photius regrets the ease of his former life[60] is paralleled in the so-called "apologetic" letter to Pope Nicholas I, written after the Council of 861,[61] while the enumeration of his griefs[62] calls to mind his letter to Bardas, written in 859.[63] The letter to Bardas may be dismissed from consideration since its alleged resemblance to our Homily XV is altogether remote. It must be admitted, on the other hand, that the letter to Nicholas I offers a very striking similarity to Homily XV, as, for example, in the following passage:

νῦν δέ, οἴμοι, καὶ λυπεῖν ἄλλους ὁ τοῦ ποιμαίνειν νόμος ἐπιτάττει, καὶ βαρὺν φαίνεσθαι, καὶ σοβαρὸν δοκεῖν, καὶ κρίνειν ἔσθ' ὅτε καὶ κατακρίνειν, τὸν ἀπ' ἀρχῆς φυγόντα τὴν τοιαύτην τάξιν .... εἰ καὶ διαφυγεῖν οὐκ ἐξεγένετο ἃ φυγεῖν εὐδαιμονία ἐκρίνετο.	νῦν δ' ἔσθ' ὅτε καὶ πικρῶς ἐπιτιμᾶν ἀνάγκη τοῖς φίλοις, καὶ τοὺς συγγενεῖς ὑπὲρ ἐντολῆς παρορᾶν, καὶ τοῖς ἁμαρτάνουσι φαίνεσθαι βαρύς ..... ἃ βλέπων καὶ πρὶν .... ἔφευγον τὴν ψῆφον .... οὐκ ἦν δὲ ἄρα φυγεῖν τὸ προορισθέν.
(Ar I. 270)	(Valettas, pp. 150-51).

There would be, therefore, some reason to place Homilies XV and XVI, not in 859 as Aristarches would have it, but in Lent of 861. It is also quite likely that a series of sermons on the Arian and Iconoclastic heresies should have been intended as a prelude to a Council of the Church. The Council of 861 met in the spring of that year, and, in addition to the case of Ignatius, dealt with disciplinary as well as doctrinal matters, among which Iconoclasm occupied an important place.[64]

---
[58] Cf. Dvornik, *The Photian Schism*, p. 83.
[59] I. 237, 253.
[60] P. 259 below = Ar I. 270.
[61] Valettas ed., pp. 149–50; PG 102, col. 597.
[62] P. 260 below = Ar I. 271.
[63] Valettas ed., pp. 491–92; PG 102, col. 620.
[64] See Dvornik, "The Patriarch Photius and Iconoclasm," *Dumbarton Oaks Papers*, 7 (1953), pp. 77 sq.

INTRODUCTION

Homily no. XVI contains, however, a passage which could be construed as suggesting a later date. In defining the Orthodox faith against heresies, Photius says that the Father is the "cause" of the Holy Ghost, for the latter is produced "One out of One," and further down, "for the One gave birth, the Other was born, and the Third proceeds beyond time and age, and beyond comprehension, neither the Ghost being included in the birth of the Son, nor the Son having a share in the procession of the Ghost (οὔτε τοῦ υἱοῦ τὴν ἐκπόρευσιν τοῦ πνεύματος συγκληρουμένου)."[65] This, though said *en passant*, seems to be a reference to the Western addition of the *Filioque*. Jugie, who has noted this passage, believes that the Homily should be dated to the end of Photius' first patriarchate.[66] His statement that "In *Homiliis quinque contra haereses*, Photius ad controversiam de processione Spiritus Sancti iam alludit; unde colligimus illas circa finem eius primi patriarchatus fuisse prolatas," needs, however, a slight correction. As we shall see, three out of the five Homilies were fabricated by Aristarches, who even went so far as to include in the fifth a few passages from the *Mystagogia*, among the bitterest that Photius ever hurled at the Roman Church.[67] After eliminating the three fictitious Homilies, the only allusion to the *Filioque* controversy that remains is the one quoted above. Now, the procession of the Holy Ghost does not seem to have been an issue between the Eastern and Western Churches until their missionaries fell afoul of one another in Bulgaria in the year 866. That does not, of course, enable us to say that Photius was unaware of the question before 866; for even if he was ignorant of the previous controversies on that score in the West, he could have known of the clash that occurred at Jerusalem in 808 between the Benedictines of the Mount of Olives and the Greek monks of St. Sabas. In 813 there arrived at Constantinople many Palestinian monks, among them St. Michael Syncellus and the brothers Theodore and Theophanes Grapti who were apparently intending to proceed to Rome in order to represent to the Pope the Oriental position on the *Filioque* dispute. They were, however, detained at Constantinople,

[65] Ar I. 295 = p. 276 below.
[66] *De processione Spiritus Sancti ex fontibus revelationis et secundum orientales dissidentes*, Rome, 1936, p. 287 and n. 3.
[67] Ar I. 321–22.

THE HOMILIES OF PHOTIUS

and never pursued their journey to the West.[68] St. Michael became after 843 abbot of an important monastery at Constantinople, which position he held until his death in 846. Thus Photius could easily have had contact with several prominent Palestinian monks who had been personally involved in the *Filioque* controversy. It is true that in his writings on the subject (namely the Encyclical Letter of 867, the Letter to the Archbishop of Aquileia and the *Mystagogia*) he gives no indication of having known of the *Filioque* addition before 866;[69] yet we are not in a position to say that he had been totally ignorant of the issue.

If the sermons on Arianism could be considered as a fitting introduction to the Council of 861, the same could also be said in connection with that of 867. We know that in the early part of that year a local synod was held at Constantinople to condemn the errors of the Latin missionaries in Bulgaria, and that Photius immediately set about convoking an oecumenical council. This was not intended to deal exclusively or even primarily with the doctrines of the Latin missionaries, as has been hitherto supposed. It was to be a general condemnation of all heresies, among which Iconoclasm occupied a prominent place.[70] If we possessed the missing sermons on the Arian heresy which carried the story from Julian the Apostate to the Second Oecumenical Council, we would be able to form a more definite judgment. It is indeed likely that Photius treated in them the heresies of Macedonius and Sabellius which were condemned at the Second Council; and it is precisely those two heresies that Photius considered to be most akin to the Latin teaching on the Holy Ghost, to the point of calling the latter a "half-Sabellian monster."[71]

The date of Homilies XV and XVI must therefore remain in the balance. If they were delivered in 861, we would have to conclude, a) that Photius had expressed himself against the double

[68] See Vailhé, "S. Michel le Syncelle," *Revue de l'Orient chrétien*, VI (1901), pp. 321 sq.; E. Amann, *L'époque carolingienne* (= Fliche & Martin, *Histoire de l'Eglise*, VI), 1947, pp. 180 sq.
[69] Cf. Jugie, "Origine de la controverse sur l'addition du *Filioque* au Symbole," *Rev. des sciences philos. et théologiques*, XXVIII (1939), p. 374.
[70] See below, pp. 302–04.
[71] *Mystagogia*, ed. Hergenröther, p. 14; cf. pp. 36, 109, and *Encyclical Letter*, ed. Valettas, p. 172 for the comparison with the heresy of Macedonius.

INTRODUCTION

procession of the Holy Ghost before the Bulgarian episode, and b) that the order of the Homilies is not strictly chronological. If, on the other hand, Homilies XV and XVI belong to the Lent of 867, then the chronological arrangement of the whole collection becomes a valid hypothesis. On the latter assumption, the following dating could be hazarded:

no. I — Lent 859 or 860.
no. II — March 24, 859 or April 12, 860 (Good Friday).
no. V — March 25, 861 or 862 (Lady Day), preferably the latter, since in 861 Photius must have been much busied with the affairs of the Synod.[72]
no. VI — April 17, 862 (Good Friday).
no. VII — March 25, 863 (Lady Day).
no. VIII — April 4, 863 (Palm Sunday).
no. IX — September 8, 863 (Nativity of the Virgin).[73]
no. XI — April 21, 865 (Easter Saturday).[74]
no. XII — April 6, 866 (Easter Saturday).
no. XIII — February 5, 867.
no. XIV — February 7, 867.[75]

---

[72] On the assumption that no. V is later than July 860 (no. IV) and earlie than April 17, 862, the suggested date for no. VI.

[73] On the assumption that no. X was preached not long after April 864. See below, p. 180.

[74] Since no. X was certainly delivered after Easter 864, which fell on April 2nd.

[75] On the assumption that nos. XIII and XIV belong to the Tyrophagy week and not the first week of Lent, as stated in their titles. Our dating of these two sermons to the same week is borne out by the similarity of their content, as well as by the *titulus* of no. XIV, as given in the Athen. 2756. See below, p. 220. It must be pointed out, however, that one passage in Homily XIV calls to mind Photius' "enthronistic" letter to Pope Nicholas I (860). Homily XIV (p. 230 below = Ar I. 193): χαίρει ... καὶ κυβερνήτης δὲ τὴν ὁλκάδα βλέπων ἐξ οὐρίου τὰ νῶτα τῆς θαλάσσης ἐπισκιρτῶσαν καὶ διατέμνουσαν ... ναὶ δὴ χαρᾶς ἀφάτου πληροῦται καὶ ἀγαλλιάσεως καὶ ὁ τῶν Χριστοῦ θρεμμάτων τὴν ποιμνιαρχίαν κληρωσάμενος, τῆς λογικῆς ποίμνης ἐνευθηνουμένης τοῖς κατορθώμασι, etc. Letter to Nicholas I (ed. Valettas, p. 136): οἶδε γὰρ, οἶδε καὶ κυβερνήτῃ καλῶς τὸ σκάφος οὐριοδρομοῦν τε καὶ πηδαλιουχούμενον εὐθυμίας καθίστασθαι πρόξενον· καὶ τὸ τῆς ἐκκλησίας πλήρωμα εὐσεβείᾳ καὶ ἀρεταῖς ἐνευθηνούμενον τὸν ἐφεστηκότα καὶ κριθέντα ποιμαίνειν εὐφραίνειν τε καὶ τὸ τῆς ἀμηχανίας ὁμιχλῶδες παρασκευάζειν ἀποτρίψασθαι. The simile is, however, rather banal, and there is no reason why it should not have been repeated at an interval of a few years.

THE HOMILIES OF PHOTIUS

no. XV – February 23, 867.
no. XVI – March 2, 867.[76]

The above table should, however, be regarded with caution. While it is true that the chronological principle was sometimes observed in contemporary Byzantine publications, it is also known that in certain cases, as with the correspondence of St. Theodore Studites[77] or that of Leo Choirosphactes,[78] the order was either not altogether accurate from the beginning or was later confused by copyists. Thus, we cannot be sure, even if Homilies XV and XVI belong to 867, that the remaining ones are placed in correct sequence.

MANUSCRIPTS

Because frequent reference to manuscripts of the Homilies is made in the course of this work, it has appeared advisable to present the following short description of them.[79] Naturally no guarantee can be offered that this enumeration is exhaustive. A full discussion of the manuscript tradition must await a critical edition of the Greek text.

A 1. Mount Athos, *Iviron 684* (late sixteenth or early seventeenth century). Contains 16 Homilies (I–XI, XIV–XVIII), pp. 37–234. This weighty tome, numbering 1052 pages, is devoted for the most part to works of Photius. It is written in an ornate hand,

---

[76] Assuming that the first sermon in the series, now lost, was preached on the first Sunday of Lent, which in 867 fell on February 16th. That leaves two more Sundays, March 9th and 16th (leaving out Palm Sunday which was on the 23rd), when Photius could have carried the story of the heresies down to the Second Council.

[77] Cf. Pargoire, "S. Théophane le Chronographe," *Viz. Vrem.*, IX (1902), pp. 73–74; B. Melioranskij, Перечень византійскихъ грамотъ и писемъ I, Записки Имп. Акад. Наукъ, VIIIe sér., Cl. hist.-philol., t. IV, no. 5 (1899), p. 52; Bury, *Eastern Roman Empire*, pp. 451–52.

[78] Cf. G. Kolias, *Léon Choirosphactès*, Athens, 1939, pp. 76–129 (letters re-edited in emended order).

[79] A somewhat misleading account of A, B and Lig is given by Ehrhard, *Überlieferung u. Bestand d. hagiogr. u. homil. Literatur d. griech. Kirche*, I 2, 1938, pp. 227–29. He states without proof that the collection of Homilies contained in A and B originated in the 14th century, and furthermore that Aristarches collated not B, but an exact copy of it. The latter statement is manifestly incorrect.

INTRODUCTION

recalling the Ottoman calligraphy of that period. Besides the Homilies, the MS contains two letters addressed to Pope Nicholas I, a letter to the Syncellus of Antioch, the canons of the Council of 861, 278 other letters, the *Amphilochia*, and two treatises, one "On the Soul" and the other "On the Body" by Nicephorus Blemmydes.[80] At one time this codex belonged to Dionysius IV, Patriarch of Constantinople (1671–1673, 1676–1679, 1683–1684, 1686–1687) who in 1678 bequeathed his library to the Iviron monastery.[81] His ex-libris is found on pp. 1, 16 and 1037.[82] The date of the MS is not known exactly. According to Porfirij Uspenskij, who first found it in 1858, the MS was completed on Saturday, the 26th of July, 1628.[83] Aristarches, who did not see the MS itself, but was using a transcription made for him by the monk Jacob of Vatopedi, states that on p. 162 of the MS was a note giving the date April 26, 1627.[84] Papadopoulos-Kerameus, on the other hand, who examined the MS in 1895, was unable to find in it any such notes, and dated the MS on palaeographic grounds to the late sixteenth century, suggesting furthermore that the scribe was Constantine Alexander Hierax, Great Logothete of the Oecumenical Patriarchate, who was active in the nineties of the sixteenth century.[85] Papadopoulos-Kerameus admits, however, that the MS had been bound and its pages cropped shortly before his time, which explains the disappearance of the notations. Unfortunately, neither Uspenskij nor the monk Jacob (who dated the MS in the fourteenth century!) gives any information about the handwriting of the missing notes, so it is impossible to say whether they in fact recorded

---

[80] Cf. A. Heisenberg, *Nicephori Blemmydae curriculum vitae et carmina*, Leipzig, 1896, pp. lxxxiii–iv; V. I. Barvinok, Никифоръ Влеммидъ и его сочиненія, Kiev, 1911, pp. 316–22.

[81] Cf. M. Gedeon, Πατριαρχικοὶ πίνακες, Constantinople, 1884, p. 601.

[82] The MS has been described by Papadopoulos-Kerameus, Святѣйшаго патріарха Фотія ... XLV неизданныхъ писемъ, St. Petersburg, 1896, pp. iv–xiv; Sp. Lambros, *Catalogue of the Greek Manuscripts on Mount Athos*, II, Cambridge, 1900, pp. 201–203. Lambros was denied access to the MS, and drew up his description of it from data supplied by the monk Jacob of Vatopedi, who transcribed the text of the Homilies for Aristarches.

[83] Четыре бесѣды Фотія, p. 51.

[84] I, p. ροι'.

[85] See above, pp. 11–12.

THE HOMILIES OF PHOTIUS

the dates of writing or were later jottings.[86] If the MS was copied in 1627–28, the scribe could not have been Alexander Hierax, who died in 1603.

B 2. *Metochion Panagiou Taphou 529*, a volume of 393 pp. Pages 1–384 are written in a hand very close to that of A, while pp. 385–393 are in a different, though contemporary, hand. According to Papadopoulos-Kerameus, this MS was written at the end of the sixteenth century by the same Hierax. It contains the same sixteen Homilies as A (pp. 89–300; the greater part of no. V is, however, missing), in addition to two fragments from the *Amphilochia*, five letters of Photius, and a number of theological tracts by other authors. The initials have not been written in. On p. 382 is the following note: τὸ παρὸν βιβλίον ὑπάρχει ἐμοῦ Πετράσκου, υἱοῦ δὲ Πέτρου βοϊβόδα καὶ Σκουλαρίου καὶ τῶν φίλων. Aristarches is wrong in identifying the Voevode in question with Stephen Petriceicu, prince of Moldavia from 1672 to 1674.[87] The owner of the MS was certainly Petraşcu, son of Peter Cercel, prince of Wallachia (1583–1585). Very little is known of Petraşcu except that he was still alive in 1630, by which time he had become a monk

---

[86] At the beginning of the treatise "On the Body" (p. 1013) the following monogram appears in the margin

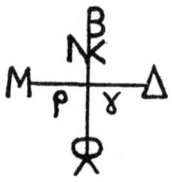

which, says Papadopoulos-Kerameus, may conceal the scribe's name in the event it was not Alexander Hierax. An almost identical monogram appears, however, in another Metochion MS (no. 252, f. 293ᵛ) in connection with the same treatises (Papadopoulos-Kerameus, Ἱεροσολυμιτικὴ βιβλιοθήκη, IV, [1899], p. 220), and, as Aristarches has convincingly shown (II, pp. 275–76), it ought to be read Νικηφόρου Βλεμίδου (sic). The Metochion 252 was written in 1566 by Ierotheus, later metropolitan of Monembasia.

[87] I, p. ροη′. The existence of this MS was first noted by Sathas, Μεσαιωνικὴ βιβλιοθήκη, I, Venice, 1872, p. 310. Described by Papadopoulos-Kerameus, Ἱεροσολυμιτικὴ βιβλιοθήκη, V, St. Petersburg, 1915, pp. 85–89, and by Κ. Moraitakes, Συμπληρωματικὸς κατάλογος κωδίκων τοῦ ἐν τῷ Φαναρίῳ Κωνσταντινουπόλεως Μετοχίου τοῦ Παναγίου Τάφου, Ὀρθοδοξία, XIII (1938), p. 184.

INTRODUCTION

under the name of Parthenius.[88] Thus the MS cannot be much later than the end of the sixteenth century.

With regard to the text of the Homilies, B often differs from A, though not substantially. Generally speaking, B tends to be more elliptical by omitting certain words which are found in A. It was Šestakov's contention that B was the more trustworthy of the two MSS, in that it reproduced faithfully what he thought to be Photius' elliptical style.[89] The relative merits of A and B should, however, be studied anew, because most of the elliptical constructions that Šestakov accepted as authentic are so harsh that one is more inclined to take the opposite view, namely that B is often at fault in such cases. The exact relationship of A to B is difficult to determine. Neither one appears to have been copied from the other, yet they obviously belong to the same family. This is made especially clear by the marginal notes ση(μείωσαι), ὡρ(αῖον) and γνώ(μη) which occur at the same places in both MSS, except that B sometimes omits a few of these notations that are found in A.

3. *Athens, National Library 2756* (late thirteenth or fourteenth century). Consisting of 209 folios, this MS is mutilated and generally in bad condition. It contains ten Homilies (nos. IX–XVIII), ff. 1–36, followed by 183 letters of Photius. The text presents a great number of short lacunae indicating either that the scribe was often unable to decipher his original and left gaps to be filled in later, or, more probably, that the original was defective. From the published descriptions it is impossible to tell if the lacunae occur at regular intervals; if they do,

---

[88] On Petraşcu, see C. Grecescu, "Pătraşcu, fiul lui Petru Cercel," *Rivistă Istorică Română*, IX (1939), pp. 178–183, who discusses a note, similar to ours, in the Dresden D. a 43. E: Γραμματικὴ Πετράσκου εὐτελοῦ (sic), υἱοῦ δὲ Πέτρου τοῦ Σκουλαρικᾶ πάσης Μεγαλοβλαχίας. The surname Cercel (= earring, from the fact that Peter learnt to wear earrings at the French court) is rendered by the Greek Σκουλάριος or Σκουλαρικᾶς from the late-Byzantine word σκουλλαρίκιον, mod. Gr. σκουλαρίκι (cf. Meursius, *Glossarium graecobarbarum*, Leyden, 1614, s.v.) I wish to thank Dr. E. D. Tappe of the School of Slavonic and East European Studies, London University, for confirming this identification. Cf. also Const. C. Giurescu, *Istoria Românilor*, II 1, Bucharest, 1943, p. 233.
[89] *Viz. Vrem.*, IX (1902), pp. 253 sq.

certain conclusions could be drawn about the form of the original.[90]

Lig 4. *Paris, Suppl. gr. 286*, ff. 454–477. Extracts from sixteen Homilies made in 1670 by Paisios Ligarides, and published in full by Jernstedt.[91] The importance of this MS for a critical edition of the *Homilies* ought to be stressed. Already Jernstedt, who collated Lig with A only in the case of Homilies III and IV, was able, on the basis of two minor variants, to express himself as follows:

"1. The codex of Ligarides is very close to A.
2. The codex of Ligarides is not identical with A.
3. The codex of Ligarides is not worse than A, but probably better.
4. The codex of Ligarides is the archetype of A."[92]

This deduction, based an a very keen philological sense, can now be further substantiated. It is quite true that Lig is extremely close to A, much more so than to B.[93] Like A, the excerpts of Ligarides begin with the two letters to Pope Nicholas I, the letter to the Syncellus of Antioch and the canons of the Council of 861. Ligarides, on the other hand, does not allude to the 278 other letters and the *Amphilochia* which are also contained in A. We should note that the *Amphilochia* had not been published in full at that time, and would have doubtless drawn the interest of Ligarides had that work been included in his MS. Here are a few examples to show that Lig is not wholly dependent on A:

---

[90] Described by G. Kournoutos and B. Laourdas in Θεολογία, XXV (1954), pp. 177–188, and by J. Darrouzès (who discovered the MS) in *Revue des études byzantines*, XII (1954), pp. 183–86. Cf. also A. Wenger, *ibid.*, XIII (1955), p. 161.
[91] *Mémoires de l'Acad. Imp. des Sciences de St. Pét.*, VIIIe série, cl. hist.-phil., VII, no. 8, 1906.
[92] *Ibid.*, p. 04.
[93] This could be proved by a confrontation of a great many passages. A glance at the titles of the Homilies is, however, sufficient to substantiate this conclusion. Thus, the title of no. II is found in B, while it is missing in A. It was likewise missing in Ligarides' MS. On the other hand, the titles of nos. VIII and IX are complete in A and Lig, while they are incomplete in B.

INTRODUCTION

Homily III (Ar II. 18): καὶ συμπένθησον καὶ πένθησον ἐπ' αὐτῇ AB: καὶ συμπάθησον καὶ πένθησον Lig, which is surely better.

Homily IV (Ar II. 32): ὅσῳ δὲ ξένη καὶ δεινὸς ἄτοπος AB: καὶ δεινὸς καὶ ἄτοπος Lig, which is probably right.

Homily VI (Ar II. 186): καρποφορήσωμεν δικαιοσύνην (δαπάνην B) τὴν κάλλιστα τὸν ἀνθρώπινον συναρμόζουσαν καὶ συμβιβάζουσαν AB: τὰ ἀνθρώπινα συναρμόζουσάν τε καὶ συμβιβάζουσαν Lig, which is precisely the way Papageorgiou emended this passage.

Homily VIII (Ar II. 413): ἐσκοτίσθη ἐν τοῖς διαλογισμοῖς αὐτῶν ἡ ἀσύνετος αὐτῶν καρδία read by A: first αὐτῶν omitted by B and Lig.

Homily IX (Ar II. 344): εἰκόνα φέρειν χαριτώσας τοῦ πλάσαντος A, B, Chalc. 1 and Vat. Reg. 15. Lig by mistake writes τοῦ πλάσματος, but the same mistake appears in Monac. 443.

Homily X (Ar II. 438$_3$): σπουδαργήσαντα (sic) Lig: σπουδαρχήσαντα corrected in the same hand from σπουδαργήσαντα A.

Homily XI (Ar II. 451): τῶν εὐαγγελικῶν ἐξαψαμένῳ ῥημάτων Lig and Coislin. 107: ἐξαψαμένων A and B.

Ibid. (Ar II. 454): χείλη δὲ συμπῆξαι παρασκευάσω Lig: συμπτύξαι Coislin. 107: συμπήξω AB.

Ibid. (Ar II. 466$_7$): τῶν ἐν τῷ βίῳ κακῶν Lig and Coislin. 107: τῶν ἐν βίῳ AB.

5. *Palatino-Heidelbergensis gr. 129* (fourteenth–fifteenth century). A miscellany of the type associated with Maximus Planudes. It contains excerpts from Homilies III and IV (f. 122^r), X (f. 122^v), XVII and XVIII (f. 141^r), which have been published by K. Müller, as well as a further quotation from no. XVII (f. 122^r) and excerpts from nos. XV and XVI (ff. 140^v–141^v) which Müller did not recognize.[94]

---

[94] See Konrad Müller, "Fragmente von Homilien des Photius," *Zeitschrift für Kirchengeschichte*, IV (1881), pp. 130–36; cf. *id.*, "Zu den planudischen Excerpten im cod. Palatinus 129," *Rheinisches Museum*, XXXVI (1881), pp. 145–50; H. Stevenson, *Codices mss Palat. gr. Bibl. Vaticanae*, Rome, 1885, pp. 61–62; H. Haupt, "Über die Herkunft der dem Dio Cassius beigelegten planudischen Excerpte," *Hermes*, XIV (1879), pp. 48 sq., and

6. *Chalki, Commercial School 64 (61)*, ff. 300ʳ–302ʳ. A miscellany of excerpts from classical and Christian works (fourteenth century), including both the Letters and the Homilies of Photius. The Homilies represented are I, II, III, IV, VIII, XI, XII, XV, XVI, XVII and XVIII. The order of these excerpts is somewhat haphazard. The MS is now at the Oecumenical Patriarchate.[95]

7. *Jerusalem, Greek Patriarchate 1* (tenth century), being a collection of lives of saints and homilies for the month of February. It contains (ff. 30ʳ–36ʳ) Homily XV, which was published after this MS by Papadopoulos-Kerameus.[96]

8. *Paris, Coislin. 107* (eleventh century), being a collection of homilies from Palm Sunday to the Decollation of St. John the Baptist. It contains (ff. 35ʳ–45ᵛ) Homily XI, the beginning of which is, however, missing.[97] This is the "Seguieranus codex" mentioned by Combefis who refrained from publishing the Homily in question because it was incomplete.[98]

9. *Cod. Vat. Reg. Svec. 15* (twelfth or thirteenth century), a menologium from September 8th to the beginning of February, containing Homily IX (ff. 32ᵛ–39ʳ).[99] It was on the basis of this MS, originally in the library of Cardinal Mazarin, that Combefis published Homily IX, the first Photian Homily to appear in print. The same Homily was transcribed from this

---

443–46; E. Piccolomini, "Intorno ai *collectanea* di Massimo Planude," *Rivista di filologia*, II (1874), p. 103, n. 1; A. Diller, "Codices Planudei," *BZ*, XXXVII (1937), p. 297, n. 1.

[95] Aimilianos Tsakopoulos, Περιγραφικὸς κατάλογος τῶν χειρογράφων τῆς βιβλ. τοῦ Οἰκουμενικοῦ Πατριαρχείου, I, Istanbul, 1953, p. 113. The Photian excerpts of this MS are not mentioned in the previous catalogue by the metropolitan Athenagoras, Κατάλογος τῶν χειρογράφων τῆς ἐν Χάλκῃ Μονῆς τῆς Παναγίας, Ἐπετηρὶς Ἑταιρ. Βυζαντ. Σπουδῶν, XI (1935), pp. 167–68.

[96] Правосл. Палест. Сборникъ, XI 1, St. Petersburg, 1892, pp. 25 sq. Cf. Ἱεροσολυμιτικὴ βιβλιοθήκη, I, St. Petersburg, 1891, pp. 3–4; Ehrhard, *op. cit.*, I, pp. 567 sq.

[97] R. Devreesse, *Le fonds Coislin (B. N. Catalogue des manuscrits grecs*, II), Paris, 1945, p. 96. Cf. Ehrhard, *op. cit.*, II, pp. 271–72.

[98] *Graecolat. Patrum bibl. novum auctarium*, Paris, 1648, cols. 1605–06.

[99] H. Stevenson, *Codices mss gr. Reg. Svec. et Pii PP. II*, Rome, 1888, p. 10; *Catalogus codd. hagiogr. gr. bibl. Vat.* (*Subsidia hagiographica*, VII), Brussels, 1899, p. 230; Ehrhard, *op. cit.*, III, pp. 470 sq.

INTRODUCTION

MS by Antonios Kateforos, whose copy is now in Venice (App. ad codd. gr. II 15 [1090], ff. 409ʳ–420ʳ).[100]

10. *Monac. 443* (fourteenth century), a two-month menologium, containing Homily IX (ff. 125–130).[101]

11. *Athens, National Library 2449* (fourteenth century). This MS, which is a *panegyrikon* without regard to the calendar, originally belonged to the monastery of St. John the Forerunner near Serres (no. II 21). Upon its transfer to Athens, it was first catalogued Suppl. 449. It contains Homily VII (ff. 74ʳ–87ʳ).[102]

12. *Chalki, Commercial School 1* (now in the Oecumenical Patriarchate), written in 1360. A collection of miscellaneous homilies, among them our no. IX (ff. 24ᵛ–29ʳ).[103]

13. *Bucharest, Rumanian Academy 595 (377)* (fourteenth century). A mixed collection of sermons and hagiographic texts, containing Homily IX.[104] See Addendum, p. 316 below.

14. *Neapol. gr. III. A.A.6* (fourteenth century). A miscellany, composed largely of profane literature. On ff. 126ʳ–133ᵛ is

---

[100] Antonios Kateforos, a priest from Zacynthus (1696–1763), was preparing a full edition of Photius, which fills seven volumes in the Marcian library (App. ad codd. gr., II, 10–15 and XI, 17). The Latin translation of Homily IX is found in II, 14 (1089), ff. 213ᵛ–217ᵛ. On Kateforos, see Edgar Martini, *Textgeschichte der Bibliotheke des Patr. Photios* (Abh. d. Phil.-Hist. Kl. d. Kön. Sächs. Gesellschaft d. Wiss., XXVIII, 6, Leipzig 1911), pp. 123–26; Sathas, Νεοελληνική φιλολογία, Athens, 1868, pp. 521–23; E. Legrand and H. Pernot, *Bibliographie ionienne*, Paris, 1910, nos. 281, 308, 313, 317, 319, 325, 406, 448, 516, 530, 2002; Lambros in Νέος Ἑλληνομνήμων, VIII (1911), pp. 106–7.

[101] I. Hardt, *Catalogus codd. mss bibl. reg. Bavaricae, Codd. gr.*, IV, Munich, 1810, p. 378; cf. Van de Vorst and H. Delehaye, *Catalogus codd. hagiogr. gr. Germaniae, Belgii, Angliae* (Subsidia hagiographica, XIII), Brussels, 1913, pp. 130–32; Ehrhard, *op. cit.*, III, pp. 33–34.

[102] Ehrhard, *op. cit.*, III, p. 763.

[103] Aimilianos Tsakopoulos, *op. cit.*, p. 10; cf. Ehrhard, *op. cit.*, III, pp. 473–75; Papadopoulos-Kerameus, Ἡ ἐν τῷ νησίῳ Σωζοπόλεως βασιλικὴ μονὴ Ἰωάννου τοῦ Προδρόμου καὶ ἡ τύχη τῆς βιβλιοθήκης αὐτῆς, *Viz. Vrem.*, VII (1900), p. 670, no. 1.

[104] Constantin Litzica, *Biblioteca Academiei Române. Catalogul manuscriptelor grecești*, Bucharest, 1909, p. 275. Litzica attributes this MS to the thirteenth century, but it cannot be earlier than the fourteenth since it contains a text by Theodore Metochites. Cf. Ehrhard, *op. cit.*, III 2 (1952), p. 821, no. 14.

THE HOMILIES OF PHOTIUS

found Homily X.[105] It was probably after this MS that the Homily in question was published by Lambeck in 1655.[106]

15. *Vat. gr. 759* (fourteenth century), a *catena* on Luke.[107] It contains extracts from Homilies V and XI, published by Mai.[108]

16. *Codex Suprasliensis* (eleventh century). A Church Slavonic menaeum for the month of March.[109] It contains a translation of Homily VIII (pp. 332–342). This bulky MS has been split up into three parts: pp. 1–236 are at Ljubljana, pp. 237–268 at Leningrad, and pp. 269–570 presumably at Warsaw.

LOST MANUSCRIPT

A manuscript containing eleven Homilies of Photius was at one time preserved in the library of the Escorial and probably perished in the fire of 1671.[110] It may have been acquired by Diego Hurtado de Mendoza († 1575) who spent twenty years as ambassador in Italy and amassed an important collection of Greek MSS, most of which, however, were copies made at his behest. In 1579 a succinct catalogue of the Greek MSS of the Escorial was made by Guill. Lindanus which lists: *Variae sequuntur Homiliae ut Photii*

---

[105] Salvatore Cirillo, *Codices graeci mss. Regiae bibl. Borbonicae*, II, Naples, 1832, p. 201. On f. 133ᵛ one sentence from Homily XI has been written twice.

[106] I am greatly indebted to my colleague Mr. John Parker for bringing this manuscript to my attention. There are strong indications that this is indeed the manuscript used by Lambeck. In a previous study by R. J. H. Jenkins and myself it was suggested that Lambeck's manuscript had been lost (*Dumbarton Oaks Papers*, 9–10, [1955–56], p. 125).

[107] R. Devreesse, *Codices Vaticani graeci*, III, Rome, 1950, pp. 276–77; cf. Ios. Sickenberger, *Die Lukaskatene des Niketas von Heracleia* (*Texte und Untersuchungen*, N. F., VII, 4, 1902), pp. 63–64.

[108] *Scriptorum veterum nova collectio*, I, Rome, 1825–31, pp. xix–xx; X, 1837, pp. 631–32, 638–39, 641, 643, 712, 716–17. Also in PG 101, cols. 1216–21, 1225–29.

[109] For the relevant bibliography, see below, p. 150, n. 1.

[110] See Kunik, "Sur un manuscrit de la bibl. de l'Escurial, renfermant un sermon du patriarche Photius," *Bull. hist.-phil. de l'Acad. imp. des Sciences*, VII (1849), no. 5; *id.*, "Nouveaux renseignements sur les deux homélies du patriarche Photius," *ibid.*, VIII (1850), no. 12; *id.* in *Mém. de l'Acad. Imp.*, VIIIᵉ série, Cl. hist.-phil., VII, no. 8 (1906), pp. 77–81.

INTRODUCTION

Constantinopolitani.[111] A fuller version of the same catalogue, communicated to Kunik by the then librarian of the Escorial, gives the following details:

Variae sequuntur Homiliae ut Photii Constantinopolitani. Photii Patriarchae Epistolae quinquaginta novem ... Ejusdem Homiliae XI. Δ. V. I. *In Parascevem, de Ascensione, in Baia et Lazarum,* εἰς τὴν ἔφοδον τῶν φωτῶν. *De Annuntiatione, in Parascevem, in Nativitatem Deiparae, De Detectione imaginis ejus, De templo, de Haeresi.*

Sed haec omnes forsan in dicto incendio periere; postea enim non apparent.

The same description was repeated in the catalogue made in 1647 by Barvoetius, with the exception that the Homily *In Baia et Lazarum* occupies not the third, but the sixth place.[112]

In 1586 a certain Valverde, who was assigned to report on the Greek MSS of the Escorial, wrote as follows: *Tenemos mas otro volúmen de las epístolas de* Libanio, *y junto el Phaedro de* Platon, *y algunos tratados de* Aristóteles, *de* Maximo Planudes, Euclides, *Homelias de* Photio *hechas en S. Sofia, y S.* Irene *sobre la Salutation angélica y Natividad de Nuestra Señora, dia de Ramos, y entrada de los Russianos en Constantinopla,* etc.[113]

It will be noticed that the Escorial MS contained one Homily that has not survived (on the Ascension), and, whereas it was said to include eleven Homilies, only ten titles are given, which probably means that there were two Homilies on the same topic. The order of the Homilies as given by Barvoetius is fairly close to that of our extant MSS:

> *In Parasceven* (I or II)
> *De Ascensione* (lost)
> εἰς τὴν ἔφοδον τῶν φωτῶν (i.e., εἰς τὴν ἔφοδον τῶν ῥῶς, III or IV, or both)[114]
> *De Annuntiatione* (V or VII)

---

[111] Reproduced by E. Miller, *Catalogue des mss grecs de la bibl. de l'Escurial*, Paris, 1848, p. 507.

[112] *Ibid.*, p. 526.

[113] Ch. Graux, *Essai sur les origines du fonds grec de l'Escurial*, Paris, 1880, p. 454.

[114] And not *in festo Epiphaniae*, as interpreted by Fabricius, *Bibl. graeca*, ed. Harles, XI, p. 32.

THE HOMILIES OF PHOTIUS

In Parasceven (VI)
In Baia et Lazarum (VIII)
In Nativitatem Deiparae (IX)
De detectione imaginis ejusdem (XVII)
De templo (X)
De Haeresi (XVIII).

Since, however, the order of Barvoetius does not wholly agree with that of Lindanus, and still less with that of Valverde, it is not advisable to make any deductions from it.

EDITIONS AND TRANSLATIONS

Homily IX was first published by Fr. Combefis, *Patrum bibliothecae novum auctarium*, I, Paris, 1648, cols. 1583–1604; and in *Bibliotheca Patrum concionatoria*, VIII, Paris, 1662, pp. 68–71 (Lat. trans. only); reprinted by A. Gallandi, *Bibliotheca veterum Patrum*, XIII, Venice, 1780, pp. 595–601.

Pater Lambeck (Lambecius) first published Homily X in his notes to Georgius Codinus, Paris, 1655, pp. 187–89 (Greek only); reprinted with Lat. trans. and notes by Combefis, *Originum rerumque Constantinopolitanarum, variis auctoribus, manipulus*, Paris, 1664, pp. 296–306; A. Banduri, *Imperium Orientale*, Paris, 1711, I, lib. IV, pp. 117–21 (text and Lat. trans.), II, pp. 804–7 (commentary); *Corpus script. hist. byz.*, along with Georgius Codinus, Bonn, 1843, pp. 194–202..

Homilies IX and X were reprinted by Eugenios Boulgaris in his ed. of Theodoret (Τοῦ μακαρίτου Θεοδωρήτου ἐπισκόπου Κύρου τὰ σῳζόμενα), V, Halle, 1775, pp. 27–34, 35–39; and after Combefis in PG 102, cols. 547–74.

Homilies III, IV, XVII and XVIII in an incomplete form and marred by many mistakes were first published, with a Russian translation and notes, by the Archimandrite Porfirij Uspenskij, Четыре бесѣды Фотія святѣйшаго архіепископа Константинопольскаго, St. Petersburg, 1864.

INTRODUCTION

A good ed. of Homilies III and IV was first given by A. Nauck, *Lexicon Vindobonense*, St. Petersburg, 1867, pp. 201–32. Re-edited by C. Müller, *Fragmenta historicorum graecorum*, V, Paris, 1883, pp. 162–73.

Twelve Homilies were published by S. Aristarches in the periodical Ἐκκλησιαστικὴ ἀλήθεια (Constantinople): vol. II (1881–2), pp. 133–40 (no. III); pp. 197–206 (no. IV); pp. 407–416 (no. I); vol. III (1882–3), pp. 17–28 (no. II); pp. 97–106 (no. VI); pp. 161–68 (no. V); pp. 305–12 (no. VII); pp. 525–31 (no. VIII); pp. 665–69 (no. XIV); pp. 786–92 (no. XV); Second series, vol. I (1885), pp. 481–507 (no. XVI); vol. II (1886), pp. 177–98 (no. XVII).

A. Papadopoulos-Kerameus, using fresh manuscript material, published Homilies XV and IX in Правосл. Палест. Сборникъ XI 1, St. Petersburg, 1892, pp. 25–52.

Homily XI was first published by P. N. Papageorgiou, Φωτίου πατριάρχου ἀνέκδοτος ὁμιλία, Trieste, 1900 (reprinted from the journal Νέα Ἡμέρα, 1900, nos. 1343–44).

A complete edition of the Homilies (except XII and XIII) was issued by S. Aristarches, Τοῦ ἐν ἁγίοις πατρὸς ἡμῶν Φωτίου ... λόγοι καὶ ὁμιλίαι ὀγδοήκοντα τρεῖς, 2 vols., Constantinople, 1900.

Homilies III and IV (after the Iviron MS) with the excerpts of Paisios Ligarides placed *en regard*, as well as Ligarides' excerpts of the other Homilies, were published by V. K. Jernstedt in *Mémoires de l'Acad. Imp. des Sciences de St.-Pét.*, VIIIᵉ sér., Cl. hist.-philol., vol. VII, no. 8 (1906), pp. 06–039; 1–45.

Homilies XII and XIII were published by G. P. Kournoutos and B. Laourdas in Θεολογία, XXV 2, Athens, 1954, pp. 177–99.

A Russian translation of Homilies III and IV by E. L(ovjagin) appeared in Христіанское Чтеніе, St. Petersburg, Sept./Oct. 1882, pp. 414–43.

A Russian translation of Homilies I and II by I. N...skij came out in Ярославскія Епархіальныя Вѣдомости, XLV (1904), pp. 127–34, 147–50, 171–84, 193–96.

THE HOMILIES OF PHOTIUS

METHOD OF THE PRESENT PUBLICATION

The translation is based on the text of Aristarches, whose pagination is indicated in the margin. The edition of Aristarches is unfortunately marred by a great number of arbitrary emendations, most of which, however, have been rectified by Papageorgiou and Šestakov. Furthermore, Aristarches has been very careless in his collation of the MSS. Consequently, I have been obliged to collate them anew. My own use of the MSS has been as follows. Nos. 1 (Iviron 684), 2 (Metochion 529), 5 (Palat. 129), 6 (Chalc. 64), 7 (Hierosol. 1), 8 (Coislin. 107), 9 (Vat. Reg. 15), 10 (Monac. 443), 11 (Athen. 2449), 12 (Chalc. 1), 13 (Bucharest 595) and 14 (Neapol. III. A. A. 6) have been consulted on photographic reproductions. For no. 4 I have relied on Jernstedt's extremely careful edition, for no. 15 on Mai's edition, and for no. 16 on Severjanov's diplomatic edition. I am sorry to report that the use of no. 3 (Athen. 2756) has been refused by the National Library of Greece.

Whenever the translation departs from the printed text of Aristarches, a note to that effect has been appended. This, however, applies only to such necessary corrections as affect the meaning, not to minor points of grammar, spelling and adherence to the manuscript tradition, which could have been dealt only with in a critical edition. Changes of punctuation have not, as a rule, been noted. For the sake of convenience, Aristarches' division into paragraphs, though not always adopted, has been indicated by means of Arabic numerals.

Homilies XII and XIII, which are absent from Aristarches, have been translated from the edition of Messrs Kournoutos and Laourdas, whose pagination is likewise given in the margin. The division into paragraphs is our own.

Whenever words not found in the Greek text had to be supplied from the context for the sake of greater clarity, such words have been italicized.

Scriptural references are, as a rule, limited to explicit quotations. Old Testament references are to the Rahlfs edition of the Septuagint.[115] No attempt has been made to determine the recensions of the Old and New Testaments used by Photius. Even a cursory

[115] *Septuaginta*, ed. Alfred Rahlfs, 3rd ed., Stuttgart, 1949, 2 vols.

INTRODUCTION

examination will show that Photius was not always following the so-called uniform Byzantine text;[116] but such an investigation, for all its interest to Biblical scholars, would have been out of place here.

The commentary is not intended to exhaust all the exegetical problems raised by the Homilies, but merely to provide the necessary historical background, whenever that is possible. Questions of religious doctrine, of literary comparison, as well as Photius' borrowings from other authors have not been dealt with at any length. To have done so would have required much more space and a wider competence than the editor possesses.

[116] See J. Neville Birdsall, "The Text of the Gospels in Photius," *Journal of Theological Studies*, New Series, VII (1956), pp. 42–55; 190–198.

NOTE ON HOMILIES I AND II

Homilies I, II and VI, according to their titles, were delivered all three on Good Friday in the old patriarchal church of St. Irene.[1] In the case of Homilies II and VI there can be no doubt that their titles are correct. As for Homily I, there is a strong likelihood, as we shall see in a moment, that it was preached not on Good Friday, but closer to the beginning of Lent.

The catechism or *catechesis* mentioned in the three Homilies refers to the instruction of new converts, the catechumens, who were to be baptized on Holy Saturday. The number of such converts must have been considerable during Photius' patriarchate owing to his vast proselytizing activities. The *Typicon* of St. Sophia, which is not much later in date, prescribes special lections for Holy Saturday in the event the patriarch is unduly delayed while baptizing new converts.[2] The *catechesis* was still a vital function of the Church, not a mere formality.

According to the ruling of the Council of Laodicea, the enrolment of the *illuminandi* had to take place not later than the second week of Lent.[3] The order of the ensuing instruction, culminating in baptism on Holy Saturday, varied greatly from region to region. For the Church of Constantinople, we know that as early as the fifth century it was the custom for the bishop to conduct the final *catechesis* on Good Friday, including, on that occasion, the *traditio symboli*.[4] The *Book of Ceremonies* refers to this practice in its account of the protocol for Good Friday: "About the third or fourth hour of the same day, the patricians, on being commanded, go to the church of St. Irene, in order that they may be present when the patriarch is performing the holy catechism in that church."[5] The

[1] Cf. A. Van Millingen in W. S. George, *The Church of St. Eirene at Constantinople*, Oxford, 1912, p. 7.
[2] A. Dmitrievskij, Описаніе литургическихъ рукописей, I, Kiev, 1895, p. 133.
[3] Can. 45, Mansi, II, 571.
[4] Theodorus Lector, *Hist. eccl.*, II. 32 (PG 86 1, col. 201 A).
[5] Bonn ed., p. 179 = A. Vogt's ed., I, Paris, 1935, pp. 167–8.

NOTE ON HOMILIES I AND II

text of such a *catechesis* has been preserved in the famous Barberini Euchology (Barb. gr. 336) of the late eighth or ninth century.[6] It also occurs in the Sinaiticus 959, ff. 113^r sq., of the eleventh century,[7] and in a manuscript Gospel of the Vatopedi monastery (no. 869, ff. 221^v sq.) of the twelfth century.[8] This text refers to the same ceremony in the church of St. Irene, and it is not unlikely that it represents, more or less, the *catechesis* that preceded Homilies II and VI, especially in view of some textual resemblances which will be pointed out below (see p. 123).

Homily I opens with a reference to the *catechesis* that went before it. This in no way indicates that the beginning of the sermon is missing, as some scholars have supposed,[9] but merely that the sermon was preached after the instruction of the catechumens. When we consider the rest of the Homily, we are at once struck by the absence of any reference to the Passion, whereas in Homilies II and VI it is dealt with at some length. Our suspicions are also aroused by the words of the opening paragraph: "So much then has been said ... for those who are already prepared for baptism, though not yet perfected," etc. It would seem that the "perfecting" here referred to was the final instruction conducted through Lent, whereas on Good Friday that instruction would have been completed. When we turn to paragraph seven, we are confronted by an even more decisive statement: "Besides, the annual course of holy fasting is upon us (καὶ γὰρ καὶ τὸ ἐτήσιον τῆς ἱερᾶς νηστείας ἐφέστηκε στάδιον), inviting us to the race, and urging us to wrestle with the foe," etc. (below, p. 54). Such an exhortation would hardly have been appropriate on the penultimate day of Passion week. We must conclude, therefore, that Homily I was not delivered on Good Friday, but rather in the beginning of Lent, perhaps on the second Sunday, when the *illuminandi* were enrolled. It would be easy for

---

[6] Printed by Goar, Εὐχολόγιον *sive rituale Graecorum*, Paris, 1647, pp. 340–44. Cf. *Dict. d'archéol. chrét. et de lit.*, s. v. Baptême, vol. II 1, col. 290.

[7] Dmitrievskij, *op. cit.*, II, Kiev, 1901, p. 59.

[8] Γέρων Ἀρκάδιος Βατοπεδινός, "Αἱ ἐν τῷ ναῷ τῆς ἁγ. Εἰρήνης κατὰ τὴν Μ. Παρασκευὴν τελούμεναι 'θεῖαι κατηχήσεις'," Ἐπετηρὶς Ἑταιρ. Βυζαντ. Σπουδῶν, VII (1930), pp. 382–387.

[9] Hergenröther, *Photius*, III, p. 233; Valettas, Φωτίου Ἐπιστολαί, London, 1864, p. 94, n. 1; Ar I, p. 463.

an editor who read only the first paragraph to assume that this Homily fell in line with nos. II and VI which were unquestionably delivered on Good Friday. Aristarches has noted the difficulty (I. 463), but has refrained from drawing the natural conclusion.

In all three "catechetical" Homilies Photius refers repeatedly to an agreement or covenant (συνθῆκαι, παραθῆκαι, ὁμολογία) "which before angels and men we have pledged to God," the text of which had been read aloud before the sermon.[10] This is, most probably, a reference to the *catechesis* which, in the Barberini codex, is entitled ἀπόταξις (i.e. renunciation of the devil) καὶ σύνταξις (i.e. pact with God), and is likened therein to a written contract. The presence of angels is also mentioned in the same office, which enjoins the catechumens to raise their arms as if to be searched by angels.

The little that can be learned about the date of Homilies I and II has been said above (pp. 19, 23). Aristarches, with his customary oversubtlety, tries to prove that no. I was spoken on the 4th of April 861 in the presence of the legates of Pope Nicholas I, for whose benefit Photius inserted a laudatory mention of St. Peter (below, p. 50), which Aristarches finds rather embarrassing and apt to "scandalise some members of the pious congregation." In Homily XVIII (below, p. 312), however, Photius again refers to St. Peter in similar terms, a passage which Aristarches arbitrarily omitted. Other statements of the "primacy" of St. Peter are found in the Letters and the *Amphilochia*.[11] More plausible is the suggestion of Aristarches that the reference to the Flood and the punishment of Sodom in Homily I (below, p. 49) is echoed in the first Homily on the Russian attack (below, p. 87), in which Photius exclaims, "Often have I pointed out to you the ashes of the Sodomites, and the flood that went before," etc. If this line of argument is followed, there is some reason for believing, since the Russian incursion occurred on the 18th of June 860, that Homily I was delivered in the early part of that year, if not the previous year.

[10] Homily I, Ar I. 470; Homily II, Ar II. 163–64; Homily VI, Ar II. 180, 183.
[11] The relevant passages have been collected by M. Jugie, "Photius et la primauté de St. Pierre et du Pape," *Bessarione*, XXIII (1919), pp. 123–29. Cf. M. Gordillo, "Photius et primatus romanus," *Orient. Christ. period.*, VI (1940), p. 30.

HOMILY I. THE BEGINNING OF LENT

I

First Homily of Photius, The Most-blessed Patriarch,[1] Ar I 469 Delivered on Good Friday from the Ambo of St. Irene, after the Conclusion of the Catechism.

1. So much then *has been said* in the preceding words for those who are already prepared for baptism, though not yet perfected, but as yet both in need of purification and debarred from the mystical table. 2. But what of us, already purified through the Spirit, perfected through Grace, deemed worthy of the Gift—the royal priesthood, the peculiar people, the holy nation,[2] whom not the blood of calves, goats and rams[3] sacrificed according to ancient rites, but the Lord Himself hath purchased with His own blood,[4] Ar I 470 who have renounced wicked deeds, and have professed goodness and justice, who have put off the old man with his desires of the flesh[5] and have put on Christ?[6] Indeed, as many of us as have been baptized into Christ have put on Christ[7] and have become members of Christ; for we have learnt from the divine Paul's teaching that our bodies are members of Christ.[8] What then of us? Have we preserved our bridal condition unsoiled, not letting it be polluted by any evil?[9] Have we maintained our earnest of the future blessedness free from trafficking, not enticed by the allurements of harlot Pleasure, nay, have we repelled and spat upon the procuress Negligence by means of a temperate mind and a diligent life? Have we, mindful of the covenant which before angels and men we have pledged to God, kept it inviolate, showing ourselves by the fulfilment of our promises faithful to the commandments of which we have been deemed worthy? Have we barred all entry to

---

[1] The title in the MSS is as follows: Φωτίου τοῦ ἁγιωτάτου πατριάρχου [so B; A has merely τοῦ αὐτοῦ] ὁμιλία α] λεχθεῖσα τῇ ἁγίᾳ παρασκευῇ ἐν τῷ ἄμβωνι τῆς ἁγίας Εἰρήνης μετὰ τὴν συμπλήρωσιν τῶν κατηχήσεων. Ar has added Κωνσταντίνου πόλεως after πατριάρχου.
[2] Exod. 19. 5–6; 1 Peter, 2. 9.
[3] Cf. Hebr. 9. 12.
[4] Acts 20. 28.
[5] Coloss. 3. 9–10; cf. Eph. 2. 3; 1 John 2. 16.
[6] Rom. 13. 14.
[7] Galat. 3. 27.
[8] 1 Cor. 6. 15.
[9] Reading: ἆρα τὸ [τὸν codd, Ar] νυμφικὸν [νυμφίον Pg] διεσωσάμεθα ἄχραντον μηδενὶ καταμολυνθῆναι παραχωρήσαντες χείρονι [χιτῶνα Ar];

the Evil one, and have we made our souls a temple of the most-holy Ghost, or rather the temple built for the most-holy Ghost—as the blessed Paul cries out, "Know ye not that your bodies[10] are the temple of the Holy Ghost which is in you?"[11]—have we kept it undefiled that we may not be destroyed? For, he testifies again, "if any man defile the temple of God, him shall God destroy."[12] Has not the gift of Grace been stolen from us, has not our liberty been enslaved, our purity soiled, our brightness darkened? Have we not betrayed our security through negligence? Is our watchman still keeping his sleepless and slumberless watch? Are we still carolled by the angels, ministers of the mysteries, who joined in rejoicing at our rebirth and stood by as unexceptionable witnesses to our covenant with God? Blessed are they whose transgressions are forgiven and whose sins are covered.[13] Do we still speak boldly to our enemies and say menacingly, "The Lord is my light and my Saviour; whom shall I fear? The Lord is the defender of my life; of whom shall I be afraid?"[14] Do we still have the courage to sing to the Lord, "I have done judgment and justice; deliver me not to them that injure me,"[15] and, "I will not be afraid of evils: for Thou art with me?"[16] If we still do these things, and are held worthy of these mysteries, and regulate our life with virtues, turning away from the seat of pestilent men[17] and avoiding their path and loathing the designs of the impious, then verily are our feats against the Evil one good and noble, but our hopes greater by far: an endless blessedness, the kingdom of heaven, rejoicing with the angels, and joy unspeakable,[18] where the patriarchs have their choirs, the fathers their assemblies, the martyrs their ranks, and all who have pleased God their gay and spacious abode. But if we have slipped away from these things, and set at nought (O, my wretchedness!) our pacts with God, and moreover the Devil laughs

---

[10] τὰ σώματα codd: τὸ σῶμα Ar.
[11] 1 Cor. 6. 19; cf. 3. 16.
[12] *Ibid.*, 3. 17.
[13] Ps. 31. 1; Rom. 4. 7.
[14] Ps. 26. 1.
[15] Ps. 118. 121.
[16] Ps. 22. 4.
[17] Ps. 1. 1.
[18] Cf. 1 Peter 1. 8.

HOMILY I. THE BEGINNING OF LENT

at our actions, seeing the tares of his wickedness sprouting up among them; if we have so fallen away from God's commands, and have denuded ourselves of assistance from above, and have slipped down to the passions, allowing all liberty and authority over us to our enemies—O, what a fall! Alas, the inconsolable disaster! We have fallen, we have been raised. For common is the plight of our ancestor, and the fall as well as the restoration is the inheritance of all. We fell again after Grace, after the restoration—a pitiable fall, a fall distressing, unpardonable, inexcusable, a fall worthy of many tears. The enemy is unarmed: for the swords of the enemy have failed utterly;[19] while we are armed with the weapons of Grace. Yet he acts shamelessly while we cover ourselves up; he attacks and we collapse, as if we were armed for the very purpose of ascribing him a more outstanding victory against us.

3. What device of salvation remains yet? What refuge of salvation?[20]. We have received the gift of baptism and have made it useless through our wickednesses. We have been illuminated with a heavenly and divine light, and we have darkened it with the murk of our deeds. We have been sealed with a precious and terrible seal (which was unapproachable to enemies and irresistible to foes), but we have torn the seal to pieces, we have broken it up, we have prepared the way against us to savage and wicked robbers—impassioned thoughts. What then do we hope for yet? Do we look to a second baptism? Do we expect a second re-birth?[21] Do we perchance await Christ coming down from heaven again, being crucified, made dead and buried, yea and baptized beforehand that He may renew our baptism again? See how Christ-loving thou art, who lovest not Christ, but desirest Christ to suffer for thee; nay, rather art thou indeed a trafficker in Christ, exceeding the Jews in folly and cruelty, who desirest thy Lord to be crucified and lashed, that thou mayest revel unstintingly in thy passions, and that no difficulty should run counter to thy dissolute wantonness. Is it for this purpose that thou expectest Christ to come again? He shall come, but to separate the chaff from the wheat, gathering the latter

[19] Ps. 9. 7.
[20] 2 Kings 22. 3.
[21] δευτέραν ἀναγέννησιν codd: δευτέραν γέννησιν Ar, who mistakenly gives it as the reading of A.

in the garner with honour, while burning the former with fire.[22] He shall come, yet not in the spirit of mercy, but exacting the penalty for our actions in life, using harshness, and uttering to the sinful that awful and inexorable sentence: "Depart from me, ye accursed, into the outer fire."[23] He shall come, but to judge, on a terrible day. "For near," says the prophet, "is the great day of the Lord, and very harsh;[24] the sound of the day of the Lord is made bitter. A mighty day of wrath is that day, a day of affliction and distress, a day of desolation and destruction, a day of gloom and darkness, a day of cloud and vapour, a day of trumpet and cry,"[25] on which, saith the Lord, "I will make the world desolate, and I will destroy the sinners out of it; and the stars of heaven, and Orion, and all the host of heaven shall not give their light. For I will command," saith He, "evils for the whole world, and *will visit* their sins on the ungodly; and I will destroy the pride of transgressors, and will bring low the pride of the haughty."[26] Seest thou how He shall come? He shall come that these things may be accomplished; for listen to Malachi too as he says, "Behold, a day cometh burning as an oven, and it shall consume them, and all the lawless shall be stubble, and the day that is coming shall set them on fire, saith the Lord Almighty, and there shall not be left of them root or branch."[27] Hearest thou, beloved one, the coming of the Lord, how terrible it is and inexorable? For He shall come not to preach repentance,[28] nor to shed compassion, but to give each man according to his works.[29] "As therefore the tares are gathered and burned in the fire," the Lord Himself saith again in the Gospels, "so shall it be in the end of this world. The Son of man shall send forth his angels, and they shall gather out of his kingdom all things that offend, and them which do iniquity, and shall cast them into a furnace of fire: there shall be wailing and gnashing of teeth."[30] He shall come as a

Ar I 474

---

[22] Mt 3. 12; Lk 3. 17.
[23] Cf. Mt 25. 41.
[24] τραχεῖα codd: ταχεῖα Ar (so Septuagint).
[25] Zeph. 1. 14–16.
[26] Is. 13. 9–11.
[27] Mal. 3. 19.
[28] Cf. Mk 6. 12.
[29] Rom. 2. 6; Ps. 61. 13; Prov. 24. 12.
[30] Mt 13. 40–42.

HOMILY I. THE BEGINNING OF LENT

judge, to part and separate those who have kept His ordinances from those who have not, bestowing on the former the unceasing kingdom, while sending the others to the everlasting worm and fire.

4. What then saith He? Since we have sinned after baptism and been polluted by transgressions, is there yet no hope of salvation for us? Is there no remedy of conversion? Is all gone? Is all vanished, the long-suffering, the love of man, the endurance, the abundant compassion? Is there no recall? Is there no return? Is there no other way of healing? Is there no other means of recovery? Insofar as it lies with our monstrous deeds, there is not. But insofar as it lies with the kindness and ineffable love of God toward man,[31] there is. What then is it? The confession by means of sincere repentance. For it says, "I said, I will confess mine iniquity to the Lord against myself; and thou forgavest the ungodliness of my heart."[32] "Confess your sins one to another," bids us the disciple and brother of the Lord, "and pray one for another, that we may be healed;"[33] and, "if we confess our sins," the beloved disciple pledges himself also, "He is faithful and just to forgive us our sins, and to cleanse us of all unrighteousness."[34] How shall I confess? By imitating the prodigal in falling down and crying out to the Lord with contrite heart and humbleness of spirit, "I have sinned against heaven and in thy sight;[35] receive me, Father, in my repentance." How shall I confess? By departing from error and by abominating sin. For if thou shalt turn, and humble thyself before the Lord, and remove unrighteousness far from thy habitation, the Almighty shall be thy helper.[36] And, "Turn ye to me, and I will turn to you," saith the Lord Almighty.[37] How shall I confess? By turning with all my heart, and by humbling myself with fasting and lamentation and rending of the heart. "For now," saith the Lord our[38] God, "turn ye to me with all your heart, and with fasting and with weeping and

Ar I 475

---

[31] Cf. Tit. 3. 4.
[32] Ps. 31. 5.
[33] James 5. 16.
[34] 1 John 1. 9.
[35] Lk 15. 21.
[36] Job 22. 23, 25.
[37] Zech. 1. 3.
[38] ὁ θεὸς ἡμῶν codd: ὁ θεὸς ὑμῶν Ar, who mistakenly gives it as the reading of B.

THE HOMILIES OF PHOTIUS

with lamentation; and rend your hearts and not your garments, and turn to the Lord your God, for He is merciful and compassionate, long-suffering and plenteous in mercy."[39] How shall I confess? By
Ar I 476 pitying the poor and the beggar, and by forgiving my neighbour's faults. For it says, "the merciful shall obtain mercy,"[40] and, "forgive, and it shall be forgiven you,"[41] and, "a man's mercy is to Him as a signet,"[42] and it is a good gift[43] to them that do it before the most High. Thus is sin wiped out, thus are we cleansed of faults. It is He again that cries out through the prophet Isaiah, "I, even I, am he that blots out thy transgressions, and they shall not be remembered. But do thou remember, and let us plead together: do thou first confess thy transgressions, that thou mayest be justified;"[44] and, "Behold, I have blotted out as a cloud thy transgressions, and thy sins[45] as darkness."[46]

But if the Evil one shamelessly plot against thee again, and inspire thoughts of fornication or, in general, of corporeal passions, inviting thee to unseemly deeds,[47] then set up against his designs this apostolic saying, put it forward like a shield: it will show the missiles ineffectual, if it is wielded wisely and vigorously in the grasp of attention and temperance: "Flee fornication. Every sin that a man doeth is without the body; but he that committeth fornication sinneth against his own body,"[48] that is, he plots against and robs his own body, tearing it away from its kinship with Christ, our true God (for indeed we are His members), and fastening himAr I 477 self onto the unclean demon. For, "he which is joined to an harlot is one body,"[49] and, "Be not deceived, none of them that commit fornication can inherit the kingdom of God,"[50] for "corruption doth

[39] Joel 2. 12–13.
[40] Mt 5. 7.
[41] Cf. Mt 6. 14.
[42] Sir. 17. 22.
[43] Prov. 4. 2.
[44] Is. 43. 25–26.
[45] τὰς ἁμαρτίας codd: τὴν ἁμαρτίαν Ar.
[46] Is. 44. 22.
[47] Reading: καὶ πορνείας βάλῃ λογισμοὺς ἢ καὶ ὅλως [so Pg: καὶ ἢ ὅλως B: ἂν καὶ ἄλλων Ar] παθῶν σωματικῶν, ἐπὶ πράξεις ἀτόπους παρακαλῶν [παρακαλῇ Ar], etc. A has καὶ πορνείας βάλῃ λογισμούς, καὶ πορνείας παθῶν σωματικῶν.
[48] 1 Cor. 6. 18.
[49] *Ibid.*, 6. 16.
[50] *Ibid.*, 6. 9–10.

HOMILY I. THE BEGINNING OF LENT

not inherit incorruption."[51] If thou art dragged down towards acquisitiveness and the insatiable desire of money, say to thyself this Davidic utterance, or rather the utterance of the Spirit: "Thou layest up treasures, and knowest not for whom thou wilt gather them,"[52] and "many have been given to ruin because of gold,"[53] and, "he that loveth gold shall not be justified,"[54] and, "behold the man who made not God his helper, but trusted in the abundance of his wealth, and strengthened himself in his vanity."[55] Add, if thou wilt, the Saviour's threat as well: "Thou fool, who remakest thy houses and buildings and renderest them more magnificent, so that the bulk and burden of thy insatiableness should be hoarded up with greater pomp, this night thy soul shall be taken away from thee, then whose shall those things be which thou hast gathered?"[56] If *the Evil one* attempts to inflame thy soul and puff it up with haughty and boastful thoughts, do not overlook that "the Lord resists the proud, but He gives grace to the humble,"[57] and that "man is like to vanity: his days pass as a shadow,"[58] and that "dust thou art, and unto dust shalt thou return,"[59] and "why are dust and ashes boastful?"[60] and, "everyone that is proud in heart is unclean before the Lord,"[61] and, "exalt not thyself, lest thou fall and bring disgrace on thy soul, and the Lord reveal thy secrets, and strike thee down in the midst of the assembly: for pride is hateful before the Lord."[62] If thou art forced to the abyss of unrighteousness, thou oughtst to say to him outspokenly, with the outspokenness[63] which the exercise of virtue has granted thee: "I have hated and abhorred unrighteousness, but the Lord's law have I loved,"[64] for he that

---

[51] *Ibid.*, 15. 50.
[52] Ps. 38. 7. Both A and B read συνάξεις [συνάζεις Ar].
[53] Sir. 31. 6.
[54] *Ibid.*, 31. 5.
[55] Ps. 51. 9.
[56] Cf. Lk 12. 20.
[57] Prov. 3. 34.
[58] Ps. 143. 4.
[59] Gen. 3. 19.
[60] Sir. 10. 9.
[61] Prov. 16. 5.
[62] Sir. 1. 30; 10. 7.
[63] The MSS read ἐπιφθέγξασθαι δεῖ μετὰ παρρησίας αὐτῷ, παρρησίας δὲ ἣν ἡ τῶν ἀρετῶν ἐργασία ἐχαρίσατο. Ar has omitted αὐτῷ.
[64] Ps. 118. 163.

works righteousness[65] shall be exalted; and, "sow to yourselves righteousness, and ye will reap the fruit of life,"[66] for, another prophet testifies, "the way of righteousness and mercy will find life and glory."[67] If he tries again to entice thee with gluttony and drunkenness, do not thou overlook Job who exhorts and reminds thee that Satan's force is in the navel of the belly.[68] Remember also the prophet Isaiah who cries out saying, "Woe to them that rise up in the morning, and follow strong drink; who wait at it till the evening: for the wine shall burn them."[69] Nor do thou disobey yet another who exhorts and counsels thee well, "Walk not in the wake of thy desires, and restrain thyself from thy appetites,"[70] and, "if thou grantest thy soul contentment of desire, it will make thee a rejoicing to thine enemies."[71] Keep also in mind the Lord's command, or rather His awesome and terrible curse, as He threatens, "Woe unto you that are full! for ye shall hunger,"[72] and, "Take heed to yourselves lest at any time your hearts be overcharged with surfeiting, and drunkenness, and cares of this life, and so that day come upon you unawares; for as a snare shall it come on all them that dwell on the face of the earth."[73] If, after attacking[74] through every species of sin, and having been repulsed with the aforesaid weapons, he falls back on God's goodness and mercy,[75] trying to persuade thee to disregard the punishments (for the enemy is shifty and resourceful, and skilled in preparing for sin our natural impulse which is prone to it), be not neglectful: thou hast again swords and shields forged by God, afforded to thee from divine Scripture, wherewith arming thyself and struggling against the enemy, thou wilt show him vanquished, and filled with every shame and dishonour: for Cain's groaning and fear,[76] and his life worse than death,

---

[65] Ps. 14. 2.
[66] Cf. Hos. 10. 12.
[67] Prov. 21. 21.
[68] Job 40. 16.
[69] Is. 5. 11.
[70] Sir. 18. 30.
[71] Sir. 18. 31.
[72] Lk 6. 25.
[73] Lk 21. 34–35.
[74] Read διὰ πάσης ἰδέας ἁμαρτημάτων προσβαλὼν with the MSS: προβαλὼν Ar.
[75] Tit. 3. 4.
[76] Cf. Gen. 4. 12, 14.

HOMILY I. THE BEGINNING OF LENT

if we make them our study, have the power to shatter and rout the battle-line of his vain designs; the floodgates of heaven opening up,[77] and inundating the whole earth for the sins of her inhabitants—that common and universal shipwreck; then again the Sodomite fire, drawn and borne down from heaven,[78] and mercilessly devouring every generation; the terrible wounds and stripes of the Egyptians visited on the Pharaoh himself and on the Egyptians for disobedience of God's commands, reducing all Egypt to the extremity of ills and dangers, and the abyss of the deep bursting open as a tomb for these same Egyptians on account of their hardness of heart;[79] the Israelites again, when they were enslaved by the passions, often mowed down by kindred hand and sword, and at other times delivered a prey to foreigners, scorched with fire and killed by snakes; and finally, that chosen people, guided by a pillar of cloud,[80] for whose sake those bitter and heavy penalties were inflicted on the Egyptians, for whose sake those great miracles were wrought—for they did not drive away those vain and demoniac thoughts, mindful of what they had suffered for[81]—these same men, who had been deemed worthy of so much and so great providence and grace, paying the penalties of ingratitude and murmuring, were overthrown in the wilderness,[82] and were condemned to banishment from the promised land; then again, Nadab and Abiud, who were of Levi's tribe and consecrated to God, being deprived of their life and made a sudden prey of fire, because they had introduced a strange fire;[83] again, the followers of Dathan and Abiron muttering at Moses and Aaron, and on this account snatched away by a chasm of the ground with all their belongings, buried before death, and

---

[77] Gen. 7. 11.
[78] Gen. 19. 24.
[79] Exod. 7–14.
[80] Exod. 13. 21.
[81] This parenthetical clause seems to make no sense as it stands in the MSS: οὗτοι δὴ ἐφ' οἷς πεπόνθασι μνημονευόμενοι, τοὺς ματαίους ἐκείνους καὶ δαιμονιώδεις λογισμοὺς διακρουέτωσαν. If this is an exhortation addressed to the Jews of the ninth century (possibly a marginal scholion which by mistake was included in the text), translate: "Let them then, remembering what they have suffered for, drive away those vain and demoniac thoughts." Correcting οὗτοι to οὗτοι and διακρουέτωσαν to διεκρούσαντο, though palaeographically not very plausible, would give a more satisfactory meaning.
[82] 1 Cor. 10. 5.
[83] Num. 26. 61.

having their life cruelly interred;[84] the uncontrollable anger of Phinees against those who had committed fornication, and their murder;[85] the severe and harsh fate of Ananias and Sapphira[86]—such and the like will suffice thee as weapons, darts and shields, and when struck with their missiles, I know well that the Insolent one[87] will be mightily repulsed. But if, beaten off by these means and repulsed, he strives again to engulf us through despair,[88] adducing the throng of our sins and the mass of our faults, and on their account showing our repentance to be ineffectual, then thou hast the repentance of the Ninevites[89] dispelling his design; thou hast David wiping off his sin by repentance, and proving this to have so much power, that he was again deemed worthy of the prophetic gift, and was numbered with the prophets, and known as God's ancestor; thou hast Peter who denied his master on being questioned by a maid, and declared under oath that he did not know Him,[90] and although convicted of perjury, yet with his tears he cleansed the pollution of his denial so thoroughly, that he was not deprived of being the chief of the apostolic choir, and has been established as the foundation-rock of the Church, and is proclaimed by Truth to be the keybearer of the kingdom of heaven;[91] thou hast the publican, the prodigal, the harlot, the robber, in a single moment, and by a single word of gratitude, both dispelling their sins and being enrolled as citizens of paradise. Using such and similar examples, scatter the murk of negligence, drive off the cloud of despair, dispel the plot, show herein too the enemy grieved, take courage in repentance: indeed, divest thyself of filth,[92] and he shall not choke our souls.[93]

[84] Num. 16. 12-33.
[85] Num. 25. 7-8.
[86] Acts 5. 1-11.
[87] ἐπηρεάζων A: ἐπιρεάζων B: πειράζων Ar.
[88] Both A and B read ἀπογνώσεως, not ἀπογυμνώσεως [so Ar].
[89] Jonah 3. 5-10; Mt 12. 41.
[90] Mt 26. 69-75.
[91] Mt 16. 18-19.
[92] Cf. Job 11. 15. The text is slightly disturbed: ἔκδυσαι [ἐκδύσῃ Ar, after Job, *loc. cit.*] γὰρ ῥύπον καὶ οὐ συμπνίγοντες [συμπνίγονται Ar] ἡμῶν [ὑμῶν Ar, who mistakenly gives it as the reading of B] τὰς ψυχὰς [αἱ ψυχαί Ar]. The general sense is clear enough, although there appears to be no altogether convincing way of emending this passage. Assuming that both ἔκδυσαι and τὰς ψυχὰς are sound, the easiest expedient would be to emend συμπνίγοντες to συμπνίξει (sc. ὁ ἐχθρός). This suggestion is due to Mr. John P. Cavarnos.
[93] Note that in the above passage (pp. 46-50), Photius is giving a list of

HOMILY I. THE BEGINNING OF LENT

5. Wilt thou attain satiety of enjoyment, and suffer no penalty, nay, rather make thyself worthy of many favours? Turn thy gaze with the wondrous David on thy blooming and fertile meadow of the Lord's commands, turn thy gaze, and do not depart from it; but fixing on it the eyes of thy mind, and dwelling on the variety of its beauty, say, "How I have loved thy law, O Lord! It is my meditation all the day,"[94] and let thy actions correspond to this utterance. Having thus filled thyself with the holy and fragrant sweetness from that source, thou shalt from true experience sing, "How sweet are thy words unto my throat! More so than honey to my mouth."[95] Such is the pleasure that the choir of the faithful enjoys; she cleanses and raises us towards a more godlike desire and enjoyment, snatching the soul away from carnal enticements, and seating it on its natural and kindred throne that is free from passion; she drives away softness, white stimulating the manly quality of unwavering in the face of matter.

Ar I 483

6. I know also of another companion and fellow lodger of this *pleasure* who has much kinship with her: for she too is begotten

---

the seven principal sins in the following order: 1. lechery (πορνεία); 2. avarice (πλεονεξία); 3. pride (ὑπερηφανία); 4. iniquity (ἀδικία); 5. gluttony (γαστριμαργία); 6. negligence (not named, perhaps ἀμέλεια); 7. despair (ἀπόγνωσις). The classification of the cardinal sins had not yet attained in the East the final formula that prevailed in Western Europe after Gregory the Great, and which, thanks to the mnemonic device *saligia*, imposed itself in the order: *superbia, avaritia, luxuria, ira, gula, invidia* and *acedia*. We know that in the East the original number was eight. In the influential list of Evagrius Ponticus, they are given as γαστριμαργία, πορνεία, φιλαργυρία, λύπη, ὀργή, ἀκηδία, κενοδοξία, ὑπερηφανία (PG 40, cols. 1272-76). In Nilus of Constantinople the same list is given, except that the order of λύπη and ὀργή is inverted (PG 79, cols. 1145-64). The same vices are enumerated by St. John Climacus (*Scala paradisi*, XXVI, PG 88, col. 1021 C), who, however, is inclined to class κενοδοξία and ὑπερηφανία under the same heading, and quotes the authority of St. Gregory of Nazianzus for the seven capital vices (*ibid.*, XXII, cols. 948-49). For the inclusion of iniquity, cf. Origen, *In Lib. Iesu Nave Hom.* I, ed. Baehrens, Leipzig, 1921, p. 296. See, amongst others, O. Zöckler, *Das Lehrstück von den sieben Hauptsünden*, Munich, 1893, pp. 15 sq.; S. Schiwietz, *Das morgenländische Mönchtum*, I, Mainz, 1904, pp. 266-74; S. Zarin, Аскетизмъ, I 2, St. Petersburg, 1907, pp. 309-353; I. Hausherr, "L'origine de la théorie orientale des huit péchés capitaux," *Orientalia Christiana*, XXX 3 (1933), pp. 164-75; Ruth Ellis Messenger, *Ethical Teachings in the Latin Hymns of Medieval England*, New York, 1930, pp. 78 sq., 93 sq., 167 sq.

[94] Ps. 118. 97.
[95] Ps. 118. 103.

THE HOMILIES OF PHOTIUS

from the persistent study of the divinely wise writ, and produces an extraordinary and wonderful delectation. For she gladdens man in his food, she gladdens him in sleep, in bodily health, in sickness, when he is invested with rule over others, when he is placed under authority, in wealth, in poverty, in each and every condition of life. Who then is she? Perhaps you wish to know. I will tell you gladly. She is the pleasure arising from the interrogation of the conscience, when the latter is found to be not altogether condemned and without excuse. For when a man examines himself upon his actions,[96] and does not find his conscience condemning him, nor wounding him with charges that he has robbed his fellows of their bare sustenance while he himself lives in luxury, or that he is sumptuously clad at the expense of his shivering brother; if he has not despoiled others of their marriage rights (and it is a proud claim to have kept his virgin purity undefiled!), if he has not made the misfortunes of others into his own delight, if he has not shared in his neighbour's prosperity with envy, if he has not been a leader of unjust hands;[97] not to mention if he has not also taken vengeance, which is a greater matter than men nowadays regard it in their everyday lives:[98] when, as I say, a man examines himself, and does not find his conscience charging him bitterly with *crimes* such as these, then, Oh me, how great a pleasure, how much happiness,

Ar I 484 what gladness does that man enjoy! It is an image of the future

---

[96] περὶ τῶν πράξεων [so Pg: πρακτέων codd: πεπραγμένων Ar]. πρακτέων seems to be wrong, since a person examines himself on the actions he has taken, not on those he ought to take.

[97] Cf. 2 Macc. 4. 40.

[98] A difficult passage which has been radically changed by Ar. Read: ὅταν [ὅτε Ar] γάρ τις ἐτάζων περὶ τῶν πράξεων ἑαυτὸν οὐκ ἔχει [ἔχῃ Pg] κατήγορον τὸ συνειδός ... ὅτι τῶν ὁμοφυῶν τὴν ἀναγκαίαν ζωὴν αὐτὸς ἀφελόμενος ἐντρυφᾷ, ὅτι ῥιγῶντα καταλιπὼν τὸν ἀδελφὸν ἐνδιδύσκεται [so Ar: ἐνδιδύσκηται A: ἐδιδύσκηται B] λαμπρῶς· ὅτι γάμων ἀλλοτρίων οὐκ [οὐκ om Ar] ἐγένετο λῃστής (μέγα γὰρ εἰπεῖν ὡς οὐκ [καὶ ὅτι Ar] ἐφθάρη τὴν παρθενίαν), οὐ [ὅτι Ar] τὰς ἄλλων συμφορὰς ἰδίας ἔθετο εὐφροσύνας, οὐ [ὅτι Ar] τῷ φθόνῳ συνεμερίσατο τοῦ πλησίον τὴν εὐημερίαν, οὐ [ὅτι Ar] χειρῶν ἦρξεν ἀδίκων· τί γὰρ δεῖ λέγειν ὡς οὐδὲ [καὶ ὅτι Ar] ἠμύνατο, μεῖζον ὂν [μειζόνως Ar] ἢ κατὰ τὴν νῦν ἐπιπολάζουσαν τῶν ἀνθρώπων πολιτείαν, etc. The negatives οὐκ ἐγένετο, οὐ τὰς ἄλλων, etc. mark an ungrammatical but very natural change in the construction. If necessary, one could read ὅτε γάμων for ὅτι γάμων. Another expedient would be to omit the first οὐκ: ὅτι γάμων ἀλλοτρίων [οὐκ] ἐγένετο λῃστής· μέγα γὰρ εἰπεῖν, etc., thus making the enumeration of good actions into a separate construction depending on μέγα γὰρ εἰπεῖν.

HOMILY I. THE BEGINNING OF LENT

felicity: it too[99] gives an undefiled joy, and as it grows old it reaches maturity, and as it matures it becomes eternal, and makes blessed and happy those in whom it is implanted. Nay, he who bears an undisturbed conscience, likewise flourishes in good things. If, on the other hand, a man's conscience hurts because he has used for luxury his neighbour's food,[100] or seized his garment or gold, or has laughed at his fall, or sharpened[101] envy like a sword, or[102] has undermined a marriage with which he had no concern, or has been guilty of any similar offence, I know not what that man can win to be happy, or what he can take his fill of and be pleased, of how such a man could be in a state of joy, and not bear about with him a conscience pricking at every point and consuming him inwardly, more so than the passion itself,[103] unless[104] he has fallen headlong[105] into the precipice of insensibility and impiety. It is not therefore possible for a man who does evil to be happy, even if every luxury flows down his throat, and the treasures of Croesus, rich in gold, lie in his power; nor if he is the acknowledged possessor of all the silken yarn in the world, will he, even so, live happily. For outside things smile favourably yet do not remain steadfast, while the condemnation of the conscience distresses inwardly, and wounds, and does not move away. It is not possible therefore for a man who is conscious of his foul deeds to live with true pleasure, nor is it possible for a good and honest man not to rejoice at the welfare of his soul, even if his bodily hunger is satisfied but with barley, and his body is clothed with rags, and all his possessions are worth but a penny.

Ar I 485

7. Ought we not to avoid on all sides the filthy and miry pleasures, and to pursue and desire those which are, as it were, sisters of

---

[99] Reading ἀκήρατον καὶ αὐτὴ [αὐτῇ codd] τὴν χάριν παρέχουσα, otherwise one would have to understand that the peace of mind resulting from a clear conscience gave an undefiled joy *to* the future blessedness, which can hardly be the right meaning.

[100] ἐφ' οἷς τροφὴν [ἐφ' ᾧ ἐν τροφῇ Ar] τοῦ πλησίον ἐνετρύφησεν codd. ἐφ' οἷς ⟨τῇ⟩ τροφῇ would be more grammatical.

[101] ἠκόνησεν rather than ἠκόντισεν, as read by the MSS.

[102] ἢ has been omitted by Ar.

[103] Meaning not entirely clear: εἰ [ἢ Pg] καὶ μὴ παρ' αὐτὸ τὸ πάθος τιτρώσκουσάν που πάντως καὶ δαπανῶσαν ἐντὸς περιφέρων τὴν συνείδησιν.

[104] εἰ μήπω codd: εἰμὴ που Ar.

[105] ἀπεκρημνίσθη [so Pg] rather than ἀπεκρημνίσθημεν codd.

purity and akin to impassivity? For the former, linked as they are with luxury, intemperance and drunkenness, generate within us the many-headed hydra of the passions, by which those who suffer this wretched plight have the faculties of their soul and body devoured, and, blind as well as maimed, they are dragged down to the abyss of complete perdition; while the pure *pleasures* grow in a pure manner out of fasting, and by them we are conveyed to the bright[106] and lovely meadow of the virtues, beautiful to behold, beautiful to dwell in and to enjoy its charms; and truly blessed it is to be transported thence to the heavenly tabernacles, where grief is banished, where gladness and joy dwell, and wherein the summit of things desirable is to be seen. Wherefore it is necessary to avoid luxury and passionate pleasures, and instead to practise fasting and self-control. Besides, the annual course of holy fasting is upon us, inviting us to the race, and urging us to wrestle with the foe, whom we ought to oppose, not by brandishing weapons and darts, or drawing bows, but by fortifying the body with fasting, bracing it with discipline, whereby the mortification of the flesh is achieved, and we re-live Christ's death, and put on the armour against the Evil one,[107] and are awarded victory if we struggle zealously to the end.

8. Let no one therefore be left out of the contest, let no one slacken, beloved ones, let no one desert the ranks. Let us all strip readily and contend valiantly. Let us endure staunchly, let us hold our ground manfully. For the crown-giver, Christ, stands in our midst, holding out the prizes of victory, granting strength to zeal, giving victory to willingness, and bestowing on us crowns for ardour. May we all win them by the grace and love of Christ, our true God, who gave Himself in exchange for us, and has wiped off our sins with His stripes,[108] has freed us from the ancient curse, has delivered us from bondage, and has deemed us worthy of adoption. Be it by the intercessions of our most-holy Lady, the Mother of God, and of all the saints. Amen.

[106] ἡμεροφόρον, an unattested word (cf. ἡμεροφαῆ). I suspect that Photius may have written ἱμεροφόρον = ἱμερτόν, although such a word is not recorded either.
[107] Cf. Ephes. 6. 11, 13.
[108] 1 Peter 2. 24.

HOMILY II. GOOD FRIDAY

II

OF THE SAME MOST-BLESSED PHOTIUS, PATRIARCH OF CONSTANTINOPLE, THE NEW ROME, SECOND HOMILY DELIVERED ON GOOD FRIDAY FROM THE AMBO OF ST. IRENE[1]

1. After the persual of the catechetical passages, to which you have listened attentively, showing the contrition of your souls, I too see myself prompted to address you at this moment. For, though you have often heard the former, and yet, once again now, you have assembled with willing intent to listen to the same things, and the fact that you have often heard them has not restrained your eagerness to listen; so also I do not think it fitting for me to keep silent, even if some who went before me possessed exceptional zeal in exhorting and teaching[2] the flock—nay, quite on the contrary, I shall look up to the choir of those blessed men as to an example, and raising myself to imitate them, to the extent of the rhetorical power that has been granted me, I shall perform my duty in exhorting you to what is needful, and inciting you to those deeds which are believed to keep our pact with God inviolate, which bring about victory over the Evil one, and yield the fruit of salvation in time of need. But it is necessary that you too should not confine what is said to the hearing only, but should also transmit it inward to your souls, so that by studying the things that are conducive to virtue, your improvement in good deeds should thereby progress. For in the study of virtue lies the root of good action; and the action, as it continues, is the more easily supported by habit and more readily attracts *other such actions as* help-mates, and becomes productive of the like when it is regulated by speech—since speech is wont, like a skilled husbandman, to sow and help increase the virtues in one and the same sacred plot of the soul, not letting them be torn apart from each other and scattered. In this wise must you be listeners of the words about to be delivered, so as to show

---

[1] In A the title is missing. B has ⟨τ⟩ οὗ αὐτοῦ ἁγιωτάτου Φωτίου πατριάρχου Κωνσταντινουπόλεως νέας Ῥώμης, ὁμιλία β' λεχθεῖσα τῇ ἁγίᾳ παρασκευῇ ἐν τῷ ἄμβωνι τῆς [ἁγίας Εἰρήνης should probably be supplied]. Ar has changed πατριάρχου to ἀρχιεπισκόπου, omitted νέας Ῥώμης, and added at the end ἁγίας Εἰρήνης, μετὰ τὴν ἀνάγνωσιν τῆς κατηχήσεως.

[2] Cf. 1 Tim. 6. 2.

yourselves the husbandmen of such deeds, and be seen as reapers of similar fruit. For he who, while admitting the exhortations into his ears, rejects them from his mind, and neither shows the benefit in his deeds, nor makes the fruit the evidence for his toils, is like unto them whose bodies are sore diseased, and who listen readily to the physician's words and promises of health, but are yet unwilling
Ar II 147 to comply with them;[3] for neither do the latter achieve health by merely hearing the words, nor do the former enjoy spiritual benefit, when the words of exhortation are not through their ears sown in their hearts, and do not produce an abundant crop of good works. But you who have come together with eager intent, try to comply with me yet more eagerly. Hearken to my call for your own salvation and for the benefit of your soul. For even if I live my own life in negligence, yet I make it my especial concern and prayer to see you conducting yourselves well, and worthily of your high calling,[4] and I derive therefrom all manner of gladness and joy; for verily the good progress of the flock is the cause of much rejoicing to the shepherd, and the abundant produce of the land fills the husbandman's soul with pleasure no less than it fills the threshing-floor with sheaves. So indeed it is with this great rational flock:[5] the harvest of virtue and the rectitude of creed are enough to gladden and exalt the leader who has been appointed to tend it, even though in his own life he is not of equal *virtue*.[6]

2. Attend, therefore, brethren, and comprehend how paltry our life is, how quickly it withers, that it is compared to a shadow, and likened to dreams,[7] and is found to be no more stable than any of those. For our life here passes by while it seems to be present, and once it has passed, does not return, but measured out and flowing away with the current of time, it combines the stationary with the passing, existence with non-existence, corruption with generation.
Ar II 148 Let us consider who we are, and no matter how long we may live here, whither we shall go hereafter, and how, unavoidably, we shall

---

[3] Cf. Aristotle, *Nic. Eth.*, 1105 b 15; Themistius, *Or.* II, 31 d.
[4] Phil. 3. 14.
[5] Reading: οὕτω δὴ καὶ τὸ [τὸ omitted by Ar] τῆς λογικῆς ταύτης καὶ μεγάλης ἀγέλης· ἡ τῶν ἀρετῶν, etc.
[6] καθ' ἑαυτὸν διακείμενος Pg: διακειμένοις codd.
[7] Sap. 2. 5; Pindar, *Pyth.*, VIII. 99.

HOMILY II. GOOD FRIDAY

pay the penalties for our deeds in this life, and let us not attach ourselves to this present life only, but let us also be mindful of the life to come. For, "remember thy end," saith the prophet, "and thou wilt never sin."[8] Let us consider the time of death, that ultimate hour, when many of our relatives and friends stand by weeping, yet unable to shed us a single drop of benefit, or to provide the hope of any assistance, and while they lament for us compassionately, they do not diminish the pains that grip us. They wail in sympathy, but do not soothe the turmoil in our soul, nor do they lighten the upheaval and that trial which is not to be assuaged—nay, they rather increase with their tears and lamentations the awaited terrors, they frighten us all the more, they disturb and confuse us. For the wailing of friends over friends both confirms the expectation of evils, and presents them as inescapable and inexorable. Who would be able to describe the distress and conflict of the soul at that moment? How could words without tears represent the suffering? For a man is lying gasping miserably, all dripping with abundant cold sweat, seeing that his natural warmth is disappearing and the controlling force is no longer able to retain the nourishing, as it were, and sustaining moisture (for the rational soul which holds together and rules *the body* is being, so to speak, drawn away from the body and being snatched up for that unavoidable migration), *that moisture* by means of which the natural heat, channelled throughout the body, achieved the compactness of the flesh, and warmed it all round.[9] Now the earth begins to sink down to the earth, and hastens to shed at once the soldering-together, as it were, and coalescing of the bodily structure. There may be seen a spectacle Ar II 149 filled with much distress and sadness. The reclining man breathes faintly, looks pitiably, sighs painfully, moves a tongue that is silent or, even if whispering, is nevertheless imperceptible; his hearing is useless, his hands paralysed. His friends cry out, they bring round his children, or set his wife before him, or else they call by name the dearest of his acquaintances, pressing him to speak to them a little or to gaze at them. However, he does not respond, being either unable or unwilling, but from time to time he lets forth a deep sigh,

---

[8] Sir. 7. 36.
[9] A full stop or semi-colon is required after περιέθαλπεν.

at another time he looks up, but with a troubled and mournful gaze, or else he remains completely motionless when spoken to. For he has those within him who are on other business and demanding other accounts, and effecting the separation of the soul from the body, severing their junction with death as with a sword.

3. It is fitting, beloved ones, that we should consider ourselves in that condition of life, and to see in the deaths of our neighbours our own death as in a mirror, and to use the demise of others for our own correction. Nor let us await others to be corrected at the sight of us, but let us correct ourselves by what we have seen and shared in suffering, and let us study death before death,[10] so that we may live after death, having slept, according to the Psalmist, a sleep "precious in the sight of the Lord."[11] As long as the market is open, let us contend zealously, that we may be provided with supplies for the voyage. The journey is at our doorstep, and the time of the end is nigh, and great[12] is the need of supplies, and the transaction whereby they can be acquired is not difficult: it does not require great toils, nor a long journey abroad, with robbers lying in ambush or obstructed by bitter cold or the unbearable scorch of the sun *beating down* on the head; nor is it necessary to sail across a vast expanse of sea, made difficult[13] by a multitude of drownings, shipwrecks and pirates, and apt to beget much hesitation. And yet to the traders of this life, these *dangers*, standing before their very eyes, do not restrain the eagerness of their will or bate their readiness, but the hopes of expected gain in the future prompt them to disdain the obvious dangers at hand. For us, however, who wish to take up spiritual trading, there is none of those obstacles, there is nothing to make us afraid, nothing adverse. The profits of the transaction are with us: we possess the fountain of tears, that most excellent and most beneficial thing, which drips down the cheeks yet washes splendidly the soul, which wells out of the eyes yet drowns the Pharaoh, our foe; which flows out of our eyelids and runs on to heaven, and waters Paradise to bear fruit for us. The face is refreshed

Ar II 150

---

[10] Cf. Plato, *Phaedo*, 67e, 81a.
[11] Ps. 115. 6.
[12] πολλή codd, changed by Ar to ὀλίγη.
[13] ἀπορούμενον codd, altered to εὐπορούμενον by Ar.

HOMILY II. GOOD FRIDAY

thereby even as the soul is sprinkled with hyssop and made whiter than snow,[14] and is presented to Christ, an acceptable offering. Thus we are easily able to purchase through it benefits of all kinds. The knowledge of sin[15] and contrition of the heart gush with this gift; for, penetrating into the soul, they somehow hew away those thoughts which result in a hardening, they open up the veins of moisture in it, and pour forth their stream, and make it the source of many graces. It is not gathered from elsewhere, but is begotten within ourselves, being the currency of the soul-benefiting trade, and serving as a purgative for sins and passions that are hard to cleanse. It washes off thoughts of fornication, it blots out the stains of perjury and abnegation of God, and blunts the stings of death.[16] Ar II 151 Let Hezekiah be to thee the witness of our argument,[17] and the harlot, and Peter, the first of the disciples and the keybearer of heaven, after his tears. If thou wilt, it breaks away Lazarus on the fourth day from the deepest hollows of Hades, where corpses dwell, and undoes[18] the loosening of his limbs, and tightens up his joints, and places him with the living, and constitutes the prelude to the wondrous miracle; for Mary and Martha wept at the feet of Jesus,[19] and He took pity of them, and wept with them, and the dead man rose up and stepped over to life, and became known as the never-silent herald of the common resurrection. Seest thou the usefulness of tears? Seest thou their strength? Seest thou their benefit? Let us weep here, that we may be comforted from above; since "blessed," it says, "are they that mourn, for they shall be comforted."[20] Let us weep from the depth of our soul, that we may wipe away the filth in it, that we may wash off the mire of the passions, that we may blot out the stains, and raise up Lazarus, made dead by our sins. Let us call in the truly faithful and genuine sisters of the deceased, I mean recognition of transgressions and confession. For, "be not ashamed to confess thy sins;"[21] and "when thou shalt turn and sigh," Ar II 152

[14] Ps. 50. 9.
[15] Rom. 3. 20.
[16] 1 Cor. 15. 56.
[17] 4 Kings 20. 2 sq.
[18] Reading ἐκλύει with the MSS: κλείει Ar
[19] Jn 11. 33.
[20] Mt 5. 4.
[21] Sir. 4. 26.

Scripture assures thee, "then thou shalt be saved."[22] And again it cries out through the same prophet, "I am the Lord of all, that blots out thy sins; but do thou remember and do thou first confess thy transgressions, that thou mayest be justified."[23] Such is the power of the outspokenness of confession and conversion for salvation! Wherefore let us invite these *sisters* to shed tears at the feet of Jesus. He is present even now, He that is close to all that call upon Him in truth, and hearkens to their voice, and suffers with the mourners, and offers them compassion, and stands by the grave, and endures the stench, and speaks to the dead one, and raises up our corpse. While yet *that corpse* has been but four days dead, let us weep and implore, lest he be further dissolved, and the bones of reason be scattered along the Hades of despair, and the firmness, as it were, and steadfastness towards piety be dispersed, and he melt away completely from the hope and desire of the future, and his source of tears be dried up, and he be deprived[24] of repentance, and be dragged down to the abyss of utter ruin. Let us weep in time, that we may not mourn endlessly. Let us weep for our sins, that we may not lament without avail at our punishments, that we may not wail forever, condemned to the gnashing *of teeth*,[25] to worms and fire[26] and darkness.

Ar II 153   4. Great is the remedy of tears. It has been given *the power*[27] to heal putrefaction of long standing; it tends the grave wounds of fornication, and removing[28] the resultant stench from our soul, suffuses it with a sweet fragrance, and blotting out the stains and scars wherewith it is bespattered, all but smoothes it out. If mercy be also added to it, the effect becomes keener, it serves as the remedy against diseases of all kind, it is seen to be a purge from every defilement. Nay, what do I say? It extinguishes the unquenchable fire[29] of that terrifying and awful hell, and wins the dew of paradise; since "blessed are the merciful, for they shall obtain

[22] Is. 30. 15.
[23] Is. 43. 25–26.
[24] ἐξαιρεθῇ Pg: ἐξαρθῇ codd.
[25] Mt 8. 12.
[26] Mk 9. 48.
[27] εἴληφεν [codd: εἴωθεν Ar] ἰᾶσθαι.
[28] ἐξαιροῦν Pg: ἐξαῖρον codd.
[29] Mk 9. 43.

HOMILY II. GOOD FRIDAY

mercy,"[30] and "the merciful shall be treated mercifully," and, as holy Scripture attests, "mercy glorieth against judgment,"[31] and the throngs of the faithful embrace *mercy* without hesitation and are sustained thereby. Pity thy fellow-slave, that thou mayest make the common Lord indebted to thee. For it is He that says, "Inasmuch as ye have done it unto one of the least of these my brethren, ye have done it unto me."[32] Do not pass the poor by, and let not his tattered rags incite thee to contempt, but let them rather move thee to pity thy fellow-creature. For he is also a man, a creature of God, clothed in flesh like thyself, and perchance in his spiritual virtue mirroring the common Creator more than thou dost. Nature has not made him indigent in this way, but it is the tyranny of his neighbours that has reduced either him or his parents to indigence, while our lack of pity and compassion has maintained or even aggravated his poverty. Give thanks that thou hast not been caught thyself by the same *ills* they suffer by making the unfortunate share in thy ease,[33] for the greatest thanks to God is compassion towards our fellow-slaves. Acquire for thyself a sure prosperity by removing the misfortune of the poor. Preserve thy good condition by visiting the sick. If thou art ill, regain thy health by alleviating in those who are ailing the hardship caused by indigence. If thou seest one whose body is withered, bruised, wounded and cast down on the ground (Oh, for our pitilessness!) do not turn away, but pay heed to it, safeguarding thyself against the uncertainty of misfortune. Tend the sick, so that thou too mayest not need the like charity in diseases like theirs. It is a great *boon* for thee not to need it; but thy guilt is equally great if thou dost not help those who do. For the measure of thy joy at having overcome thine own troubles will be the same as of thy guilt, if thou refusest aid to those whom thou seest in distress. Take pity on the poor, and push him not aside when he begs, nor make him through the pitilessness of thy manner into a Lazarus down here, that he may not show thee from over

Ar II 154

---

[30] Mt 5. 7.
[31] James 2. 13.
[32] Mt 25. 40.
[33] Reading: εὐχαρίστησον [Ar unnecessarily adds θεῷ: τῷ θεῷ Pg] ἐφ' οἷς ἅπερ [ἐφ' οἷς περ Ar] ἐκεῖνοι κακῶς πάσχουσιν οὐχ ἥλως [ὅλως Ar] αὐτὸς τῷ [Pg: τὸ codd, defended by Šest., p. 534] μετόχους ποιεῖν [ἀμετόχους ποιῶν Ar] τοὺς δυστυχοῦντας, etc.

there to be the rich man. Consider the rich man's unquenchable fire,[34] and extinguish in thyself the flame of avarice; withdraw not thy hand from the poor, that thou mayest not be refused when begging for the finger that refreshes. Have the poor man share thy goods, that thou mayest not hear, "Thou receivedst thy good things in thy lifetime."[35] Take pity on *human* nature, beware of the judgment, look to the recompense,[36] reverence the adoption.[37] Give little things here, that thou mayest receive great things over there. Shed here drops of sympathy, that thou mayest draw for thyself streams of mercy. Do not hold *human* nature cheap, that thou mayest escape condemnation; propitiate the Judge, that thou mayest receive the recompense, or even be deemed worthy of the adoption. What is more valuable or more painless than this transaction? And what is more wretched than to disregard these things? If therefore thy hand is prosperous, give money to him that begs. If, however, thou hast kept thyself in a middling estate, and entrenched thyself in self-sufficiency in such wise that nothing superfluous or unnecessary is stored away in thy chests, then wherefrom thou farest daintily give also food to the poor, or rather, wherefrom thou nourishest thyself nourish also the poor. Cast a garment about him that shivers; receive the roofless in thy house; show thyself hospitable to strangers, remembering Abraham's hospitality,[38] while entertaining and cherishing the hope of the blessing that was repaid to him by God. But if even these things thou lackest, then give a cup of cold water.[39] Christ receives that from thee no less than the luxurious gifts of the rich; for He accepts the willingness, weighing not the bulk of the gift, but the manner of the intention. Thus far does He extend the bounds of charity! Or rather, He does not stop them even here. But if thou lackest even these things, and whereas thy inclination moves thee to compassion, indigence keeps thy willingness in check, then go to the sick, visit the prisoner, sympathise heartily with thy fellow-sufferer, sigh from thy very soul at

---

[34] Mk 9. 43.
[35] Lk 16. 20–25.
[36] Hebr. 11. 26.
[37] Cf. Galat. 4. 5.
[38] Gen. 18.
[39] Mt 10. 42.

HOMILY II. GOOD FRIDAY

the misfortune that has befallen him, shed a tear to refresh the victim: for a neighbour's sincere sympathy is a great consolation for the sufferer. If thou too hast at one time been overtaken by the same ills, then lighten his misfortune by thy personal story; for even the mere conversation of those who have suffered the same is found to be comforting to those in distress. God does not turn away from any of these things: He accepts everything, everything He repays with mercy, on everything He pours compassion, by every means He calls us together to the kingdom of heaven. Seest thou how the Lord of all has set this common gift before everyone, rich, middling, poor, indigent? How He has not forbidden anyone to draw from the springs of pity? But just as He has afforded the light of the sun and the splendour of the moon equally to all, and has compounded the temperance of the air for everyone to breathe alike, and has wisely devised the orderly succession of the seasons, and poured out the timely showers of fructifying rain, Ar II 157 making the enjoyment thereof common, so also He has spread out evenly the boon of charity and mercy to all men, thereby both granting a useful wealth to the rich, and affording poverty to the poor not as an obstacle, but indeed as a helper to salvation.

5. What then? If the poor to the best of their strength have drawn and stored away the oil beforehand, while those who rely on wealth and are cramped by its bulk do not purchase any oil, except what is sufficient for their wounds, is there any license to answer[40] left to them, or rather, will not the gates of paradise be rightly shut in their face? Yet for the poor and indigent the very rejection by the rich is sufficient to draw upon them mercy from above; for just as the hardness of heart of the prosperous and their indifference towards their fellow-slaves shuts to them[41] the gates of the Lord's compassion, so unmercifulness and disregard of the unfortunate opens to the latter some access to divine acceptance. Let us not therefore open wide the heavenly gates for others and close them for ourselves, nor let us feast others splendidly on our own inconsolable misfortunes and gladden them with our mourning.

---

[40] Acts 25. 16.
[41] αὐτοῖς codd: αὐτοῦ Ar, who mistakenly gives it as the reading of the MSS.

THE HOMILIES OF PHOTIUS

For those who have not pitied their distraught[42] and needy fellow-men, but showed themselves unfeeling towards them, make the Lord's compassion gush more abundantly for the latter, while diverting it from themselves. Nor let us imitate the foolish virgins, Ar II 158 but let us emulate the wise ones. For they were truly foolish who, having quenched the hot coals of the passions and kindled the flame of virginity—a big task requiring great intentness—did not take along the oil, a thing so easy to accomplish, and so simple to procure. Let us not liken ourselves to the senseless virgins, lest, by making the hour of the Kingdom an hour of trafficking, we be sent away from the bridal chamber, lest we hear, "I know you not."[43] For if we feed not the poor, nor admit the homeless under our roof, if we do not clothe the shivering, nor receive the stranger in our house, if we do not give even some cold water[44] for the thirsty to drink, if we do not visit the sick or the prisoner, nor join in sympathy for their sufferings, then the Judge shall come upon the throne of glory,[45] and He shall speak (but may none of us, O Lord, hear that distressing and harsh voice!) saying, "Depart from me, ye cursed, into everlasting fire, prepared for the devil and his angels: for I was an hungred, and ye gave me no meat: I was thirsty, and ye gave me no drink: I was a stranger, and ye took me not in: naked, and ye clothed me not: sick, and in prison, and ye visited me not."[46] Let us not place ourselves in this miserable condition, beloved ones, so as not to be submitted to such terrible threats. For even if we answer saying (Oh, Oh, with how many tears and sighs!), "Lord, when saw Ar II 159 we thee an hungred, or athirst, or a stranger, or naked, or sick, or in prison, and did not minister unto thee?", then shall He answer them (but not us, O Lord, not us!), "Inasmuch as ye did it not to one of the least of these, ye did it not to me."[47]

6. Hearest thou, O man, that terrible and inexorable threat, and dost thou not yet aid those that beg? Thou lendest to Christ by making them a loan—and dost thou not do this with great eager-

---

[42] Surely πενθοῦντας καὶ πενομένους [πενθοῦντες Ar, probably a misprint].
[43] Mt 25. 12.
[44] ψυχροῦ ὕδατος codd: ποτήριον ὕδατος Ar.
[45] Mt 25. 31.
[46] Mt 25. 41-43.
[47] Ibid., 44-45.

HOMILY II. GOOD FRIDAY

ness? Thou seest unmercifulness to be the fuel of the curse, of darkness and of perpetual punishment, and mercy, on the other hand, to be the price for the kingdom of heaven—and dost thou disregard the latter, while turning to the former? Do this not if thou believest me, or rather if thou obeyest the commands and injunctions of God our Saviour; for He saith, "The King shall say unto them on the right, Come ye blessed of my Father, inherit the kingdom prepared for you from the foundation of the world: for I was an hungred, and ye gave me meat: I was thirsty, and ye gave me drink: I was a stranger, and ye took me in: naked, and ye clothed me: I was sick, and ye visited me: I was in prison, and ye came unto me. Inasmuch as ye have done it unto one of the least of these my brethren, ye have done it unto me."[48] Seest thou His kindness? Seest thou His mercy? How He takes upon Himself the plight of the poor? How He transfers the charity unto Himself? How so? That He may alleviate their great shame and distress, and render thee more willing to do them good, and offer thee manifold and more abundant recompense for having done a service not only to a fellow-slave,[49] but through him, to the common Lord also. Seest thou His condescension? Seest thou the Lord's compassion? He is not ashamed to assume the rank and name of thy fellow-slaves and brethren, that He may prove thee to be a companion of the angels. He is not ashamed to acknowledge thee His nourisher and provider, He that fills every living thing with pleasure,[50] that He may make thee a citizen of paradise. "For I was an hungred, and ye gave me meat,"[51] and "inasmuch as ye have done it unto one of the least of these my brethren, ye have done it unto me,"[52] He cries out expressly. "Come, ye blessed of my Father, inherit the kingdom prepared for you."[53] Hearest thou His call? Rise up, prepare thyself, and "do not postpone from day to day," as Scripture counsels thee, "for the Lord's wrath shall come suddenly, and thou shalt be destroyed in a time of vengeance."[54]

Ar II 160

[48] *Ibid.*, 34–36, 40.
[49] ὁμόδουλον [sc. εὐεργετηκότι] codd: ὁμοδούλῳ Ar.
[50] Ps. 144. 16.
[51] Mt 25. 35.
[52] *Ibid.*, 40.
[53] *Ibid.*, 34.
[54] Sir. 5. 7.

7. Wherefore, let us make haste, brethren; let us prepare ourselves. Let us call together the poor, and buy the oil from them, that we may keep our lamps unextinguished, and hearken to that blessed voice, and be deemed worthy of the blessing. Do good to the poor, even if it is not for the inborn compassion due to thy fellow-creature, but that thou mayest receive the recompense, or if not for that, then, that thou mayest escape hell and be delivered from that fire. What Ar II 161 is more profitable or easier than to pity the poor man, and through him make Christ thy debtor? What is more blessed than to take him as thy table-companion, and to dine with Christ, and be judged worthy of the bridal chamber? Who is this senseless and wretched man,[55] that when he is so easily and readily thought fit for such company at table, and is shown to share in the endless glory and salvation, yet passes these things by, swept away by the tide of pitilessness, and is borne down into the snare of hell,[56] as the saying goes? Is he not wretched who does not understand that all ephemeral things must be dismissed on account of the lasting[57] happiness hereafter, lest he be driven away ignominiously from the portion of the saved?[58] When, moreover, the ephemeral things required of us are so small—food and drink, a garment, a roof, a movement of the limbs, sharing pain with sufferers, that we may receive in return the kingdom of heaven, yet we do not choose so—does this leave room for greater folly or wretchedness? Do we not rather vote for our own condemnation, and bring into court[59] a deed that renders ourselves undeserving of all sympathy?

8. Why hoardest thou thy wealth, O man, and buriest it in the ground,[60] and liest awake with cares, and administerest what is not thine, and whereof thy will is not master, picturing in thy imagination the enlargement of houses, the multiplication of money, advancement in dignity, and submitting thyself to a twofold evil, on the one hand, being oppressed and torn asunder by everyday cares, and awaiting, on the other, the condemnation of the judgment

---

[55] τίς οὗτος codd: οὕτως Ar.
[56] Prov. 9. 18.
[57] Read τὰ πρόσκαιρα προΐεσθαι μακρᾶς [so Pg: μικρᾶς codd, Ar] ἕνεκα τῆς ἐκεῖθεν εὐμοιρίας.
[58] Cf. Coloss. 1. 12.
[59] εἰσάγομεν, a legal term, unnecessarily corrected by Ar to ἐπάγομεν.
[60] Cf. Mt 25. 18.

HOMILY II. GOOD FRIDAY

to come for thy acquisitiveness and vain fancies, and being worn and wasted away by that *thought*? Why clingest thou to the earth and what flows into the earth, fixing thy heart, as the Lord's saying goes, where thy treasure lies buried?[61] Why dost thou store away for thyself the purchase price of hell, and kindlest all the more that fire which is fanned by a pitiless mind, is fed and increased for thy[62] destruction by thy merciless way? Why, when others are wasted away by hunger, dost thou live luxuriously, and hamperest nature, and crampest thy stomach, and fattenest thy flesh, and thickenest thy body, to be, alas,[63] shortly laid out for worms to devour, and to be ground into dust? Why raisest thou thy eyebrows, and puffest up thy cheeks, and lookest lordly, forgetting or disregarding that "dust thou art and unto dust shalt thou return,"[64] and that "man is like to vanity: his days pass as a shadow."[65] Why disregardest thou the hungry, and abominatest the poor—because thou livest more daintily than they, or rather, because thou hast wasted their necessary food on thy dissolute wantonness, and deprived them of drink by intoxicating thyself to excess, or because thou hast made the misfortunes of others thy own pleasures? Do these things make thee disdain thy neighbour? Do these move thee to be arrogant to thy fellow-men? Do these, contrary to all reason, incite thee to overbearing and contempt for moderation? Dost thou swagger arrogantly on account of those very things over which thou oughtst to groan, to look downcast, to lament and to repent, and dost thou puff out thy inflated vainglory, even perchance in the face of a famished man, when it is considered even by the most boastful that seeking to lord it over such a one is a degradation of their dignity?

9. Knowest thou not that the books contain the records of all these things?[66] Dost thou not know that thou hast angels closely observing and writing down thy actions? Do ye not know that we have abjured in their presence the acts of the Evil one, and have

---

[61] Lk 12. 34.
[62] εἰς σὴν [codd: τὴν Ar] δαπάνην.
[63] εἰς σκωλήκων βορὰν οὐδὲ μετὰ βραχὺ προκεισόμενον, codd, which is meaningless. Ar omits οὐδέ. It could, perhaps, be emended to οὐαί.
[64] Gen. 3. 19.
[65] Ps. 143. 4.
[66] Rev. 20. 12.

parted with him, but have made a covenant with God to live according to His commandments? How then dost thou set the covenant at nought, but what thou hast spat upon thou shrinkest not from doing again? How dost thou shun the merciful Lord, and take refuge with the tyrant? The latter, if he takes thee under his sway, will give thee darkness, worms and gnashing of teeth, and he is pleased thereat, that he may not be alone in suffering hell. While the King of glory and Guardian of the universe apportions thee paradise, and grants thee most splendid light, and enrols thee in the choir of the angels. Dost thou, however, disdain these, yet pressest on readily to those? Dost thou neglect the latter and desire the former? Dost thou not even move a limb for those things which are rich in reward for thee, but contract for and wretchedly pursue those which are followed by hell and condemnation? Seest thou into what evils we are tossed, and what things we exchange for what? Not gold for brass, as the Homeric students would say,[67] but the incorruptible we let go for the corruptible, and the eternal for the perishable. Yea indeed, we abandon for the painful pleasures and foul passions things that are truly fair, good and blessed, when we take no thought of the beggars, nor care for the poor, nor succour the indigent; if we do not support the weak,[68] or are arrogant to our fellow-slaves, if we glut ourselves beyond need, but do not bend down to those who ask for food.

10. Let us look at the table of agreements which has been read out to us, and each man setting up his own conscience as his judge and examiner, let us consider which of our pledges we have kept, and which we have neglected. And those we have kept—if, in fact, we have kept any—let us multiply, while those we have betrayed let us retrieve. Nor let us be proud in case we have done well in anything, but let us be ashamed of our errors, and let us hasten to fulfil what we have left out. Nay, a righteous deed is not an acquittal for our sins, but our righteous deed itself is spoilt by our sins, or rather, we are condemned by our righteous deeds for our sins. For the observance of like commandments renders the transgression of the rest voluntary and inexcusable. Thus, if even he who does not

Ar II 164

---

[67] *Iliad*, VI. 236.
[68] Cf. Acts 20. 35.

HOMILY II. GOOD FRIDAY

pay back his debt with interest[69] is not guiltless, then surely he who has not even restored the principal in full must be guilty: for if he who failed to multiply the talent[70] is to be judged, how shall he who did not even make good the debt escape condemnation? And if he who prays and gives thanks that he has not done anything of what the many do is guilty of boastfulness[71], then he who takes pride in things he ought to be ashamed of, is he not worthy of the worst punishment? Nay, if he who has no wedding garment is cast out of the bridal chamber,[72] is he not banished whose very soul and body are full of stains? Let us, therefore, seek diligently which of the agreements have been disregarded[73] by us and have escaped us, and let us readily take them upon ourselves. Let us not appear beliers of our profession, nor put it off from day to day,[74] for thou knowest not what the next day will bring forth. And it is said, "Watch, for ye know not what hour your Lord doth come,"[75] and, "if the evil servant shall say in his breast, My lord delayeth his coming; and shall begin to smite his fellow servants, and to eat and drink with the drunken; the lord of that servant shall come in a day when he looketh not for him, and in an hour that he is not aware of, and shall cut him asunder, and appoint him his portion with the hypocrites: there shall be weeping and gnashing of teeth."[76] Who fears not the threat? Who can resist the wrath? Who does not shudder at so great a punishment? Who does not tremble at the harshness of the cutting asunder? For that servant is severed asunder who does not watch, but treats his fellow-slaves offensively, and he is condemned with the hypocrites, and is given over to the gnashing of teeth and inconsolable weeping.

Ar II 165

---

[69] τὸ πολὺ τοῦ χρέους, as read by the MSS, can be right only if it means "the overpayment of the debt," which is perhaps possible, though the normal meaning would be "most part of the debt." τὸ πολυ ⟨πλάσιον⟩ may be suggested instead. Note that πολυπλάσιος, which is the spelling of the MSS, has been needlessly emended by Ar to πολλαπλάσιος (II. 160₂, 161₁₇, 164₁₀). Cf. Šest. p. 535. Another possible emendation would be τὸ πλέον τοῦ χρέους.
[70] Mt 25. 24 sq.
[71] Lk 18. 11 sq.
[72] Mt 22. 11–13.
[73] παρωράθη, needlessly emended by Ar to παρεώραται.
[74] Sir. 5. 7.
[75] Mt 24. 42.
[76] Ibid., 48–51.

11. He then reaps such fruit from such seed, but what sayest thou? Do not even these things tear thee away from drunkenness and gluttony? Do not even these make thee sober and awake? Do not even these choke thy brother-hating, haughty thoughts, and guide thee on to fellow-love and equity? Thou seest thy like severed asunder, and dost thou not expect, while committing the same iniquities, to undergo the same condemnation, thou who art liable to pay even more? For thou, didst thou but wish it, hadst him as an incitement to correction and as a moderator of thy life, while he was tripped up before thy time, and without thy example in sight was induced to do deeds for which he was condemned to suffer what he was fit to suffer. There will not come another judge, but the same will judge thee who has already shown His judgment on him. He indicates the judgment beforehand, not that He may inflict it, but that He may deliver thee from it, if thou art but willing thyself; and He puts forth the threat not that He may plunge thee in despair, but that He may save thee through repentance. He makes Himself the implanter of the threat that thou mayest reap repentance, and He sows the condemnation so that with the fear of hell as with a scythe thou mayest cut away the very roots of hell, and harvest the crop of joy. If then He both shows and does everything[77] that He may save thee in divers ways, and yet thou art not converted by any of these[78]—nay, even turnest up, as they say, every stone to appear neglectful of them all—thou severest thyself asunder, usherest in disaster, and renewest the pain of punishment.

12. Let us not too, therefore, beloved ones, cause a future so bitter and terrible to come upon us, nor let us make the time of reward[79] a time of condemnation, nor prepare the day of resurrection as a day of downfall. For God has appointed the day to come to be

---

[77] εἰ δ' ὁ μὲν πάντα καὶ δείκνυσι καὶ ποιεῖ Pg: εἴδομεν πάντα codd: ἰδοὺ πάντα Ar.
[78] οὐδενὶ τούτων ἐπιστρέφῃ is right: οὐδενὸς τούτων ἀποστρέφῃ Ar. The question mark after ἀλογήσας should be replaced by a comma [so Pg].
[79] The MSS read ἀναρρήσεως (literally "proclamation" or "commendation"), which is probably right. Ar has ἀναρρύσεως (= "deliverance"), which he mistakenly ascribes to B. On ἀνάρρησις in a laudatory sense, cf. Suidas, s. v. (A 2045): τοὺς μὲν ἀναρρήσεων καὶ στεφάνων ἀξιοῖ, τοὺς δὲ διηνεκεῖ παραπέμπει τιμωρίᾳ. On the liturgical use of the word, cf. Goar, Εὐχολόγιον sive rituale Graecorum, Paris, 1647, pp. 257-58.

HOMILY II. GOOD FRIDAY

a day of resurrection and joy, not of sorrow and sentence.[80] Those, however, who prefer the transgression of the commandments to their observance, and whose love for God has been quenched by mutual hate, those have made for themselves the time of enjoyment into a time of torment, and find the resurrection not a resurrection but an ultimate fall. To such evils are submitted the disdainers of the Lord's commands, and the furtherers of their own wishes, who have fallen into forgetfulness of good works, while keeping the memory of transgressions fresh through practice, whose manner and deeds we ought to avoid with every effort, and not to envy their conduct, even though the prosperity of life may smile at some of them. Fret not thyself because of evil-doers, neither be thou envious of them that do iniquity: for they shall soon be withered like grass, and shall soon fall away as the green herbs.[81] Fret not thyself because of evil-doers, for the same David, God's ancestor, cries out, "I saw the ungodly highly exalted and lifted up like the cedars of Lebanon. Yet I passed by, and lo! he was not: and I sought him, and his place was not found."[82]

13. Let us not, therefore, envy those men in anything. Let us rather avoid greed, through which injustice thrives and justice is banished, brotherly love is spat on and hatred of mankind is embraced. Let us avoid drunkenness and gluttony, which are the parents of fornication and wantonness: for excess of every kind is the cause of insolence, and outflow is the begotten child of plenitude, from which fornication and wantonness are hatched. Let us avoid strife, division, seditions, whereof plots are born and murders begotten; for from evil seed grow evil crops. Let us avoid foul speech, whereby those who are accustomed to it slip easily into the pit of evil deeds. For what one is not ashamed to say, one will not be ashamed to do either; and what one enjoys hearing one will be drawn into committing.[83] Let us abominate these things and spit upon them, but let us love the Lord's commandments and adorn ourselves with them. Let us honour virginity, let us attain gentle-

---

[80] ἀποφάσεως is read by the MSS, and should probably be retained (cf. Homily XIV, Ar. I. 197₄): ἀπογνώσεως Ar.
[81] Ps. 36. 1–2.
[82] *Ibid.*, 35–36.
[83] Cf. Photius, *Letters*, ed. Valettas, p. 227.

ness, let us preserve brotherly love, let us give lodging to hospitality, let us cling to fortitude, let us cleanse ourselves with prayers and repentance, let us welcome humbleness that we may draw nigh to Christ. For the Lord is near to them that are of a contrite heart, and He will save the lowly in spirit.[84] Let us embrace moderation; let us practise the judgment and distinction of the good from the bad. Let the soul be undaunted by the evils of life, especially if they are inflicted on us on account of Christ and His commandments, for we know that justice will follow, and it is thanks to them that we are easily carried up to heaven.

14. Let us consider in our mind, if nothing else, at least the mystery of this day: how the Lord and Creator of the universe, the unbounded and uncircumscribable, who holds the earth aloft by His word alone, and moves the sky with His nod, and grasps the world in His palm—let us consider how, having come forth for us,[85] incarnate from a virgin's blood, He is hanging on the cross, and surrenders His hands to the nails, and His feet are transfixed, and His side is pierced, and He is spat on and smitten—He at whom the Cherubim tremble, and by whose providence the universe is governed. Why does He suffer these things? That He may pour forth salvation for thee, that He may deliver thee from the bondage of the devil,[86] that He may snatch thee away from the ancient domination. He, then, suffers these things that He may redeem us that have once been sold through sin, yet do we try by such foul and unseemly pleasures and negligence to sell ourselves back again? He is lashed that He may remove[87] from us the lashes of our sins, and do we submit to them[88] again as to good masters? He surrenders His body to death that He may vivify our soul, and do we, by goading our own body with unnatural deeds, allow it to wage war and breathe death against the soul? He is tasting death that He may give us immortality, and do we strive to strangle ourselves with

---

[84] Ps. 33. 19.
[85] ἐμοί codd, unnecessarily changed by Ar to ἡμῖν. The graphic use of the first person singular, where we would use the plural, is very common in Photius.
[86] Hebr. 2. 14–15.
[87] ἀποστήσῃ Pg: ἀποτήσῃ A: ἀποτίσῃ B: ἀπωθήσῃ Ar.
[88] ὑποκατακλινόμεθα αὐταῖς Pg: ὑποκατακλινόμεθα ἑαυτοῖς codd: ὑποκατακλίνομεν ἑαυτοὺς Ar.

HOMILY II. GOOD FRIDAY

the noose of our passions? The earth quakes, the sun is darkened, the veil of the temple is rent,[89] because they see the Lord crucified for us, and do we not even grieve for our sins? The elements are altered, and dost thou not change for the better even so, do not even these things call thee to repentance, do they not soften the hardness of thy soul?

15. Let us take thought of these matters, beloved ones, and taking thought, let us strive to show that the foregoing are not reproaches and accusations directed against us, but that they fulfil the function of exhortation and incitement to what even we cannot achieve without toil. For the judges of the games too, as they watch those that race eagerly for a prize, do indeed take pride in the contest, but do not tire of exhorting and urging on the contestants, until they have won their wreaths. You also I behold by the grace of Christ filled with contrition, gushing tears, and showing supplication on your faces. May I be assured that they remain with you! May I rejoice in your righteous deeds and take pride in your godly ways! Would that the expressions of compassion and contrition which I see now be confirmed in very deeds, and that your souls be kept in this condition and state, that I too through you and together with you may be made worthy of the heavenly kingdom[90] in Jesus Christ our Lord, by whose help emperors reign and tyrants rule the earth;[91] let Him also, who has brought to light our Christ-loving and pious emperor to be provident for the Roman race, and anointed him with the imperial unction, adorn him all the more with virtues, and make him walk unswervingly and unhesitatingly in the way of truth, showing him invincible to all the enemies, merciful to subjects, and worthy of his empire, through the intercessions of our most-holy Lady, the Mother of God, and of all the saints who from the beginning of time have pleased God, to whom be glory and power for ever and ever. Amen.

[89] Mt 27. 51; Lk 23. 45.
[90] 2 Tim. 4. 18.
[91] Prov. 8. 15–16.

NOTE ON HOMILIES III AND IV

The following two Homilies, dealing as they do with the same historical event, the Russian attack on Constantinople in 860, can best be considered together. They are, besides, the only ones in the whole collection to have received adequate attention from historians, culminating in an exhaustive monograph by the late A. A. Vasiliev.[1] This will absolve us from the necessity of discussing the whole setting of the following two sermons; here we intend only to extract the historical information they contain, to point out wherein this information differs from that given by later and less reliable sources, and to determine the approximate dates when the two sermons were preached. For although we are dealing with documents of some notoriety, which have been the subject of an immense, if often conflicting, literature, it seems to us that an attentive reading of the text can provide some fresh data on the attack of 860, the first impact of the *Rhos* on the Byzantine world.[2]

From the first sermon (no. III) we can gather the following facts: that the raid was completely unexpected, that the outskirts of the city were ravaged, that there was general consternation, that the emperor and the army had departed to ward off another barbarian

[1] *The Russian Attack on Constantinople in 860*, Cambridge, Mass., 1946, with full bibliography of previous literature. See now also M. V. Levčenko, Очерки по истории русско-византийских отношений, Moscow, 1956, pp. 57–76. Among older studies, A. Chassang, "Deux homélies de Photius au sujet de la première expédition des Russes contre Constantinople," *Annuaire de l'Association pour l'encouragement des études grecques en France*, V (1871), pp. 75–85; C. De Boor, "Der Angriff der Rhos auf Byzanz," *BZ*, IV (1895), pp. 445–66; E. Gerland, "Photius und der Angriff der Russen auf Byzanz," *Neue Jahrbücher für das Klassische Altertum*, VI, B. XI (1903), pp. 718–22; V. Lamanskij, "Житіе св. Кирилла какъ религіозно-эпическое произведеніе," Журн. Мин. Нар. Просв., Nov.–Dec. 1903, pp. 370–96.

[2] Discounting the alleged raid before 842, which has been inferred from the *Life of St. George of Amastris* (in spite of recent Russian attempts to substantiate that raid: E. E. Lipšic, "О походе Руси на Византию ранее 842 года," Исторические Записки, XXVI [1948], pp. 312–31; M. V. Levčenko in *Viz. Vrem.*, IV [1951], pp. 150–52; *id.*, Очерки, pp. 46–55). It is to be noted that the name Rhos appears only in the titles and not in the text of the Homilies. The Rhos are, of course, again mentioned in Photius' encyclical letter to the Oriental patriarchs, written in 867 (ed. Valettas, p. 178).

NOTE ON HOMILIES III AND IV

attack, that the Russians were not a well organized expedition but a rabble equipped "in servile fashion," and finally that the inhabitants of Constantinople implored divine help in night-long litanies, calling especially on the Virgin. The second sermon (no. IV), delivered when the danger had just passed, gives us the following facts: the unexpectedness, swiftness and inhumanity of the attack were unprecedented; the barbarians, whose very name had been unknown, appeared suddenly in the outskirts of Constantinople, and even hoped to capture the city; they came down in boats from the north; no resistance was offered, and the barbarians made themselves rich with booty; the slaughter and destruction were appalling; the enemy retired, however, when divine help was invoked; Photius and the inhabitants of the city carried the Virgin's garment round the walls, at which point the enemy suddenly turned their backs and departed.

Such are the facts to be gleaned from the two sermons, and it is idle to upbraid Photius for the paucity of his information, as many modern authors have done, since his purpose was not to chronicle events which were all too familiar to his audience, but to draw from them a moral and religious lesson. It must be borne in mind, on the other hand, that being public pronouncements made at the very time of the event,[3] the two sermons are the most authoritative of all Greek sources dealing with the attack of 860. The rest of the Greek sources amount to no more than a couple of references by Nicetas Paphlagon, who wrote some fifty years after the event,[4] an entry in the Brussels Chronicle, a brief reference in the Continu-

---

[3] It has been suggested (Vasiliev, *op. cit.*, pp. 93, 214; cf. Bury, *History of the Eastern Roman Empire*, p. 420) that the text of the two Homilies, as it appears today, would have been quite incomprehensible to a 9th century congregation and that it must have been embellished and remodelled for publication. If that were so, then the sermons could not be said to be absolutely contemporary documents since we do not know when such a "remodelling" took place. These two sermons, however, are in no way more difficult than the rest of Photius' homiletical works or, indeed, those of his contemporaries. And if the inhabitants of Constantinople, well educated as they were, could not follow the involved yet always meaningful prose of Photius, how could they have understood the incomparably more bombastic sermons of, say, Leo VI, unless those too, and in fact the whole of contemporary Byzantine homiletics, were rewritten for publication?

[4] On the date of the *Vita Ignatii*, probably *ca.* 907–909, see R. J. H. Jenkins in Ἑλληνικά, XIV (1956), p. 346.

ation of Theophanes (echoed by Cedrenus[5] and Zonaras[6]) and a more detailed but less trustworthy account found in several chronicles, all of which derive from Symeon Logothete.

The statements of Nicetas Paphlagon, the Brussels Chronicle and the Continuation of Theophanes do not contradict those of Photius. Nicetas tells us that the Russians came down from the Black Sea, ravaged the Bosphorus straits, and extended their depredations to the Princes' Islands, on one of which the Patriarch Ignatius was then living in exile.[7] The Brussels Chronicle (compiled presumably in the eleventh century) is the only source that gives the exact date of the attack as the 18th of June 860, and therefore draws on a reliable document. Here is what it says: "During his (Michael's) reign, on the 18th of June of the 8th Indiction in the year 6368, the fifth year of his reign, the Russians came in 200 ships and were, through the intercession of the all-hymned Mother of God, overpowered by the Christians, utterly defeated and destroyed."[8] The Continuation of Theophanes says that the Russians devastated the Black Sea coast and even surrounded the city at a time when Michael was leading an expedition against the Arabs. "Having, however, on that occasion taken their fill of God's wrath, they (the Russians) returned home, after Photius, who then held the helm of the Church, had propitiated the Godhead."[9]

Quite different is the account of Symeon Logothete, as represented in the works of his plagiarizers. We are told that Michael III undertook an expedition against the Arabs, leaving the prefect Oryphas in charge of Constantinople, but when he had gone out as far as Mavropotamon (or Mavros Potamos), news reached him that the Russians were threatening Constantinople: they had penetrated into the Bosphorus with 200 ships and surrounded the city. Thereupon Michael came hurriedly back and, with great difficulty, made his way across the strait. After invoking divine aid in the Blachernae church of the Virgin Mary, he and Photius took up the holy

---

[5] Vol. II, p. 173 (Bonn).
[6] Vol. III, p. 404 (Bonn).
[7] *Vita Ignatii*, PG 105, cols. 516–7; cf. col. 532 C.
[8] F. Cumont, *Anecdota Bruxellensia*, I, p. 33 (Université de Gand, *Recueil des travaux publ. par la Fac. de Philosophie et Lettres*, fasc. 9, 1894).
[9] P. 196.

NOTE ON HOMILIES III AND IV

maphorion and dipped it in the sea. Immediately a storm arose and the ships of the barbarians were smashed up. Few of the Russians were able to escape home.[10]

That this story stands in contradiction to the two sermons, at least as regards two essential points, has been observed by most historians, although many of them have hesitated to take the next logical step, viz. to deny the miraculous dipping of the *maphorion* and the emperor's return to Constantinople while the Russians were still investing the city. In this case indeed the *argumentum ex silentio* is decisive. Photius could not have failed to mention either the miraculous storm if it had in fact occurred (indeed, what better material could there be for a sermon?) or the participation of the emperor in the religious procession, since he never missed an opportunity to extol Michael's achievements. Instead he says, "As the whole city was carrying with me her raiment for the repulse of the besiegers and the protection of the besieged, we offered freely our prayers and performed the litany," etc.[11] Since Photius could not have included the emperor in the words πᾶσα ἡ πόλις, it must be deduced that the Russians withdrew before the emperor's return. Whether it was a superstitious fear that prompted them to do so, or the realization of their inability to capture the city, or a report that Byzantine forces were hastening against them,[12] remains an unsolved question. Another important point is that at the time when the second sermon was delivered, the Russians had not been defeated by the Byzantine forces. Indeed, the second sermon is full of reproach for the cowardice and dejection of the citizenry. Instead of being moved to anger and revenge, they were paralysed.[13] The barbarians, on the other hand, were fully successful, and seized rich booty ("an obscure nation ... but now risen to a splendid height and immense wealth").[14] Moreover, the departure of the Russians was sudden and quasi-miraculous. Surely, if Michael

---

[10] Leo Grammaticus, pp. 240–1 (Bonn); Theodosius Melitenus, ed. Tafel, Munich, 1859, p. 168; Georgii Hamartoli Continuator, ed. Muralt, St. Petersburg, 1859, pp. 736–7; *id.*, ed. Istrin, Хроника Георгия Амартола, vol. 2, Petrograd, 1922, pp. 10–11; Pseudo-Symeon, p. 674 (Bonn).
[11] See p. 102 below.
[12] So Bury, *History of the Eastern Roman Empire*, p. 421.
[13] See p. 97 below.
[14] P. 98 below.

had annihilated the invaders before the second sermon was delivered, Photius could not have called the deliverance of the city "unhoped for" and "inexplicable."[15]

If these inferences are accepted, three possible explanations present themselves: 1) the Russian raid was successful to the extent that the invaders looted the environs of Constantinople without opposition and then returned home; 2) the Russians withdrew of their own accord, but ran into a storm on their homeward journey and were shipwrecked; 3) the emperor's hasty return and the destruction of the Russians took place after the second sermon was preached. The first possibility has actually been accepted by several authors,[16] but that entails rejecting not only the somewhat dubious testimony of Symeon Logothete, but also that of Theophanes' Continuator and the Brussels Chronicle which appear to be more credible. Nor is it at all likely that a Russian success would not have found a magnified echo in the Russian chronicles which, on the contrary, speak of a failure.[17] The second possibility is that the

[15] Pp. 102-03 below.
[16] Loparev in *Viz. Vrem.*, II (1895), pp. 617 sq. (see, however, Vasil'evskij in *Viz. Vrem.*, III [1896], pp. 83-95); A. Šachmatov, Древнѣйшія судьбы русскаго племени, Petrograd, 1919, p. 60 (following Loparev); G. Laehr, *Die Anfänge des Russischen Reiches*, Berlin, 1930, p. 94; substantially the same conclusion in Levčenko, Очерки, pp. 74-75. The chief evidence for this view has been thought to be the statement of John the Deacon that the Normans attacked Constantinople with 360 ships and returned home in triumph (MGH, *Scriptores*, VII, 1846, p. 18. Repeated by Andrea Dandolo, *Chronicon Venetum*, in Muratori, *Rer. ital. script.*, XII, 1728, col. 181). Vasiliev (*op. cit.*, pp. 55 sq.) believes that the event recorded by John the Deacon is not the attack of 860, but a piratical raid from the south in 861. The occurrence of a second raid is, however, entirely undocumented. It is with reference to both raids that Vasiliev interprets the statement of Pope Nicholas I in 865 that the pagans who had devastated the environs of Constantinople remained unpunished (MGH, *Epistolae*, VI, 1925, pp. 479-80). At first sight, the Pope's statement may appear to be a strong argument in favour of the view that the Russian raid was successful. It must be observed, however, that the pontiff is speaking in very general terms, and not specifically about the Russians (if indeed he has the Russians in mind). What he says is that the pagans who had invaded Crete, subjugated Sicily, conquered numerous Byzantine provinces, and burnt the very outskirts of Constantinople, did all these things with impunity. The Pope is referring, therefore, to the general military situation of the Empire which, with obvious exaggeration, he represents as uniformly disastrous, whereas we know, for instance, that a crushing defeat was inflicted on the Arabs in 863. Hence it would be a mistake to draw from the Pope's rhetorical statement any specific conclusion regarding the Russian raid.
[17] Laurentian Chronicle (which merely reproduces Hamartolus), Полное

NOTE ON HOMILIES III AND IV

Russians, perhaps weakened by their own excesses and demoralized by the sight of religious processions along the walls, hastily withdrew and caused their own destruction by running into a storm.[18] In favour of this view may be quoted the "divine wrath" which, according to Theophanes' Continuator (along with Cedrenus and Zonaras) fell on the Russians, a phrase more suited to an act of God than to a regular military defeat. If, at the cost of rejecting the evidence of the Brussels Chronicle, such a course of events is accepted, it must be assumed that the second sermon was preached before news of the Russian disaster reached the capital, which is possible, but there still remains the question of the emperor's return. Lamanskij contended that Michael had no reason to come back to Constantinople and remained on the eastern front, where he had more formidable enemies to face; but that was before Grégoire's discovery that the battle of Anzen, presumed to have taken place in the summer of 860, is wholly apocryphal.[19]

This brings us to the third possibility. Did Michael who, after the exchange of prisoners with the Arabs in May, somewhat unexpectedly undertook another expedition, come hurrying back to Constantinople? The little we know of the hostilities of that year (discounting the misplaced accounts of Genesius, pp. 91-93 and Theoph. Cont., pp. 177-179) is not decisive on this point. Taking into account, however, the several successful Arab raids mentioned by Tabari and, on the other hand, the absence of any important Byzantine offensive, it is reasonable to assume that Michael was prevented from carrying out the expedition he had organized.[20] This conclusion is corroborated by other considerations as well. We know that the exchange of several thousand prisoners took

---

Собрание Русских Летописей, I, 2nd ed., Leningrad, 1926, pp. 21-22 = S. H. Cross and O. P. Sherbowitz-Wetzor, *The Russian Primary Chronicle*, Cambridge, Mass., 1953, p. 60; Hypatian Chronicle, ПСРЛ, II, 2nd ed., St. Petersburg, 1908, p. 15; etc. The Russian sources have been discussed by Vasiliev, *op. cit.*, pp. 107 sq.

[18] So Lamanskij, *op. cit.*

[19] "Etudes sur le neuvième siècle," *Byzantion*, VIII (1933), pp. 520-24; *Id.*, "Manuel et Théophobe," *ibid.*, IX (1934), pp. 184-5, 202-3.

[20] See Vasiliev, *Byzance et les Arabes*, I, Brussels, 1935, pp. 245-6, where it is likewise assumed that the Arab inroads were encouraged by the emperor's absence. Tabari's account is on p. 320.

place in May 860,[21] at which time there must have been a truce. Hence Michael could hardly have set out from Constantinople at the head of an army before early June, which agrees very well with Symeon's statement that news of the Russians' arrival reached him when he was still on his way and had not as yet done anything against the Arabs. It is quite natural that Oryphas should have dispatched a messenger with all speed to inform the emperor of the new danger, and it is equally natural that Michael should have come back with a small force at the very least.

If the emperor's hasty return is granted, and the great majority of historians accept it, certain conclusions follow. In the first place, Photius' second sermon must have been preached before the emperor's arrival. Secondly, the main body of the Russians had already left,[22] so that Michael cannot be said to have broken up the siege. But he may have taken some measures of retaliation, since it is unlikely that later historical tradition, generally unfriendly to Michael, should have put to his credit an incident that had never happened.[23] There is, of course, no way of disproving that a sudden storm fell upon the retreating Russians. The third and most important inference to be drawn from Michael's precipitate return is that the duration of the Russian attack was shorter than the time required to cover the distance to and from Mavropotamon. Unfortunately, the name Mavropotamon (Black River) was a common one, and it is a matter of uncertainty whether it should be identified with the Mavropotamon which is a tributary of the Sangarius (close to Nicomedia) or its namesake in Cappadocia.[24] Even accepting the

[21] *Ibid.*, p. 240, n. 2.
[22] It is conceivable that some Russian stragglers continued to loot the shores of the Bosphorus after the bulk of the fleet had left.
[23] Unless it is supposed that Symeon Logothete drew his account from some fictitious *logos* extolling the miracles of the Holy Robe. A document of this sort (presumably relating to the Avar raid of 619) devotes considerable space to a religious procession headed by the emperor and the patriarch (published by Loparev in *Viz. Vrem.*, II [1895], pp. 581–628).
[24] Vasiliev, *The Russian Attack*, pp. 195–6, is in favour of the latter, while Grégoire (in Vasiliev, *Byzance et les Arabes*, I, p. 196, n. 2) prefers the former. As Vasiliev points out in his later study, Photius' statement in his first sermon that "the emperor endures far distant labours beyond the frontier" seems to indicate that Michael had gone some distance, although Photius had probably no means of knowing at the time how far the imperial army had advanced.

NOTE ON HOMILIES III AND IV

latter alternative, the time interval could not have been more than a month, and probably less. The first sermon was therefore delivered immediately following the 18th of June 860, possibly on the 23rd which was a Sunday,[25] the second very soon afterwards, perhaps in the beginning of July. The theory first propounded by Papadopoulos-Kerameus[26] and followed by several other historians, viz. that the Russian attack lasted several months, almost a year, is not only incredible in itself, but quite out of keeping with Photius' second sermon, in which the patriarch likens the incursion to a thunderbolt, and says that it was like no previous one in swiftness and suddenness.[27] Besides, by December 860 legates were already arriving at Constantinople for the Council which was to be held in March of the following year.

It may be added that the two Homilies on the Russian attack formed, to some extent, the basis for the unfortunate theory, put forward by Papadopoulos-Kerameus, that Photius (or George of

[25] This date has been suggested by Gerland, *op. cit.*, p. 719, n. 2.
[26] "Акаѳистъ Божьей Матери," *Viz. Vrem.*, X (1903), pp. 391–3.
[27] The following arguments have been adduced in favour of a prolonged siege: 1) an entry in the Constantinopolitan Synaxarium commemorating a miraculous liberation from unnamed enemies on the 5th of June (Delehaye, *Synax. eccles. CPanae, Propylaea ad Acta Sanct. Nov.*, cols. 729–31; Dmitrievskij, Описаніе литургическихъ рукописей, I, pp. 78–9); 2) the fact that Pseudo-Symeon (whose chronology, however, is completely unreliable) speaks of the Russian attack under two successive years (p. 674); 3) a sermon preached by George of Nicomedia on the feast of the Presentation of the Mother of God (Nov. 21st), at the close of which he calls on the Virgin Mary to avert the "godless madness" of unnamed enemies (PG 100, col. 1456). As regards the first argument, Constantinople had undergone a great many attacks before the 9th–10th century when the above-mentioned Synaxarium was compiled, and besides, as Vasil'evskij has pointed out (*Viz. Vrem.*, III [1896], p. 95), the entry could well refer to the Avar invasion of 619 which was averted from the capital precisely on the 5th of June (*Chronicon Paschale*, I, p. 712). The second argument hardly requires any discussion. As for the third argument, we do not know that the sermon was preached in 860, so that George of Nicomedia could be referring to some other barbarian invasion (possibly the Arab naval raid which reached Proconnesus). Grégoire and Orgels ("Les invasions russes dans le Synaxaire de Constantinople," *Byzantion*, XXIV [1954], pp. 141–45) suggest that the commemoration of June 5th refers to the Russian attack of 941, whereas another commemoration on June 25th (τῶν Σαρακηνῶν καὶ τῶν ῾Ροῦν ἡ ἔλευσις, καὶ λιτὴ ἐν Βλαχέρναις) records the liberation of the capital from the Russians in 860. Whether the entry of June 25th concerns the events of 860 or not (its relevance was denied by Vasil'evskij in *Viz. Vrem.*, III, p. 95), it must be pointed out that the Synaxarium speaks of the *arrival* of the Saracens and Russians (?) and the litany at the Blachernae, so that the exact date of the Russians' *departure*, while certainly very close to June 25th, remains unknown.

Nicomedia) was the author of the Acathistos Hymn.[28] The verbal similarities, if they are significant, certainly point in the opposite direction, viz. that Photius borrowed from the hymn which, indeed, may have been recited by the inhabitants of Constantinople during the Russian raid. The first Homily on the Annunciation, with its concluding χαιρετισμοί (see below, page 121), and that on the Nativity of the Virgin also show points of contact with the Acathistos. As to the latter, the consensus of modern opinion places its composition in the sixth century.[29]

It may be of some interest to note that an address delivered by Dorotheus, metropolitan of Mitylene, during the siege of Constantinople by the Turks in 1422 is made up entirely of passages excerpted from Homilies III and IV.[30]

III

Ar II 5 OF THE SAME MOST-BLESSED PHOTIUS, ARCHBISHOP OF CONSTANTINOPLE, FIRST HOMILY ON THE ATTACK OF THE RUSSIANS[1]

1. What is this? What is this grievous and heavy blow and wrath? Why has this dreadful bolt fallen on us out of the farthest north? Ar II 6 What clouds compacted of woes and condemnation have violently collided to force out this irresistible lightning upon us? Why has this thick, sudden hail-storm[2] of barbarians burst forth, not one that hews down the stalks of wheat and beats down the ears of corn,

---

[28] ʻΟ ʼΑκάθιστος Ὕμνος, οἱ ʻΡῶς καὶ ὁ πατριάρχης Φώτιος, Athens, 1903; "Акафистъ Божьей Матери," *Viz. Vrem.*, X, pp. 357–401; ʻΟ πατριάρχης Φώτιος καὶ ὁ ʼΑκάθιστος Ὕμνος, Trieste, 1904 (polemical); ʻΗ σημερινὴ θέσις τοῦ περὶ ʼΑκαθίστου ζητήματος, *Viz. Vrem.*, XV (1908), pp. 357–83; Πηγαὶ καὶ δάνεια τοῦ ποιήσαντος τὸν ʼΑκάθιστον Ὕμνον, Βυζαντίς, I (1909), pp. 517–40. In the last-named study the author promises a monograph proving that George of Nicomedia rather than Photius was the author of the Hymn. This monograph has not appeared. The arguments of Papadopoulos-Kerameus were refuted by M. Théarvic (= J. Pargoire) in *Échos d'Orient*, VII (1904), pp. 293–300; VIII (1905), pp. 163–166.

[29] The bibliography on this subject is immense. Cf. the latest study by E. Wellesz, "The 'Akathistos.' A Study in Byzantine Hymnography," *Dumbarton Oaks Papers*, 9–10 (1956), pp. 141–174.

[30] Loparev in *Viz. Vrem.*, XII (1906), pp. 166–71; cf. V. Laurent in *Rev. des ét byz.*, IX (1952), pp. 166–8.

[1] In the Palat. 129 the extracts from this Homily are entitled εἰς τὴν τῶν βαρβάρων ἔφοδον.

[2] θάλασσα is read by the MSS, but the sense requires χάλαζα.

HOMILY III. THE RUSSIAN ATTACK

or lashes the vine-twigs and dashes to pieces the unripe fruit, or strikes the stems of plants and tears the branches apart (which for many has often been the extent of its most grievous damage), but miserably grinding up men's very bodies, and bitterly destroying the whole nation? Why or how have the lees (to call them no worse) of so many and great disasters been poured out on us? Is it not for our sins that all these things have come upon us? Are they not a condemnation and a public parading of our transgressions? Does not the terror of things present indicate the awful and inexorable judgment of the future? Is it not the apprehension of us all, nay the sight before the eyes of each, that not one will have been left any longer to survive, so that not even the fire-tender[3] can escape the calamity to tell the tale?[4] Verily, sins diminish tribes,[5] and *sin* Ar II 7 is like a two-edged sword for those who indulge in it. We were delivered from evils which often had held us; we should have been thankful, but we showed no gratitude. We were saved, and remained heedless; we were protected, and were contemptuous. For these things punishment was to be feared. O cruel and heedless minds, worthy to suffer every misfortune and distress! From those who owed us small and trifling things we made relentless exaction; we chastised them. We forgot to be grateful when the benefit had gone by. Nor did we pity our neighbours because we had been pardoned ourselves. But in being freed from the impending fears and dangers, we became yet more cruel to them, and we neither considered the number and magnitude of our own debts which the Saviour had forgiven, nor did we respect the debt of our fellow-servants, tiny as it was, and not to be weighed against our own even in the measure of speech. Having been ourselves mercifully delivered from many great *debts*, we unmercifully enslaved others for little ones.[6] We Ar II 8

---

[3] A proverb. Cf. Herodotus 8. 6; Zenobius 5. 34 in E. L. Von Leutsch and F. G. Schneidewin, *Corpus paroemiographorum graecorum*, I, p. 134; cf. *ibid.*, p. 289; II, pp. 44, 580, 582; Theoph. Cont., p. 25₁₃.

[4] Read τοῖς ἔπειτα with the MSS: τῆς ἔπειτα Ar.

[5] Prov. 14. 34. Delete ἀνθρώπων, which Ar has added after ἁμαρτίαι.

[6] In Uspenskij's *ed. princeps* this sentence read as follows: πολλῶν καὶ μεγάλων ἐλευθεροθέντων, ὀλίγους ἁλοεῖς ἀφιλανθρώπως ἐδουλώσαμεν. This led to the belief that the Russian attack was brought about by the persecution of certain Russian threshers established at Constantinople. This notorious error, although refuted by Nauck (p. xxx, n. 29) and by Vasil'evskij ("Русско-византійскіе отрывки," Журн. Мин. Нар. Просв., March 1878, p. 175, n. 2),

enjoyed ourselves, and grieved *others*; we were glorified, and dishonoured *others*; we grew strong and throve, while waxing insolent and foolish. We became fat, gross and thick, and although we do not forsake God as Jacob of old, yet like the beloved one, we have been filled and we kicked,[7] and like a maddened heifer[8] we raged against the Lord's commandments, and we disdained His ordinances. For this reason there is a sound of war and great destruction in our land.[9] For this reason the Lord hath opened His treasury and brought forth the weapons of His anger.[10] For this reason a people has crept down from the north, as if it were attacking another Jerusalem, and nations have been stirred up from the end of the earth, holding bow and spear; *the people* is fierce and has no mercy; its voice is as the roaring sea. We have heard the report of them, or rather we have beheld their massed aspect, and our hands have waxed feeble; anguish has seized us, and pangs as a woman in travail. Go not forth into the field, and walk not in the ways, for the sword lingers round about.[11] "What shall I testify to thee, or what shall I compare to thee," Jeremiah will cry out with me today, "O queenly city? Who shall save thee and comfort thee, for the cup of thy destruction is enlarged? Who shall heal thee?"[12] Now you are weeping. I too was nearly overwhelmed by the misfortune, and cut short in my speech. But why do you cry out to me? Why do you lament? Listen to me. Stop weeping awhile, and give access to words. I too weep with you, but neither do little drops quench a fire that has long been fanning (need I say that they kindle it all the more?), nor has a transient tear the power to expiate God's wrath fired by our sins. I too weep with you, but we have overlooked the tears of many sufferers—I pass over those that we have caused.[13]

Ar II 9

---

re-appears from time to time in historical handbooks. Examples in Vasiliev, *The Russian Attack*, pp. 185–86. The correct reading is probably ⟨ἀντ'⟩ ὀλίγων ἄλλους καὶ ἀφιλανθρώπως ἐδουλώσαμεν (cf. Mt 18. 21–35). Pg corrects ὀλίγων to ἀλγεινῶν which, however, does not fit the context.
[7] Deut. 32. 15.
[8] Hos. 4. 16.
[9] Jer. 27. 22.
[10] Jer. 27. 25.
[11] Jer. 6. 22–25.
[12] Lament. 2. 13.
[13] Reading ἐκινήσαμεν with Müller (so also Ar). Cf. Ar. II. 10₇: μείζους ἂν ποταμούς ... ἐκίνησεν αἵματα. The MSS read ἐκενώσαμεν.

HOMILY III. THE RUSSIAN ATTACK

I too weep with you, if the present time be a time for tears, and the misfortune that has overtaken us be not too great for the flow of tears; for there are—indeed, there are—many misfortunes too great for tears, when the inward parts are inflamed[14] by a deep-seated *ill*, or else violently contracted and stopped up, so that oftentimes even the moisture that distils from the eyes does not flow down.[15] I do not see now any benefit even in the shedding of tears.[16] For when before our eyes the enemy's swords are drenched in the blood of our fellow-countrymen, and we, as we behold this, do not take it upon ourselves to help, as we ought to, being at a loss what to do, but instead collapse in tears, — what kind of consolation is this for the victims? Even more copious streams than the tears welling from our eyelids might the blood of the severed[17] bodies have prompted, but since the gory flood that flows therefrom cannot wipe off the pollution of our transgressions, how can the rivers of our eyes wash it clean? It is not now, my beloved ones, that we ought to weep, but we should have hated sin from the start; not mourn now, but have formerly avoided the pleasures which have caused us this sorrow. It is as though we had delivered ourselves into bondage to cruel masters and were unwilling to bear the torture of the whip, if, having given ourselves over to wicked deeds, we were to beg off the punishment which God's righteous judgment[18] inflicts on us. Not now ought we to wail, but to have been temperate through life; not to scatter now our wealth, when thou dost not know thyself if thou shalt still be[19] its possessor, but to have formerly abstained from the property of others, when the present plague had not yet descended on us. Not to open a booth for mercy now, when the fair of life is about to be broken up by the ills which are upon us, but never to have committed injustice, while the ability remained

---

[14] Reading διαφλεχθέντων with Chalc. 64 and Nauck: διαφραχθέντων proposed by Müller: διαληφθέντων Pg: διαφυλαχθέντων A and B.

[15] Ar's correction καταλείβεται [καταλείπεται A and B] is confirmed by Chalc. 64 which reads καταλείπεται.

[16] Read τῶν δακρυόντων with the MSS: τῶν δακρύων proposed by Nauck, adopted by Ar.

[17] Read διαιρεθέντων with the MSS: ἀναιρεθέντων Ar.

[18] Rom. 2. 5.

[19] ἔτι καταστήσῃ codd: ἐπικαταστήσῃ Ar, who mistakenly gives it as the reading of A.

HOMILIES OF PHOTIUS

in our power. Not to attend vigils now, and run to litanies, and beat the breast, and sigh deeply, and raise the arms, and bend the knees, and weep mournfully, and look dejected, when the pricks of death[20] are sharpened against us: we should have done these things long ago, we should have long ago devoted ourselves to good works, we should have long ago repented over our evil ones. For in so acting now, indeed before a Judge who is, above all, righteous, and whose heart is not overly inclined to pardon,[21] it is not to pity, I think, that we are moving God, but we make ourselves the fierce accusers of the sins which were by us committed. Surely those who, as we see, have both knowledge and strength to live soberly and godfully now, yet who, before the tide of ills swept over us, did nothing in the way of virtue and salvation, but with such negligence and indifference stained their souls with their passions, do they not present them-

Ar II 12 selves self-convicted? Thou who mournest now, why didst thou not formerly abstain from incontinent laughter, licentious songs and theatrical plays?[22] Thou who lookest distraught now, why didst thou contract thy eyebrows, and puff up thy cheeks, showing a face filled with overbearing? Thou who pridest thyself on pitying the wronged and sympathizing with them, why didst thou fall like an unexpected plague on whomever it chanced to be? In a word, why didst thou, who now art kindly to all and in all matters, treat nobody with moderation in former times? But thou didst boast thyself in the command of unrighteous hands,[23] and if thou hadst not succeeded in taking revenge on a suspected enemy, thou didst think thy life was not fit to live. The poor was cast out of thy doors, hungry and an object of abomination, while clowns, gorging themselves from thy table and thy wealth, took all the more advantage of thy simplicity. Thou didst overlook as being of little profit the love of friends, thou spatst upon the nature of kinship, and brokest the bonds of assistance, eager to become, as it were, a fury, a man who hateth his kind. I am far from enumerating all the thefts and

[20] 1 Cor. 15. 56.
[21] Reading with the MSS καὶ μὴ παραπολὺ τὴν γνώμην πρὸς τὴν συγγνώμην ἐπιρρεπῶς ἔχοντι [καίτοι παραπολὺ Ar].
[22] Here Rossejkin ("Первое правленіе Фотія," Богословскій Вѣстникъ, 1909, p. 474, n. 1) sees a direct allusion to Michael's favourite occupations, but is this not rather the usual censure of the ever-popular mime?
[23] Cf. 2 Macc. 4. 40.

HOMILY III. THE RUSSIAN ATTACK

robberies, the fornications and adulteries, and all those other unspeakable deeds, excellent and durable fuel for this fire that has been kindled and poured around us. I know that now as you revolve these matters, you mourn and look downcast. But time is pressing, the Judge incorruptible, the danger terrible, the mass of sins great, and the repentance insufficient. Often have I sown words of reproof, words of threat in your ears, but, it seems, they grew up amidst thorns.[24] I implored you, I castigated you. Often have I pointed out to you the ashes of the Sodomites, and the flood that went before, when the earth was covered with the waters, and the universal destruction of the human race was effected.[25] Often have I represented the Jewish people, the chosen one, the beloved one, the royal priesthood,[26] for its murmuring, its rebelliousness, its ingratitude, and similar trespasses, being lashed and humbled by the foe it had defeated, and over whom it had itself triumphed—diminished, falling, perishing. Often have I admonished you: be on your guard, mend yourselves, convert yourselves; do not wait for the sword to be furbished: the bow is being bent.[27] Do not take *God's* long-suffering as an occasion for contempt; do not act wickedly in the face of His extreme gentleness. But why do I irritate[28] your hearts which are already inflamed? Surely it is better to castigate you as you are now sorrowing, than to send you away unreproached to suffer punishment from above, and to use the present misfortune as a helper in convicting you, rather than, respecting your plight, leave the disobedient and the sinners unreproved. What now? We have admonished and threatened you, using the name of God: our God is jealous and long-suffering, but when He is angered, who shall withstand Him?[29]

2. These things have I been saying, but, it seems, it was like carding *wool* into the fire[30]—a proverb that is timely for me to quote

---

[24] Cf. Lk 8. 5–6.
[25] See above, p. 40.
[26] Exod. 19. 6.
[27] Ps. 7. 13.
[28] ἐπιξέσω A: ἐπιλύξω B: ἐπινύξω Pg. But the meaning requires a present tense, so that ἐπιξέω, ἐπινύσσω, or even ἐπιζέω would be better readings.
[29] Cf. Nahum 1. 2, 3, 6.
[30] Cf. Plato, *Laws*, 780c; Zenobius 5. 27 in Leutsch and Schneidewin, *Corpus paroem. graec.*, I, p. 130.

now (would it were not so!).³¹ For you have not been converted, nor have you repented, but you have made your ears heavy so that you should not hear the word of the Lord.³² For this reason His wrath has been poured upon us, and He has kept watch over our sins,³³ and He has set His face against us.³⁴ "Woe is me, that my sojourning has been too long,"³⁵ will I cry out with the psalmist David, short as it has been.³⁶ It has been too long because I have not been heard in my entreaties, because I see a cloud of barbarians deluging with blood our city which has been parched by sins. Woe is me that I have been preserved to see these evils, that we have become a reproach to our neighbours, a scorn and derision to them that are round about us,³⁷ that the unbelievable³⁸ course of the barbarians did not give rumour time to announce it, so that some means of safety could be devised, but the sight accompanied the report, and that despite the distance,³⁹ and the fact that the invaders were sundered off *from us* by so many lands and kingdoms, by navigable⁴⁰ rivers and harbourless seas.⁴¹ Woe is me, that I see a fierce and savage tribe fearlessly poured round the city, ravaging the suburbs, destroying everything, ruining everything, fields, houses, herds, beasts

Ar II 16

---

³¹ Read ὤφελεν with A [ὤφελε B: ὤφελον Ar] and construe with εἶναι.
³² Zech. 7. 11.
³³ Bar. 2. 9.
³⁴ Ezek. 15. 7.
³⁵ Ps. 119. 5.
³⁶ With reference, perhaps, to his two years as patriarch.
³⁷ Ps. 78. 4.
³⁸ Read ἄπιστος with the MSS: ἄπυστος Ar after a suggestion of Müller's. Further down keep περινοηθείη of the MSS [προνοηθείη Ar].
³⁹ A difficult passage. The MSS read: καὶ τότε πόθεν καὶ χώραις πόσαις ... τῶν ἐπελασάντων διειργομένων. The text is probably right. For the idiomatic use of καὶ τότε (= 'and especially'), cf. Homily XIII, KL p. 195₁₈: καὶ τότε τίνες; Nauck corrects καὶ τότε πόθεν to καὶ τὸ πεπονθέναι: Pg to καὶ τότε πόλεσιν, while Ar reads καίτοι γε πολλαχόθεν καὶ χώραις πολλαῖς.
⁴⁰ ναυσιπόροις codd: ἀναυσιπόροις Ar.
⁴¹ This sentence seems to favour the view that the invaders came from Kiev rather than from the Crimea or the Black Sea coast in general. For a survey of older literature on this subject, see N. Polonskaja, "Къ вопросу о христіанствѣ на Руси до Владимира," Журн. Мин. Нар. Просв., Sept. 1917, pp. 45 sq. The Tmutorokan (or Black Sea) theory still has its adherents, among them G. Vernadsky ("Byzantium and Southern Russia," *Byzantion*, XV [1940–41], p. 73; *Ancient Russia*, New Haven, 1943, pp. 343–4. In the latter work it is suggested that the expedition was undertaken jointly by the Khaganates of Tmutorokan and of Kiev). Vasiliev (*The Russian Attack*, pp. 173–4) has shown cogent reasons why the attack could hardly have come from the Tauric or the Taman Peninsula.

HOMILY III. THE RUSSIAN ATTACK

of burden, women, children, old men, youths, thrusting their sword through everything, taking pity on nothing, sparing nothing. The destruction is universal. Like a locust in a cornfield, like mildew in a vineyard, or rather like a whirlwind, or a typhoon, or a torrent, or I know not what to say, it fell upon our land and has annihilated whole generations of inhabitants. I deem them happy who have Ar II 17
fallen prey to the murderous barbarian hand, because, having died, they have avoided sooner the awareness of the calamities which have seized us unexpectedly. If the departed had any consciousness of these things, then they too would have bewailed with me those who are still left behind for the things they are suffering continually, and because they have taken their fill of so great pain without being relieved of it, and seeking death they find it not. For it is much preferable to die once than to expect continually to die, to be constantly grieved by the sufferings of one's neighbours, and to have one's soul lacerated.

3. Where is now the Christ-loving emperor? Where are the armies? Where are the arms, the engines, the military deliberations and preparations? Is it not an attack of other barbarians which has removed and drawn to itself all these things?[42] The emperor endures long labours beyond the frontier, and the army has marched away to toil with him; whilst we are worn down by the ruin and slaughter before our eyes, which have overtaken some and are about to overtake others. As for this fierce and barbarous Scythian tribe,[43] having crawled out of the very outskirts of the city, like a wild boar it has Ar II 18
devoured all round about.[44] Who then will defend us? Who will array himself against the foe? We are deprived of everything, we are helpless on all sides. What lament may equal our misfortunes?

---

[42] If this statement is taken at its face value, the unexplained resumption of hostilities between the Empire and the Arabs must have been caused by an Arab attack. On the events of the year 860, see Vasiliev, *Byzance et les Arabes*, I, Brussels, 1935, pp. 240 sq.

[43] The use of the name "Scythian" is taken as evidence by Levčenko (*Viz. Vrem.*, IV, [1951] p. 153; Очерки, p. 43) that the invaders were Slavs and not Scandinavians. No such far-reaching conclusions can, however, be drawn from Photius' statement. That Slavs participated in the attack can hardly be denied, but the question of Scandinavian leadership is quite a different one, and may not have been known to Photius at the time. Besides, the word "Scythian," though often applied to the Slavs, also meant "barbarous" in general.

[44] Cf. Ps. 79. 14.

HOMILIES OF PHOTIUS

What tears will be able to suffice for the magnitude of the calamities that surround us? Come unto me, O most compassionate of prophets, bewail Jerusalem with me—not the ancient one, the metropolis of one nation, which grew up from a root with twelve offshoots,[45] but *the metropolis* of the entire universe, as much of it as is adorned by the Christian creed, which lords it in antiquity, in beauty, size, splendour, in the multitude and magnificence of its inhabitants. Bewail with me this Jerusalem, not yet captured and fallen down, but standing nigh to being captured, and rocked by *the calamities* we behold.[46] Bewail with me the queen of cities, not as she is led away captive, but whose hopes of salvation are in captivity. Seek water for the head and fountains of tears for the eyes,[47] pity her [48] and mourn for her, since she weeps sore in the night, and her tears are on her cheeks, and there is none to comfort her;[49] since Jerusalem Ar II 19 has sinned a sin; therefore has she come into tribulation[50] and those who had been awed by her might have sneered at her; since the Lord has sent fire into her bones,[51] and has made heavy His yoke on our neck, and has laid pains on our hands[52] which we shall be unable to withstand. Weep with me since mine eyes have failed with tears,[53] my belly is troubled, and my heart is turned within me for I am embittered with much bitterness; abroad the sword has bereaved me;[54] and the enemy has opened his mouth against me, and gnashed his teeth, and said: I shall swallow her up.[55] O queenly city, what a throng of evils has poured around thee, as the depths of the sea and the mouth of fire and sword[56] have cast lots according to barbarian custom for the children of thy belly,[57] yea, those settled so splendidly

---

[45] Reading with Pg: οὐ τὴν παλαιὰν ἐκείνην ἔθνους ἑνός, ἐκ μιᾶς ῥίζης δωδεκαστελέχου βλαστήσαντος, [omit τὴν] μητρόπολιν, etc.: ἐκείνην, ἔθνους ἑνός ... δώδεκα στελέχους βλαστήσαντος τὴν μητρόπολιν Ar.
[46] τοῖς ὁρωμένοις in the MSS: τοῖς ὠρυγμένοις Ar.
[47] Jer. 8. 23.
[48] Read συμπάθησον καὶ πένθησον with Lig, which is surely better than συμπένθησον καὶ πένθησον, as read by the other MSS.
[49] Lament. 1. 2.
[50] *Ibid.*, 1. 8.
[51] *Ibid.*, 1. 13.
[52] *Ibid.*, 1. 14.
[53] *Ibid.*, 2. 11.
[54] *Ibid.*, 1. 20.
[55] *Ibid.*, 2. 16.
[56] Cf. Gen. 34. 26; Josh. 19. 48; 2 Kings 15. 14, etc.
[57] Is. 48. 19.

HOMILY III. THE RUSSIAN ATTACK

outside the town, and are devouring them.[58] O fair hope of many men, what a calamitous threat and what a mass of horrors have innundated thee all round, and have humbled thy celebrated glory! O city reigning over nearly the whole universe, what an uncaptained army,[59] equipped in servile fashion,[60] is sneering at thee as at a slave! O city adorned with the spoils of many nations, what a nation has bethought itself of despoiling thee! O thou who hast erected many trophies over enemies in Europe, Asia and Libya, see how a barbarous and lowly hand has thrust its spear against thee, making bold to bear in triumph victory over thee![61] Everything with thee has come to such a pitch of misfortune, that thy unassailable strength has sunk to the dregs of extreme infirmity, and thy enemies, beholding thy infirmity and subjection,[62] display the strength of

---

[58] In other words, the barbarians threw some of their victims into the sea to drown, burnt others in their suburban homes, and killed others with the sword. The Greek text offers some difficulties: καὶ τὰ σὰ τῆς κοιλίας ἔκγονα [ἔγγονα A] καὶ τὰ [ἃ Ar] πρὸ τοῦ ἄστεως [ἃ add. Nauck] λαμπρῶς ἐπεπόλιστο, λαγόνες θαλάσσης καὶ πυρὸς καὶ μαχαίρας στόμα βαρβαρικῷ νόμῳ διακληρωσάμενα [διακληρωσάμενον B] κατεσθίουσι. It is not entirely clear whether καὶ ἃ (following Ar) πρὸ τοῦ ἄστεως λαμπρῶς ἐπεπόλιστο is epexegetic of τὰ σὰ τῆς κοιλίας ἔκγονα; in other words, whether the casualties were limited to inhabitants of the suburbs or included city-dwellers as well. I do not understand Šestakov's suggestion (p. 526) that τὰ πρὸ τοῦ ἄστεως λαμπρῶς ἐπεπόλιστο, i. e. the suburbs, are the same as the λαγόνες θαλάσσης (which he presumably takes in the sense of "banks"). Palat. 129 has τὰ πλείω δὲ λαγόνες θαλάσσας, etc., which does not help to clarify the meaning.

[59] The word ἀστρατήγητος can be understood in two ways, either as 1) unskilled in the art of war, or 2) lacking a general. The second meaning seems to be more appropriate here (cf. Procopius, *Bell. Pers.*, II, 25, 13 and *Chronicon Paschale*, I, p. 695, schol.) This epithet need have no bearing on the question whether the incursion was led by Askold and Dir, as reported by the Russian chronicles. That the expedition was under the command of a leader or leaders is only natural, but compared to a regular Byzantine force it must certainly have appeared like a disorganised band of pirates.

[60] Read δουλικῶς with the MSS: δούλοις Ar.

[61] The MSS read τὸ κατὰ σοῦ κράτος ... τροπαιοφορῆσαι [κατὰ τοῦ σοῦ κράτους suggested by Nauck, adopted by Ar].

[62] The above translation is tentative, since the Greek text is obviously corrupt. The MSS read: ὥστε καὶ τὴν ἀπροσμάχητόν σου ῥώμην εἰς τρύγα ἐλάσαι βαθυτάτης ἀρρωστίας, καὶ τὸ ἀρρωστοῦν καὶ τεταπεινωμένον τῶν ἀντιπάλων φιλάνθρωπον [ἀφιλάνθρωπον Ar] ὄμμα χειρὸς ἰσχὺν ἐν σοὶ ἀποφαίνειν, etc. The trend of the argument suggests that τὸ ἀρρωστοῦν καὶ τεταπεινωμένον should refer to the weakness of the Byzantines, which the enemy tries to exploit; but I am unable to supply any plausible emendation that would yield such a meaning. If, on the other hand, τὸ ἀρρωστοῦν καὶ τεταπεινωμένον could refer to the weakness of the enemy, an easier, though not altogether convincing correction would be ⟨ὢ⟩φιλάνθρωπον ὄμμα (as a parenthetical exclamation). In the latter case, translate: "so that thy enemies, infirm and humble as

their arm against thee, and try to bedeck themselves with a glorious name. O queen of queenly cities, who hast saved many others from dangers by thy alliance, who hast with thy arms raised up many that had been forced down to their knees, now lying a prey deprived of helpers! O grace and splendour, size and beauty, elegance and adornment of venerable shrines, O sanctuary of bloodless victims,[63] place inviolate and holy of the dread sacrifice and the mystical

Ar II 21 table, see how enemies' feet are threatening defilement! O pure veneration, stainless faith, undefiled worship, see how the mouth of the impious and the arrogant is opened wide against us![64] O white hairs, unction and ministry of the priests! O me, holy shrine of God and God's Wisdom,[65] sleepless eye of the universe! Wail ye virgins, daughters of Jerusalem. Weep ye young men of the city of Jerusalem. Mourn ye also, mothers. Shed tears, ye babes, shed tears; for the magnitude of the calamity forces even you to awareness. Shed tears, for our ills have been multiplied,[66] and there is none to deliver,[67] none to help.

4. But until when the weeping? Until when the mourning? Until when the wailing? Who will hearken, and how will the plague

Ar II 22 cease?[68] Who will make atonement? Who will cry out on our behalf? If there were a Moses, he would have said to the Lord, "If Thou wilt forgive them, forgive, and if not, blot me too out of the book of life, which Thou hast written,"[69] and to us, "The Lord shall fight for us, and we shall hold our peace."[70] But there is not, because the godly man hath failed from the earth.[71] There is no Moses, there is no Abraham to open his mouth and speak boldly, and say to God, "Destroy not the righteous with the wicked, that the righteous be as the wicked."[72] There is none who will repeat those merciful and

---

they are, should try (O *God's* merciful eye!) to show on thee the might of their hand," etc.
[63] Deleting ὦ after τραπέζης.
[64] Cf. Ps. 34. 21.
[65] I. e. the church of St. Sophia. Cf. below, Homily VII, p. 140.
[66] I Macc. 1. 9.
[67] Hos. 5. 14.
[68] Num. 17. 13.
[69] Exod. 32. 32.
[70] Exod. 14. 14.
[71] Ps. 11. 2.
[72] Gen. 18. 23.

HOMILY III. THE RUSSIAN ATTACK

wondrous arguments, by means of which *Abraham* pleaded that a multitudinous town, borne headlong beyond *the laws of* nature, should find salvation on account of ten righteous men and hear the God of the universe *say* that, "If there be found ten in the city, I will not destroy it for the ten's sake."[73] There is then no Moses, there is Ar II 23 no Abraham; but if you will (a strange thing will I say, yet true), you can make unto yourselves a Moses, you can show an Abraham. For it was not strange that even Moses, when his people were heedless, should have been disregarded for all his pleading;[74] though it was indeed very dreadful that he should have often with his own hand slain many, for whose sake he did everything. Abraham, too, had to see those on whose behalf he had begged and implored *God*, destroying their life by fire, for they had cultivated the thorns of passion. You are able, if you will, that such an one may say to you, "The Lord shall fight for us, and we shall hold our peace."[75]

Do you wish to know how afraid I am of your weeping, that it is temporary; your charity, that it is for a short while; your temperance, that it is ephemeral; your brotherly love, that it *will last only* as long as the threat of the enemy around, being as it is a common ill, compels you to concord; the humility and moderation of your character, that they are while servitude is imminent; that your Ar II 24 vanity is suppressed and your anger held in check, and your tongue is the vehicle of spiritual hymns and not of shameful words as long as the shouts of the enemy impinge on your ears; that the litanies, and the all-night standing at prayers, and the fasting and the sighs are while death by the sword is before you? 5. These things trouble and agitate me much more than the barbarians' arms. This is what I fear, on seeing actions now performed readily and by everybody, which aforetime were not even done by some, even in a corner and grudgingly. It frightens and distresses me that while calamity is standing by, then we take pride in our conversion; that when

---

[73] Gen. 18. 32.
[74] The reading of the MSS is defended by Pg: ἀνεπιστρόφως ἔχοντος τοῦ λαοῦ, δεινόν, οὔπω δεινὸν εἰ πρεσβεύων παρηκούετο, ἀλλ' ἐκεῖνο λίαν φοβερόν, etc.: τοῦ λαοῦ (δεινὸν εἴπω, δεινόν), καὶ πρεσβεύων Ar. The omission of the first δεινόν seems, however, to be called for; οὔπω, if it is right, must be understood in the sense of οὐδέν.
[75] Cf. Exod. 14. 14. Read κύριος πολεμήσει ὑπὲρ ἡμῶν καὶ ἡμεῖς σιγήσομεν [ὑπὲρ ὑμῶν καὶ ὑμεῖς σιγήσετε Ar, in conformity with the text of the Septuagint].

grievous things occur, then we have recourse to good deeds. For this reason there is no Moses now, nor Abraham. If, when the misfortune that now grips us is passed, you kept the same decorum, order and disposition, then you would have put forward many a Moses and an Abraham to fight for you and make atonement to God for us all.[76] And why do I say Moses and Abraham? You would Ar II 25 make the Lord Himself, common to us and to them, our champion and defender; Him Who has brought on the enemy for our sins, to break the might of the enemy; the Punisher to heal; the wrathful One to be merciful. For great is the charity of our God, and His forgiveness of those that return to Him.[77] "Make godly and amend your ways and your works," He crieth out through Jeremiah, "and hearken to the voice of the Lord; and the Lord shall cease from the evils which He has pronounced against you."[78] But you do not wish it so. Cry not, nor make ye agitation: it would have been better to give thanks quietly for the ills we did not suffer, instead of crying out vehemently for fear of suffering *the punishment* that attends those who live perversely; *to have done that* while those abundant fountains of good things were gushing for us in our lifetime, instead of trying to escape the throng of numberless ills[79] which is now standing over us on the razor's edge.

6. But check the weeping, stop, become firm keepers of these *injunctions*. I am so bold as to say: I am the surety for your salvation. I say this, encouraged by your pledges, not by my own actions; by your promises, not by my own words. I pledge your salvation, if Ar II 26 you yourselves observe the agreements staunchly; I *pledge you* liberation from your hardships, if you *pledge* your steadfast conversion; I *pledge* the retreat of the enemy, if you *pledge* withdrawal from the passions. Or rather, it is not I who am the surety for these things, but on my own and your behalf I put you forward as the

[76] Reading καὶ ὑπὲρ ἡμῶν [ὑμῶν Nauck, Ar] ἐξιλεοῦσθαι προεβάλλετε θεόν [so Pg, confirmed by Dorotheus of Mitylene, *Viz. Vrem.*, XII, p. 170_{12}, who paraphrases ἐξιλεοῦσθαι ὑπὲρ ἡμῶν τὸν δεσπότην προεβάλλεσθαι (sic)]: προεβάλετε θεός! codd: προεβάλετο θεός Nauck, Müller, Ar.
[77] Sir. 17. 29.
[78] Jer. 33. 13.
[79] Read ἀλλὰ μὴ περὶ τοῦ δεδιέναι παθεῖν [μὴ περιδεδιέναι τοῦ παθεῖν Ar] ... ἀλλὰ μὴ τῶν χαλεπῶν ἡμῖν ἀπείρων ὄχλον [τὸν τῶν χαλεπῶν ... ἄπειρον ὄχλον Ar].

HOMILY IV. DEPARTURE OF THE RUSSIANS

bondsmen and make you the pleaders, if you fulfil the agreements without reservation. For the Lord Who is merciful and repenting of men's evil[80] will say to you, "Behold, I am blotting out as a cloud thy transgressions, and thy sins as darkness; turn to me and I will redeem thee,"[81] and again, "Turn to me, and I will turn to you,"[82] and again, "I shall pronounce an end upon a nation or upon a kingdom to cut them off and to destroy them," and again, "If that nation turn from their sins, then I also will repent of all the evils which I purposed to do to them."[83]

Ar II 27

7. Finally, beloved ones, the time has come to have recourse to the Mother of the Word, our only hope and refuge. Imploring, let us cry out to her: save thy city, as thou knowest how, O Lady! Let us set her up as our intermediary before her Son our God, and make her the witness and surety of our compact, her who conveys our requests and rains down the mercy of her Offspring, and scatters the cloud of enemies, and lights up for us the dawn of salvation. May we be delivered through her pleading of this present wrath, and be delivered also of the endless condemnation to come, in Jesus Christ our Lord, to whom be all glory and thanks and veneration, together with the Father and the Holy Ghost, now and for ever and ever. Amen.

IV

OF THE SAME MOST-BLESSED PHOTIUS, ARCHBISHOP OF CONSTANTINOPLE, THE NEW ROME,[1] SECOND HOMILY ON THE ATTACK OF THE RUSSIANS

Ar II 30

1. I know that you are all aware—both those who are skilled in comprehending God's rejection of men,[2] and those who are somewhat more ignorant of the Lord's decrees—indeed, I believe that all of you alike perceive and understand that the danger let loose

Ar II 31

---

[80] Joel 2. 13.
[81] Is. 44. 22.
[82] Zech. 1. 3.
[83] Jer. 18. 7–8.
[1] The words νέας 'Ρώμης have been omitted by Ar.
[2] ἀποστροφὴν πρὸς ἀνθρώπους θεοῦ, probably in the sense of "aversion to" (not "turning to," hence "submission" as in Gen. 3. 16 and 4. 7). Cf. Pseudo-Dioscorides, *De venenis*, 30 (*Medicorum graec. opera*, ed. Kühn, XXVI, Leipzig, 1830, p. 38$_2$).

on us, and the sudden incursion of the tribe came upon us from no other source than the wrath and anger of the Lord Almighty. For, to be sure, the Godhead is good and above anger and every passion, inasmuch as its nature surpasses every material affection (which has been allotted a position of subordination beyond all comparison), yet He could be said with propriety to be wrath and angered, whenever an action, deemed worthy of anger and wrath, draws from Him fitting condemnation for its perpetrators; in which manner the calamity which has just overtaken us has also burst out, revealing to our faces the censure of our sins. Nay, nor did it
Ar II 32 resemble other raids of barbarians, but the unexpectedness of the attack, its strange swiftness, the inhumanity of the barbarous tribe, the harshness of its manners and the savagery of its character proclaim the blow to have been discharged like a thunderbolt from heaven. Nor shall I keep silent because you all know it, and because both the acuteness of the misfortune and the critical time have inscribed in your hearts the cause of our accumulated ills; nay, the more since I have yourselves as witnesses of what I am going to say, for this reason will I rather speak in just reproach, dramatizing and acting out to you those things for which by our own sins we have set up a stage and have jointly prepared a tragedy, making our state the theatre of multiform woes. For the wrath of God comes upon us for our transgressions,[3] and the stuff of the perilous *drama* is the acts of the transgressors, and the exaction of punishment is *for* unrepented-of errors. And the more strange and terrible and extraordinary[4] the assault of the invading nation, the more clear is the proof of the abundance of sins; and again, to the extent that *that nation* was obscure, insignificant, and not even known[5] until
Ar II 33 the incursion against us, so much the more is the enormity of our shame set down and the parading of our disgrace proclaimed, and so much the bitterer is the pain caused by the lash. For the victory of the weaker and ignored over those who were effulgent in fame

[3] Cf. Eph. 5. 6.
[4] The right reading seems to be δεινὸς καὶ ἄτοπος [so Lig]: δεινὸς ἄτοπος A and B: δεινῶς ἄτοπος Nauck: δεινὴ καὶ ἄτοπος Ar, but see Šest. p. 528, who gives other examples of a masc. adj. agreeing with a fem. noun.
[5] Read μηδὲ μέχρι τῆς καθ' ἡμῶν ἐπελεύσεως γινωσκόμενον. Nauck's suggested addition of ὀνόματι after μηδὲ [adopted by Ar], though paralleled by Ar. II. 35₄, is not justified.

HOMILY IV. DEPARTURE OF THE RUSSIANS

and unbeatable in strength makes the blow unsurpassable, ushers in an inconsolable disaster, and keeps the memory of the misfortunes ineffaceable. Thus have we been lashed by our unjust deeds, distressed by our passions, humbled by our transgressions, stupefied by evils, becoming a scorn and derision to them that are round about us.[6] For those to whom the very repute of the Romans once appeared irresistible, have taken up arms against their empire itself, and have clapped their hands together, puffed up with the hope of taking the queenly city as a nest of birds.[7] They have ravaged its environs, they have laid waste the approaches to the town, they have harshly destroyed those who fell into their hands, they have poured round about it with all impunity, so encouraged and uplifted by our[8] ill-fortune, that the inhabitants could not even look at them with straight and undaunted eyes; nay, on account of those very things which ought to have incited them to engage the enemy more courageously, they were unnerved and collapsed. For whereas they ought to have been filled with righteous anger at the murder of fellow-countrymen by barbarians, and to have hastened[9] to demand a requital with fair hopes *of success*, they, cowering and panic-stricken, were paralysed; indeed those who had been saved, and who ought to have avenged the victims, imagined the plight of the prisoners as their own capture. For once the sudden fright had fallen into the depths of the heart, and the infection had festered into a wound, then the flow of cowardice was conveyed from the ulcer of the heart as from a fountain and source throughout the whole body, and made those on whom the outcome of the war rested appear with limbs paralysed. Thus we became the plaything of the barbarous tribe, and we thought their threat to be irresistible, their intention incapable of being put to shame, and their attack invincible. For where there is the wrath of God, there also is every dread thing[10]; and when He turns away, destruction most readily

Ar II 34

---

[6] Ps. 78. 4.
[7] Cf. Is. 10. 14.
[8] Read ἡμετέρας with the MSS, not ὑμετέρας [so Ar].
[9] The MSS read ἐπείγεσθαι, not ἐπάγεσθαι, as printed in all the editions.
[10] The correct reading is presumably ἔνθα γὰρ ὀργὴ θεοῦ, ἐκεῖ καὶ τὸ τυχὸν φοβερόν [so Cod. Chalc. 64, f. 300ᵛ, confirmed by Dorotheus of Mitylene, *Viz. Vrem.*, XII, p. 168₁₉]: ἐκεῖ καὶ τὸ τυχόν A, B, Lig: ἐκεῖ καὶ τὸ ἀτυχεῖν Nauck, Müller, Ar.

Ar II 35 creeps in, and those He delivers to chastisement fall an easy prey into the hands of assailants; and, except the Lord guard the city, the watchmen watch in vain.[11]

2. An obscure nation, a nation of no account,[12] a nation ranked among slaves, unknown, but which has won a name from the expedition against us,[13] insignificant, but now become famous, humble and destitute, but now risen to a splendid height and immense wealth, a nation dwelling somewhere far from our country, barbarous, nomadic, armed with arrogance, unwatched, unchallenged, leaderless, has so suddenly, in the twinkling of an eye, like a wave of the sea, poured over our frontiers, and as a wild boar[14] has devoured the inhabitants of the land like grass, or straw, or a crop (O, the God-sent punishment that befell us!), sparing nothing
Ar II 36 from man to beast, not respecting female weakness, not pitying tender infants, not reverencing the hoary hairs of old men, softened by nothing that is wont to move human nature to pity, even when

[11] Ps. 126. 1.

[12] Both A and B read ἀναρίθμητον [ἀνάριθμον Ar], which in this context cannot mean "countless," since "obscure and countless" is nonsense. For ἀναρίθμητος in the sense of "unregarded," see Euripides, *Ion*, 837; *Hel.*, 1679; cf. also the famous oracle which declared the Megarians to be οὔτ' ἐν λόγῳ οὔτ' ἐν ἀριθμῷ (Schol. Theocr., XIV. 48). Nauck (p. L) put forward the plausible correction εὐαρίθμητον = "few," which I would hesitate to adopt because of its far-reaching historical bearing.

[13] The interpretation of this famous passage strikes at the very heart of the problem of Russian origins. The most natural way of understanding it would be that the name Rhos was unknown in Byzantium until the attack of 860, on account of which it became famous overnight. It is true that a Russian embassy did appear at the court of Theophilus in 838, and the envoys must have called themselves by the name Rhos (as they did at Ingelheim), but that brief visit went unnoticed, so that the very existence of the Rhos remained unknown to the general public. Vasil'evskij's objection that ἄγνωστον should be translated "obscure" or "unnoted" and not "unknown" (Труды, III, Petrograd, 1915, pp. cxxv–cxxvii) has some philological backing, but insofar as it is intended to support the now discredited theory of Russian naval raids before 842, it may be set aside. It is not necessary to consider here the derivation of the name Rus, i. e. whether it is of Scandinavian origin (still the more plausible hypothesis) or native to South Russia. See Dvornik, *The Making of Central and Eastern Europe*, London, 1949, pp. 62, 305–314. For the South Russian theory see G. Vernadsky, "The Origin of the name Rus'," *Südostforschungen*, XV (1956), pp. 167–179. There is yet a third theory, that the name Ros was invented by the Greeks who identified the invaders of 860 with the Ros of Ezek. 38–39 (so V. Parchomenko, У истоковъ русской государственности, Leningrad, 1924, pp. 55–56).

[14] Cf. Ps. 79. 14.

HOMILY IV. DEPARTURE OF THE RUSSIANS

it has sunk to that of wild beasts,[15] but boldly thrusting their sword through *persons of* every age and sex.[16] One could see babes torn away by them from breast and milk and life itself, and *finding* an improvised grave in the rocks against which, alas, they were dashed; mothers wailing miserably, being slaughtered over their infants who were still convulsed and gasping—a piteous thing to hear and more piteous to see, much better to be passed over in silence than to be told, and worthier of its perpetrators than of its victims. Nay, nor did the savagery stop with human beings, but over all speechless animals, oxen, horses, fowl and others, which they fell upon, did their cruelty extend. There lay an ox and a man by its side, a child and a horse found a common grave, women and fowl stained each other with their blood. Everything was full of dead bodies; the flow of rivers was turned into blood; some of the fountains and reservoirs it was no longer possible to distinguish, as their cavities were made level with corpses, others retained but Ar II 37 faint traces of their former outline, the missing *traces* being overlaid by the bodies that lay scattered alongside them.[17] Corn-land was rotting with dead bodies, roads were obstructed, forests took on a wild and desolate aspect because of corpses rather than because of bushes and solitude, caverns were filled up, mountains, hills, ravines and gullies differed in no way from city cemeteries. Thus the calamitous[18] destruction spread on, and the plague of war, borne on the wings of sin, flew all round about, destroying everything it encountered.

3. Nobody would be able to describe in words the Iliad of

---

[15] Reading ὑπ' οὐδενὸς τῶν ὅσα [so Nauck: ὅσῳ codd] δυσωπεῖν εἴωθεν ἀνθρώπου, κἂν εἰς θηρίων ἐκδράμῃ [so Nauck: ἐκδράμοι codd], φύσιν μαλασσόμενον. But Müller is perhaps right in correcting ἀνθρώπου to ἄνθρωπον. Ar has ἀνθρώπους ... ἐκδράμοιεν.

[16] A and B have ἀλλὰ ἰδίᾳ [ἀλλ' ἰδίᾳ Lig] πάσης ἡλικίας καὶ φύσεως τὸ ξίφος ὠθεῖν θρασυνόμενον. ἰδίᾳ corrected to διὰ by Nauck, is, however, defended by Šest. p. 528 (in the sense of 'indiscriminately'), but that would still require the addition of διὰ or κατά.

[17] The meaning is not altogether clear. The MSS have: ταῖς δὲ παντελῶς ἀμυδρὰ τοῦ προτέρου σχήματος ἴχνη ἐφαίνετο τῶν παρακειμένων αὐτοῖς [αὐταῖς Ar] ἀναπληρούντων τὰ λείποντα. There seems, however, to have been some uncertainty about the words τὰ λείποντα, since in A a smooth breathing has been written over the grave accent of τὰ, while B has τάλείποντα. This suggests that the original reading may have been τὰ ἐλλείποντα or τὰ ἐκλείποντα.

[18] Read τοῦ πάθους ἡ θραῦσις [τοῦ πλήθους Ar].

ills[19] which overtook us then. And who, on seeing these things, would not admit that the cup mixed by the Lord's anger, which had boiled over[20] at our transgressions, was not poured out on us to its very dregs? Who is it that, studying and revolving these matters, will not walk all through life, even unto the very end, in mourning and melancholy? How everything was confounded then, and how the

Ar II 38 city could almost be said to have been captured by the spear! For while her capture was easy and her inhabitants had no means to defend her, that is to say, while it rested in the power of her foes whether she should suffer or not suffer; and while the safety of the city was in the hands of the enemy, and her fate was at the mercy of their good pleasure; then, I say, it made but small odds, or rather, it was much harder if the city had not yet fallen than if[21] she had fallen earlier; for the latter, by the suddenness of the blow, might perhaps have concealed the reason for her immediate fall;[22] whereas the former, by the lapse of time and by arousing the enemies' goodwill (since she would thus have fallen to their mercy), and so adding to the disaster the insult of their clemency, would make yet more painful the feeling of captivity.[23] Do you remember the turmoil, the tears and wails to which the whole city descended then in utter despair? Do you recollect that murky and terrible night when the orb of all our lives was setting with the orb of the sun, and the light of our life was sinking into the deep darkness of death? Do you

Ar II 39 recollect that unbearable and bitter hour when the barbarians'

---

[19] A proverbial saying. Cf. Demosthenes, *De falsa legatione*, 148; Leutsch and Schneidewin, *Corpus paroem. graec.*, I, pp. 96, 256; II, p. 34; D. K. Karathanasis, *Sprichwörter und sprichwörtliche Redensarten des Altertums*, Munich, 1936, p. 35, no. 38. Cf. also below, p. 196, n. 16.

[20] Read ὑπερζέσας [ὑπερφυέσι Uspenskij, Ar].

[21] Reading τοῦ [τῷ Ar] πάλαι πεσεῖν with the MSS.

[22] The MSS have τῆς μὴ παραυτίκα ἁλώσεως τὴν αἰτίαν, but Ar is probably right in omitting μή.

[23] A difficult and obscure passage. The MSS read: τὸ δὲ τῷ μήκει τοῦ χρόνου καὶ τὴν τῶν ἀντιπάλων ἐπαίρειν [ἐπαῖρον Ar, which he incorrectly gives as the reading of B] φιλανθρωπίαν [ἀφιλανθρωπίαν Ar] ὡς τῇ ἐκείνων οὔπω συγκατενεχθείσης εὐσπλαγχνίᾳ, καὶ τῷ πάθει συνάπτον τὴν ἀπὸ τῆς συμπαθείας [ἀσυμπαθείας Ar] ἀδοξίαν, etc. It appears necessary either to omit οὔπω, or change it to οὕτω, since the Russians would hardly have become more compassionate if the city had *not* submitted to their clemency. This passage seems to imply that the Russians first made an unsuccessful attempt to storm Constantinople, and then offered it a surrender on terms.

HOMILY IV. DEPARTURE OF THE RUSSIANS

boats came sailing down at you,[24] wafting a breath of cruelty, savagery and murder? When the sea spread out its serene and unruffled surface, granting them gentle and agreeable sailing, while, waxing wild, it stirred up against us the waves of war? When the boats went past the city showing their crews with swords raised, as if threatening the city with death by the sword? When all human hope ebbed away from men, and the city was moored only with recourse to the divine? When quaking[25] and darkness held our minds, and our ears would hear nothing but, "The barbarians have penetrated within the walls, and the city has been taken by the enemy"? For the unexpectedness of the event and the unlooked-for attack induced, so to speak, everybody to imagine and hear such things—a symptom that is indeed common among men in such cases: for what they fear excessively they will believe without verification to have happened even when it has not; whereas that of which they have had no previous apprehension they will reject by the arbitrary power of their judgment even when it has come upon them. Verily, there was mourning then, and lamentation and woe.[26] Then each man became the unbiased judge of his own sins, not railing at the "slander" of his accusers to escape the accusation, not demanding external proofs, not pretending to call in witnesses in order to "triumph over the knavish trick," but each man, placing the wrath of God before his eyes, admitted his own transgression, and on account of what he had foolishly done against the commandments, considered himself within the pale of danger; and, being torn away from pleasures by the experience of misfortune, he was converted and reformed to a temperate life, and[27] to confessing to the Lord with sighs, confessing with tears, with prayers and appeals. For a common misfortune and the expectation of death are able—indeed able—to make men aware of their sins, and bring them to their senses, and improve them by their actions.

4. When we made such amends, when we set up our reason as

---

[24] Read ὑμῖν with the MSS: ἡμῖν incorrectly given by Ar as the reading of A: ἡμῶν proposed by Nauck, adopted by Ar.
[25] σεισμός codd, gratuitously changed to σκότος by Ar, and to σκοτισμός by Pg.
[26] Cf. Ezek. 2. 10.
[27] Keep καί after μετερρυθμίζετο, which has been omitted by Ar.

the inflexible arbiter of our sins, and we, the accused, pronounced the verdict against us to be valid, when we invoked God in litanies and hymns, when we offered our repentance with affliction of the heart, when, extending our hands to God all night long, we implored His compassion, and placed in Him all our hopes—then we were delivered from the calamity, then we received liberation from the ills that surrounded us, then we saw the danger being crushed, and the Lord's wrath was seen lifted away from us. For we beheld our enemies retiring, and the city that had been threatened with capture being freed from pillage; at the time when, denuded of all help, and deprived of human alliance, we were spiritually led on by holding fast to our hopes in the Mother of the Word, our God, urging her to implore her Son, invoking her for the expiation of our sins, her intercession for our salvation, her protection as an impregnable wall for us,[28] begging her to break the boldness of the barbarians, her to crush their insolence, her to defend the despairing people and fight for her own flock. When, moreover, as the whole city was carrying with me her raiment[29] for the repulse of the besiegers and the protection of the besieged, we offered freely our prayers[30] and performed the litany, thereupon with ineffable compassion she spoke out in motherly intercession: God was moved, His anger was averted, and the Lord took pity of His inheritance. Truly is this most-holy garment the raiment of God's Mother! It embraced the walls, and the foes inexplicably showed their backs; the city put it around itself, and the camp of the enemy was broken up as at a signal; the city bedecked itself with it, and the enemy were deprived of the hopes which bore them on. For immediately as the Virgin's garment went round the walls, the barbarians gave up the siege

---

[28] Lig seems to have preserved the original reading: ταύτης τὴν σκέπην εἰς τεῖχος εὑρεῖν ἀπολιόρκητον (literally, "for us to have as an impregnable wall"). A and B add τῆς after ταύτης. Ar, following Nauck, has changed εὑρεῖν to ἡμῖν, while Müller has emended it to τηρεῖν.

[29] The "garment" of the Virgin (variously called ἐσθής, πάλλιον, ὠμοφόριον, μαφόριον) was, according to tradition, found at Capernaum, and brought to Constantinople by two patricians in the reign of Leo I (457–474). It was kept in the Blachernae church. See, amongst others, J. Ebersolt, *Sanctuaires de Byzance*, Paris, 1921, pp. 45 sq.; N. H. Baynes, "The Finding of the Virgin's Robe," in *Byzantine Studies and Other Essays*, London, 1955, pp. 240–47.

[30] Read τὰς ἱκεσίας [ἑκουσίας Ar] ἑκουσιαζόμεθα. In A the scribe had first written ἑκουσίας, but then corrected it to ἱκεσίας.

HOMILY IV. DEPARTURE OF THE RUSSIANS

and broke camp, while we were delivered from impending capture and were granted unexpected salvation. For the Lord looked not on our sins but on our repentance, nor did He remember our iniquities,[31] but He looked on the affliction of our hearts, and inclined His ear[32] to the confession of our lips. Unexpected was the enemy's Ar II 43 invasion, unhoped-for appeared their departure; extreme was *God's* irritation, but His mercy inexpressible; unspeakable was the fear they inspired, but they became contemptible in flight; *God's* wrath accompanied them in the attack against us, but we have found God's compassion, routing them[33] and checking their onset.

5. Let us not, therefore, make *God's* love of man an excuse for negligence, nor consider His compassion an incitement to indifference, nor make the beginning of salvation an open gate to our perdition, nor let us be softened by His mercy, so that the end may not be worse than the beginning,[34] and we draw upon ourselves the curse of the Jews: "Ah sinful nation, a people full of sins, why should ye be smitten any more, adding to your iniquities," as Isaiah says, "and it is not possible to apply a plaister, nor oil, nor bandages."[35] Let us not, therefore, beloved ones, render ourselves Ar II 44 guilty of so great evils, nor become oblivious of the compact we pledged to God when we were seeing that terrible danger pressed hard against our face. For you know—you surely know[36]—each man being taught anew by his own conscience, how at that time whoever had done an unjust act pledged himself to God never to do it again, whoever had abandoned his body to fornication was seen, out of loathing for that passion, to make free profession of temperance, yea the habitual drunkard was sober and promised to remain sober in the future; another, who was hard and inhuman of heart, gave

---

[31] Ps. 78. 8.
[32] Ps. 114. 2.
[33] Reading συνελαύνουσαν αὐτούς with the MSS [αὐτοῖς Ar].
[34] Cf. 2 Peter 2. 20.
[35] Is. 1. 4–6.
[36] Read ἴστε γάρ, ἴστε πάντως [πάντες Ar]. It may be cautiously suggested that the meaning of this sentence would benefit by a transposition, viz. instead of ἴστε γάρ, ἴστε πάντως, ὑπὸ τῆς οἰκείας ἕκαστος ἀναδιδασκόμενος συνειδήσεως, ὡς κατ' ἐκεῖνο [so Nauck; ἐκείνου codd] καιροῦ ὁ μὲν ἀδικόν τι δεδρακὼς μηκέτι πράσσειν τοῦτο θεῷ συνετίθετο, etc., transposing ἴστε γάρ, ἴστε πάντως, ὡς κατ' ἐκεῖνο καιροῦ, ὑπὸ τῆς οἰκείας ἕκαστος ἀναδιδασκόμενος συνειδήσεως, ὁ μέν, etc. ("For you know, you surely know, how at that time, each man being taught anew by his own conscience," etc).

HOMILIES OF PHOTIUS

himself entirely over to charity, begging God's mercy as a pledge of his charity towards his neighbours; while he who was malicious to his friends and the ruin of his rivals, an executioner to slaves and a tyrant to free men, seized with weeping and lamenting, tamed and amended the savagery of his character. One could see the haughty humble and voluptuaries fasting; those whose life had been spent in laughter and play moistened their cheeks with torrents of tears; those who had devoted themselves to the acquisition of money shared with the poor, rejecting the disease of avarice, and, to sum up, after close examination of their own defects, they cast them off with much zeal and did away with them. And each man who had lived in negligence and indifference professed himself with hand and foot and every effort to embrace virtue, and they all prayed and pledged themselves to walk thereafter in all purity and

Ar II 45 without turning back along the path of their promises. So let none of us be forgetful of these things; let no one ruin these promises with oblivion, for oblivion of them can kindle God's wrath. Moreover, we have also taken the Mother of the Word, our God, as surety for these our pledges to Him, and the mercy that thereby came upon us has delivered us from captivity. Having with these *pledges* cleansed and tilled our hearts, we have reaped the fruit of repentance; having in this wise reformed our minds, we have been rid of our misfortunes. Having established these foundations for our future life, let us not heap up wood, hay or stubble,[37] the inflammable material of sin which destroys those that are laden with it, but let us build with gold and silver,[38] the sincerest and purest of deeds, into which the poison of wickedness is not injected, so that we may

Ar II 46 have an indestructible bulwark for refuge and an undefiled sanctuary when temptations rear their heads. Nor let us turn back, that we may not be convicted of being unfit for the kingdom of heaven,[39] that we may not cause by our deeds the past ills to repeat themselves and remain with us. Let each man turn away from his evil deeds with all his heart,[40] scrutinizing and searching himself as to which of his acts has so vexed God as to have drawn on such great wrath,

[37] 1 Cor. 3. 12.
[38] *Ibid.*
[39] Cf. Lk 9. 62.
[40] Joel 2. 12.

HOMILY IV. DEPARTURE OF THE RUSSIANS

which is so excessively wicked as to cause so great a danger; for which of our deeds has His anger been kindled, and which have contributed to our being overshadowed by the cloud of His mercy; why was the punishment inflicted, and how was the blow averted; wherefore were we wounded, and with what medicines were we healed. If we seek after these things, and busy ourselves in such wise, and make them a matter of concern, then I know that the Lord will shed His mercy more abundantly, for He is near to all that call upon Him in truth, and will perform the desire of them that fear Him, and will hear their supplication and save them,[41] and He is the protector of all that hope in Him.[42] But if we cling to our former sins, which God forbid (Oh, that there be not one amongst us so insensitive and incorrigible as to disregard such great vexation sent by God!), if then we pollute ourselves with these same passions and stain ourselves with the mire of pleasures, instead of expiating past *calamities* with persevering repentance, and using bygone ills to guard our future life, into what ruin, alas, are we casting ourselves again, of what disasters are we digging a pit,[43] how great a storm of evils are we, in our mad folly, raising against ourselves! For it is said, "If ye will not repent, He will furbish His sword; He has bent His bow and made it ready; and on it He has fitted the instruments of death";[44] and, "He shall rain upon sinners snares, fire and brimstone, and a stormy blast shall be the portion of His cup";[45] and, "Fire and hail, famine and death, sword and lash, all these have been created for the sinners."[46] We have no need of the example of others for our own chastisement. We must use ourselves for our own correction and admonition, our misfortune as our remedy, the past for the future. For when we were wallowing and luxuriating in dissolute and wanton haunts—not to mention the rest—then we saw the Lord's wrath falling down on us like a mass of hail on a harvest of crops.[47] Repentance stopped the destruction: let us not stir it up with

---

[41] Ps. 144. 18-19.
[42] Ps. 17. 31.
[43] Cf. Is. 51. 1.
[44] Ps. 7. 13-14.
[45] Ps. 10. 6.
[46] Sir. 39. 29; 40. 9-10.
[47] Cf. Is. 30. 30.

negligence. His anger was softened by the streams of our tears: let us not kindle it again with outbursts of incontinent laughter, with addiction to theatrical plays. The sword sharpened against us has been sheathed, withdrawn by our litanies and prayers: let us not furbish it again by devoting ourselves to sleep,[48] drunkenness and the tending of our intemperate belly. God heard the groaning of our hearts, *He heard* that cry, and did not overlook it; let us not cease from doing so, that God's mercy may assist us continually. Drunkenness is an evil, fornication is an evil, injustice is an evil, Ar II 49 hatred of one's brother is an evil, anger at one's neighbour, haughtiness, murder, envy *are evils*. Negligence and indifference are evils. Let us avoid these things with every effort, beloved ones. These passions are common to rulers *and ruled*,[49] rich and poor, men and women; so let the righteous deeds be common also. These things inflame God's wrath, increase the danger, repress His mercy, and while making us weak before the enemy, they raise up the foe against us. Let us abominate and reject these things with all our heart, that we may not be condemned to rejection from God.

6. For indeed whenever Israel of old was convicted of having surrendered to the passions, then it was delivered to the edge of the sword—that *famous* Israel, not an ordinary nation, nor a disregarded people, but one that was glorified as the portion of the inheritance,[50] and was blest as the chosen people. That very *nation* then, when it sinned, was chastised with enemies, but when Ar II 50 it was righteous, won and prevailed over them; when it earnestly observed the commandments, it was rewarded in war with alien land and enjoyed other men's toils, but when it despised the Law, it was taken captive and saw its own land allotted to the enemy, *saw them* singing martial hymns and dancing the war-dance—and that most wisely and justly. For the people beloved and favoured by God ought not to rely on the strength of the hand, or to think much of the power of the arm, or to lean on military preparations, but to be certain of vanquishing its opponents and being victorious by the

---

[48] Read ὕπνοις καὶ μέθαις καὶ θεραπείᾳ τῆς ... γαστρός, which Ar has changed to δείπνοις καὶ μέθαις, τῇ θεραπείᾳ τῆς ... γαστρός.
[49] ἀρχομένων is absent from the MSS, and has been supplied by Nauck.
[50] Ps. 104. 11.

HOMILY IV. DEPARTURE OF THE RUSSIANS

alliance of the Most High, knowing that *alliance* to attend excellence of actions and to accompany the plenteousness of good deeds. So if one slips away from the good and from virtue, one also, of necessity, slips away from God's assistance; but if one embellishes one's life with good works, and wears virtue like a corselet, then one has His invincible help as ally against the foes. While then God's people waxes strong and triumphs over its enemies by His alliance, the rest of the nations, whose religion is at fault, are not increased in strength on account of their own good works, but on account of our bad ones, through which they are made powerful and exalted to Ar II 51
our detriment. For they are let loose upon us like lashes, and our sins are the material that these lashes are made of, and dominion over us is handed to them to the extent to which we defeat ourselves with our passions and, through our tendency of retreating towards evil, we abandon the ranks in which the holy law of salvation has appointed us. So since, on the one hand, by doing right we become closer to God, and victory over the enemy accrues to us through victory over our passions; while, on the other hand, when we sin we are paid with rejection from God and falling into the power of the enemy, ought we not then to avoid and abominate transgressions, but to seek good works, to flourish with them, and constantly enhance our life with them? How could a man even venture to prevail over the foe, when he cherishes within himself inward enemies and factions that are defeating him, when senseless anger rules over the empire of reason, and incites muderous thoughts against Ar II 52
his neighbour, who perhaps has done him no harm? How dost thou expect victory over the enemy to abide with thee, when the greed of desire has taken under its hand the absolute power of reason, and drags it hither and thither, leading it round like a captive in any direction the passion may ordain? How could the prize over the foe accrue to men who are thus being defeated and enslaved? It is impossible, utterly impossible, for a man who has been fettered and subjugated by intestine enemies, and who has sold himself to his passions, to be able to overcome outside enemies. If we wish to destroy the latter, let us first of all take heed to subjugate our internal foes, let us end their rebellion and strife. Let reason be the complete ruler of the passions, and then we shall

overcome our opponents who have license to strike and wound us from without. For if thou hast abandoned to the passions the reason which thou hast received from God to be absolute master, and hast subjected it to them like a captive, how canst thou wish to overpower the enemies who are attacking thee from outside? How canst thou despoil the munitions of thy foes, thou whose mind is constantly despoiled by internal revolts and conspiracies? Let us first expel the intestine *enemies* from our thoughts, and then we shall easily despoil the might of aliens. Dost thou not see how Israel, when it overcame its passions, overcame also its enemies (for God joined in leading its army), but when it was enslaved by sin, then it was also delivered over to its enemies (for the might of God which shared the leadership had abandoned it)? This *nation*, while it pleased God, escaped thanks to Moses the terrible and crushing hands of the Egyptians; and not that only, but even the raging sea became unto it a straight path in a manner surpassing words, while it opened up as an eternal tomb to the pursuing Egyptians, wondrously destroying horses, chariots, Pharaoh and all.[51] Whereat the people beloved by God was pleased and overjoyed, and struck up in its happiness a song of deliverance to God, the general Who grants victory. But on another occasion, when they were seduced into becoming guilty of murmuring, and equipped themselves for war without God's command, and were led away into putting their trust in the law of might rather than in a sign from God, they were utterly worsted and defeated, swelling the power and exalting the fame of their opponents by their own transgression. And again, when they were led by God's law and obeyed the words of Moses, they captured many cities of their enemies, took many prisoners, plundered much booty, and were filled with much gladness and joy. And that gladness and pleasure of victory would have remained with them, had they not, through ingratitude, marshalled serpents against themselves;[52] for there was no nation at hand to fulfil and demonstrate with the sword God's righteous vexation at their ingratitude. In this way is a sinning people chastised: either mowed down by the enemies' swords, or devoured by the teeth of wild

[51] Exod. 14. 21 sq.
[52] Num. 21. 6.

HOMILY IV. DEPARTURE OF THE RUSSIANS

beasts, or punished[53] with earthquakes and violent eruptions, or burnt up by thunderbolts from heaven, or oppressed by dearth of crops, or destroyed by pestilential air. A means of punishment is never lacking to fit the peculiarity of the sin. If a man has escaped this one, he is impaled on that,[54] and again, if he has perhaps avoided that one, he is caught by another, and *generally* he who lives unjustly and has accounts to render will not be able to shun punishment. Why do I have to relate the remaining *history* of Israel? Its victories against the foe when it lived with moderation, its unexpected defeats when it was foolish again; its captivity, its return, its second rebellion, its restoration, the very destruction of Jerusalem, and again its rebuilding? Their good *fortunes* bloomed over good deeds, while wicked ones were repaid with calamities. Therefore, beloved ones, using for our own betterment *the evils* that have been heaped upon us, the same that aforetime have been manifested in the case of Israel,[55] let us hate sin and cleave to virtue. Let us avoid those everyday soul-destroying trespasses—drunkenness, fornication, envy, slander, greed, injustice, imposture, hatred of one's brother, *and* the offspring of these *sins*,[56] so that we may be rewarded with victory in wars, and not forego[57] our heavenly inheritance.

7. But since we have been delivered from the threat, and have escaped the sword, and the destroyer has passed by us,[58] who have been covered and marked out with the garment of the Mother of the Word, let us all in common with her send up[59] songs of thanksgiving to Christ our God Who was born of her—every house that has escaped the sword, *persons of* every age, women, children, youths and old men. Indeed, those to whom a common destruction was impending, ought to consecrate and offer to God and His Mother a common hymn. We have enjoyed a common deliverance: let us offer common thanks. Let us say to the Mother of the Word

---

[53] Read παιδευόμενοι [σαλευόμενοι suggested by Müller, adopted by Ar].
[54] Reading περιεπάρη [περιεπάγη Ar, who mistakenly ascribes it to A].
[55] τὰ κατὰ τὸν Ἰσραὴλ πάλαι προϋποδειχθέντα [codd] may be retained: κατὰ τὰ τῷ Ἰσραὴλ Ar.
[56] ⟨καὶ⟩ τὰ τούτων ἔκγονα should probably be read.
[57] ἀστοχήσωμεν, needlessly changed by Ar to ἀτυχήσωμεν.
[58] Cf. Exod. 12. 23.
[59] Read ἀναπέμψωμεν with the MSS [ἀναμέλψωμεν proposed by Nauck, adopted by Ar].

with rectitude of mind and purity of soul: "Unhesitatingly we keep[60] our faith and love for thee. Do thou save thy city, as thou knowest how and willest. We put thee forward as our arms, our rampart, our shield, our general: do thou fight for thy people. We shall take heed to the best of our strength to make our hearts pure before thee, having torn ourselves away from filth and passions. Do thou dispel the plots of them that rise up arrogantly against us. For even if we are amiss in the commandments made unto us, it is thine to set us straight, it is thine to proffer a hand to us who are kneeling down, and to raise us up from our fall." Thus let us address the Virgin, and let us not speak falsely, that we may not be belied in our fair hopes, that we may not be balked of our expectation, so that having

Ar II 57 overcome the tossing, the waves and storms of life's evils, we may come to anchor in the harbour of salvation, and be deemed worthy of the heavenly glory, by the grace and mercy of Christ our true God, to Whom is due all glory, honour and veneration, together with the Father and the Holy Ghost, the consubstantial and life-giving Trinity, now and for ever and ever. Amen.

[60] Read φυλάττομεν [φυλάξομεν Nauck, Ar].

NOTE ON HOMILY V

There was a widespread tradition in Byzantine literature harking back to St. Luke's narrative that homilies on the Annunciation should be cast in a semi-dramatic form.[1] The present one is an example in point. Written in poetic prose, it is rich in assonances, and contains a dialogue between Mary and Gabriel (purely rhetorical in character) amplifying the Gospel narrative. It should be noted that neither in this nor in the other Homilies does Photius make use of apocrypha, unlike his contemporary George of Nicomedia.[2] Apocryphal details, drawn from the Protoevangelium of James and other sources, are particularly plentiful in sermons on the Annunciation, e. g. the one by Andrew of Crete,[3] those attributed to the Patriarch Germanus,[4] St. Gregory the Wonderworker,[5] etc. Our Homily concludes with a series of Chairetismoi (*Salves*) and a prayer for one emperor. The date advanced by Aristarches (II. 229), to wit the 25th of March 865, is quite gratuitous.

Both as regards the dialogue form and the litany of Chairetismoi, the present Homily does nothing more than follow a tradition which had become firmly entrenched by the ninth century. It is generally believed that the Syrian soughîthâ was the precursor of Byzantine dramatic and semi-dramatic homilies. The progress of the latter is difficult to follow as most of the supposedly early examples are either of doubtful authenticity or clearly spurious. The *genre* is said to have been established in Byzantine literature by the fifth century.[6]

---

[1] See G. La Piana, *Le rappresentazione sacre nella letteratura bizantina*, Grottaferrata, 1912, pp. 99 sq.; *id.*, "The Byzantine Theater," *Speculum*, XI (1936), pp. 176 sq.

[2] On the use of apocrypha by George of Nicomedia cf. L. Bréhier, "Les miniatures des 'homélies' du moine Jacques," *Monuments Piot*, XXIV (1920), pp. 104 sq. In the *Amphilochia* (quaest. 151, PG 101, col. 813) Photius applies the term "profane" (ἔξω) to the O. T. apocrypha.

[3] PG 97, cols. 881–913.

[4] PG 98, cols. 320–340.

[5] PG 10, cols. 1172–77.

[6] La Piana, *Rappresentazione sacre*, pp. 63–68. A short dialogue is found in the Annunciation homily by Hesychius of Jerusalem who lived in the first

HOMILIES OF PHOTIUS

As for the Chairetismoi with their rich répertoire of Marian symbolism, they were fully developed by the sixth century (witness Romanus[7] and the Acathist Hymn). Such litanies were addressed to other saints as well, e. g. to St. Euphemia (by Photius' contemporary Constantine of Tius).[8] For purposes of comparison, the Annunciation homilies by Sophronius of Damascus,[9] Andrew of Crete,[10] as well as one falsely attributed to Basil of Seleucia[11] should especially be mentioned.

This Homily, as well as nos. VII and IX, have been analysed by M. Jugie in relation to the dogma of the Immaculate Conception.[12]

V

Ar II 230 OF THE SAME PHOTIUS, MOST-BLESSED PATRIARCH OF CONSTANTINOPLE, HOMILY DELIVERED ON THE ANNUNCIATION OF THE MOST-HOLY MOTHER OF GOD[1]

1. Gay is today's festival, and splendid is the joy it conveys to the ends *of the earth*. The joy it yields scatters old sorrow; the joy
Ar II 231 it yields banishes the curse of the world, inaugurates the raising of him who fell long ago, and pledges salvation to all of us. An angel converses with a virgin, and the whispering of the serpent is made idle, and the impact of his plot is averted. An angel converses with a virgin, and Eve's deceit fails, and convicted nature, seen *to rise* above condemnation, as it had been before condemnation, is enriched with the possession of paradise as its portion. He speaks to the Virgin, and

---

half of the 5th century (PG 93, cols. 1453 sq.). It is considered authentic by Vailhé, *Échos d' Orient*, IX (1906), p. 142.
  [7] For example, the hymn on the Annunciation in N. B. Tomadakis, Ῥωμανοῦ τοῦ μελῳδοῦ ὕμνοι, Athens, 1952, pp. 303 sq.
  [8] *Acta Sanctorum*, Sept. V, pp. 282 C–283 A. Cf. Loparev in *Viz. Vrem.*, XVIII (1911), p. 35.
  [9] PG 87 ter, cols. 3217 sq.
  [10] See n. 3 above.
  [11] PG 85, cols. 425 sq.
  [12] "Photius et l'Immaculée Conception," *Échos d'Orient*, XIII (1910), pp. 198–201; *L'Immaculée Conception dans l'Écriture Sainte et dans la tradition orientale*, Rome, 1952, pp. 164–69.
  [1] In A and B the title is given as follows: Τοῦ αὐτοῦ Φωτίου ἁγιωτάτου πατριάρχου Κωνσταντινουπόλεως ὁμιλία λεχθεῖσα εἰς τὸν εὐαγγελισμὸν τῆς ὑπεραγίας θεοτόκου. Lig adds Μαρίας after θεοτόκου.

HOMILY V. THE ANNUNCIATION

Adam receives a pledge of liberty, and the serpent, instigator of evil, is deprived of his tyranny over our kind, and is dispossessed of his authority, and learns now that he had armed himself in vain against Creation. His devices against us weaken, as an incorporeal being brings the message of the invincible trophy against sin: for Christ's cross and willing suffering are death and sin swallowed up in victory,[2] and such also is His suffering through the Incarnation. The angel is now bearing the good tidings of the Incarnation, in which *tidings* we are rejoicing today, and whose festival we are celebrating. An angel is being sent to the Virgin, and human nature is renewed; for, having quaffed the tidings like a remedy of salvation, it spits out all the poison of the serpent, and is cleansed from the spots of its disease. An angel is being sent to the Virgin, and the bond of sin is being torn up, and the penalty for the disobedience is abolished, and the universal recall is pledged in advance. Today the tidings Ar II 232 of joy have arrived, since the archangel is exchanging words with the virgin maiden, since the commander of the invisible host is conversing with Mary, espoused to Joseph but designated and preserved for Jesus. But what is he uttering and what *tidings* is he bringing? What? O, unspeakable words of an awful mystery, and incomprehensible manner of a strange speech! What he is uttering and what *tidings* he is bringing I am led on to say, and I cower with anguish. I cower as I begin to fathom the sea of the Lord's love of man. I cower, being required to plumb the depths of the divine dispensation. My mind reels at grappling *with the subject*,[3] speech withdraws, and my tongue shrinks from speaking. Once more, as though striving with eagerness, speech wants to talk freely, but perplexity arms silence against it, and makes the latter prevail.

2. But come, O wisest of the Evangelists, and joining in the beginning of my speech, cast out my anguish by thy help, and reviving my faint heart, pledge me courage by thy support, saying: "In the sixth month the archangel Gabriel was sent from God unto a city of Galilee, named Nazareth, to a virgin espoused to a man whose name was Joseph of the house and lineage of David; and the

---

[2] Cf. 1 Cor. 15. 54.
[3] The reading of A, the only MS at this point, should probably be retained: καὶ νοῦς μὲν ἰλιγγιᾷ προσβάλλειν [προβάλλειν Ar]. Cf. below, p. 148, n. 40.

virgin's name was Mary. And the angel came in unto her and said, Hail, much-graced one, the Lord is with thee."[4] Seest thou what it was he was bringing, and what he spoke to her? Seest thou the cause of the conversation? "Hail," saith he, "much-graced one, the Lord is with thee." O strange mystery, that escapes every mind and every apprehension! A mystery which is believed, not investigated; wondered at, not searched into; a mystery which is worshipped, but not examined; praised in song, not scrutinized; honoured, not weighed; longed for, not apprehended. An angel is sent to a virgin, pledging the Lord's presence, announcing God's coming among men, bringing the good tidings of the re-creation of Creation. An angel is sent to a virgin, disclosing the Lord's descent, and the Lord comes with the message. The former brings the good tidings, and the Lord accompanies the words. The former cries out to the Virgin, "Hail, much-graced one," and the Lord fulfils the joy by His action. The former calls out to the Virgin, "Hail, much-graced one," and the whole world reaps through her the fruit of joy. He utters the fair salutation to the stainless maid, and the Virgin is troubled by his strange greeting, while the whole Creation leaps with joy at the good news of its salvation.

3. The honoured maid is troubled, but she does not reject. She is troubled by the words, but does not turn away from the bounty. For it says, "When she saw *him*, she was troubled at his saying, and cast in her mind what manner of salutation this should be."[5] She was troubled, she did not turn away; she was troubled, but she cast in her mind; she cast in her mind inquiring into the manner of the salutation, yet perceiving that its cause escaped understanding: what manner of salutation this should be. "For I see," says she, "that it does not fall within the limits of the usual, that it has overleapt the laws of nature, is not circumscribed by human actions: what manner of salutation this should be. I see the messenger standing reverently, and I am moved to receive his message joyfully; but he addresses me bridal words, and changes the joy to fear, and troubles my soul with his message. I see his face restrained by modesty, but he announces to me the coming of a bride-

---

[4] Lk 1. 26–28.
[5] Lk 1. 29.

HOMILY V. THE ANNUNCIATION

groom. I see him conversing wisely, but he utters words of conception, and the love of virginity forces me to suspect his saying as a wile. What manner of salutation this should be. For this reason," says she, "I am troubled, seeing the matter evenly balanced in my mind. For the messenger's rank and manner, and his seemly aspect indicate that the message comes from God. His words, however, which give the impression of being those of a suitor, prompt me to refuse assent." For indeed, saith the Evangelist, "seeing *him* she was troubled." Seeing what, and wherefore was she troubled? Seeing the angel looking at her with chaste eyes, yet bringing tidings of a suitor; *seeing him* attend with a seemly gaze, yet speaking of a marriage contract. Having heard these bridal words, and seeing the manner of the conversation to be untouched by the passions, the holy Virgin was troubled by her conflicting thoughts and, seized by a prudent fear, was amazed by the strangeness of the salutation.

4. But what does the angel say to her? Did he leave her to be troubled by opposing thoughts? Did he forsake her to be tossed by the waves of perplexity? Would he not have been proved *in that case* to be a worthless minister of the command? Would he not have rightly paid a penalty because he had left the Virgin to be disturbed? What then says he? "Fear not, Mary,[6] I have not come to speak to thee in deceit, but to introduce the abolition of deceit. I have not arrived to lead thee into error, but to pledge deliverance from error. I have not visited thee to violate thy inviolate virginity, but to bring the good tidings of the inhabitation of the Creator and Guardian of virginity. Fear not, Mary. I am not the servant of the serpent's wickedness, but the delegate of Him who suppresses the serpent. The former, by means of his words, instilled the poison into human nature, and having mixed death into the potion, poured out the plague on everyone; I come to graff in[7] by means of the Lord's commands unending life to the world,[8] whereby the disease of our kind is removed, and the blessedness in paradise is made free to all. The former, by the deceit of divinisation, pushed Adam into dis-

[6] Lk 1. 30.
[7] Rom. 11. 23.
[8] τοῖς πέρασι cod: τοῖς πεσοῦσι Ar.

obedience, and made him exchange his painless existence for a toilsome life; I bring thee the good tidings that the universal Creator shall truly make man divine in thy virginal and stainless womb, and dispel the spurious divinisation. I have come as a bridal escort, not as a plotter; an instigator of joy, not a cause of sorrow; as a herald of salvation, not a counsellor of perdition. Fear not, Mary. I will heal thy thoughts with the Lord's commands, I will undo the bonds of thy perplexity. Thou hast found favour with God.[9] The salutation is of divine favour, not an instrument of *human* nature; it Ar II 236 is of a godly favour, and not of a human plot; of a godly favour, and not of bodily intercourse. It is of a favour which overleaps human understanding."

But when thou hearest of favour, O man, think not that this gift was granted to the Virgin in vain, nor consider the present as an empty honour. For the Virgin found favour with God because she had made herself worthy before her Creator, because, having adorned her soul with the fairness of her purity, she had prepared herself as an agreeable habitation for Him who by His word has established heaven.[10] She found favour with God not only because she had kept her virginity inviolate, but also because she had maintained her desires unsullied; because since she was a babe she had been sanctified to God as a living and unquarried temple, built for the King of glory, for the stainlessness of her body, the exceeding splendour of her virginity, her undefiled chastity, the great purity of her disposition, her soul unwavering to sin and clinging[11] to the best. "For this reason thou shalt conceive in thy womb and bring forth a son whom the Cherubim praise in fear. Thou shalt conceive in thy womb and bring forth a son whom the ranks of the angels tremble to see, and the entire Creation is unable to contain. Thou shalt conceive in thy womb and bring forth a son, the Creator of thy inviolate womb, not corrupting thy virginity, but sealing the bolts Ar II 237 of virginity; not destroying the purity of thy pregnancy, but showing it uncorrupted by fornication. Thou shalt conceive in thy womb Him who is present everywhere, but is contained by nothing,

[9] Lk 1. 30.
[10] Cf. Ps. 32. 6. Read with Vat. gr. 759: τοῦ [τῷ A] λόγῳ τοὺς οὐρανοὺς στερεώσαντος [τῷ Λόγῳ, τῷ τοὺς οὐρανοὺς στερεώσαντι Ar].
[11] καὶ [delete τὸ added by Ar] τοῦ κρείττονος ἀμετάπτωτον.

HOMILY V. THE ANNUNCIATION

whom only thy womb is believed to receive and contain without being straitened. Thou shalt conceive in thy womb the Creator of thy first ancestor. For it was about thee that the Prophet also cried out, saying, "Behold, a virgin shall conceive in the womb, and bring forth a son, and they shall call his name Emmanuel, which being interpreted is, God with us."[12] He is the mighty God, the Prince of peace, and the Father of the future age.[13] The prophecies made concerning thee I too announce to thee today, and I am not come to offer my own words, but to bring the commands of Him who has sent me. It is He that inspired the prophet Isaiah to prophesy concerning thee; it is He again who entrusted me also to announce today the outcome of that prophecy which is soon to be fulfilled: "And behold, thou shalt conceive in thy womb and bring forth a son, and they shall call his name Emmanuel, which being interpreted is, God with us." And because through Him they will enjoy salvation, they shall call Him Jesus who has delivered them of their sins: His title *comes* from His bounty, His style from His function, His fair name from His deeds. They shall call Him Jesus, through whom the inexhaustible wealth of salvation flows to them; through whom the stings of death[14] are broken, while the grace of immortality flourishes, and the might of sin collapses, while the nature of the fallen one rises triumphant. He shall be great, and shall be called the Son of the Highest.[15] He shall be great, as He had been, although He assumes the smallness of the flesh, although He puts on the humbleness of the body. He shall be great: nay, nor does the assumption of humanity debase the greatness of divinity, but the humbleness of humanity is rather exalted with it. He shall be great even after the incarnation, or, if thou wilt, even after His labours, even after His sweat has poured down in great drops,[16] even as He takes upon Himself all that the nature of the flesh is wont to suffer. Wherefore, even if thou seest Him hungry, even if sweating, even if labouring, even if insulted and lashed, even if finally crucified, made dead and buried, do not consider it with

Ar II 238

[12] Is. 7. 14; Mt 1. 23.
[13] Is. 9. 6.
[14] 1 Cor. 15. 56.
[15] Lk 1. 32.
[16] Lk 22. 44.

reference to the divine Word as being in any way paltry and unworthy of God. For thus too[17] shall He be great, as He had been, although by the law of our nature He has willingly assumed in His own flesh the things of the flesh. He shall be great, and shall be called the Son of the Highest. Thou shalt not call Him so, but He shall be called. Thou shalt not set this name upon Him, but He shall be called. And by whom shall He be called? Clearly, by the consubstantial Father who knows exactly the nature of the Son,

Ar II 239 since no man knoweth the Son, but the Father, and no man knoweth the Father, but the Son.[18] For He of whom the Son was ineffably and timelessly begotten, possesses also the unerring apprehension of Him; and He who has the true knowledge of the offspring, may be trusted also to apply an appropriate name. Wherefore saith the God of all and Father of our Lord Jesus Christ, "This is my beloved Son, in whom I am well pleased; hear ye him."[19] He is forever, though the name is given to Him now for our instruction and cognizance. For this reason, it says, "He shall be named," not "He shall become": for before all time He had been enthroned together with His consubstantial Father. Him thou wilt conceive in thy womb, and His mother thou wilt be proclaimed; Him thy virginal womb receives. Whom the heavenly vault could not contain, in the hollow of whose hand everything is held,[20] the work of whose providence is the maintenance and continuance of existent things, Him thou shalt conceive in thy womb."

5. But what did the most-holy Virgin *reply* to this? Was she immediately softened by these words, and having opened her ears wide

Ar II 240 with pleasure, did she allow her thoughts to give assent without scrutiny? Not at all. But what says she? "Now I know clearly that thou describest to me conception, pregnancy and the birth of a son, but thou hast increased my perplexity all the more. For how shall this be to me, seeing I know not a man?[21] For every birth comes from intercourse with a man, while abstention from relations with

[17] οὗτος ἔσται [so A, Ar] should probably be changed to οὕτως ἔσται on the authority of Vat. gr. 759, which gives this passage in condensed form: κἂν γοῦν πτωχεύῃ τὴν σάρκα, ἀλλὰ καὶ οὕτως μέγας ἔσται ὥσπερ ἦν.
[18] Mt 11. 27.
[19] Mt 17. 5.
[20] Cf. Is. 40. 12.
[21] Lk 1. 34.

HOMILY V. THE ANNUNCIATION

a man does not so much as permit one even to hear of conception. How then shall I have offspring, whose begetter is unknown? How shall this be?"—"And who knows how to interpret the Lord's counsel? Who dares to inquire into the motives of the King's command, and to unfold the reason of a mysterious dispensation? Who is able to relate the manner of the strange birth? Who has the strength to scrutinize an inscrutable mystery? How shall this be? One thing I know, one thing I have been taught, one thing I have been sent to tell. This I say: the Holy Ghost shall come upon thee, and the power of the Highest shall overshadow thee.[22] It is that which shall teach thee how thou shalt be pregnant. It shall interpret how thou shalt conceive. It is a participant in the Lord's wish, since they are enthroned together, while I am a slave. I am a messenger of the Lord's commands, not the interpreter of this *particular* command. I am the servant of His will, not the expounder of His intent. The Spirit shall set everything in order, for it searcheth all things, yea, the deep things of God.[23] I cry out, 'Hail, much-graced one,' and I praise the miracle in song, and worship the birth, but I am at a loss to tell the manner of the conception. But if thou wishest to accept credence of my tidings by means of examples, inferring great things from small ones, and confirming the things to come by things past,—thou shalt conceive in thy womb and bring forth a son in the same manner as Aaron's rod was budded without cultivation, acting like a rooted plant.[24] As the rain borne down from heaven on the fleece watered that alone but did not refresh the earth,[25] thus thou too shalt conceive in thy womb and bring forth the Lord. This thy ancestor also, David, announces in advance, inspired by God of thy pregnancy: 'He shall come down like rain upon a fleece, like a drop falling upon the earth.'[26] As the bush received the fire, and feeding the flames was not consumed,[27] thus shalt thou conceive a son, lending Him thy flesh, providing nourishment to the immaterial fire, and drawing

[22] Lk 1. 35.
[23] 1 Cor. 2. 10.
[24] Num. 17. 23.
[25] Judges 6. 37.
[26] Ps. 71. 6.
[27] Exod. 3. 2.

incorruptibility in return. These things prefigured thy conception, announced in advance thy delivery, represented from afar thy pregnancy. Those strange things have been wrought that they might confirm thy *child's* ineffable birth. They happened beforehand that they might delineate the incomprehensibility of the mystery: for the flaming bush, and the bedewed fleece, and the rod bearing leaves would not have contributed anything useful to life, nor would they have incited man to praise the Wonder-worker, nay, the miracle would have fallen to no purpose, unless they had been set down as prefigurations of thy giving birth, and been, as it were, the advance proclamations of the Lord's coming. Thou hast, if thou

Ar II 242 willest, thy neighbour and kinswoman Elizabeth as an example, for behold, she hath also conceived a son in her old age: and this is the sixth month with her, who was called barren; for with God nothing shall be impossible.[28] He who releases the bonds of barrenness can also make unto Himself a birth without a man's mediation. He who has renewed a withered root into a fruit-bearing stem, He shall also change unto Himself the unmoistened ground into fertile land."

6. Such things the archangel was saying, drawing the spotless maiden to assent. But to this what *was the reply of* the honoured virgin, the heavenly chamber, the holy mountain,[29] the sealed fountain,[30] kept for Him only who had sealed it? "Since," says she, "thou hast clearly explained that the Holy Ghost shall come upon me, I no longer demur, I no longer object. Be it unto me according to thy word.[31] If I am judged worthy for the Lord, I will gladly serve His will. If the Builder desires the thing built to become a temple to the Builder, let Him construct a house unto Himself as He has pleased. If the Creator rests on His creature, let Him

Ar II 243 mould in me His flesh as He knows how and wishes. Behold the handmaid of the Lord: be it unto me according to thy word.[32] Let thy words be unto me fulfilled in the act. Let thy words be unto me in accordance with the deeds."

[28] Lk 1. 36–37.
[29] Ps. 98. 9.
[30] Song 4. 12.
[31] Lk 1. 38.
[32] *Ibid*.

HOMILY V. THE ANNUNCIATION

7. The holy and uncorrupted Virgin for her part, having shown in such words her obedience to the Lord's ambassador, put an end to the conversation. As for us, what shall we offer to the Virgin? What words of praise[33] shall we weave for her? What other, than those whose beginning Gabriel has first provided to us, saying, "Hail much-graced one, the Lord is with thee. Blessed art thou among women, and blessed is the fruit of thy womb."[34] Hail, because we see the sun of righteousness rising out of thee, illuminating both the heavenly and the earthly order, driving away the murk of error, and irradiating the universe with the splendour of Grace. Hail, much-graced one, because having raised for us without husbandry the soul-nourishing grain, thou hast destroyed the seeds of the soul-corrupting growth. Hail, because thou hast brought to all of us the ambrosia of the life-giving bread, baked in thy flaming womb as in an oven, having removed like yeast[35] the pest of the death-giving food. Hail, because thou hast made the tree of life bear fruit for us, which withers the offshoots of the tree of decay[36] and yields the sweetness of knowledge. Hail, much-graced one, because thou hast stored away the pearl of great price,[37] conveying[38] the wealth of salvation to the ends of the universe. Blessed art thou among women, because thou hast requited the discomfiture of woman's transgression, having turned the reproach of deceit into a laudation of the sex; because in thee, a virgin, He who first moulded Adam out of virgin earth, today remoulds man from thy virginal blood; because, having woven the fleshy garment of the Word, thou hast covered up the nakedness of the first-formed. Why should I enumerate each count? Hail, much-graced one, because super-human things were wrought in thee, and the blessing of all good things has bloomed for us through thy pregnancy.

Ar II 244

8. O thou, Virgin and Mother—this new and strange thing under

---

[33] φωνὰς ὑμνολογίας unnecessarily corrected by Ar to τερπνὰς ὑμνολογίας (cf. Šest., p. 536).
[34] Lk 1. 28, 42.
[35] Cf. Exod. 12. 15.
[36] τοῦ ξύλου τῆς βρώσεως. A pun on the double meaning of βρῶσις = 1) "eating," with reference to the Tree of Knowledge which was καλὸν εἰς βρῶσιν (Gen. 3. 6), and 2) "corrosion" (Mt 6. 19, 20).
[37] Mt 13. 46.
[38] διαπορθμεύουσα cod: διαπορθμεύσασα Ar.

the sun—extend to us now also thy intercession for our protection. Send us thy help to guard us. Strengthen thy faithful slave, our pious emperor, with virtue and reverence to God, guiding him to steer with godly mind the helm of the kingdom down here, and showing him heir of the kingdom[39] of Christ, our true God, thy Son and Master, over there, which may we all win through the grace and compassion of Christ Himself, our true God, conceived without seed, unutterably gestated, and inexplicably born. For it is He who has made us, and we are His people, and the sheep of His pasture,[40] and to Him we send up praise and worship, together with the co-eternal and consubstantial Father, and the life-giving, conjoined and co-everlasting Spirit,[41] now and for ever and ever. Amen.

[39] James 2. 5.
[40] Ps. 99. 3.
[41] συμφυεῖ τε καὶ συναϊδίῳ πνεύματι.

NOTE ON HOMILY VI

On the nature of the *catechesis* which preceded this sermon, see above, p. 39, where it has been suggested that the office preserved in the Barberini Codex probably resembles the one used by Photius. Besides the closeness in date, certain textual similarities are in favour of this view, e. g.

Goar, Εὐχολόγιον, p. 340:
σήμερον μέλλετε τῷ Χριστῷ τῆς πίστεως ἐκτίθεσθαι γραμματεῖον

Photius (Ar II. 183):
τὸ γραμματεῖον ἡμῖν τῶν συνθηκῶν ὑπαναγινώσκεται σήμερον

Ibid.
βλέπετε οὖν πῶς τὴν ὁμολογίαν χειρογραφεῖτε

Ar II. 180
τῆς ὁμολογίας τὸ χειρόγραφον προκομίζεται.

Very noteworthy in this sermon is the appeal to certain seditious elements to return to the bosom of the Church (below, pp. 134–36). There is no doubt that Photius is here referring to the followers of Ignatius, since his only reproach against the purity of their faith is that they had created a rift and parted company with the body of the faithful. The assertion that they constituted "a small and tiny party, and perhaps not even a party" agrees well with recent research into the extent of the Ignatian opposition. While the majority of the hierarchy submitted to Photius, hardly more than a score of metropolitans and bishops remained refractory, and even in monastic circles, which were traditionally attached to Ignatius, the opposition was not nearly as serious as has been generally believed.[1] Photius further insinuates that far from undergoing persecution, the Ignatians turned their "uprising against the Church into a means of livelihood and a practice of trafficking." It is difficult to say what particular cases he had in view. We have, however, an instance of some Studite monks who, upon leaving

[1] See Dvornik, *The Photian Schism*, pp. 63 sq.

their monastery, found a wealthy patron to house and feed them,[2] not to speak of the abbot Theognostus who made for himself an influential position in Rome. The Council of 861 adopted a number of rulings against monastic laxity, such as the holding of property by monks, their moving from one establishment to another, or even into private households, etc.[3] Bearing in mind that a large proportion of the Ignatian party were monks, and that the rulings of the Council were, if not exclusively, yet to some extent aimed against them, this may be regarded as a further illustration of the charge made by Photius.

The date of the sermon falls, of course, within the reign of Michael III in view of the concluding prayer for one emperor. One is even tempted to see an allusion to Michael's irregular ways in the wish that God should bedeck him with the "flowers of *sophrosyne*." The weakness of the Ignatian party and Photius' confident tone would suggest a date after the Synod of 861, which confirmed the deposition of Ignatius. Thereafter, with the success of government policy and the flight of many prominent Ignatians to Rome, the strength of the opposition party must have been considerably impaired. On the other hand, if our views are correct the sermon must be earlier than 866 when the popularity of Photius and that of the government he represented had begun to decline (see below, p. 222).

VI

Ar II 180 THIRD HOMILY OF PHOTIUS, THE MOST-BLESSED ARCHBISHOP OF CONSTANTINOPLE, DELIVERED FROM THE AMBO OF ST. IRENE ON GOOD FRIDAY, AFTER THE PERUSAL OF THE USUAL CATECHISM

1. When the devil's might is being despoiled, when the sting of death[1] is being blunted, when the trophy over Hades is set up, then the table of agreements is read out to us, then the document of the covenant is brought forward, then the written record of our promises

---

[2] Van de Vorst, "La Vie de S. Evariste," *Analecta Bollandiana*, XLI (1923), pp. 307 sq.
[3] Mansi XVI, cols. 536–549. Cf. Dvornik, "The Patriarch Photius and Iconoclasm," *Dumbarton Oaks Papers*, 7 (1953), pp. 78–80.
[1] I Cor. 15. 56.

HOMILY VI. GOOD FRIDAY

is carried in triumph. Why so? In order that, as we see the common enemy vanquished and lying low, and the common Lord being praised in song[2] for having through His own suffering and experience of death won victory and granted victory unto us, we should know clearly of what we stand in debt, and that we have made our life a contradiction of the hymns we sing, and that those of us who have departed from the covenant have deprived ourselves of every excuse. For when Christ fights for me as He is hanging on the cross, or rather awards me a brilliant victory, while the enemy of our kind is lying low helpless, and I not only do not exert myself[3] against the prostrate one, but offer and dedicate myself entirely to passion-provoking indolence, breaking by my transgression the pact with God, and of my own free will handing to the enemy the power over me, what other refuge of excuse is left to me? What device will be found that I may not suffer an irrevocable and cruel *punishment*? For if those who set at nought imperial commands pay the unavoidable penalty when they render accounts for what they have been ordered to do, will not those who, not only disregard and pass by the commands of the King of kings and Lord of lords[4] and Creator of all, but trample and spit upon the pacts they have made with Him, pay the ultimate penalty, and one which cannot be exceeded? Tell me, O man: Christ, fastened to the wood, is crucified for thee, and suffers the death of criminals; out of that, grace and victory over the foe accrue to us; the enemy fails, for the swords of the enemy have failed utterly;[5] our free will has been liberated from the disabilities caused by the transgression; the pacts with God lie before us. Why do we not fulfil our promise? Why do we not repay at least a small part of our debt, but instead increase, and that[6] every day, our obligation by heavy interest, having wretchedly forfeited[7] our body and our very soul? Is it not out of negligence? Is it not from an indolent mind and an inclination prone to passions? If

---

[2] Read with the MSS χορηγὸν ἐμοὶ [ἡμῖν Ar] τῆς νίκης ὑμνολογούμενον [ὑμνολογοῦντες Ar].
[3] Supplying ⟨οὐ⟩ μόνον οὐκ ἐπαγωνίζομαι.
[4] 1 Tim. 6. 15.
[5] Ps. 9. 7.
[6] Read καὶ [καὶ omitted by Ar] καθ' ἑκάστην.
[7] ὑπερήμερον ... παρασκευάσαντες codd: παρασκευάζοντες Ar.

through indolence and negligence we are brought to barter away a wealth of so great and so many goods—the Lord's victory, the foe's defeat, the grace proferred to us, our free will, the covenant itself—, then those who have betrayed all these things through the enjoyment of the passions, and considered their safeguarding and maintenance of no account, what room for forgiveness have they left themselves? Have they not shown themselves guilty of a multitude of evils? Are they not the enemies of their own salvation? Are they not the foes of the Cross? He saves, we destroy. Are we not fighting for the enemy? For by doing those things in which his strength against us lies, we are thereby proven to be fighting on his side and, worst of all, against our very selves. Are we not the denouncers of our liberty? For we have made it useless by remaining subservient to the pleasures. Are we not inconsiderate of the grace? Are we not ungrateful for the beneficence? For those who live contrariwise to the grace and the beneficence render a great insult and blasphemy both to that grace and to that beneficence.

2. But let us reverence Him who has been crucified for us. Let us be ashamed of the lance, the nails (Oh, what forbearance and long-suffering!⁸), the stripes, the blows, the buffeting, the spitting, the crown of thorns, which the Lord of all has willingly suffered for our sake, so that by rising above passions and sin, we may conduct ourselves worthily of our portion in paradise. Let us be shamed by our own pacts which we have pledged to God before angels and men. For if indeed⁹ those who transgress mutual agreements do not remain unpunished by the laws, how great a penalty will be exacted from us who have set at nought our pacts with God? Nay, let us sober down, beloved ones, let us awake, and though late, let us at last come to our senses. For this reason is the record of our agreements read out today, so that having considered all these matters, Christ's sufferings, our promises, the deeds of our life, and impressed them well in our minds, we may arise from our heedless torpor and avoid the noose of deceit and error, and walk along the unswerving path of the Fathers, which is not beset by the serpent that bites

⁸ Rom. 2. 4.
⁹ ἐπεί γε μὴν [not μέν, as indicated by Ar] γὰρ οἱ τὰς, Lig. A and B omit the four initial words, which makes for too harsh a transition from the previous sentence.

HOMILY VI. GOOD FRIDAY

the heel.[10] Having thus received in our heart the teaching of the Spirit, and having fostered it well by continuous study, and, by our application to this study freed our eagerness for action, let us cultivate for ourselves the copious fruit of salvation. Let us not liken ourselves to the rocky and stony-hearted, who, receiving with joy the seed of the word, do not even allow it to grow roots, but as Ar II 184 soon as a little grief befalls them, they wither up together with the shoot, having bloomed with salvation but a short time. Nor let us receive the catechism of Scripture as in passing, lest rousing up Satan against ourselves, we make him a robber and a thief of the good seed which has been sown, and through lack of spiritual food, destroy our life by wretched famine; lest the Lord say of us also, "And these are they by the way side, where the word is sown; and when they have heard, Satan cometh immediately, and taketh away the word that was sown in their hearts."[11]

3. Let us not reduce ourselves to this condition, beloved ones, nor show our soul to be thorny ground by rearing tares through our worldly preoccupations, and running to wood with the desires of the flesh, and being choked, but after cleansing her of the passion-causing pleasures, and watering her in advance with tears, and rendering her fertile,[12] let us thus receive the seed of the word in the furrows of our hearts, and bear fruit, if possible, as with the best husbandmen, an hundredfold. If we do not reach an hundred, let us bear fruit sixtyfold; and if our tilling has not thriven even to this point, let us bear fruit thirtyfold.[13] In any case, let us bear fruit Ar II 185 lest, like that barren fig-tree,[14] we draw the curse on ourselves and be condemned to be cut down before a Judge who is righteous and whose judgment none gainsays. For it is not only the fig-tree that has remained fruitless, the barren and harsh synagogue of the Jews,

---

[10] Gen. 49. 17.
[11] Mk 4. 15.
[12] Delete full stop after ἐργασάμενοι, and read οὕτω τε [δὲ Ar].
[13] Cf. Mt 13. 8; Mk 4. 8; Lk 8. 8. A curious scholion on Mt 13. 8 attributed to Photius explains that bringing forth a hundredfold denotes a rigorously ascetic life and a faultless ministry, sixtyfold an earnest pursuit of virtue and abstention from every base instinct, thirtyfold a chaste marriage coupled with the doing of good works. See Правосл. Палест. Сборникъ, XI 1 (1892), p. 90. A similar scholion in L. Thomas, *Les collections anonymes de scolies grecques aux Évangiles*, II, Rome, 1912, p. 68, no. 229.
[14] Mt 21. 19; Mk 11. 13.

whose produce amounted only to the growth of leaves, it is not the only one that is withered and cut at the root, but if any one, like all of us, has been deemed worthy of having Grace as his root, and does not show the branch worthy of the root, nor puts forth fruit appropriate to the plant, he too is subjected in like fashion to punishment and hewing down. For "every tree," the Planter of all good things hath said, "that bringeth not forth good fruit is hewn down, and cast into the fire."[15] Let us fear the threat, let us avoid the punishment. Let us consider who it is that has delivered this decree: not a man, nor an angel, nor one who is reckoned among a higher rank of incorporeal beings,[16] but the Lord of all Himself, the Judge Himself, who is going to judge the whole world in righteousness.[17] Nobody has the power to annul the Judge's verdict; there is none else to seek refuge with, whereby one could escape these *punishments*; there is no supplication on the other side, no begging for pardon, no means of mercy, no benefit in tears, nor in sighs: everything must yield before the Judge's sentence. Merciful He is, but just; compassionate, but He sets a bound and does not pass it;[18] long-suffering, but when we are unrepenting He gives a verdict of great harshness. Every tree that bringeth not forth good fruit is hewn down, and cast into the fire.[19]

4. Let us bring forth fruit unto God,[20] lest we are cut out, roots and all, and wretchedly wither away together with every hope of life and salvation, lest we end our life consumed in the unquenchable fire. Let us bring forth righteousness, which joins together and compacts[21] human things[22] most admirably, meting out to our neighbours[23] by the same standard by which we wish to be measured ourselves; since unrighteousness is the worst of all sins, and easily

[15] Mt 7. 19.
[16] I. e., presumably, an archangel, or a member of the seven other higher ranks of celestial hierarchy. Read οὐκ ἄλλος τις τῶν μετὰ ταύτην [ταύτην om B] τὴν [τὴν om A] πρώτην φύσιν τῇ [τὴν Ar] τῶν ἀσωμάτων συνεξεταζόμενος.
[17] Acts 17. 31.
[18] Cf. Ps. 103. 9.
[19] Mt 7. 19.
[20] Rom. 7. 4.
[21] Eph. 4. 16.
[22] Read τὰ ἀνθρώπινα συναρμόζουσάν τε καὶ συμβιβάζουσαν with Lig: τὸν ἀνθρώπινον συναρμόζουσαν καὶ συμβιβάζουσαν AB: τὸν ἄνθρωπον συναρμολογοῦσαν καὶ συμβιβάζουσαν Ar.
[23] τοῖς πλησίον ἐπιμετροῦντες codd: τοὺς πλησίον Ar.

HOMILY VI. GOOD FRIDAY

seen by all men, at least those of good sense, to be a mean thing and a work of the Evil one. For a man surely knows that he should not have done to his neighbour what he does not wish to suffer himself. Art thou grieved when another deprives thee of thy farm, or thy field, or thy garment, or thy beast of burden? Neither do thou Ar II 187 wrong thy neighbour in any such way. Thou hast an unwritten law, clearer and more obvious than any written one, namely thy own feeling and disposition over similar plights, when thou art let to suffer the same at the hands of others. Use the same standard for thyself as for thy neighbour. Whatever grieves thee, harms thee and distresses thee, consider that same thing grievous, distressing and damaging to thy neighbour. The precept is simple, the law is common to Greeks, barbarians[24] and, if thou willest, to faithful and unfaithful. Many infidel nations live by this inborn law; many barbarians, while being barbarians in other respects, observe steadfastly this natural law, having made sure, by not wronging others, that they are not themselves wronged by them. What then? Is justice sought after by infidels and barbarians, even without a written law, that they may live and keep *society* together, while for us faithful, who call on Christ, who possess written laws, to whom inexorable penalties have been appointed, and heavenly rewards promised, is it not a shame to be called faithful unless we observe justice towards one another in purity and steadfastness? And will not Thy name, O God, be on our account and through our actions blasphemed among the gentiles,[25] when the infidels excel[26] and surpass in their way of life the conduct of those who call themselves "faithful"?

5. But may none of you be, God forbid, either more cruel than Ar II 188 barbarians or more wretched than infidels; rather let us all conduct ourselves worthily both of our faith and of our vocation,[27] maintaining fairness towards each other rightly and unalterably, and storing up mercy for ourselves for the expiation of our sins at the time of judgment. For mercy rejoiceth against judgment,[28] and the merciful

[24] Rom. 1. 14.
[25] Rom. 2. 24.
[26] Keep ἀποκρυπτόντων, i. e. "eclipse" [ἀποκαλυπτόντων Ar].
[27] Eph. 4. 1.
[28] James 2. 13.

shall obtain mercy,[29] and blessed are the merciful, for they shall obtain mercy.[30] What is easier than this transaction? What is more profitable than this contract? What is more wretched than to disregard this commerce? Hast thou seen a beggar in distress? Hast thou overlooked a fellow-man crying out? Then thou hast barred to thyself the stream of the Lord's mercy; and by not having given here a drop of thy overflowing wealth to the poor, thou hast kindled over there the unquenchable flame of Hell for thy mercilessness. But hast thou pitied him? Hast thou given him mercy according to thy means? Thou wilt find mercy, and wilt quench that fire which the thorns of thy other faults have lit, as it dies down and is wasted away by the drops of mercy. The property of oil is to feed the fire on earth, and kindle it, and produce great flames when poured on it; while the grace of mercy wilts that other fire, and the more abundantly one sheds it, the more it lessens it and quenches it. Even one who is liable to that insufferable and terrible fire places himself above condemnation because of compassion. Faithful is the guarantor of this pledge—the Judge Himself, the Lord Himself. In judging He shall not forget His own words. He Himself crieth aloud, "Blessed are the merciful, for they shall obtain mercy."[31] The beggar has running wounds, and sleeps out naked, and looks up to thy hands, O man. Does not his plight abash thee? Art thou not ashamed of *human* nature? Does not his misfortune bend thee to pity? Wipe his wounds with water, that thou mayest rid thyself of the ulcers of thy soul. Clothe him that thou mayest bedeck thyself with a fair cloak—charity. Receive him under thy roof that thou mayest have him prepare thy way in the heavenly tabernacles, knowing that inasmuch as thou doest it unto one of these thy fellow-slaves, thou doest it to the common Lord.[32] Let us give Him small things out of the wealth wherewith He has endowed us; let us bring Him *offerings* through the poor, out of what He has granted us Himself. Nor let us ask for another Lazarus to correct us, since the correction yields great and unspeakable pain and repentance, but does not result in any benefit or salvation. Let that *Lazarus* in the Gospels, by the

[29] Cf. Prov. 22. 9.
[30] Mt 5. 7.
[31] *Ibid.*
[32] Mt 25. 40.

HOMILY VI. GOOD FRIDAY

example of the rich man at whose gate he was laid,[33] suffice for thy correction. Let not that miserable rich man, more wretched than all beggars, be erased from our memory, as he is standing in the midst of the flames, melting away, wasting away, calling out to Lazarus, and seeking to lick, as if from a fountain, a drop *of water* from the finger of the beggar, whom he had abominated, as a respite from the burning fire. Remember him straightway, and Lazarus too,[34] when thou seest a beggar, and remembering them, abominate such behaviour, that thou mayest escape Hell. Instead take him in thy arms, clothe him, feed him, that thou mayest hear those blissful words, "Come, ye blessed of my Father, inherit the kingdom prepared for you."[35]

6. Having thus watered ourselves with charity, and tilled well the fallow land[36] with sympathy for the poor, let us bring forth the crowning virtue, love, through which peace and calm accrue to our own life, and also piety and faith in God are expressed. For "by this they will know," saith the Lord, "that ye are my disciples, if ye love one another."[37] It is from the same source that the friend of peace, the bosom disciple, has drawn for us his flowing streams, which he pours out saying,[38] "If a man say, I love God, and hateth his brother, he is a liar: for he that loveth not his brother whom he hath seen, how can he love God whom he hath not seen?",[39] well nigh meaning, "O man,[40] when thou severest from thyself and hatest one with whom thou dwellest in the same city, who breathes the same air as thou, who cherishes the same manner of life, and perchance embraces the same pursuit, and bears the same aspect,

Ar II 191

---

[33] Lk 16. 19 sq.
[34] Keep the reading of the MSS, but punctuate: εἰς ἀναψυχὴν τοῦ φλογίζοντος. ἐκείνου παρευθὺ καὶ τοῦ Λαζάρου μνήσθητι, etc. [τοῦ φλογίζοντος ἐκείνου πυρός. εὐθέως καὶ τοῦ Λαζάρου Ar: τοῦ φλογιζομένου σώματος. ἐκείνου παρευθὺ καὶ τοῦ Λαζάρου Pg]. τὸ φλογίζον can stand as a substantive here. For its intrans. use, cf. Exod. 9. 24.
[35] Mt 25. 34.
[36] Cf. Jer. 4. 3.
[37] Jn 13. 35.
[38] Read with all the MSS: καὶ ὁ τῆς εἰρήνης φίλος καὶ μαθητὴς ἐπιστήθιος ὢν ἐκεῖθεν ἤντλησεν ἡμῖν τὰ ῥεῖθρα τῷ λόγῳ πηγάζων, ἐὰν εἴπῃ τις, etc. Ar has μαθητὴς ἐπιστήθιος ὢν ... τὰ ῥεῖθρα τοῦ [which he mistakenly ascribes to A] λόγου [which he mistakenly ascribes to A and B] κραυγάζων.
[39] 1 John 4. 20.
[40] ἄνθρωπε codd: ἄνθρωπον Ar.

and has shared of the same blood, and to whom thou hast been bound with the unbreakable bond of nature, then how wilt thou be believed when thou sayest thou lovest God, whom it is impossible to see with human eyes, and who, we know, is above all human intercourse?" It is impossible to be man-hating and not be God-hating, as it is impossible to be man-loving without being God-loving. Wherefore, let us love one another, beloved ones, using again the Divine as a good counsellor and exhorter, who crieth out in a loud voice, "Love is from God; and he that loveth is born of God, and knoweth God; for God is love,"[41] and, "if a man saith he is in the light, and hateth his brother, he is in darkness, and he that loveth his brother abideth in the light, and there is none occasion of stumbling in him; he that hateth his brother is in darkness, and goeth in darkness, and knoweth not whither he goeth, because darkness hath blinded his eyes."[42] Hearest thou, O man, how he who has divorced himself from the love of his neighbour, is also torn away from love of God, and is filled with darkness, and having had the eyes of his mind blinded, he wastes away his life in distant straying and deceit and deep murk, neither perceiving the light, nor knowing wherein he is walking; while he that loveth his neighbour is acknowledged as God's friend, inasmuch as he provides clearer evidence of his love for the common Lord by his affectionate actions towards his fellow-slave; and he is further held to have been born of Him, since he has not darkened the splendour of his exalted birth with any base and alien seed of man-hating, and he is illuminated by the rays of light, and irradiated, as much as man is able, by knowledge of God.

7. Such and so great is the power of love, and in this way it provides the enjoyment of all manner of good things to those who embrace it, and when it falls away, all grace is gone, every virtuous practice disappears, every kind of intercourse is severed, every commonwealth with its laws and men is hurled into disaster; for just as when the bodily joints, wherewith an animal's members are bound and held together, are broken and rent asunder, immediately the whole animal is dispersed and destroyed, so when love, which

[41] 1 John 4. 7–8.
[42] *Ibid.*, 2. 9–11.

HOMILY VI. GOOD FRIDAY

joins and holds everything together, is excised from our life, all virtue and order and every other good thing is likewise broken up and ruined, while wickedness, corruption and disorder are introduced instead, and generally no good thing is brought to a profitable end without love. Nay, nor is the possession of gifts useful without love, nor is the gift of prophecy precious, nor is faith, even if it removes and brings down mountains, considered piety without love; nor is the giving away of all one's possessions to the needy, and denuding oneself of all one's wealth accounted as charity. What say I? Nor is a martyr's death by fire free of loss in the absence of love. Thinkest thou that what I have said is rash? The trumpet of the Spirit, the great Paul, sounds and speaks in accord with me, wherefore it is better to hear his clarion call. What then saith he? "If," quoth he, "I speak with the tongues of men and angels, and have not love, I am become as sounding brass, or a tinkling cymbal; and though I have prophecy, and understand all mysteries and all knowledge, and though I have faith, so that I could remove mountains, and have not love, I am nothing; and though I bestow all my goods to feed *the poor*, and though I give my body to be burned, and have not love, it profiteth me nothing."[43] Seest thou what an awesome and terrible utterance he has given out? What sayest thou, Paul? What? When thou bestowest all thy goods to feed the beggars, and hast faith that removes mountains, and offerest thy body to be burned with fire for Christ, thou findest no profit at all, but in vain and with harm dost thou abide in all these things, thy gifts, thy toils, thy sufferings? Yes, saith he, unless love be present, through which the rest is put in order and perfected, no single one of the aforesaid yields any profit to anyone, but even results in a harmful end for its user. Thus without love no gift, no virtue is of any benefit; on the contrary, it rather has its own usefulness perverted, and becomes on a par with wickedness for its possessor, and is seen to be the cause of great damage to those who have it. For he who has bestowed all his goods to feed *the poor*, and has given his body to the fire, and who has profited nothing without love, what great damage has he suffered! It is with good reason that in its absence the rest should remain useless: for just as when a source is

Ar II 194

Ar II 195

[43] 1 Cor. 13. 1–3.

stopped,[44] the streams flowing from it dry up, and though some remnants of water are left in the crevices, they are useless and unfit for drinking, nay, rather cause great harm and nausea to anyone wishing to drink *of them*; so also when love, from which flow the graces of the virtues and gifts, is dried up by hate, they are likewise quenched and destroyed; and if thou shouldst perhaps see some remnant of righteousness, or mercy, or knowledge, or prophecy, or faith left in the depths of the soul, it is feeble,[45] spurious, putrid and faded, and yields no benefit to him who tries to pride himself on it.

8. Wherefore, beloved ones, let us diligently cleave to love. Let us pursue it earnestly, let us take it in our home, let us make it our companion in market-places, in places of seclusion, in cities, in the wilderness, in councils, in tribunals; or rather, if we cling to it in all purity, we shall not see any tribunals at all. For it is the source of long-suffering, of kindness, of lenience, of absence of anger, of meekness, of faith, of hope, of patience. Where these *qualities* are present, strife and wranglings and trials and tribunals vanish, their use being clearly proved to be unprofitable and vain. That it gushes forth with these streams, hear again from the same wondrous Paul as he crieth: "Love suffereth long, and is kind; love envieth not, vaunteth not itself, is not puffed up, doth not behave itself unseemly, seeketh not her own, is not provoked; love thinketh no evil, rejoiceth not in iniquity, but rejoiceth in the truth, covereth all things, believeth all things, hopeth all things, endureth all things; love never faileth."[46] Let us, therefore, love one another, beloved ones,[47] that we may keep the possession of the gifts given us by God, that we may not render useless the grace of the virtues. Let us love one another that we may be deemed worthy of becoming and being called God's children,[48] that we may be made heirs to the kingdom of heaven.

9. But come today, thou seditious one, whoever thou art, who attemptest to rend asunder Christ's flock, but rather partest thyself

[44] Cf. Prov. 25. 26.
[45] Read ἀσθενές τε ἐστὶ [πανάσθενές τε ἐστὶ Ar].
[46] 1 Cor. 13. 4–8.
[47] 1 John 4. 7.
[48] Jn 1. 12.

HOMILY VI. GOOD FRIDAY

from Christ, and fallest away from thy mother, the Church, even if thou dost not wish it so, come, listen again to Paul's advice and exhortation, or rather his verdict, as he clearly testifies saying, "Though I have faith so that I could remove mountains, and though I bestow all my goods to feed *the poor*, and though I give my body to be burned, I am nothing, it profiteth me nothing."[49] But being thyself devoid of love, and having a faith which, far from removing mountains, is not even, so to speak, unadulterated (for how could one who tears himself away from the faithful and breaks off from the rightly-believing Church?), and neither bestowing thy goods to feed the beggars (for thou wouldst not have made thy uprising against the Church into a means of livelihood and a practice of trafficking), nor indeed hastening to a martyr's death by fire, what hope of salvation dost thou leave thyself? What apology will suffice thee for the judgment over there? What kind of tribunal[50] will face thee on that day? Art thou ashamed to come up and ask forgiveness for thy distant straying? And does the murk of despair cover thy thoughts? And art thou afraid lest approaching thou be pushed away, and hastening towards love, thou fallest away from thy fellow-rebels, and be not received in the bosom of the Church? Do these things frighten and trouble thee and urge thee to be timid in the face of thy salvation? I make the first gesture of love, I stretch out my hand and welcome those who are willing, or rather I will strive to welcome even the unwilling; and neither will I reproach them for the rift, nor condemn them for vanity, nor overlook them because they are a small[51] and tiny party, and perhaps not even a party. But joining and adding them completely to the body of the Church,[52] I will, strengthened by Christ, show the love and affection to be mutual, and the diligence mutual; or rather, if you will, I shall imitate my Lord, and seeing what had been dead coming back to life, and what had been lost hastening back to its mother, the Church, I will receive them with outstretched hands, and kill the fatted calf, the best, that is, of what I have to contribute in the way of

---

[49] 1 Cor. 13. 2–3.
[50] Reading with the MSS ποταπόν [ποταπῷ Ar] σοι ... τὸ κριτήριον.
[51] μικρὰν (Ar's μακρὰν is a misprint; the correct reading appears at Ar II, p. 179₁₁).
[52] Cf. Eph. 4. 16.

making merry,⁵³ and put a ring *on their finger*, helping eagerly to mark their repentance with the inviolate seal of a sincere return, and I will call together the friends, and they will join in rejoicing,⁵⁴ all those who consider their neighbour's salvation and recall as their own pleasure and delight. Only do you approach with willingness, and do not allow any longer the Deceiver, who first tore us⁵⁵ away from the commandment, to check your eagerness and your intentions. For he who at that time by guileful speech contrived to banish our ancestors from the commandment and from paradise,⁵⁶ is the same who every day entraps the human race with plots and deceits, and catches different men in different pits of perdition, but strives especially to break away and separate some men from the choir of the Church, so that finding the sheep gone astray and deserted both by the flock and the shepherd,⁵⁷ he may thus⁵⁸ easily devour it. But recognizing his complex wiles and his multifarious devices, let us flee his advice, let us watch for the treachery, and never break ourselves away from Christ's fold and flock. Thus we may render vain the contrivances and wiles of the wild beast who seeks to snatch away our soul.

10. But the God of peace,⁵⁹ our Lord Jesus Christ, who by His own death has destroyed the partition-wall of enmity and reconciled us, who had fallen away and sinned, to His own Father,⁶⁰ may He now also maintain the Church, whom He has purchased with His precious blood, spotless and irreproachable, like a chosen bride standing on His right, radiating piety through the beauty of her teaching, and pacify her, drawing up to Himself those who are not yet entirely corrupted and engulfed by irreverence, and recalling them, binding and joining them to the Church with the indissoluble bonds of love; showing our pious and Christ-loving emperor acting

---

⁵³ Reading ὅ τι ποτ' ἂν εἰς εὐφροσύνης λόγον ἐμοὶ συντελοῦν τυγχάνῃ τὸ κάλλιστον (epexegetic of μόσχον). Ar adds ποιήσω after κάλλιστον.
⁵⁴ Cf. Lk 15. 20 sq.
⁵⁵ πρώτως ἡμᾶς codd: πρῶτον ὑμᾶς Ar.
⁵⁶ καὶ τῆς ἐντολῆς codd: ἀποσπάσας τῆς ἐντολῆς Ar.
⁵⁷ Cf. 1 Peter 2. 25.
⁵⁸ Reading with the MSS: τὸ πρόβατον ἔρημον, οὕτω λοιπὸν εὐχερῶς, etc.: τὸ πρόβατον εἰς ἔρημον τόπον εὐχερῶς Ar.
⁵⁹ Rom. 15. 33.
⁶⁰ Cf. Eph. 2. 14–16.

HOMILY VI. GOOD FRIDAY

within the limits of justice, and bedecked with the flowers of temperateness, thriving in truth and meekness, so that having David, God's ancestor, to say to him, "Bend *thy bow*, and prosper, and reign, because of truth, and meekness, and righteousness, for the right hand of the Most High will guide thee wonderfully,"[61] he may be deemed worthy also of the heavenly kingdom. May we all win it too by the intercessions of our most-holy Lady, the Mother of God, and of all those saints in whose counsels God is glorified.[62] Amen.

[61] Ps. 44. 5.
[62] Ps. 88. 8.

NOTE ON HOMILY VII

The title of this Homily indicates that it was preached before the Emperor, and therefore probably in the church of St. Sophia which, as we learn from the exordium, was gaily adorned for the occasion. It may be that the redecoration of the church with images was already under way (see p. 139, n. 4). In the tenth century the protocol for the feast of the Annunciation was the same as the standard procession for great feasts described in ch. I of the *Book of Ceremonies*,[1] unless Annunciation fell on the Sunday of the third week of Lent (as it did in 865), in which case the order of events was different: the emperor paid but a short visit to St. Sophia, and heard the liturgy in the church of St. Mary Chalkoprateia.[2] Normally, however, the patriarch would meet the emperor at the narthex door of St. Sophia, and together they would proceed through the nave and into the sanctuary. After the customary *proskynesis* and burning of incense in the sanctuary, the emperor retired to his robing-room (*metatorion*), and came out thereafter only for the Great Entrance, the Kiss of Peace and the Communion. The *Book of Ceremonies* does not refer to a sermon, which would have followed the lections, i. e. at a time when the emperor had withdrawn to the *metatorion*.

This sermon was delivered during the sole reign of Michael III, certainly a few years after Photius had become Patriarch, since in § 7 (p. 147 below) he says, "For a long time and often have I advised you to be ready," which indicates that he had been preaching for some years past.

It will be noticed that this Homily, like the other three that were delivered in the presence of emperors (nos. X, XVII and XVIII), is a rhetorical show-piece, more florid in style than those intended for less stately occasions.

---

[1] Bonn ed., p. 33 = A. Vogt's ed., I, Paris, 1935, p. 26.
[2] Bonn ed., pp. 162 sq. = Vogt, I, pp. 151 sq.

HOMILY VII. THE ANNUNCIATION

VII

OF THE SAME MOST-BLESSED PHOTIUS, PATRIARCH OF CONSTANTINOPLE, SECOND HOMILY ON THE ANNUNCIATION OF THE MOST-HOLY MOTHER OF GOD, DELIVERED IN THE EMPEROR'S PRESENCE

1. "How amiable are thy tabernacles, O Lord of hosts,"[1] the occasion invites me to cry out with the prophet David, as I behold the courts of the church thronged with the multitude of her rational flock, assembled together in the gaiety and variety of their many hues. Verily, "how goodly are thy habitations, Jacob, and thy tents, Israel, as gardens by the rivers, and as tents which the Lord hath pitched."[2] These matters too have been well and fittingly expressed by the prophet who, though he stood outside our fold, yet included in his prophecy our state also.[3] Rejoicing myself, and seeing fulfilled in deeds the oracles admirably delivered by those men in former times, I too proclaim them now by way of preamble in a proud voice and with gladness. Goodly indeed and fair to behold are the tents of the new Jacob, deemed worthy to see God in the flesh, and they are able to elevate the soul constantly towards divine love, to those whose zeal, aroused by the beautiful sights before their eyes, is drawn on to the intelligible and divine beauty.[4]

2. But wherefore, O God's people and most Christ-loving of emperors, have you assembled thus eagerly and splendidly, and

---

[1] Ps. 83. 2.
[2] Num. 24. 5–6.
[3] I. e. Balaam, whose unwilling praise of Israel is again referred to in Homily X (below, p. 188).
[4] Cf. Plato, *Sympos.*, 210–211. Jacob denotes the Christian people (cf., for example, Cyril of Alexandria, *Glaphyra in Gen.*, PG 69, cols. 153 sq., and esp. col. 160), and it was the advent of Christ that Balaam was considered to have foretold in his prophecy (Procopius of Gaza, *Comment. in Num.*, PG 87, cols. 867–68).It may be argued that Photius is here referring to images of "God in the flesh," which the Christian people were privileged to see, just as Jacob had seen God face to face. It was not until 867 that the first major mosaic, that of the Virgin and Child, was put up in St. Sophia following the defeat of Iconoclasm (see below, pp. 283–84). We do not, of course, know to what extent portable icons were exhibited in St. Sophia before any mural mosaics had been completed. It would be unwise, therefore, on the basis of this somewhat ambiguous passage to draw any inference about the date of the seventh Homily.

have adorned this holy and august temple, which[5] one might well call, without missing the mark, the eye of the universe, and especially so today when, mixing the white with the black, out of which colours the natural constitution of the eye is wrought, you have filled with your bodies the voids of this wondrous place, forming, as it were, the socket of the eye?[6] What is this haste of yours, and this graceful gaiety, and this smiling assembly? Surely you have come to celebrate the betrothal of the daughter of mankind, and to dance because of the joy of the Mother of the Word; and you have striven, after showing such fair and great preparation, to make into a magnificent festival the beginning and foundation of our common salvation. For verily, the betrothal of the ever-virgin is the foundation and groundwork of our salvation; it does not prop up the roof of one house threatening collapse, nor does it set up and hold together a village or a town that is falling to the ground, but it does raise, renew and support our entire human race, which had taken a great fall. For just as when the foundations of a house have been well and firmly established, joy and gladness, prevailing over all difficulties, already seize the prospective lodgers, so when the foundations of our salvation are laid in such wise and holy manner by Logos the artificer, humankind inaugurates the founding of its happiness and joy,[7] and scraping off the senility of disobedience like

---

[5] Note that what appears to be the right reading is given by Lig: ὅπερ ὀφθαλμόν τις εἰπών [so Ar]. The other MSS have ὃν ὀφθαλμόν τι [τις Athen. 2449] εἰπών, which is surely wrong, since ὅν does not agree with τέμενος.

[6] The meaning of this laboured simile seems to be the following: the church of St. Sophia might be called the eye of the universe, and this is especially apt today, when the contrasting garments of the congregation form the white and the black (i. e. pupil) of the eye, while the empty shell of the church is the socket. Cf. Šest., p. 541. Ar's text is probably right, though his apparatus is incorrect. The MSS read: τὸ λευκὸν τῶν χρωμάτων οἱονεὶ τῷ μέλανι κερασάμενοι [not κερασάμενον, as noted by Ar; διακεκερασμένῳ τῷ μέλανι Lig] . . . τοῖς ἡμετέροις [surely ὑμετέροις] σώμασι τὰ κενὰ τοῦδε τοῦ θεσπεσίου χώρου, καθάπερ ὀμμάτων κοῖλα μορφοῦντες, ἀνεπληρώσατε. The participle μορφοῦντες should be either μορφοῦντα (but that would form an ugly hiatus) or μορφοῦντος (to agree with χώρου), since it is the κενά, the voids of the church, and not the congregation, that formed the empty socket. It is not impossible, however, that Photius was so confused by the intricacies of his own simile, that he inadvertently wrote μορφοῦντες.

[7] Placing the comma after θεμελίων instead of after ἀγαλλιάσεως as in Ar. Or, if Ar's punctuation is retained, translate: "so when rejoicing and gaiety are laid in such wise and holy manner by Logos the artificer as the foundations of our salvation, humankind inaugurates the construction work," etc.

HOMILY VII. THE ANNUNCIATION

a disease, servant of death, it bedecks itself instead with immortality as with a new creation. With good reason, therefore, does human kind betroth itself to joy; for it takes to itself the grace of being made divine, and having spat out the deceitful love of impiety like demoniac frenzy, it decks itself out like a pure bride for none other than its Creator and Maker. With good reason does human kind leap *with joy* and cry aloud;[8] for it receives the glad tidings that its daughter has been designated as a chosen bride for her Creator. With good reason does human kind bear itself proudly and Ar II 371 rejoice; for upon receiving the news of a marriage contract with the Lord, it casts off the shameful yoke of slavery.

3. This festival, therefore, is the beginning of all *the other* festivals, in that it gives us the contract for heavenly commerce, enriches the world with the inviolate wealth of the Lord's advent, and both effects the cleansing of our human frame, and offers us the enjoyment of the undefiled goods. In it joyfully appears the choir of the prophets, strengthened with the eye of divine vision, and upborne on the wing of that spiritual life[9] which, even in our present, material world they were known to have led beyond *the ability* of mortal men, and wearing the truth of their prophecies like a bright garment, they deck out the chamber of the Lord's betrothal. In it the band of the apostles assembles too, and, as they gather together the ends of the world and establish the preaching of the salutary word, they display with pure hands the wealth of the Virgin's dowry. In it the troops of martyrs also crowd together, and letting fall the dye of their martyrs' blood, make bright the purple of the imperial bride-chamber. In it the contingents of the incorporeal beings appear also, Ar II 372 and joining choir with the archangel Gabriel, bear as a gift[10] the condescension of the divine sojourn among men, and life on earth puts on[11] heavenly raiment. For today the Virgin on behalf of our whole race is being betrothed to the common Lord, and human kind, having broken off[12] its intimacy with that alien adulteress and

[8] παρρησιάζεται codd: παρουσιάζεται Ar.
[9] Cf. Plato, *Phaedr.*, 248 b–c.
[10] δωροφοροῦσι codd: δορυφοροῦσι = "escort," Ar, which is a likely emendation.
[11] περιβάλλεται [so Athen. 2449], rather than προβάλλεται [AB].
[12] διασπάσασα codd: διασπῶσα Ar.

slave, sin, returns after a long time to its fellow and comrade, virtue, and embraces both temperately and passionately a conjugal love for her. Today the Virgin is being set apart from among men, offered to the Creator as the first-fruits of *our human* clay, and the great and eternal mystery of our re-creation[13] is being accomplished in a wondrous manner. Today Adam's daughter, having retrieved the transgression of the first mother Eve, and cleansed herself of the stain that emanated thence, fair and beautiful in the eyes of the Creator, pledges salvation to the human race. For today the commander of the incorporeal beings comes flying from the arches of heaven to Mary, and in announcing to the Virgin the glad tidings of the Lord's coming, enfolds her with the glorious words: "Hail, much-graced one, the Lord is with thee,"[14] and through her all Creation is enriched with joy.

4. The archangel comes to Mary, that fragrant and never-fading flower of the Davidic race, that admirable, great and God-carved ornament of human kind. For this virgin having been, so to speak, from the very swaddling clothes steeped[15] in the virtues, and grown with them, devoted herself to leading a life of the spirit on earth, and having opened the gates of the road to virtue, made entrance possible by her example to those[16] who have an inborn and unquenchable desire to wait on the heavenly bride-chamber. For who, from childhood up, was ever so self-controlled towards pleasures, not those only which disregard bounds and career beyond nature's limits, nor those which, though we see them practised without the infringement of written laws, yet spring from human motives, but even such as have their seat in the mind and indulge their raptures no further? Nay, the blessed Virgin did not permit even her thoughts to incline towards any of those, but was entirely possessed by divine love, showing and proclaiming in these and all other respects that she had been truly set apart as a bride for the Creator of all, even before her birth. For moreover, having also fettered anger, like

Ar II 373

---

[13] τῆς ἐμῆς [codd: ἀνθρωπίνης Ar] ἀναπλάσεως.
[14] Lk 1. 28.
[15] ὑποτρεφομένη Athen. 2449 (bearing out Pg's conjecture). This also appears to be the reading of A: ὑπροστρεφομένη (?) B: ὑποστρεφομένη Ar.
[16] ὅσοις codd: ὅσαις Ar.

HOMILY VII. THE ANNUNCIATION

some uncouth beast, with her impassive mind as with indissoluble threads, she made her whole soul a holy shrine of meekness, having with steady judgment at no time appeared to weaken the strength of her fortitude, and even at the Lord's passion, at which she was present, having let fall no word of blasphemy or indignation, which distressed mothers are wont to do at such great suffering of their children. Sufficient evidence of the fortitude and courage which she possessed from the beginning is her strength herein; and the exaltation of her soul was of noble growth. Her unequalled[17] gift of sagacity and a clear understanding bloomed out in deeds and words, by means of which she prudently and on all sides composed and trimmed herself against all the storms of life's temptations, even those which were roused by the violent hurricane of evil spirits, never allowing any of her wares as much as to touch for a moment the brine of evil.

5. Thus, while the Virgin by surpassing human standards showed herself worthy of the heavenly bride-chambers, and brightened with her own beauty our unsightly aspect, which the pollution of our ancestors had stained, there appeared Gabriel, ministering to the mystery of the King's coming, and cried out with unconstrained voice and tongue, "Hail, much-graced one, the Lord is with thee, delivering through thee the whole race from its ancient sorrow and curse." For this reason David also, the ancestor of God, as he holds his spiritual lyre, appears to dance in his soul at his daughter's betrothal, and running his prophetic fingers over the psalmic strings, strikes up a sweet song, one that is worthy of the Virgin's bridal-chambers, and brings salvation to the whole world: "Hear, O daughter, and see, and incline thine ear, and forget thy people and thy father's house. Because the King hath desired thy beauty, and he is thy Lord,"[18] and of us all; and along with the whole Creation we worship Him with all reverence as our common Lord and the Maker of everything. Hear, O daughter, and incline thine ear to Gabriel's message, for it is through that, through the most pure tidings given thee, that we have washed off, like a briny sound

Ar II 374

---

[17] ἀμίμητον ἐπήνθει τὸ χάρισμα Athen. 2449; ἀμίμητον is omitted by A, B and Ar.
[18] Ps. 44. 11-12.

HOMILIES OF PHOTIUS

with the sweet water of speech,[19] the poison of disobedience which the Serpent's advice instilled into Eve's ears and so made all humankind to share of that venomous drop, and that we are enabled to submit and hearken only to the commands of our Creator. Hear, O daughter, and receive obediently the tidings of conception: for the substantial[20] and co-eternal Word of the Father, not departing from His own essence, nor turning into mere flesh (for that would have been both harmful to humankind, and an extreme insult to divine essence), but keeping[21] each of the components unmingled in an indissoluble unity, has in a manner befitting God chosen to inhabit thee for our renovation, and mercifully opens wide the heavenly tabernacles for us to dwell in.

Ar II 375

6. What is pleasanter than this joy? What is more splendid than this festival? What is more exalted than the present feast? We are lifted up from the earth; we are raised to the skies. We put off corruption; we put on incorruptibility. We have escaped[22] the labours and thorns of the curse; we are enriched with the fruitfulness of the blessing. But having been endowed with the boons of divine grace, let us also contribute the fruits from our own good will: let the soul too be adorned with bridal ornament, and gleam splendidly, bringing in her train no meretricious work of darkness, nor obscuring and dimming the bright attire of our bodies with her own murkiness. Towns often make a marriage connection with other neighbouring towns,[23] and houses arrange a matrimonial exchange between one another, and attract a great crowd, especially persons belonging to the same family, and they are all happy, and flock together, even if no other benefit accrues to them through that exchange. For what great thing is there for them to gain when others are being bound in the child-producing bond of wedlock, and that without having a clear end? And yet each man with great readiness brings wedding gifts to the maiden, one man gold,

---

[19] Plato, *Phaedr.*, 243 d; Leutsch and Schneidewin, *Corpus paroem. graec.*, II, p. 267.
[20] ἐνυπόστατος.
[21] φυλάττων codd: φυλάττειν Ar.
[22] διεφύγομεν codd: διαφεύγομεν Ar.
[23] The reading of the MSS, πόλεις (acc.) πολλάκις τὰς ἐκ γειτόνων ἄλλαι πόλεις εἰς κῦδος [read κῆδος] συνάπτουσι, may be kept: ταῖς ἐκ γειτόνων ἄλλαις πόλεσι κῆδος συνάπτουσι Pg: τὰς ἐκ γειτόνων ἄλλας πόλεις Ar.

HOMILY VII. THE ANNUNCIATION

another silver, another precious stones,[24] others strings of pearls, another something else of especial value to adorn and enrich the recipient. But how shall I liken the incomparable, or how shall I delineate that of which no example has existed from the beginning of time? Should not one be afraid *to make* a comparison,[25] and stand Ar II 376 in amazement? Yet He who is God, and suffers me to be a man, has Himself mercifully provided me license to draw this comparison too.[26] The fellow citizens then, when a girl of their city is given away in marriage, do those things, and not those only, but they also carry lights, and perchance sing the wedding song, and clap their hands, and escort her, and perform every service which is pleasing and agreeable to their hosts. As for us, members of mankind, when the stainless maid, Mary forever virgin, the unblemished daughter of our race, is chosen, not from one city, nor from one nation, but from among all the other maids of the entire universe, alone as bride for the absolute King and Lord of all, what are we to do as an offering worthy of the bridal ceremony? Who will have the means to offer a gift that has attained such measure of value?[27] Shall I tell you? And let no one cry out on the hardness *of the sacrifice*! Hard indeed is the injunction on those who receive it in sloth of spirit; yet is it not *the duty* of those who proclaim and show to what height the dignity of our nature can attain?[28] Nay, the word is not mine, but is of the teaching of the Spirit. Let those not yet married *offer* virginity:[29] for nought is so sweet and pleasing as virginity to the Ever-Virgin. Let those who are bound in matrimony *offer* their experience of life, and indulgence of nature for procreation, and

---

[24] The words ὁ δὲ τῶν τιμίων λίθους are found only in the Athen. 2449. Further down in the same sentence read ἄλλο τι [so Pg; ἄλλό τι codd; ἀλλ' ὅ, τι Ar] τῶν εἰς κόσμον καὶ πλοῦτον ... κεκτημένων τὴν συντέλειαν.

[25] δεδιέναι τοῦ παραδείγματος [codd] is probably correct (defended by Šest., p. 542). So also φοβεῖσθαι with gen. [τὸ τοῦ παραδείγματος Pg: περὶ τοῦ παραδείγματος Ar].

[26] Following the reading of A, B and Ar, καὶ τοῦτο παραδειγματίζειν τὴν ἄδειαν. Note, however, the variant of Athen. 2449, καὶ τοῦ παραδειγματίζειν (= "to draw comparisons").

[27] Following the text of A, B and Ar, τίνι δὲ δῶρον εἰς τηλικοῦτον μέτρον ἀξίας ἀναδραμὸν προσάγεσθαι πορισθήσεται; Note, however, the variant reading of Athen. 2449, ὥστε προσαγαγέσθαι ("Who will have a gift of sufficiently high value *to be presented*?").

[28] Delete Ar's brackets, and print question mark after ἀξίωμα.

[29] Cf. 1 Cor. 7. 25 sq.

thereafter continence preserved intact,[30] nor insult the former with a second marriage: for continence is akin to, though somewhat different from virginity, fulfilling the blessing of God by the begetting of children, yet preserving traces of virginity by abstaining from wantonness. Let them who have slipped from these two *virtues offer* repentance for it, and tears, and forgiveness to their debtors, and charity to the poor: for it is good to offer these things as a gift to the Lord, even as a gift that is not owed; and if this be so, then to settle our debt, and thus convert our obligation into free gifts, both in name and in function—which is a windfall exceeding all hope,—is a task requiring great determination, and no lack of eagerness and effort. Let others *offer* righteousness and regard for alien property: for why dost thou hasten[31] to cause thy neighbour things which, hadst thou suffered them at the hands of another, thou wouldst have bewailed and bemoaned in lamentation? Let others *offer* patience in misfortunes and endurance, for suffering these things patiently is not without recompense. Let others *offer* meekness and hospitality, for these too are conducive to seeing God.[32] In any case, let each man who has come to this heavenly and kingly wedding contribute some gift agreeable to the Virgin and worthy of such a bride: for what is offered her, thereat the Bridegroom, our God, rejoices. And by bringing nothing[33] in honour of the betrothed, one will be harshly cast out of the wedding chamber for having insulted the Bridegroom.

7. If one takes to mind Gabriel, commander of the host, the Virgin's initiator, the messenger and spokesman of our salvation,[34] if one considers that he is sent by the Lord that he may observe each man's gift, do you think that the contest that lies before everyone of us is a paltry one, and that we are not to run for our very soul, seeing, besides, that he is accounting and busily inquiring as to which of the guests are bringing gifts? Furthermore, if he also put a seal on the one who bore a gift, and registered him worthy

---

[30] Cf. 1 Tim. 2. 15.
[31] τρέχεις Athen. 2449 (bearing out Pg's conjecture): τρέχει AB: τρέχειν Ar.
[32] Cf. Mt 5. 8.
[33] The reading of A and B, καὶ οἶς τις [οἶα τις Athen. 2449: ὅστις Ar] οὐδὲν εἰς τιμὴν τῆς μνηστευθείσης συνεισήνεγκεν, is probably correct.
[34] τῆς σωτηρίας ἡμῶν Athen. 2449: ἡμῶν is omitted by A, B and Ar.

HOMILY VII. THE ANNUNCIATION

of the bridal-chamber and of this holy celebration, while thrusting away and driving out those who brought nothing at all, then would not the one who bore nothing, even before the examination reached him, have been struck and perplexed by the expulsion and condemnation of his like, and so have exposed his own self, even prior to the trial, by the pallor of his face,[35] and proclaimed himself unworthy of the festival? I, for one, am afraid lest even now in our midst (for it is not proper that the minister of the divine wedding should be left out of its celebration), indeed I am greatly afraid and alarmed lest even now he is come in our midst, although he is not visible to everybody, to inquire, and to proclaim some worthy of the bride-chamber, others to be thrust far away from its very doors. Therefore, I have fears for both yourselves and for me. As for you, I have for a long time and often advised you to be ready, nor do I cease now from such exhortations as lie in my duty and power; as for me, since I have prepared no worthy gift, I have decided to take refuge in the bridal song of the Ever-Virgin, a song not of passion and coupling, whereof I have as teacher and initiator the minister of this great festival and overseer of the celebration. Perchance, as I sing of him, and busy myself around him, the investigator will spare me and will not send me away, nor, binding me with fetters, inflict upon me the punishment of the guilty for having insulted the King's wedding, but will count me among the choir of the gift-bearers. For there is, yea, there is such a thing before the merciful Judge, as intensity of desire to take the place of a gift for the otherwise destitute, even if the offering contains nothing worthy of the zeal. Hail, therefore, do I cry out with great striving and desire, both with my mind and my tongue, O Virgin, refuge of my weakness and indigence. Hail, much-graced one, through whom what had Ar II 379 been diseased is strengthened, and what had been crushed is recreated, and the devil who strikes with the heel and is the cause of our crushing is slain, suppressed and trampled down. Hail, much-graced one, through whom the bitter verdict against our kind is wiped off by the sweetness of thy tidings, and putting off the ugliness of transgression, we are crowned with the beauty of the divine

---

[35] No need to correct δι' ὧν ἦν ἠλλοιωμένος, i. e. "by the change of his features," to δι' ὧν ἦν ἐληλαμένος [so Pg].

advent that is from thee. Hail, much-graced one, intelligible and God-made mirror of the inspired prophets' mystical discernment, in which they mysteriously saw reflected the condescension of the Word to us, and, like trumpets resounding with the divine Spirit, they encompassed the ends of the entire world, noising abroad thy pregnancy. Hail, much-graced one, workshop of the world's joy, in which the condemnation of the first curse has been melted down, and the dignity of joy through thee has been forged. Hail, much-graced one, whose beauty, kept pure in soul, body and thought, the King of all hath desired,[36] for the renovation and recreation of the image decayed through the devices and various rebellions of the Evil one. For this reason the nations will supplicate thee with gifts,[37] who through thee have been enriched with piety, and have rid themselves of those ugly wrinkles of alien semblance.[38] Mayest thou rejoice, palace not built by hand, in which the King of glory has put on our garment, dyed red with thy virginal blood like imperial purple, and has clothed the unseemly nakedness of our first father. Mayest thou rejoice, who didst lend flesh to the Creator and absolved us from our debt, who didst not undo the bonds of virginity and who torest up the document of sin. Mayest thou rejoice, living ark of God, in which the second Noah, having come to dwell, took in and saved well nigh our entire human race, that had been submerged by the storm of sins, and afforded us models and examples of a second life and a more divine conduct. Mayest thou rejoice, furnace forged by God, in which the Creator, having leavened anew our nature with thy most-pure and virginal substance,[39] has cleansed us of that sour and distressing staleness, renovating man into a new creature.

8. But why attempt to fathom in words a story which even angels are unable to tell, by which all strength of discourse is defeated, every law of laudation is proved inadequate, every human mind becomes dizzy as it begins to grapple *with the subject*,[40] and desists,

Ar II 380

[36] Ps. 44. 12.
[37] *Ibid.*, 13. Read λιτανεύσουσί σοι with the MSS [σοι om Ar].
[38] Cf. 2 Tim. 3. 5; Rom. 2. 20.
[39] Literally "dough" or "lump." Cf. 1 Cor. 5. 6.
[40] Note that, whereas A, B and Lig read λογισμὸς δὲ σύμπας ἀνθρώπινος προβάλλειν ἀρχόμενος, Athen. 2449 has προσβάλλειν, which is probably correct. Cf. above, p. 113, n. 3.

HOMILY VII. THE ANNUNCIATION

and is held in perplexity? Wherefore it is better to honour the mystery with grateful silence than to incur the accusation of rashness in speech. Already the Bridegroom too, having prepared the time for the banquet, and inviting to the mystical and immortalizing table those who have not been wholly banished from it by their actions, mercifully grants my humble self to perform the sacrifice and act as priest, urging me to the ministration of the mystery. May we all without condemnation be deemed worthy of it through the mediation of the ever-virgin[41] Mother of God, at whose intercession may Christ, our true God, born of her in a manner surpassing words and understanding, show our pious and faithful Emperor terrible to the foe, beloved by his subjects, and deem him worthy, along with us, of the heavenly bridal-chamber. For His is the kingdom, and to Him we send up glory, together with the Father and the Holy Ghost,[42] now and for ever and ever. Amen.

[41] After τῆς ἀειπαρθένου, Athen. 2449 adds καὶ ἀπειρογάμου νύμφης ("and unwed bride").

[42] Athen. 2449 adds τῇ ὁμοουσίῳ καὶ ζωαρχικῇ τριάδι ("the consubstantial and life-giving Trinity").

NOTE ON HOMILY VIII

Perhaps the most noteworthy thing about this sermon is that at a very early date, probably at the end of the ninth or the beginning of the tenth century, it was translated into Church Slavonic. The Slavonic version is contained in the famous Codex Suprasliensis (eleventh century), the bulkiest among Old Church Slavonic manuscripts and one of the most ancient in the Cyrillic alphabet.[1]

The Cod. Supr. is a pre-Metaphrastian menologium for the month of March, and contains, in addition to the relevant saints' lives, a number of homilies covering the period from the Saturday τοῦ Λαζάρου to the Sunday after Easter. No Greek archetype of the Cod. Supr. has yet been found, and the question is further complicated by the fact that its component parts seem to have been translated by different persons and at different times, and then collected into a single book, which may have been modelled on a Greek menologium of a kind that we no longer have.[2] The manuscript itself is said to have been written in central or eastern Bulgaria, and it is believed that its redactor revised to some extent the language of the original translations, which had been written at first in Glagolitic characters. If there was a Greek original, it must have dated from the second half of the ninth century at the

---

[1] Published by F. Miklosich, *Monumenta linguae Palaeoslavonicae e codice Suprasliensi*, Vienna, 1851, pp. 245-52; and by S. Sever'janov, Супрасльская рукопись, St. Petersburg, 1904 (Памятники Старославянскаго Языка, II 1), pp. 332-42. The relevant bibliography is very extensive. See esp. A. Marguliés, *Der altkirchenslavische Codex Suprasliensis*, Heidelberg, 1927; Karl H. Meyer, *Altkirchenslavisch-griechisches Wörterbuch des Codex Suprasliensis*, Glückstadt & Hamburg, 1935; id., *Fehlübersetzungen im Codex Suprasliensis* (Schr. d. Königsberger Gelehrten Gesellschaft, 15/16 J., Geisteswiss. Kl., h. 2, Halle, 1939). Full bibliography previous to 1933 is given by G. A. Il'inskij, Опыт систематической Кирилло-Мефодьевской библиографии, Sofia, 1934, pp. 151-54.

[2] See A. Ehrhard, *Überlieferung u. Bestand d. Hagiogr. u. Homilet. Lit. d. Griech. Kirche*, I 5 (1937), pp. 593-603. Ehrhard believes that the Cod. Supr. is a direct translation of a Greek menologium, a view, however, that requires further proof.

NOTE ON HOMILY VIII

earliest, since the Cod. Supr. contains a chapter on the Forty-two Martyrs of Amorium († 845).³

The reign of King Symeon of Bulgaria (893–927) was a particularly active period in the translation of Greek Church texts, and it may have been at that time that our Homily was turned into Slavonic. Leaving aside the many thorny problems that are associated with the Cod. Supr., it is sufficient to note that the version of our Homily, apart from a few blunders,⁴ is extremely faithful, and even helps in a few cases to establish the Greek text.⁵ If it were known that the Cod. Supr. had an exact Greek counterpart, then the presence in it of a Photian homily would not raise any further questions. If, on the other hand, the selection of homilies was made in Bulgaria or for Bulgaria, it would be reasonable to enquire why this particular Homily of Photius was chosen, and whether it was not on account of its marked anti-Jewish tone.⁶

A sally against the ingratitude and blindness of the Jews was, of course, a perfectly commonplace feature of homilies dealing with Christ's entry into Jerusalem. Even so, the pronounced anti-Jewish feeling of this Homily, as well as of no. XI, may call for some ad-

---

³ See the posthumous study by Vasil'evskij in *Mém. de l'Acad. Impér. des Sciences de St.-Pét.*, cl. hist.-phil., VIIIᵉ sér., VII, no. 2 (1905), pp. 91–113.

⁴ In addition to two minor mistakes pointed out by K. Meyer, *Fehlübersetzungen*, p. 78, attention should be drawn to Supr. 332₁₉: ЗЪЛО БО АШТЕ РАДОСТИ ПРѢДОЛѢЕТЪ ПОУСТОШЬНОЕ ЮСТЬСТВО (= δεινὸν γὰρ ἡ χαρὰ χρῆμα καινοποιῆσαι τὴν φύσιν), where the translator took δεινόν to mean "bad" and mistook καινοποιῆσαι (= "to renew") for something like κενὴν νικῆσαι τὴν φύσιν (= "to overcome vain nature"). Other mistranslations on pp. 335₁₄, 336₁₈, 337₂₂, 339₁₄.

⁵ See below, p. 153, n. 3, p. 154, n. 5, p. 155, n. 9, p. 158 n. 25. The correct reading συναγελάζομαι σκιρτῶν τοῖς νηπίοις (cf. p. 153, n. 4), altered by Ar to συναγάλλομαι, is confirmed by СЪМѢШАА СѦ СКАЧѪ СЬ ДѢТЬМИ (Supr. 332₂₄; СЪМѢША = ἀναφύρειν, μειγνύναι); οἱ παῖδες οἱ πολιόφρονες (cf. p. 157, n. 21), unnecessarily corrected by Ar to πολύφρονες, is confirmed by Supr. 337₁₆ СТАРЧЪ ОУМЪ ИМѢѪШТЪ.

⁶ The existence of Jewish missionary work in Bulgaria, suggested by the *Responsa ad consulta Bulgarorum*, § 104 (PL 119, col. 1011), is discussed by Zlatarski, История на Българската държава, I 2, Sofia, 1927, pp. 65–66. There would have been, therefore, a natural demand for anti-Jewish polemics. For a similar situation in south Russia, see I. I. Malyševskij, "Русскія извѣстія о Евреяхъ въ Кіевѣ и въ Южной Руси въ X–XII вѣкахъ," Чтенія въ Ист. Общ. Нестора Лѣтописца, II, Kiev, 1888, pp. 20–24, 49–58.

ditional comment, being, as it was, very typical of ninth-century Byzantium.[7] To some extent, the reaction against Jews was caused by Iconoclasm which, rightly or wrongly, was ascribed by Byzantine authors to Jewish influence.[8] Michael II (820–829) is said to have been brought up by Jews and Athingani,[9] and, after he had become emperor, to have exempted Jews from the payment of taxes.[10] Most defenders of images, including Photius,[11] liken or equate Iconoclasm with Judaism. We have numerous examples of anti-Jewish polemics in contemporary Byzantine literature. The Patriarch Nicephorus composed a treatise on the subject which he addressed to the emperor Michael I,[12] while disputations with Jews hold a prominent place in the Life of St. Theodore of Edessa[13] and that of St. Constantine, apostle of the Slavs.[14] St. Constantine is said to have composed a book on this topic, which his brother Methodius translated into Slavonic.[15] Roughly of the same period are the anti-Jewish works by Basil of Neopatrae,[16] Gregory Asbestas, friend and supporter of Photius,[17] as well as one falsely attributed to Anastasius Sinaita.[18] Photius himself was interested in the conversion of Jews, as we learn from his letter to the archbishop of Kerch.[19] We have, however, no reason to hold him responsible for the persecution of the Jews which was undertaken by Basil I

---

[7] See esp. Dvornik, *Les légendes de Constantin et de Méthode*, Prague, 1933, pp. 198–202.

[8] Cf. Vasiliev, "The Iconoclastic Edict of the Caliph Yazid II," *Dumbarton Oaks Papers*, 9–10 (1956), pp. 26 sq.

[9] Theoph. Cont. (Bonn), pp. 42 sq. Cf. J. Starr, "An Eastern Christian Sect: the Athinganoi," *Harvard Theol. Rev.*, XXIX (1936), pp. 93–106. It is even stated that Michael's grandfather was a converted Jew (Michael Syr., *Chronique*, ed. Chabot, III, Paris, 1905, p. 72).

[10] Theoph. Cont., p. 48; Cedrenus, II, p. 73 (Bonn).

[11] Epistle to Boris, PG 102, col. 652.

[12] *Vita Nicephori*, ed. De Boor (*Nicephori opuscula historica*, Leipzig, 1880), pp. 158–59.

[13] Ed. Pomjalovskij, Житіе иже во святыхъ отца нашего Θеодора архіепископа Едесскаго, St. Petersburg, 1892, pp. 94–97.

[14] Ch. IX–XI.

[15] *Ibid.*, ch. X (Dvornik, *Légendes*, pp. 367–68).

[16] Unpublished except for some extracts. See Krumbacher, *Gesch. d. Byz. Litt.*², p. 131.

[17] See G. Mercati, "Un' antisemita bizantino del sec. IX, che era Siciliano," *Didaskaleion*, IV (1915), pp. 1–6.

[18] PG 89, cols. 1203–1282. Cf. Krumbacher, p. 66.

[19] PG 102, col. 829 A.

HOMILY VIII. PALM SUNDAY

ca. 873,[20] since Photius was not patriarch at the time.[21] This persecution, which did not attain any sincere conversions, may be considered as the climax of the anti-Jewish feeling prevalent in ninth-century Byzantium.

VIII

HOMILY OF PHOTIUS, THE MOST-BLESSED PATRIARCH, ARCHBISHOP OF CONSTANTINOPLE, ON PALM SUNDAY AND LAZARUS[1]

1. When, as the children cry out, "Hosanna in the highest,"[2] the Church sounds her clarion call, and I draw into my ears that splendid and most God-becoming sound, I am altogether transported with zeal (for joy is a mighty thing to renew nature, and desire knows not how to wait when time bids); and I go about Bethany in the course of godly thought,[3] and I clap my hands and dance, and leaping I join the troop of infants,[4] and fashion with them a victorious anthem for the Lord: "Hosanna in the highest. Blessed is he that cometh in the name of the Lord." And when again I behold them bearing branches, and going forth to meet Christ, forming choirs and spreading out their garments, I rejoice likewise in that I see children with unconstrained tongue and deed proclaim the King, and at that moment especially it comes upon me to deplore and hate the perversity of the Jews, inasmuch as children are grateful, while their fathers think of murder, and babes speak

---

[20] As suggested by Fr. Cumont, "La conversion des Juifs byzantins au IXe siècle," *Revue de l'instruction publique en Belgique*, XLVI (1903), pp. 8–15. On the persecution in general, see Joshua Starr, *The Jews in the Byzantine Empire* (*Texte u. Forsch. zur Byz.-Neugriech. Philologie*, no. 30, Athens, 1939), pp. 3–6, 127–136.

[21] Cf. Vogt, *Basile Ier*, p. 302, n. 4.

[1] In A and Lig the title is as follows: Φωτίου τοῦ ἁγιωτάτου πατριάρχου ἀρχιεπισκόπου Κωνσταντινουπόλεως, ὁμιλία εἰς τὰ βάϊα, καὶ εἰς τὸν Λάζαρον. In B it is incomplete. The Cod. Suprasliensis has: "Sermon of Photius, Patriarch of Constantinople, on Palm Sunday and Lazarus" (p. 332$_{12}$).

[2] Mt 21. 9; Mk 11. 10.

[3] The MSS read: λογισμῶν θειοτέρων θειοτέρῳ δρόμῳ περιέρχομαι τὴν Βιθανίαν (sic) [λογισμῶν θειοτέρων δρόμῳ θέων Ar]. The Slavonic version (p. 332$_{22}$) has: "and with a swift mind I go about Bethany" (И оумомъ быстромъ объхождѫ видании҄ѫ), which suggests something like λογισμῶν θέοντι δρόμῳ in the original.

[4] Read συναγελάζομαι with the MSS [συναγάλλομαι Ar].

of God, while old men fight against God. Then do I see even the wisdom of the scribes collapsing; for in their fancy and assumed knowledge they have been lifted to an evil eminence, and have fallen away from the true and verily divine wisdom. Then do I also bewail the hardness of heart of the teachers themselves; for, though presuming to teach others, they have not even been deemed worthy of joining the choirs of their pupils because of the wilful wickedness into which they had been swept, and while professing to cure diseases of the soul in others, they themselves have been taken sick with the lowest ignorance, having miserably inflamed their whole soul with the disease of conceit, and in truth ailing a double ailment, inasmuch as they are in a low state, and, being as they are in the last extremity, they are not even aware of their sickness. 2. For if they had accepted the physician who was at hand and present with them, and had availed themselves (an easy matter and free of cost)

Ar II 412 of the cleansing *waters*, while the streams of healing were gushing for their benefit,[5] they could have washed off thereby the stains of their disease. But having of their own free will shut the eyes of their senses and of their very understanding, to their own detriment, they turned away from their treatment, and did not wish to recognize their Saviour and Creator. "For had they known Him," as the divine Paul testifies, "they would not have crucified the Lord of glory."[6] They did not know Him, they did not even want to recognize Him. And where the will is recalcitrant, both the judgment falls prey to the disease which has seized it, and the freedom of the mind is enslaved and cannot mount to the noble apprehension of truth. They did not know Him who is escorted by angels, and who is proclaimed by prophets. They did not know Him who sits on the right hand of the Father, and is carried in a virgin's arms, and sustains everything with a word alone. They did not know Him who is borne on the cherubic throne, yet is upheld by a beast of burden, who is hymned by children, yet comes willingly to suffer.

Ar II 413 They did not know Him; they did not even choose to understand,

[5] There appears to be no reason to change the reading of the MSS: καὶ ῥείθρων αὐτοῖς προχεομένων ἰαμάτων, ῥᾴδιον ὂν [ὃν B] καὶ χωρὶς δαπάνης τοῦ ῥύπτοντος [τοὺς ῥυπῶντας Ar] ἀπαρύσασθαι. The Slavonic version faithfully reproduces τοῦ ῥύπτοντος by ОТЪ ОМЪІВАЮЩТААГО ИХЪ (p. 333₂₀).

[6] I Cor. 2. 8.

HOMILY VIII. PALM SUNDAY

but professing themselves to be wise, they became fools,[7] and in their reasonings their foolish heart was darkened.[8] This the prophet also said, foreseeing from afar, "They shall indeed hear, but they shall not understand; they shall indeed see,[9] but they shall not perceive. For the heart of this people has become gross, and their ears are dull of hearing, and their eyes have been closed; lest they should see with their eyes, and hear with their ears, and understand with their heart, and be converted, and I should heal them."[10]

3. Tell me then, O Jew, why dost thou boast of the prophets, but blasphemest against Him who has been prophesied? Why dost thou adhere to the letter, but disregardest the spirit of the writings? Why dost thou gather the gleanings of the Law, but leavest it to others to reap its fruit? Why watchest thou vainly in the quarries of the letter, but dost not dig up, neither dost thou treasure away the gold that lies concealed in them? Others have diligently plucked the flowers from the meadows of the Law and, brilliantly crowned, surround with their choirs the bridal-chamber of the Church, and they exude the fragrance of the piety which is of Grace; while thou hast wasted away thine eyes on the petals of the leaves, and thou art completely bent on them, and neither art thou distressed by their harshness, nor dost thou transfer thy gaze to the contemplation of the flowers. Thou dwellest miserably on the oystershell which encases the pearl,[11] while Christ's people neatly open it and extract therefrom the truly white glow of truth. Thou sittest with long labour by the bridal-chamber, but thou dost not receive the bridegroom who has come, seized as thou art by love of harlotry. Verily is your synagogue husbandless, brooding alone senselessly on bare words. Verily is this people foolish and unwise;[12] for, having been placed in the front ranks of the Law, they have not been enrolled even in the last place as regards the knowledge of God. Hast thou not heard King David singing under divine afflatus, "Out

Ar II 414

[7] Rom. 1. 22.
[8] Rom. 1. 21.
[9] The words καὶ οὐ μὴ συνῶσι καὶ βλέποντες βλέψουσι are missing in A and B, and have been supplied by Ar. Their presence in the original is borne out by the Cod. Supr.
[10] Is. 6. 9–10.
[11] Cf. Mt 13. 46.
[12] Deut. 32. 6.

of the mouth of babes and sucklings hast thou perfected praise, because of thine enemies, that thou mightest put down the enemy and avenger?"[13] Dost thou not believe him as a prophet? Then believe him as a kinsman, if thou hast not repudiated the kinship in words too: for it has long been evident that in deeds thou hast abandoned it. Dost thou despise him as a shepherd? Then fear him as a king. For he knows how to threaten in kingly fashion when he perceives those who take no heed of him or treat him insolently, and he lays on with his gleaming sword,[14] and rules with a rod of iron,[15] and dashes to pieces as potter's vessels[16] those who rely on the rottenness of their hearts. Repeat then with him in a loud voice, "Out of the mouths of babes and sucklings hast thou perfected praise." The Saviour has come for thy vindication; for thy vindication is He perfecting the praise of babes. Why dost thou begrudge thyself thine own salvation? Why art thou so mean in requiting *an act of* grace, unless this too, though easy, is yet above the powers of thy perversity? Disbelievest thou what thou hast heard? Believe what thou seest. Even to the prophet Isaiah dost thou refuse compliance, who cries out saying, "Stammering tongues shall learn to speak peace?"[17] Are not stammering tongues clearly proclaiming the truth? Have not babes learnt to praise peace? For Christ is our peace Who hath broken down the middle wall of enmity,[18] and through Him we have been reconciled with our Father and Creator, from Whom we had wickedly parted ourselves in former times.[19] Does not Zechariah too, seized by God, foretell the Grace to Sion: "Rejoice greatly, O daughter of Sion, proclaim it, O daughter of Jerusalem. Behold thy king is coming to thee, just and a Saviour; he is meek, and riding on a beast of burden and the foal of an ass?"[20] Hast thou not thine eyes to witness what has been prophesied? Those things which thou hast been hearing from the prophets, dost thou not see them standing before thee? Are things not concordant with

[13] Ps. 8. 3.
[14] Cf. Ps. 7. 13.
[15] Ps. 2. 9.
[16] *Ibid.*
[17] Is. 29. 24; 32. 4.
[18] Ephes. 2. 14–15.
[19] Cf. Rom. 5. 10.
[20] Zech. 9. 9.

HOMILY VIII. PALM SUNDAY

the words? Is He not meek? Is He not just? Is He not a Saviour? Is He not riding on a beast of burden? Are not stammering tongues splendidly proclaiming peace? Are not children, with the wisdom of old men,[21] bringing their gift of praise?

4. It is the children who bring their gift of praise so that the story may expose as unfounded any suspicion of insincerity, in the event that some deliberate evil-doer might say that the singers of praise offered their hymn to the Lord with some artifice and in order to curry favour.[22] For the nature of babes knows not how to devise craftiness, nor is it subject to the disease of flattery, but just as the grace of the Spirit sounds in them, so do they proclaim the miracle. Children offer their gift of praise so that all may be taught in very deed[23] that the grace of the Mystery is comprehended not by those who have a curious turn of mind and are shamelessly inquisitive, but that the knowledge of piety is revealed to those who approach it with an unaffected mind and thoughts unused to evil. For if a man forces that which is above scrutiny to be subjected to scrutiny, instead of following the divine writings, he will grievously tear asunder those very rules of nature by which he is so elated, and will altogether forsake the laws of theology, which he is insulting, and will be driven afar from his laboriously-sought speculation. Children are offering their gift of praise so that they may both make public the transgression of their parents and inaugurate the believers' knowledge of God. For what surpasses understanding and is incapable of being learned by the judgment of the mind requires a more divine inspiration, which, impinging upon pure and unaffected hearts, reveals through them the knowledge of truth to others. Thou, however, dost thou not even see Lazarus rising up from his tomb, the dead man coming to join the living, and reclining at the Lord's table?[24] Thou loosest the swathings of the dead, but dost thou not loose thy unbelief? Thou rollest away the stone from the tomb, but dost thou not roll away envy from thy heart which

Ar II 417

---

[21] Read πολιόφρονες with the MSS: πολύφρονες Ar.
[22] χάριτι προσπαθείας codd [χάριν κολακείας Ar]. χάριν προσπαθείας would probably be better.
[23] Read ἵνα πάντες ἔργῳ διδαχθῶσιν with B [παῖδες πάντες ἔργῳ διδαχθῶσιν A: ἵνα τοὺς πάντας ἔργῳ διδάξωσιν Ar].
[24] Cf. Jn 12. 2.

causes a worse corruption in thee? Thou seest Hell at the Lord's command give up the four-days-dead, yet dost thou arm thy prophet-slaying hands to kill both the resurrected and the Resurrector?

Ar II 418 5. Oh, what folly! Oh, the incurable hardening of their thoughts! They have perverted their minds to such a degree of impiety, that whence they ought to have derived belief, they derive unbelief; for what they ought to give praise, they blaspheme; for what they ought to render glory and exult, they are ungrateful; what they ought to honour and pay homage to, they speak ill of and battle against God. Such a thing is madness! Such a thing is possession by conceit! For, intoxicating the mind with the error[25] of phantasies, it does not allow the eye of reason to peer through the murk that has poured all around it, and to gaze at the light of truth. Such is the disease of the pharisees and the scribes who, though they make much of the first seat at table, and puff themselves up at being called Rabbi, and boast of keeping the Law by broadening the borders of their garments,[26] take not the least heed of truth, or account piety for anything. Such is the sting of envy! Once it has pierced[27] the soul, it disables the whole man. For it destroys the power to be watchful, and ruins miserably the senses, through the use of which lies the road to knowledge, allowing one neither to comprehend the advantageous, nor to preserve what is heard by means of memory, nor even to see clearly what is presented to the sight.

Ar II 419 6. As for us, my beloved ones, let us escape these soul-destroying diseases. Let us escape vainglory, through which the first of the incorporeal beings suffered the first fall. Let us escape envy, if for

[25] A textual puzzle. A and B have τοὺς γὰρ λογισμοὺς τῆς πλάνης καὶ ἁπάσης τῶν φαντασιῶν ἐκμεθύσκουσα (sc. ἡ ἐπιληψία τῆς οἰήσεως). Ar makes the plausible emendation τῇ πλάνῃ καὶ ἀπάτῃ. The Cod. Supr. reads оүмъі бо ихъ прѣльштенніа мечъ тъштанню оупоивъ which, as it stands, could mean only something like "for the sword of error having inebriated their minds with eagerness." It would appear, however, that мечъ тъштанню is a mistake for мечътанню (= τῇ φαντασίᾳ), which in turn suggests τῆς πλάνης τῇ φαντασίᾳ in the original.
[26] Cf. Mt 23. 5–7.
[27] Pg is surely right in correcting ἐνεσπάρη to ἐνεπάρη (sc. τὸ κέντρον). Supr. has въглѫбнѫ въ доүши = "gone deep into the soul."

HOMILY VIII. PALM SUNDAY

no other reason than that it saps its possessor, and distresses not at all, or very little, the envied one. Let us escape conceit and the striving for fame, through which the apprehension of truth is put to flight. Let us escape ingratitude and blasphemy, for these things threw the high priests and scribes into the pit of perdition; these things inflamed the high priests and scribes of the Jews to kill Christ; these things have shown the high priests and scribes more foolish than the babes. Let us not, therefore, imitate the ingratitude of the Jews, but let us emulate the gratefulness of the children; not the godlessness of the old men, but the godly speech of the babes; not the blindness of the envious, but the knowledge of God of those who sing praise; not the wickedness of those who thirst for blood, but the guilelessness of the infants. Let us too become like children. For, saith the Lord, "Except ye turn and become as little children, ye shall not enter into the kingdom of heaven."[28] Let us become children in guilelessness, by not inserting anything wicked or deceitful in our soul, but by receiving and inscribing the pious faith in a soul entirely clean and freed from the marks of impiety,[29] that we may enter the kingdom of heaven. Ar II 420 Let us bring branches of charity and fellow-love to the Lord, that we may enter the eternal joy of the righteous. Let us go forth to meet Him as He comes riding on a young ass, and is proclaiming the folly of the Jews, and is adopting the gentiles as His children. Let us go forth to meet Him spreading out our garments. How are we to spread them out? By spreading them under the poor; for He takes upon Himself the plight of the poor, and cries out, "Inasmuch as you have done it unto one of these my brethren, ye have done it unto me."[30] Oh, what merciful and divine words! You are spreading out your garments under my feet, He says, when you clothe the poor; you are cherishing me when you release them from the bitter sting of the cold. Let us spread out our garments for Him, that we may be entitled to cry out with the children, "Hosanna in the highest. Blessed is he that cometh in the name of the Lord."[31]

[28] Mt 18. 3.
[29] The MSS read ὅλῃ καθαρᾷ καὶ τῶν τῆς δυσσεβείας ἀπηλλαγμένη χαρακτήρων [ὅλοι καθαροὶ ... ἀπηλλαγμένοι Ar].
[30] Mt 25. 40.
[31] Mt 21. 9.

Blessed is He that cometh to spread out His arms on the cross, and to gather the gentiles unto Himself. Blessed is He that cometh to make Hell a prisoner, to release Adam from his bonds, and to raise him from his fall. Blessed is He that cometh to destroy the power of tyranny, and to bestow liberty on them that are sore distressed. Blessed is He that cometh to empty out the storehouses of Hell, and to fill the heavenly mansions with the throng of the saved. Blessed is He that cometh to offer Himself as a sacrifice for our sake,[32] to expiate all our sins, and to reconcile us with the Father. Blessed is He that cometh to suppress death, to inaugurate our resurrection, to free us from servitude, and to bestow on us His adoption.

7. For it is Thine, Who art our Creator, to have given us existence and fashioned us out of nothing, and after we had fallen and been crushed, to have raised us again and restored us. It is part of Thy love of man to seek that which is gone astray,[33] and to convert from error,[34] and to make us worthy of our ancient inheritance. For we are Thy people and the sheep of Thy pasture,[35] and all of us depend on Thee. And to Thee we send up praise and thanks, together with the Father and the Holy Ghost, the consubstantial, life-giving and all-powerful Trinity, now and for ever and ever. Amen.

[32] Cf. Ephes. 5. 2.
[33] Mt 18. 12.
[34] James 5. 20.
[35] Ps. 78. 13.

NOTE ON HOMILY IX

The present Homily, preached on the birthday of the Virgin (September 8th), is found in more manuscripts than any other Homily of Photius. Its most interesting feature is a digression on the absurdity of Greek mythological fables.[1] The *fictus adversarius* whom Photius is refuting (§§ 4–6) is not, of course, a pagan,[2] but a sceptic who opposes natural law to the miraculous birth of the Virgin from a barren woman, yet who, allegedly, gives credence to the absurd creation-myths and metamorphoses of classical mythology.

There is no reason to think that this tirade, admittedly very typical of early Christian apologetics,[3] is a mere rhetorical device. Considerable evidence exists that in the course of the ninth century certain intellectual circles of Constantinople were won over by the charms of classical literature and became somewhat critical of Christian writings. To what extent this trend went beyond the general revival of classical studies is not an easy question to answer. The accusations of paganism made against some of the intellectual figures of the time could be, of course, regarded as the reaction of obscurantists towards the resurgence of classical learning, no matter how innocuous; yet such an explanation does not, by itself, appear to be adequate.

It is in the reign of Theophilus (829–842) that a more emancipated attitude towards classical antiquity becomes apparent. It is associated especially with the somewhat shadowy figure of Leo the Mathematician, appointed by the Iconoclasts Bishop of Thessalonica (840–843), and later made professor at the University of

---

[1] The passage in question has been noted by Étienne Chastel, *Histoire de la destruction du paganisme dans l'Empire d'Orient*, Paris, 1850, pp. 318–19.

[2] There is no evidence for the survival of paganism in Constantinople as late as the 9th century. There is, however, a somewhat unclear statement which may indicate that pagans still lived at Nicaea *ca.* A.D. 800 (Epiphanius, *Vita S. Andreae*, PG 120, col. 229 B–C).

[3] Cf., for example, Greg. Naz., *Or.* XXXIX, §§ 3–7, PG 36, cols. 336–41.

Constantinople.[4] Leo was accused of paganism, perhaps unjustly;[5] but he almost certainly dabbled in astrology and studied books of a compromising nature.[6] It may have been the same Leo who criticized certain grammatical solecisms in the Bible and drew a rebuke from Photius.[7] Attachment to ancient lore was also apt to provoke charges of sorcery, such as were made against Leo, the Patriarch John VII the Grammarian (837–843) and even Photius.[8] At the beginning of the tenth century the scholar and diplomat Leo Choirosphaktes was assailed for his pagan leanings, his interest in ancient drama and music, and his criticism of the Lives of saints; his exile may have resulted from that very charge.[9]

[4] On Leo, see Bury, *A History of the Eastern Roman Empire*, pp. 436 sq.; L. Petit, "Les évêques de Thessalonique," *Échos d'Orient*, IV (1900–1901), p. 217; F. Fuchs, *Die Höheren Schulen von Konstantinopel im Mittelalter* (Byzantinisches Archiv, no. 8, 1926), pp. 18 sq.; Dvornik, "La carrière universitaire de Constantin le Philosophe," *Byzantinoslavica*, III (1931), pp. 59–67; *id.*, *Les légendes de Constantin et de Méthode* (1933), pp. 42 sq.; E. E. Lipšic, "Византийский ученый Лев Математик," *Viz. Vrem.*, II (1949), pp. 106–149; Bertrand Hemmerdinger, *Essai sur l'histoire du texte de Thucydide*, Paris, 1955, pp. 35 sq.

[5] See the violent attack on Leo by his former pupil Constantine and the justification by the same Constantine for having assailed his master. Printed by Matranga, *Anecdota graeca*, II, Rome 1850, pp. 555–559; PG 107, cols. lxi sq., 660 sq. That these texts refer to Leo the Mathematician has been shown by G. Kolias, *Léon Choerospactès*, Athens, 1939, pp. 66–68. Cf. also *Anthol. Pal.*, XV. 12 (*lemma*): Λέοντος φιλοσόφου εἰς ἑαυτὸν τοῦ ἐπονομαζομένου Ἕλληνος.

[6] The chroniclers mention several instances of astrological predictions made by Leo, as well as the application by him of astral sympathy to agriculture. See Theoph. Cont., pp. 189, 191, 197, 232; Pseudo-Symeon, p. 677; Continuator of Georgius Monachus, p. 829 (Bonn ed.); Cedrenus, II, p. 170; Genesius, p. 104; Glycas, p. 541. It is probably the same Leo who is the author of several significant epigrams in the *Palatine Anthology*. In one of these he praises the astrologer Paul of Alexandria for having opened to him the secrets of divination (IX. 201 = PG 107, col. 664). Leo the Mathematician may also be the author of the astrological work contained in the Paris. gr. 2420 and 2424 under the title Λέοντος φιλοσόφου περὶ βασιλείας καὶ ἀρχόντων.

[7] *Epistolae*, ed. Valettas, pp. 403–4 = *Amphil.*, quaest. 106, PG 101, cols. 640–41.

[8] Pseudo-Symeon, pp. 670, 672–73. The youthful Photius is here represented renouncing Christ in exchange for having "every Hellenic writing at the tip of [his] tongue, and surpassing all men in wisdom."

[9] As argued by Kolias, *op. cit.*, pp. 55 sq. Leo Choirosphaktes was the target of two accusations of paganism: one by Constantine Rhodius (published by Matranga, *Anecd. gr.*, II, pp. 624–25); the other by Arethas, entitled Χοιροσφάκτης ἢ μισογόης (published by J. Compernass in *Didaskaleion* I (1912), pp. 295–318; and again by M. A. Šangin in Византийский Сборник, Moscow-Leningrad, 1945, pp. 228–48).

NOTE ON HOMILY IX

Such was the context of Photius' tirade against Greek fables. It may also be added that the Caesar Bardas (864–866) destroyed a number of ancient monuments which were thought to have an occult connotation, as well as a statue of Tyche.[10] When we turn to the writings of Photius, we discover several references to the prevalence of a critical attitude towards Holy Scripture, in addition to the one instance quoted above. George of Nicomedia who devoted much time to the study of ancient poets found fault with a barbarous word used by St. Peter[11] and criticised St. Paul's style;[12] another scholar was displeased by the obscurity of prophetic books.[13] The literary standard which these critics employed was obviously that of the Greek classics.

It is not altogether clear what prompted Photius to assail Greek mythology from the pulpit. Was it a deliberate move on his part to state publicly his own attitude towards pagan antiquity, and clear himself of any accusations on that score, such as were circulated in monastic circles? Admittedly, Photius was deeply versed in classical authors, among them the *mythographi* and *paradoxographi*.[14] But even a cursory reading of the *Bibliotheca* will show what Photius' position as regards ancient authors was: he admired them for their style and educative value, while castigating them for their fabulous tales and religious views. A more plausible explanation would be that there were two rival schools in the ninth-century classical revival: on the one hand, the school of Photius which gave preference to Aristotle in philosophy and to the orators and historians in literature (the poets are not represented in the *Bibliotheca*); on the other hand, a school more inclined towards Plato[15] and the Neoplatonists (and hence perhaps to the occult), the

---

[10] *Script. orig. Constantinopol.*, ed. Preger, II (1907), p. 184.
[11] PG 101, col. 557.
[12] *Ibid.*, cols. 576–592.
[13] *Ibid.*, col. 948.
[14] Including Apollodorus, our most valuable compendium of Greek mythology (*Biblioth.*, cod. 186, p. 142 in Bekker's ed.) and Lucius of Patras (*ibid.*, cod. 129, p. 96). The manuscript tradition of Apollodorus can be traced back to the milieu of Photius. See A. Diller, "The Text History of the Bibliotheca of Pseudo-Apollodorus," *Trans. of the Amer. Philol. Assoc.*, LXVI (1935), pp. 296–313.
[15] Photius was, on the whole, critical of Plato, both as regards the theory of ideas (on which he composed a treatise now lost: cf. PG 101, col. 480) and the ideal state, which he considered absurd and indecent.

tragedians and lyric poets. At any rate, Photius' tirade calls to mind the vitriolic accusations hurled by Arethas at Leo Choirosphaktes, namely his questioning hagiographical exaggerations,[16] his renouncing Christianity in favour of paganism, his being as impious as the Jews, his admiring Porphyry and Julian, etc. It is not unlikely, therefore, that Photius was denouncing that other, more dangerous, trend in ancient studies, and his attack, coming as it does from a champion of learning, shows, more clearly than the defamatory *libelli* and the biased statements of chroniclers, that the classical revival was something more than a literary phenomenon.

IX

Ar II 330 OF THE SAME MOST-BLESSED PATRIARCH PHOTIUS, ARCHBISHOP OF CONSTANTINOPLE, HOMILY ON THE NATIVITY OF OUR MOST-HOLY LADY, THE MOTHER OF GOD[1]

1. Every festival and every celebration at which the concourse of the faithful is gladdened dispels mutual differences and quarrels, and brings together men of opposed opinions who have broken the bond of love by strife, by offering as it does the harmony of the chants as an invitation to the recall of concord. It also shows that Ar II 331 the congregation are the creatures and handiwork of the same Lord and Creator; and, by indicating the equal dignity of the creation through the unity of worship, it soothes and calms down those who are bitterly irritated with one another, persuading them to think with moderation and humanity, and teaching them to look up all alike to the Creator's hand and to consider themselves the same clay of creation. To this end, in my opinion, has the rule proper to Christians instituted the celebration of festivals: one shows Christ as He is born, another bears witness to His baptism, another has Him transfigured, another working miracles, curing men possessed by demons, giving sight to the blind, stemming torrents of blood, knitting together the lame and the paralysed, raising up the dead;

---

[16] Compernass, *op. cit.*, p. 304.
[1] That is how the title appears in A and Lig. In B it is incomplete. Ar omits ἀρχιεπισκόπου and δεσποίνης ἡμῶν.

HOMILY IX. THE BIRTH OF THE VIRGIN

finally, another exhibits Him as He is hanging on the cross, yet another as He is rising up and inaugurating our resurrection in visible deeds.

2. Thus, while each holy festival both affords the enjoyment of common gifts and lights up its peculiar glow of grace, the present feast honouring the birth of the Virgin Mother of God easily carries off the glittering prize of seniority against every competitor. For, just as we know the root to be the cause of the branches, the stem, the fruit and the flower, though it is for the sake of the fruit that care and labour are expended on the others, and without the root none of the rest grows up, so without the Virgin's feast none of those that sprang out of it would appear. For the resurrection was because of the death; and the death because of the crucifixion; and the crucifixion because Lazarus came up from the gates of Hell on the fourth day, because the blind saw, and the paralytic ran carrying the bed on which he had lain, and because of the rest of those wondrous deeds (this is not the time to enumerate them all) for which the Jewish people ought to have sent up glory and chanted praise, but were instead inflamed to envy, on account of which they perpetrated the Saviour's murder to their own destruction. And this because Christ, having submitted to baptism, and having released[2] men from their error, taught the knowledge of God in deed and word. The baptism was because of the nativity; and Christ's nativity, to put it briefly and aptly, was because of the Virgin's nativity, by which we are being renovated, and which we have been deemed worthy to celebrate. Thus the Virgin's feast, in fulfilling the function of the root, the source, the foundation (I know not how to put it in a more appropriate way), takes on with good reason the ornament of all those other *feasts*,[3] and it is conspicuous with many great boons, and recognized as the day of universal salvation.

3. For today the Virgin Mother is born of a barren mother, and the palace of the Lord's advent is being decked out. Today the

---

[2] ἀπολυσάμενος codd: ἀπολουσάμενος Ar.

[3] All the MSS, with the exception of Lig, read ἐκείναις τε πάσαις εἰκότως [εἰκότων Vat. Reg. 15] ἐναγλαΐζεται. Presumably ἐκείναις refers to πανηγύρεσι understood. Lig has ἐκείναις πάσαις εἰκότως ταῖς εὐφημίαις ἐναγλαΐζεται, but he may have himself supplied ταῖς εὐφημίαις for greater clarity.

bonds of barrenness are loosed, and the locks of virginity are sealed. For inasmuch as a womb[4] unfruitful and deadened for purposes of childbirth, brought forth unexpectedly a fair fruit, by that very fact the incorruptibility of virginity is assured, and the miraculous pregnancy is heralded by manifest deeds. To be sure, birth without a man is a marvellous thing, as is the preservation of virginity after the delivery; but a barren woman, made fruitful in her old age and giving birth, also surpasses the laws of nature, and heralds the Virgin's giving birth, for the sake of which this miracle is wrought.[5] Today Anna is shorn of the reproach of sterility, and the world reaps the crop of joy. Joachim is called the father of a child, and we receive by way of earnest the dignity of the adoption. Today the Virgin comes forth from a sterile womb, while barrenness overtakes the offspring of sin. The congregation of the Jewish Synagogue is bereaved, while from the womb of the Church her children appear, divinely increased and multiplied by Christ, the Bridegroom. The Virgin comes forth from a sterile womb, at a time when, had it been fruitful, her birth would have been strange What a miracle! When the time of sowing had passed, then came the moment of bearing fruit. When the flame of desire had been extinguished, then the torch of childbearing was lit. Youth did not produce a flower, yet old age puts forth a shoot. When nature was in her prime, the belly was not seen to swell, yet the ever-virgin child is seen to be the offspring of a withered womb.

4. But art thou puzzled, O man, that a barren woman gave birth? Or rather, seekest thou to belittle the wondrous fact, at which thou too shouldst wonder even as we?[6] And how, arguest thou, could a barren woman give birth? For if she is barren, she cannot give birth, and if she does give birth, she is not barren. How can dried-up breasts gush with streams of milk? For if old age is unable to store away blood, how can the teats whiten into milk what they have not

---

[4] Reading οἷς γὰρ νηδὺς ἄγονος with Chalc. 1, Monac. 443 and Ar: ἧς γὰρ A, B, Lig and Vat. Reg. 15. If the latter reading is adopted, place a full stop or semi-colon after προήνεγκε, and translate: "For she whose womb was unfruitful," etc. But cf. below, n. 20.

[5] Reading δι' ὃν τερατουργεῖται with A, B and Lig: δι' ὧν Vat. Reg. 15, Chalc. 1 and Monac. 443. If the latter reading is preferred, translate, "and heralds by its miraculous nature the Virgin's giving birth."

[6] δι' ὧν θαυμάζομεν codd: δι' ἃ Ar.

HOMILY IX. THE BIRTH OF THE VIRGIN

received? How does a deadened womb bring to maturity, quicken, encompass and feed the foetus? Such *arguments* dost thou devise against thyself and thy salvation? In what capacity? For thou couldst not be of the faithful who are worthy of the miracle. Nay indeed, the faithful person will never be misled into disbelieving those things by which faith *is established*, but the Jew will.[7] Yet what of Sarah—or did that escape thee? Did she not have in Isaac a child of her old age and barrenness? If Anna confuses and disturbs thy mind, Sarah should rather *do so* since she *came* first. If the former be the cause of thy hesitation, dost thou not perceive that thou art rejecting the latter from thy kinship, and cutting the roots whereof thou art the branch, and art proved to have departed from Jewish laws?[8]

5. As for me, if I said[9] that the birth had happened by a natural concatenation, and then invited thee to agree, the woman's barrenness, her old age, nature *itself* would rightly[10] have aroused difficulty in reasoning. But if I represent it as an act of divine grace, why dost thou force grace to be subservient to nature, of whom she has always been the mistress? Dost thou accept Adam to have been moulded out of clay and produced without *natural* birth,[11] dost thou accept Eve to be the offspring not of intercourse but of a rib, yet being unable to ascribe these things to natural law?[12] For the successive multiplication and birth of men, keeping as it does a different order of procession, does not permit us to believe the procreation of those to have been the work of nature, nor, on the other hand, contrary to nature. For it is the origin of men's natural constitution. Therefore it is *the work* of divine decree and power. What then? Thou grantest the Godhead to have had at that time

---

[7] Reading with the MSS: οὐδὲ γὰρ οὐδὲ τοῖς δι' ὧν ἡ πίστις ἀπιστεῖν, οὔμενουν, ὁ πιστὸς παραχθήσεται [ταραχθήσεται Chalc. 1], ἀλλ' Ἰουδαῖος. Ar has οὐδὲ γὰρ ἐξὸν τοῖς, δι' ὧν ἡ πίστις, ἀπιστεῖν· οὔμενουν ὁ πιστὸς ταραχθήσεται, ἀλλ' ὁ Ἰουδαῖος. The revised punctuation was kindly suggested to me by Prof. Paul Alexander.
[8] Read ἐκεῖνο σὺ [σοῦ Ar] καὶ τῆς σῆς οὐκ αἰσθάνῃ παραγράφων συγγενείας ... καὶ τῶν [καὶ οὐ τῶν Ar] Ἰουδαϊκῶν θεσμῶν ἐξελέγχῃ κατενηνεγμένος.
[9] Keep λέγων of the MSS: ἔλεγον Ar.
[10] καλῶς codd, changed to οὐδόλως by Ar.
[11] γεννήσεως codd: γυναικὸς Ar, which he erroneously ascribes to A.
[12] οὐκ ἂν εἰπεῖν ἔχων of the MSS is right [οὐκ ἂν ἔχοις εἰπεῖν Ar], but punctuate: δέχῃ ... γεννήσεως, δέχῃ ... γέννημα, λόγῳ ταῦτα φύσεως οὐκ ἂν εἰπεῖν ἔχων;

the power to do even the most unbelievable of things, and thou dost not arm natural law against its Creator; now, however, as if convicting of advanced senility that most omnipotent and perfect power, thou declarest it too weak for these *wonders*; though, schooled as thou art in those that went before, thou shouldst more fittingly have accorded the same unhesitating faith to the latter as well. Nay, he who will doubt could not even be a Jew—if he were a Jew[13]—but a pagan in his mind and judgment.

6. So thou disbelievest that a child was born of a barren woman, and scoffest at it, thou who imaginest men to be the children of putrefaction,[14] who hast invented dragon teeth to be the wombs from which thy ancestors sprang[15] (would that thou who sayest such things proved them[16] to be their tombs!), who commandest[17] stones to become men,[18] drawing the lineage of thy forefathers as befits thyself, and tracing it to ants' blood?[19] These things thou believest, although they are utter nonsense, and thou hast no advocate anywhere, neither in grace, nor mind, nor nature, nor sensation, nor other men's opinion, nor thine own, nor anything else, except thy shamelessness and folly, and yet thou cherishest them and preachest them. But that which conflicting opinions confirm, forced by truth to speak the same language, whereof sight and sensation are the first witnesses, and which is corroborated, apart from the aforesaid *instances*, by many similar events of

Ar II 338

---

[13] Read: οὐδὲ Ἰουδαῖος ὁ ἀμφισβητήσων ⟨ἂν⟩ εἴη [εἴης Ar] ἄνπερ Ἰουδαῖος εἴη [εἴης Ar].

[14] It is not clear what ancient myth or doctrine is referred to here. The creation of men out of putrefying matter seems to be unknown to Greek mythology.

[15] Dragons' teeth were sown by Cadmus at Thebes. Thereupon armed men arose from the ground and slew one another, only five of them remaining. Euripides, *Phoenissae*, 939 sq.; Pausanias, IX. 10. 1; Apollodorus III. 4. 1; etc. A similar story is reported of Jason in Colchis. Apollonius Rhodius, III. 401 sq., 1176 sq.; Apollodorus, I. 9. 23; etc.

[16] Read with all the MSS ταῦτα λέγοντί σοι τούτους ἐδείκνυς [λέγων σὺ τούτοις Ar].

[17] προστάσσων or προστάττων codd: προτάσσων Ar.

[18] After the flood that followed the Bronze Age, Deucalion and Pyrrha were commanded by Zeus to take up stones and throw them over their head. The stones that Deucalion threw became men, those that Pyrrha threw became women. Pindar, *Olymp.*, IX. 41 sq.; Apollodorus, I. 7. 2; etc.

[19] After Zeus had carried off Aegina to the island later called by her name, he begot a son, Aeacus. As Aeacus was alone on the island, Zeus made men for him out of ants. Apollodorus, III. 12. 6; Strabo, VIII. 6. 16; etc.

HOMILY IX. THE BIRTH OF THE VIRGIN

antiquity, that thou attemptest to ridicule and make light of? I do not mean to say that we ought to speak proudly of our *beliefs* on account of the fact that the pagans have preached such gross absurdities,[20] nor—far from it—that light should be brightened by darkness, or truth to stand with the help of lies, or faith to be supported by error; but that it was altogether not permissible for them, who had sunk as far below as we are above nature, to honour Ar II 339 and admire unnatural things which can in no manner be substantiated, while trying to undermine by misleading speech what is far above telling and nature, and what even recently martyrs' tombs sometimes miraculously testify, when need requires it and Providence so dispenses.[21] Consider this also: is our nature not governed by its affects, by sickness, old age, even by youth that has not yet reached maturity or makes in some other way for impotence in procreation?[22] And the astonishing thing is, had not familiarity robbed it of its strangeness, that *youth* itself, in which a man comes to be a father,[23] prevents him for a while from becoming a father. What then? Is nature to be overcome by *these* affects, if not by some other affect that is an offscouring of nature,[24] and shall grace, which formed nature, not be able to repair her? Is old age to chill

---

[20] καὶ οὐ τοῦτο φαίην ἂν ἔγωγε ὡς, οἷς ἐκεῖνοι τὰ ἀτοπώτατα πεπρεσβεύκασι, τούτοις ἡμᾶς δεήσει σεμνολογεῖν τὰ ἡμέτερα. This could also be translated, "that we should speak of our *traditions* in the solemn terms in which they preach their gross absurdities"; but I believe that the rendering given above is more appropriate to the trend of the argument. Photius often uses οἷς rather loosely, to mean something like "by the fact that." Cf. above, p. 166 and n. 4 (= Ar. II. 333₉): οἷς γὰρ νηδὺς ἄγονος ... καρπὸν παρ' ἐλπίδας ὡραῖον προήνεγκε, τούτοις καὶ τὸ τῆς παρθενίας μνηστεύεται ἀδιάφθορον.

[21] This passage has been completely perverted by Ar. I would suggest reading: ἀλλ' ὡς ὅλως οὐκ ἐξῆν ἐκείνοις, κάτω παντελῶς κατενεχθεῖσι [κατενεχθῆναι Ar] καὶ ὅσον ἡμεῖς [οὕτως ἡμῖν Ar] ἄνω τῆς φύσεως, τὰ [ἃ Ar] μὲν παρὰ φύσιν καὶ ἃ μηδ' ὁστισοῦν τρόπος συγκροτήσειε, ταῦτα τιμᾶν καὶ θαυμάζειν, ἃ δὲ πολλῷ κρείσσω [so Chalc. 1: κρεῖσσον A, B, Vat. Reg. 15, Monac. 443] καὶ λόγου καὶ φύσεως καὶ ἃ νέως [νεὼς AB; καὶ ἀνέσεως Chalc. 1, Vat. Reg. 15; καὶ λόγῳ ἀνέσεως Monac. 443; καὶ αἰνέσεως Combefis, Ar] καὶ εἰσέτι καὶ μαρτύρων τάφοι ... ἐπιμαρτύρονται, ταῦτα δὴ [so Ar: δὲ codd] λόγῳ καὶ πλάνῃ πειρᾶσθαι παρασαλεύειν.

[22] The MSS read νεότης οὔπω [οὕτω Vat. Reg. 15, Monac. 443: οὕτως Chalc. 1] ἡβάσκουσα εἰ [ἢ would be better] καί τι ἄλλο ἀσθένεια καθεστῶσα τῆς τεκνώσεως: ἢ καί τις ἄλλη Ar.

[23] The reading of the MSS, δι' ἧς ἔρχεταί τις [τι AB] τοῦ εἶναι πατήρ, should probably be retained: ἄρχεταί τις εἶναι Ar.

[24] A difficult passage: τί οὖν; τὰ πάθη νικᾷ τὴν φύσιν, εἰ μή τι ἄλλο πάθος καὶ περίττωμα ταύτης ὄν, etc. It would appear that Photius has two kinds of πάθη in mind, on the one hand natural conditions, such as youth and old age, and on the other hand the refuse, so to speak (περίττωμα), or vices of nature.

HOMILIES OF PHOTIUS

Ar II 340 and dry up the fountains of generation, and cannot the Creator warm and irrigate that which has grown old? Shall nature bear easily the fate to which she has not yet been reduced (for her time is not yet), and the worse plight into which she is being dragged down,[25] and shall not the Creator easily at His will restore her to the state in which He set her at first? Dost thou disbelieve my words? Thou doest well. For these things do not resemble, not by far, thy noble metamorphoses, which I will enumerate to thee; or rather, it is thy task to recount them, that thou mayest have more opportunity in thy most edifying stories to be arrogant towards us. Tell us of the human poplars, from whose eyes drips the mythical amber,[26] whence thou drawest thy wealth of silliness. Enumerate thy laurel-trees[27] and palm-trees,[28] thy nightingales and swallows,[29] Ar II 341 thy musical swans[30] and halcyons,[31] and thy friendly dolphins.[32]

[25] A most obscure passage. The MSS give: ἐκεῖνα πρὸς ἃ μήπω κατηνέχθη, τοῦ καιροῦ [καὶ τοῦ καιροῦ Chalc. 1, Vat. Reg. 15, Monac. 443] μήπω παραστάντος, καὶ χειρόνων ὄντων [so Chalc. 1, Vat. Reg. 15, Monac. 443: χείρονος ὄντων AB: καὶ πρὸς ἃ χείρονα ὄντα Ar] πρὸς ἃ καθέλκεται, φέρει ὅμως εὐμαρῶς. What Photius appears to be saying is that if human nature can submit to the infirmities of old age and to death, then surely God can reverse the process. If such is the meaning, however, it is rather strange that the condition to which nature has submitted in this case, i. e. presumably old age, should be said to be worse than the condition to which she will eventually submit, i. e. death. There may, therefore, be some justification for a transposition, namely, ἐκεῖνα πρὸς ἃ καθέλκεται, καὶ χειρόνων ὄντων πρὸς ἃ μήπω κατηνέχθη, τοῦ καιροῦ μήπω παραστάντος.

[26] The Heliades, daughters of the Sun, were changed into poplars, and wept amber. Eurip., *Hippol.*, 740; Apoll. Rhod., IV. 603 sq.; Philostratus, *Imag.*, I. 11; etc.

[27] Daphne, daughter of the river-god Peneus (or, according to other versions, of Ladon or of Amyclas), was pursued by Apollo, who was enamoured of her, and when she was on the point of being overtaken, she was turned into a laurel-tree. Pausan., VIII. 20; X. 7. 8; Philostratus, *Vita Apoll.*, I. 16; Parthenius, *Narrat. amat.*, 15; etc.

[28] Probably with reference to the sacred palm-tree of Delos, which was believed to have sprung up when Latona landed on the island. It was while clinging to it that Latona gave birth to Apollo and Artemis. *Odyssey*, VI. 162; Pausan., VIII. 48. 3; Aelian, 5. 4; etc.

[29] Procne and Philomela were turned into a nightingale and a swallow respectively when they were being pursued by Tereus, who had successively married both of them. Apollodorus, III. 14. 8, and others.

[30] Several persons were turned into swans: Cycnus, son of Apollo, Cycnus, son of Sthenelos, and Cycnus, the Ligurian king. Antoninus Liberalis, 12; etc.

[31] Halcyone was married to Ceyx. They were so presumptuous as to call each other Zeus and Hera, and were turned in punishment into a halcyon (kingfisher) and a gannet respectively. Apollod., I. 7. 4; cf. Antonin. Lib., 11; etc.

[32] Dolphins were thought to be friendly to men, several of whom they

HOMILY IX. THE BIRTH OF THE VIRGIN

Sing of thy[33] androgynous Tiresiases that they may resolve the strife of the gods, worthy of the latter's wantonness; who, moreover, having given a greater share of pleasure to the goddess, were rewarded with punishment for their outspokenness.[34] Dost thou wish me to remind thee of the sea-voyaging bulls, steered by love for an unfortunate girl,[35] the lengthy absences, the many journeys, and the residences very far from Olympus? I am silent about the rest. Nor is it, I think, proper for the unguent of faith to be mingled with the mire of error, or the light of piety to be insulted with the deep murk of impiety. Wherefore, bidding a definite farewell to this tedious nonsense and chatter, and pitying for their folly those who are in a flutter about these things, while abominating their imposture, let us now proceed with the initial course of our speech.

7. Humanity therefore, having, long been enslaved by the power of ancestral sins, the birth of its daughter, heralding Him who shall remove these *sins*, gives[36] manifest signs of our deliverance from that domination and our release from servitude. Wherefore Adam, too, along with Eve, having cleansed themselves of the ancient stains of their transgression, and putting off the sullenness of despondency, gladly join the choir of the Virgin's feast with a confident voice and face, or rather, they are become its leaders. For they, through whom the seed of sin had become ingrown in the whole race and had perverted it, are especially fit, once the seed has been uprooted, to lead the joyful choir, to seek out and call together their descendants. Since, moreover, the disease of the trespass has been transmitted from the first transgressors down through all men, and since everyone needs the same treatment; since universal salvation is being founded today with the Virgin's birth, it was

Ar II 342

---

saved from drowning, notably Arion, Enalos and Koiranos. See esp. Plutarch, *De sollert. anim.*, 36; Aelian, *De nat. anim.*, II. 6.

[33] ὕμνει σου Chalc. 1, Vat. Reg. 15, Monac. 443: ὕμνεις σου AB: ὕμνει καὶ Ar.

[34] Tiresias the seer, who had been a woman for seven years, was consulted in a dispute between Zeus and Hera as to whether men or women derived more pleasure from love. He answered that women had nine shares of pleasure out of ten, while men had only one. Hera was angered, and blinded him. Apollod., III. 6. 7; Phlegon, *Mirabilia*, 4; etc.

[35] Zeus, who had fallen in love with Europa, turned himself into a tame bull and, having mounted her on his back, carried her off across the sea to Crete. Apollod., III. 1. 1; etc.

[36] παρέχεται codd: παρείχετο Ar.

fitting that we should organize a common festival of all nations, and strike up public songs of thanksgiving transcending our world, since universal salvation requires thanks that transcend our world. Let us send up songs of thanksgiving because Adam is re-created and Eve is renovated with him, because the curse is abolished, and our nature, putting off the dead leathern mask of sin, is remoulded after the pristine dignity of the Lord's likeness. Let us send up songs of thanksgiving and organize public choirs, because, coming forth from a sterile womb, the Virgin sanctifies the sterile womb of nature and grafts into its fruitlessness the fruitfulness of virtue. For in lending to the Lord and Husbandman of the world the streams of her stainless blood to moisten the whole desiccated lump, she fittingly receives on that account the blessing of fruitfulness. The ladder leading up to heaven is being built, and earthly nature, leaping over her proper boundaries, comes to dwell in the heavenly tabernacles. The Lord's throne is being prepared on earth, earthly things are sanctified, the heavenly hosts are mingled with us, and the Wicked one, who first deceived us and was the contriver of the plot against us, has his power crushed, as his wiles and devices rot away.

8. Who will be able to tell God's wonders?[37] What words will express the might of what is above words? Will not every mind[38] be numbed in extending its comprehension to the magnitude of the facts? God formed man[39] in the beginning, moved by an ineffable wealth of love, the work of His own hand, graciously giving him to bear the Creator's image—the handiwork indicating the nobility of the flesh, the image that of the spirit. A garden, agreeable and lovely, had been planted eastward,[40] breathed over by the unfading flowers of its meadows, abounding in various seasonable fruit of plants, while rivers which flowed in the middle and watered the face of the plain with their clear stream lent to the place an extraordinary beauty. In this spot the Creator settled the work of His Lordly hand, appointing him master of everything, and showering him abundantly with every good thing. Thereafter He brought

---

[37] Cf. Ps. 105. 2.
[38] πῶς δὲ νοῦς ἅπας codd: ποῖος δὲ νοῦς Ar.
[39] Gen. 2. 7.
[40] Gen. 2. 8.

HOMILY IX. THE BIRTH OF THE VIRGIN

forth into being a companion from the rib of the ineffably born, that she might know the lender, wherefrom she had been taken, to be the head,[41] and look up to him with her obligation in mind, and that through their natural bond the bond of concord[42] should abide with them. Having bestowed *on man* the enjoyment and mastery over everything in the garden, and since it was also meet for him who was entrusted with so great an authority to be disciplined and trained with some command, God appointed a law unto him, in accordance with which it was not difficult to live, nor yet altogether easy to keep on guard, and whereby either reward or culpability was dispensed. For, having explicitly marked off from the rest a tree with fair bloom, He gave out a command decreeing not to eat of that alone. But a wicked beast, the instigator of evil, whose deed caused him to be named the Slanderer, eyed man jealously from the very creation. Using as a tool another beast of those that crawl, and addressing alluring and seductive words to the woman, with a great sprinkling of blasphemy against the Lawgiver, he persuaded the woman, and through her the husband, to neglect the command, and to eat whereof it had been decreed to abstain. They forthwith transgressed against the order, and were deprived of all their gifts, which was the plotter's goal; for to this end his whole device had been contrived. From this point on, as the transgression spread from the ancestors to their descendants, the plotter held our whole race enslaved in his power.

9. But what of the Creator and Protector? Did He utterly overlook His creature, distressed and plunged in such great error, and constantly enslaved by his passions? By no means. For how could He have gladly suffered to see that which He had created with pride being led away captive and seduced? Wherefore, the oneness of the Trinity having, if it is permitted to say so, consulted with Itself (and it is permissible to say this of the re-creation, since it is said of the creation, "Let us make man in our image and likeness,"[43] with reference to the single purpose of the mind),[44] made disposition

---

[41] Cf. 1 Cor. 11. 3.
[42] Read ὁ τῆς [τοῖς Ar, probably a misprint] ὁμονοίας ... σύνδεσμος.
[43] Gen. 1. 26.
[44] Cf. Athanasius, *De Synodis*, PG 26, col. 737, § xiv; Procopius of Gaza, *Commentarii in Gen.*, PG 87, col. 113; further references in H. Pinard's

HOMILIES OF PHOTIUS

for the re-creation of the creature that had been crushed. It sought a man (for human kind had become grievously savage and desolate, and would not be brought back either by threats, or penalties, or laws, or prophets) possessing the same nature as ourselves, in whom could be seen the inviolate observance of the law, so that human kind, in seeing the ways of its kin and fellow, could imitate him, and so that the contriver of the plots against us should be deprived of his mastery by a lawful victory and struggle, by the same means through which he had gained his ascendency over us. It was needful, therefore, for one person of the Trinity to become man, to make it manifest that the re-creation too, like the creation, was Its own work. And it was altogether meet that He should be the Son on earth and not derogate from His celestial rank, who had been the Son from all eternity, in being and in glory. But it would have been impossible to be one of the sons[45] of men without incarnation. For incarnation is the road to birth, and birth is the conclusion of pregnancy, which, entailing as it does a mother, naturally requires that such a one
Ar II 348 be provided beforehand. So it was needful that a mother should be prepared down below for the Creator ,for the re-creation of shattered *humanity*, and she a virgin, in order that, just as the first man had been formed of virgin earth, so the re-creation, too, should be carried out through a virgin womb, and that no transitory pleasure, even lawful, should be as much as imagined in the Creator's birth: since a captive of pleasure was he, for whose deliverance the Lord suffered to be born.[46]

10. But who was worthy to serve as the minister of the mystery? Who was worthy to become the mother of God, and lend flesh to

---

article "Création," *Dict. de théol. cath.*, III 2, cols. 2111 sq. The above argument has led to the artistic representation of the Trinity deliberating in council about the incarnation of Christ. Such a representation is found in the Paris and Vatican MSS of Jacob Kokkinobaphos: H. Omont, "Miniatures des homélies sur la Vierge du moine Jacques," *Bull. de la Soc. française de reproductions de manuscrits à peintures*, XI (1927), pl. XIX; C. Stornajolo, *Miniature delle omilie di Giacomo Monaco*, Rome, 1910, pl. 48. Cf. Adelheid Heimann, "Trinitas Creator Mundi," *Journal of the Warburg Institute*, II (1938), p. 46.

[45] εἰς ἀνθρώπων υἱούς codd: υἱὸν Ar.
[46] The reading of all the MSS, ὃν ὁ δεσπότης ἐλευθερῶσαι τὴν γέννησιν κατεδέξατο, should probably be retained: τῇ γεννήσει Ar.

HOMILY IX. THE BIRTH OF THE VIRGIN

Him who is rich in everything? Who then was worthy? Clearly it was she who this day strangely issued from Joachim and Anna, the barren root, whose nativity we are celebrating in splendour, whose birth is the prelude to the greatest mystery—I mean the birth of the Word in the flesh—, and for whom this public and holy celebration is held. It was needful, yea needful, that she who from the very cradle had by a superior reason preserved her body pure, her soul pure, her thoughts pure, should be marked out to be the Creator's mother. It was needful that she who had been brought to the temple as an infant, who had trodden the untrodden places, should appear as a living temple for Him who gave her life. It was needful that she who had been born in a wondrous manner from a sterile womb, and had removed her parents' reproach, should also make good the failure of her forefathers: for she, the descendant, was able to repair the ancestral defeat, who brought forth the Saviour of our race by a husbandless birth, and moulded His body. It was needful that she who had formed herself beautifully with spiritual comeliness should appear as a chosen bride, fitting for the heavenly Bridegroom. Is was needful that she who with her virtuous ways, as with stars, had likened herself to the heavens, should be revealed to all the faithful as giving rise to the sun of righteousness. It was needful that she who had dyed herself once with the dye of her virginal blood should serve as the purple of the universal Emperor. Oh, what a miracle! Whom the entire creation cannot contain, the Virgin's belly bears without being straitened. Whom the Cherubim do not dare to behold, the Virgin carries in her arms of clay. From the barren and fruitless womb comes forth the holy mountain, from which has been cut without hands[47] a precious cornerstone,[48] Christ our God, who has crushed the temples of the demons and the palaces of Hell together with their domination. The living and heavenly oven is being forged on earth, wherein the Creator of our clay, having baked the first-fruits with a divine fire and burnt up the crop of tares, makes unto Himself a bread of wholly pure flour.[49] But what is one to say, what would one not

---

[47] Dan. 2. 45.
[48] Is. 28. 16; 1 Peter 2. 6; Eph. 2. 20.
[49] Cf. Rom. 11. 16; Num. 15. 19–21.

experience, sailing over the high sea of the Virgin's gifts and achievements? One fears and rejoices, one is calm and excited, one is hushed again and cries out, one cowers and expands, sometimes drawn by fear, sometimes by love.

11. Having now given myself to the love rather than to the fear, I would gladly, as you know, come forward to you flowing with an abundant, even if useless,[50] flow of speech, enabled by the Virgin's miracles to form lakes and flood over, and especially on seeing that you eagerly open your ears, while applying and consecrating your mind to the praise of the Ever-Virgin—that is, had I been at all initiated in the Virgin's mysteries. But already time urges me on to other matters, to another *manifestation of* honour for the Virgin—I mean, to begin the mystical and bloodless sacrifice (since the recollection of the Son's willing sufferings is an honour to the mother), which claims our attention, and over which it is high time to officiate.

12. But, O Virgin and Mother of the Word, my mercy-seat and refuge, who hast been strangely produced of a barren woman, and stranger still, hast brought forth for us fruit, the crop of life, do thou plead and mediate before thy Son, our God, and prove the singers of thy praises, after they have wiped off[51] all filth and pollution, worthy of the heavenly bridechamber, to be eternally illuminated by the triple light of the supernal Trinity, and enjoying its marvellous and unspeakable sight, in Jesus Christ our Lord, to whom be all glory and power, for ever and ever. Amen.

[50] Read εἰ καὶ ἀχρήστῳ with A and B: καὶ εἰ καὶ ἀχρήστῳ Vat. Reg. 15 Chalc. 1, Monac. 443: καὶ ἀχρήστῳ Ar.
[51] ἀποσμηξαμένους codd: ἀποσμηξαμένη Ar.

NOTE ON HOMILY X

The present Homily, which has been known since its first publication by Peter Lambeck in 1655, is generally considered to have been preached at the inauguration, on May 1st, 880,[1] of the Nea Ekklesia, or New Church, built by the Emperor Basil I in the Great Palace of Constantinople. On this assumption, the Homily has been widely used by art-historians and archaeologists.[2] In fact, however, this Homily was delivered at the inauguration by the Emperor Michael III of the palatine church of Our Lady of the Pharos, probably in the year 864. As the arguments in favour of the latter interpretation have been stated elsewhere,[3] it will be sufficient to summarize them here.

The reason why this Homily came to be connected with the Nea Ekklesia is because in Lambeck's *editio princeps* and in later reprints, the Homily appeared under the title: Φωτίου πατριάρχου Κωνσταντινουπόλεως ἔκφρασις τῆς ἐν τοῖς βασιλείοις νέας ἐκκλησίας τῆς ὑπεραγίας θεοτόκου, ὑπὸ Βασιλείου τοῦ Μακεδόνος οἰκοδομηθείσης, to wit, "Description by Photius, Patriarch of Constantinople, of the New Church of the Most-Holy Theotokos, built in the Palace by Basil the Macedonian." As has been said above (p. 32), the MS used by Lambeck appears to have been the Neapol. gr. III. A.A.6 in which, however, the title is completely different (see p. 184, n. 1). One may conclude, therefore, that it was Lambeck himself who composed the title of his edition, possibly on the strength of the

---

[1] For the date, see A. Vogt, *Basile I*^{er}, Paris, 1908, p. 398, n. 4. Most authorities, however, place the event in 881 on the basis of the valueless chronology of Pseudo-Symeon (*Scriptores post Theophanem*, p. 692).

[2] J. Labarte, *Le Grand Palais de Constantinople et ses abords*, Paris, 1861, pp. 88–90; J. P. Richter, *Quellen der Byzantinischen Kunstgeschichte*, Vienna, 1897, pp. 356–57; Kondakov, Византійскія церкви и памятники Константинополя, Odessa, 1886, pp. 61–63; Ebersolt, *Le Grand Palais de Constantinople*, Paris, 1910, pp. 130–32, and many others.

[3] R. J. H. Jenkins and C. A. Mango, "The Date and Significance of the Tenth Homily of Photius," *Dumbarton Oaks Papers*, 9–10 (1956), pp. 125–140.

statement in Pseudo-Symeon's chronicle[4] that Photius officiated at the inauguration of the Nea Ekklesia.

It will be noticed that in the four extant MSS in which this Homily appears, the title is entirely different: "Sermon delivered in the form of a description of the renowned church in the Palace." When we proceed to examine the contents of the Homily, the following facts appear:

1) The church was dedicated to the Mother of God.

2) The government of the day consisted of one emperor and a newly-appointed Caesar. The Emperor had won a series of brilliant victories, had received tributaries, had rebuilt and restored a number of cities. As for the Caesar, he is invited to join in the general rejoicing because he had attained his high office not by human machinations, but by God's decree. That there were no other imperial personages at the time is made clear by the statement: "For it is through you twain (διὰ γὰρ τῆς ὑμετέρας δυάδος) that the Trinity ... steers wisely and governs Her subjects" (p. 189).

These facts are inapplicable to the reign of Basil I in general, and to the Nea Ekklesia in particular. In the first place, the Nea Ekklesia was not dedicated to the Virgin alone, but, on the authoritative evidence of the *Vita Basilii*, to Christ, the archangels Michael and Gabriel, Elijah, the Virgin and St. Nicholas.[5] Almost from the very beginning, however, it came to be known as the church of the Archangels,[6] and later as that of St. Michael.[7] Had Homily no. X been preached at the inauguration of the Nea, Photius could not have omitted mentioning the multiple dedication of the church, especially in view of Basil's particular devotion to Gabriel and the prophet Elijah.[8]

Even more telling is the discrepancy regarding the imperial persons. We know that Basil I conferred the title of emperor on

---

[4] P. 692.

[5] *Script. post Theoph.*, pp. 319, 325; cf. Credenus, II, p. 233.

[6] Typicon of the Great Church (end of the 9th century) in Dmitrievskij, Описаніе литургическихъ рукописей, I, p. 150; *Vita Theophanus*, ed. Kurtz (*Zwei griechische Texte über die hl. Theophano*, St. Petersburg, 1898), p. 13.

[7] Luitprand, *Antapodosis*, I. 10, and most later authors and pilgrims.

[8] Thus, in the Paris. gr. 510, f. C^v Basil is pictured receiving the imperial insignia from Gabriel and Elijah. Omont, *Miniatures des plus anciens manuscrits grecs de la B. N.*, Paris, 1929, pl. XIX and p. 13.

NOTE ON HOMILY X

three of his sons. His eldest son Constantine died most probably on the 3rd of September, 879.[9] Leo was crowned emperor on the 6th of January, 870,[10] while Alexander was crowned certainly before November, 879[11] and probably before August of that year.[12] Thus, from 870 until Basil's death there were never fewer than three emperors reigning simultaneously. It is impossible to assume that Photius, had Homily no. X been delivered at the inauguration of the Nea, would have, a) excluded Alexander in such definite terms, and, b) described Leo as Caesar. The rank of Caesar, which must have had unpleasant associations to Basil, could not have been confused with that of emperor, be it even junior emperor. Besides, if Photius was addressing Leo, Basil's eldest surviving son and heir,[13] how could he have congratulated him on attaining office not by human machinations but by God's decree?

It must therefore be concluded that the emperor and the Caesar are Michael III and his uncle, the Caesar Bardas. Once this is granted, everything becomes clear. Bardas was created Caesar on April 12, 864.[14] In the previous year Michael had won two brilliant victories against the Eastern Saracens,[15] while in the spring of 864 Bulgaria was humbled without fighting.[16] In 858 and 859 Michael rebuilt and fortified the cities of Ancyra and Nicaea.[17] Thus all the

[9] See F. Halkin, "Trois dates historiques précisées grâce au Synaxaire," *Byzantion*, XXIV (1954), pp. 14–17.

[10] Scholium of Anastasius Bibliothecarius in Mansi XVI, col. 143, corroborated by the fact that Leo is first mentioned in the 9th session of the anti-Photian Council (Feb., 870), while he is not mentioned in the 8th (Nov., 869): Mansi XVI, cols. 381, 389.

[11] Since he is mentioned in the acts of the Photian Council in Nov., 879 (Mansi XVII, col. 393 B and ff.).

[12] The letter of Pope John VIII to the Byzantine Emperor, dated August 879, is addressed to Basil, Constantine and Alexander (MGH, *Epist.*, VII[1912], p.167). The Greek version of this letter substitutes Leo's name for Constantine's.

[13] It is fairly certain that Leo was the legitimate son of Basil I. See Adontz, "La portée historique de l'oraison funèbre de Basile I," *Byzantion*, VIII (1933), pp. 501–13; A. Vogt, "La jeunesse de Léon le Sage," *Revue historique*, 174 (1934), pp. 389–428.

[14] See Stein in *Mélanges Bidez* (*Annuaire de l'Inst. de philol. et d'hist. orient.*, II, 1934), p. 899, n. 2.

[15] Cf. Vasiliev, *Byzance et les Arabes*, I, Brussels, 1935, pp. 251–56.

[16] Cf. Vaillant and Lascaris in *Rev. des ét. slaves*, XIII (1933), pp. 13–14.

[17] Cf. Grégoire in *Byzantion*, V (1929–30), p. 328; Vasiliev, *op. cit.*, p. 236. For the inscriptions of Nicaea, see A. M. Schneider, *Die Stadtmauer von Iznik*, Berlin, 1938 (*Istanbuler Forschungen*, 9), pp. 51–52. On the rebuilding of Selymbria (before 856), cf. *CIG*, no. 8683.

encomiastic statements contained in our Homily have a precise contemporary relevance. It may be noted by way of contrast that the year 880 appeared under particularly gloomy auspices: in May 878 Syracuse had been captured by the Arabs, while in September 879 Basil's eldest son Constantine died. The emperor went into mourning and did not even appear at the Council of November 879—March 880 until the two closing sessions.[18]

Thus the date of our Homily falls after April 12, 864 and certainly before April 21, 866, when Bardas was murdered.[19] The reference to Bardas' undertaking his high office (p. 189) points, however, to a date closer to the former rather than to the latter *terminus*. Moreover, since the conversion of the heathen was a regular concomitant of a Byzantine encomium,[20] and since Photius does not allude to the conversion of King Boris of Bulgaria, which took place in 864,[21] it may be argued with some cogency that the sermon must be earlier than the end of that year.

It remains to identify the renowned church of the Theotokos which forms the subject of our Homily. In the Great Palace of Constantinople there were several churches and chapels dedicated to the Mother of God, among which the most famous was that of the Pharos, situated in the closest proximity to the throne room and the imperial apartments,[22] and considered to be the *capella palatina* more specifically than any other shrine in the palace. That this is the church in question is confirmed by a brief entry in the chronicles derived from Symeon Logothete.[23] They tell us that

---

[18] As conjectured by Dvornik, *The Photian Schism*, pp. 194–95. Cf. Halkin, *loc. cit.*

[19] *Script. post Theoph.*, p. 206.

[20] Cf. *Vita Basilii*, cap. 95–97 (pp. 341–344), on which see Jenkins, "The Classical Background of the *Scriptores post Theophanem*," *Dumbarton Oaks Papers*, 8 (1954), pp. 29–30.

[21] Vaillant and Lascaris, *op. cit.*, pp. 5–15.

[22] On the church, see Ebersolt, *Le Grand Palais de Constantinople*, Paris, 1910, pp. 104–109; Janin, *La géographie ecclésiastique de l'Empire byzantin*, I 3, Paris 1953, pp. 241–45.

[23] Theodosius Melitenus, ed. Tafel (*Monumenta saecularia*, III cl. 1, Munich, 1859), p. 174; Leo Grammaticus (Bonn ed.), pp. 248–49; Continuator of Georgius Hamartolus, ed. Muralt, St. Petersburg, 1859, p. 746; *id.* after Cod. Vat. 153 in Istrin, Хроника Георгия Амартола, II, Petrograd, 1922, p. 15; *Script. post Teoph.*, pp. 834–35; Pseudo-Symeon, *ibid.*, p. 681; Slavonic version of Georg. Hamart., Istrin, *op. cit.*, I (1920), p. 516. Ebersolt (*Le Grand*

NOTE ON HOMILY X

Michael exhumed the remains of the iconoclast Emperor Constantine V, whose green marble sarcophagus he ordered to be sawn up and made into parapets for the church of the Pharos *which he had built* (ὑπ' αὐτοῦ κτισθέντι). Actually, "rebuilt" would have been a more precise term than "built," since the church of the Pharos was already in existence in the year 769.[24] That this valuable piece of information has come down to us is in itself a happy accident. There can be no doubt that Michael's activity in the building and redecoration of churches, like so many of this Emperor's other achievements, has been deliberately suppressed by the historians of the Macedonian dynasty. Had it not been for the sawing-up of the iconoclast emperor's sarcophagus and the public profanation of his bones—an anecdote intended to illustrate Michael's eccentricity—we probably would not have heard about the re-building of the Pharos church.

The present Homily is particularly valuable for the desription it provides of the palatine church. From other sources we know that the church was a small one,[25] that it had a narthex[26] which communicated with the nave by means of "royal doors,"[27] a right-hand side or aisle,[28] and a *diakonikon* on the south side of the apse[29] (consequently a *prothesis* on the north side). We also know that the front door leading from the atrium to the narthex was perforated and made of silver,[30] and that the south wall of the church had glass windows set in a wooden lattice.[31] We can now supplement these data from our Homily. Photius mentions the atrium, the marble revetment of the façade (πρόσοψις), the intricate tessellated pavement, the polychrome marble which covered the interior walls, and

---

Palais, p. 104) misunderstood this passage to mean that the church had been built by Constantine V.

[24] Theophanes, ed. De Boor, p. 444.
[25] Anthony of Novgorod, ed. Loparev, Правосл. Палест. Сборникъ, XVII 3, St. Petersburg, 1899, p. 19.
[26] *De Ceremoniis*, pp. 119, 137, 178 (Bonn).
[27] *Ibid.*, p. 120.
[28] *Narratio de imagine Edessena*, § 64 in Dobschütz, *Christusbilder* (*Texte u. Untersuchungen*, N. F. III, 1899), p. 85**.
[29] Nicholas Mesarites in A. Heisenberg, *Die Palastrevolution des Johannes Komnenos*, Progr. d. K. alten Gymnasiums zu Würzburg, 1907, pp. 35–36.
[30] *Ibid.*, p. 29.
[31] *Ibid.*, p. 34.

the dome which seems to have been ribbed.[32] By combining these data we obtain a church of the transitional ninth-century style, of which St. Clement at Ancyra is either a representative or a precursor.[33] It is, of course, only natural that a ninth-century church should have been domed and conformed to that general type; nevertheless, the evidence of our Homily is important, as the Pharos church has sometimes been represented as a basilica owing, no doubt, to the uncertainty concerning its date.

Photius further describes the profusion of gold and silver which were lavished on mosaic tesserae, on plaques, capitals, cornices (περιζώματα) and chains. The holy table was made of a composition more valuable than gold, probably referring to incrustations of precious stones and to enamels. The ciborium, surmounted as usual by a conical roof, as well as the columned chancel-screen were covered with silver. Particularly interesting is the description of the mosaics. In the centre of the dome was a "man-like" image of Christ, who seemed to oversee the orderly government of the world. The iconographic type of the Christ is not specified, but it may be suspected that it was a full seated figure rather than the traditional bust of later time. In Constantinople itself the first authentic example of a bust-Pantocrator in the dome of a church is at the church of Stylianos Zaoutzes (end of the ninth century), described in a sermon by Leo VI.[34] Around the figure of Christ, says Photius, in the "concave segments" of the dome, was a throng of angels escorting the Lord. In the apse was a standing Virgin with arms raised (*orans*), as in the apse of St. Sophia at Kiev, or that of Nea Moni on Chios. The rest of the church was decorated with individual images of martyrs, apostles, prophets and patriarchs, among whom David and Jacob are mentioned by name, and appear to have been carrying scrolls inscribed with their respective utterances (Ps. 83. 2–3; Gen. 28. 17).

[32] See below, p. 188.
[33] For a description of this church, see G. de Jerphanion, *Mélanges d'archéologie anatolienne* (Mélanges de l'Université Saint-Joseph, XIII), Beirut, 1928, pp. 113–143 and pls. LXII–LXXX). For the date (7th–9th cent.), see E. Weigand in *BZ*, XXXII (1932), p. 372.
[34] Akakios, Λέοντος τοῦ Σοφοῦ πανηγυρικοὶ λόγοι, Athens, 1868, p. 275; cf. A. Frolow in *Études byzantines*, III (1946), p. 60.

NOTE ON HOMILY X

The mosaic decoration of the church consisted therefore of individual figures arranged in a hierarchical order, to the exclusion of Gospel scenes. Such a scheme of decoration is typical for the period immediately following the re-establishment of Orthodoxy. We find it in the Chrysotriklinos, adorned with pictures between 856 and 867,[35] in St. Sophia, the decoration of which was certainly conceived under Michael III, although not under way until 867,[36] and, towards the end of the century, in the monastery of Kauleas.[37] An instance of a Gospel cycle is found early in the reign of Basil I,[38] and from that time onwards it becomes the prevailing formula. We have no information whatsoever on the mosaics of the Nea Ekklesia, and it may now be doubted that they were limited to individual figures.

It is likely that the mosaics described by Photius were replaced or supplemented by a Gospel cycle at a later date. Nicholas Mesarites, who was sacristan of the church *ca.* 1200, may be referring to such a cycle in a passage which is, however, highly ambiguous.[39] If he is in fact referring to mural decoration, it was one of considerable complexity, including scenes such as the Washing of the Feet, the Last Supper, the Transfiguration, Christ before Pilate, St. Peter submerged, the miracles, Christ annointed by Mary Magdalen, etc. This cycle (if such it was) could well have been added under the Comnenian dynasty. It was precisely at that time, towards the middle of the twelfth century, that the Pharos church by a process of gradual accumulation became the foremost repository of relics pertaining to Christ.[40]

---

[35] See S. Der Nersessian in *Actes du VIe Congrès intern. d'ét. byzantines*, II, Paris, 1951, pp. 321–330.
[36] See below, p. 283.
[37] Akakios, *op. cit.*, pp. 245–46; Frolow, *op. cit.*, p. 70.
[38] In the church of the Virgin of the Source (τῆς πηγῆς), decorated before the death of Basil's son Constantine (*Anthol. Palat.*, I. 109–117).
[39] *Op. cit.*, pp. 31–32. Ebersolt (*Le Grand Palais*, pp. 108–9) takes the existence of a mosaic cycle as an established fact.
[40] On the relics, see Janin, *op. cit.*, p. 244; Ebersolt, *Sanctuaires de Byzance*, Paris, 1921, pp. 23–29.

HOMILIES OF PHOTIUS

X

Ar II 428 Homily of the Same Most-Blessed Photius, Archbishop[1] of Constantinople, Delivered in the Form of a Description of the Renowned Church in the Palace

1. Gay is the gathering I see today, and such as no human effort could have assembled without divine inspiration. Wherefore I accept the sweet gifts of Grace and, joining Christ's flock as it thrives and rejoices, I exult therein, knowing full well that the pleasure and gladness of the festival are not confined to us alone, but that its holiness is carried up to our common Lord Himself. For the splendour of a festival, inasmuch as it is the ornament and pride Ar II 429 of the celebrants, so does it make manifest the tokens of the Lord's love. But when it does not celebrate a commemoration which is carried out in the usual yearly fashion, but introduces a fresh and newly-come honour to God, would it not appear all the more to light up God's love *for us*, and further enhance the decorousness and splendour of the celebrants? But what is this so great a concourse and gathering of people? What is the celebration? What has called together and stirred up all of us? Do you wish me to say it? Or would it be better to let him tell and explain the object of this celebration, who is both its instigator and its wise architect? For he is also able to describe the subject in words who, having preconceived in his soul the forms of these things, has in his great wisdom created on earth this inimitable work.

2. Tell us then, most Christ-loving and pious of emperors, who both surpassest all thy predecessors and honourest them splendidly by sharing in the office, tell an audience which, as thou seest, is eager to listen, for what reason thou hast called us together. Show in words what thou hast already shown in deeds. Hast thou again won victories and trophies over the barbarians, with which time and time again thou hast graciously greeted us, and is this why thou hast convoked us, to gladden us and at the same time to send up in common our universal thanks to Him Who has granted the victory? Or, having received new tributaries and humbled the bold and inso-

---

[1] ἀρχιεπισκόπου A, B, Lig: πατριάρχου Ar. Neapol. gr. III.A.A.6 has Φωτίου πατριάρχου Κωνσταντινουπόλεως ἔκφρασις τοῦ ἐν τοῖς βασιλείοις περιωνύμου ναοῦ.

HOMILY X. INAUGURATION OF A CHURCH

lent mind of the foreigner,[2] *dost thou wish* to ascribe with pious intent all thy achievements to God's strong hand? Or hast thou re-erected subject cities which have long lain low, and built others from the foundations, and repeopled others, and consolidated the frontiers through *the settlement of* towns?[3] Or is it because thou art rich[4] and makest thy subjects prosperous? Instruct us who are looking up to thee as to the all-embracing eye of the universe, for which of these reasons thou hast called us together. Or dost thou keep silent out of modesty, not wishing thyself to recount to us thy achievements, into which praise must of necessity be woven, and designatest me to sound in words, under the inspiration of thy deeds, the cause of this gathering?

3. It is a different celebration today, friends, and a different mystery. A Virgin's temple is being inaugurated on earth,[5] a worthy house for the Mother of God, as much as any in this world. A Virgin's temple is being inaugurated today on earth,[6] a truly praiseworthy work of imperial magnificence, a church in the midst of the very palace, rising up as a second palace, divine and venerable, which makes the *first* palace appear, when compared and likened to it, as a private house, or rather, by its own fairness and inherent splendour, illumines and beautifies it also, and adds more dignity to its former ornament. On beholding it thou mightest say that it is not the work of human hands, but that a divine power superior to ours has formed its beauty.

4. The atrium of the church is splendidly fashioned: for slabs of white marble, gleaming bright and cheerful, occupy the whole façade,[7] and by their evenness and smoothness and close fitting

---

[2] Read ὑψηλὸν καὶ γαῦρον ἀλλόφυλον φρόνημα with A and B. Neapol. gr. III.A.A.6 and Lambeck have καὶ after γαῦρον, which likewise appears in Ar.

[3] Or perhaps, "made the boundaries secure for the towns." The Greek text, as given by all the MSS, is ταῖς πολιτείαις πυκνώσας τὰ ὅρια [τῆς πολιτείας Ar].

[4] Read πλουτῶν with the MSS: πλουτίζων Ar.

[5] The MSS read ἐπὶ γῆς ἐγκαινιζόμενος [ἐπὶ γῆς ἐγκαινίζεται σήμερον Combefis, Ar].

[6] The words ἐπὶ γῆς are omitted by B and Ar.

[7] πρόσοψις in the Greek. The west façade of St. Sophia likewise had a revetment of white Proconnesian marble. Ebersolt (*Le grand palais de Constantinople*, pp. 131–32) is surely wrong in thinking that Photius is referring to the marble pavement of the atrium.

they conceal the setting of one to another and the juncture of their edges, so that they suggest to the beholder's imagination the continuousness of a single *piece of* stone with, as it were, straight lines ruled on it—a new miracle and a joy to see. Wherefore, arresting and turning towards themselves the spectator's gaze, they make him unwilling to move further in; but taking his fill of the fair spectacle in the very atrium, and fixing his eyes on the sight before Ar II 432 him, the visitor stands as if rooted *to the ground* with wonder. Legends proclaim the lyre of Thracian Orpheus,[8] whose notes stirred inanimate things. If it were our privilege also to erect truth into legends and make it awe-inspiring, one might say that visitors to the atrium were turned with wonder into the form of trees: so firmly is one held having but seen it once.

5. But when with difficulty one has torn oneself away from there and looked into the church itself, with what joy and trepidation and astonishment is one filled! It is as if one had entered heaven itself with no one barring the way from any side, and was illuminated by the beauty in all forms shining all around like so many stars, so is one utterly amazed. Thenceforth it seems that everything is in ecstatic motion, and the church itself is circling round. For the spectator, through his whirling about in all directions and being constantly astir, which he is forced to experience by the variegated spectacle on all sides, imagines that his personal own is transferred to the object.

Ar II 433 Gold and silver cover the greater part of the church, the one smeared on tesserae, the other cut out and fashioned into plaques, or otherwise applied to other parts. Over here are capitals adorned *with gold*, over there are golden cornices. Elsewhere gold is twined into chains, but more wonderful than gold is the composition of the holy table. The little doors and columns of the sanctuary together with the peristyle[9] are covered with silver; so also is the

---

[8] The MSS read Ὀρφεῖ μὲν οἱ μῦθοι τῷ Θρᾳκὶ κιθάραν κρούουσι, which is not very satisfactory [κροτοῦντες διδόασι Ar]. Lambeck by mistake read κούουσι, which Combefis emended to κροτοῦσι. In view, however, of the dat. Ὀρφεῖ, one might suggest ποιοῦσι. Cf. Greg. Naz., *Or.* XXXIX. 5 (PG 36, col. 340 B): οὐδὲ Ὀρφέως τελεταὶ καὶ μυστήρια, ὃν τοσοῦτον Ἕλληνες ἐπὶ σοφίᾳ ἐθαύμασαν, ὥστε καὶ λύραν αὐτῷ ποιοῦσι, πάντα τοῖς κρούμασιν ἕλκουσαν.

[9] Referring to the chancel-screen with its peristyle of little columns.

HOMILY X. INAUGURATION OF A CHURCH

conical roof set over the holy table with the little pillars and canopy that support it.[10] The rest of the church, as much of it as gold has not overspread or silver covered, is adorned with many-hued marble, a surpassingly fair work. The pavement, which has been fashioned into the forms of animals and other shapes by means of variegated tesserae, exhibits the marvellous skill of the craftsman, so that the famous Pheidias and Parrhasius and Praxiteles and Zeuxis are proved in truth to have been mere children in their art and makers of figments. Democritus would have said, I think, on seeing the minute work of the pavement and taking it as a piece of evidence, that his atoms were close to being discovered here actually impinging on the sight.[11] So full of wonder is everything. In one respect only do I consider the architect of the church to have erred, namely that having gathered into one and the same spot all kinds of beauty, he does not allow the spectator to enjoy the sight in its purity, since the latter is carried and pulled away from one thing by another, and is unable to satiate himself with the spectacle as much as he may desire.

Ar II 434

6. But something has escaped me, although it should have been said first (for the wonder of the church does not permit the orator to do his own task fairly even in words), so it shall be said now. On the very ceiling is painted in coloured mosaic cubes a man-like figure bearing the traits of Christ. Thou mightest say He is overseeing the earth, and devising its orderly arrangement and govern-

---

[10] The text presents a slight difficulty. All the MSS read καὶ αὐτὸς ὁ κωνοειδὴς καὶ τῇ θείᾳ τραπέζῃ ἐπικείμενος σὺν τοῖς ὑπερείδουσι στυλίσκοις ὑπωρόφοις ὄροφος. Combefis added καὶ after στυλίσκοις. So also Banduri who, however, by mistake omits ὄροφος. Ar has αὐτὸν τὸν κωνοειδῆ ... ἐπικείμενον ... ὄροφον. If ὑπωρόφοις is an adj. agreeing with στυλίσκοις (i. e. "the columns under the roof"), then it should be preceded by τοῖς. If, on the other hand, ὑπωρόφοις is used as a subst. (? = "canopy"; cf. Diod. Sic. XVIII. 26. 5), then the addition of καὶ is necessary.

[11] The text is rather awkward. The MSS give Δημόκριτος εἶπεν ἄν ... μὴ ἂν πόρρω εἶναι τῷ [τὸ Neapol. gr. III.A.A.6] μὴ οὐχὶ καὶ τὰς ἀτόμους αὐτοῦ καὶ ὑπ' ὄψιν πιπτούσας ἀνευρῆσθαι. The pleonasm τὸ [rather than τῷ] μὴ οὐχὶ is certainly strange, but cf. Homily XI, p. 208, n. 70 (= Ar II. 465[1-3]): οὕτως οὐκ ἔστι τοῖς ἐπηρεάζουσι τὴν ἀνάστασιν ἐφ' ᾧ τῶν ἐλέγχων τὸ ἀναπόδραστον διαδράσαντες, τὸ μὴ οὐχὶ λυσσᾶν αὐτούς ... τὴν ἀναχώρησιν ἕξουσιν. In place of τὸ μὴ οὐχὶ Ar makes the ingenious correction τὸ μὴ ὄν. Cf. Aristotle *Metaph.*, 985b on the technical use of τὸ μὴ ὄν in the philosophy of Democritus to denote the void (which in this case would presumably refer to the interstices between the mosaic cubes).

ment,[12] so accurately has the painter been inspired to represent, though only in forms and in colours, the Creator's care for us. In the concave segments next to the summit of the hemisphere[13] a throng of angels is pictured escorting our common Lord. The apse which rises over the sanctuary glistens with the image of the Virgin, stretching out her stainless arms on our behalf and winning for the emperor safety and exploits against the foes. A choir of apostles and martyrs, yea, of prophets, too, and patriarchs fill and beautify the whole church with their images. Of these one,[14] though silent, cries out his sayings of yore, "How amiable are thy tabernacles, O Lord of hosts! My soul longeth, yea, even fainteth in the courts of the Lord";[15] another,[16] "How wonderful is this place; this is none other but the house of God";[17] another, though he is not of our company and is not represented here,[18] might well exclaim, prophesying these our things even against his will, "How goodly are thy houses, O Jacob, and thy tabernacles, O Israel! As the gardens are they by the river's side, and as the tents which the Lord hath planted,"[19] and not man.[20]

In olden days a tabernacle was, upon divine command, built by Moses, beholder of God, to offer up sacrifice to God and expiate his people's transgressions; and later by King Solomon the temple of Jerusalem, a fair work which eclipsed all the temples before it in beauty, size and magnificence. But as a shadow and a figure are below truth and reality, so are those *inferior* to the temple which has now been built by our faithful and great Emperor,[21] not only because this one is of Grace and the Spirit, while those were of the Law and the Letter, but also because in point of beauty and execution and ingenuity they take second place.

[12] A similar passage in Leo VI, *Orat.*, XXVIII, ed. Akakios, p. 245. Cf. Frolow, "Deux églises byzantines," p. 61.
[13] τμήμασιν ἐγκοίλοις, the reading of all the extant MSS, is to be preferred to τμήμασιν ἐγκύκλοις given by Lambeck.
[14] David.
[15] Ps. 83. 2–3.
[16] Jacob.
[17] Gen. 28. 17.
[18] Balaam who, of course, was not pictured. Cf. above, p. 139 and n. 3.
[19] Num. 24. 5–6.
[20] ἄνθρωπος codd: ἄνθρωποι Ar.
[21] The title πιστὸς καὶ μέγας βασιλεύς was particularly affected by Michael III, and is found on his coins. Cf. Grégoire in *Byzantion*, IV (1927–28), pp. 441–42.

HOMILY X. INAUGURATION OF A CHURCH

7. But how can one attempt in so short a time to describe in words the wonders of this renowned church, when even sight itself, though it surpasses the other senses in alacrity, is proved incapable after a length of time of comprehending them in any way? Yet, even if my speech has fallen below the mark, I am not any the less content than if it had risen to the level[22] of an adequate description. For my purpose was not to make an exhibition of eloquence, but to show that the church is most excellent and beautiful and that it defeats the canons of an *ekphrasis*.[23]

8. But let the course of my speech steer round and turn towards thee,[24] the instigator of this gathering. Rejoice, therefore, among emperors most blest and beloved of God, and be thou renewed in thy bodily and mental prime that bears fruit in good works. As thou celebratest the inauguration both of the renowned church and the works of thy wisdom and thy hand, do thou bend *thy bow* and prosper and rule, because of truth and meekness and righteousness;[25] for thou art guided, as is plain to see, and shalt be guided by the right hand of the Most High, who formed thee and anointed thee from the cradle itself to be king over His own peculiar people. Rejoice with him and be with him renewed thou also, pride of all Caesars whom the sun has looked upon, who surpassest thy predecessors in wisdom and intelligence, and in the fact that thou hast received this high office by divine ordinance and not through ambition nor the canvassing of men. Join, therefore, in rejoicing and renewing thy spirits with him who has taken thee as partner and sharer of the imperial dignity for the common salvation of the subjects and as befits *thy* loyalty and most sincere love for him. For it is through you twain that the Trinity, piously worshipped and revered, while spreading and conveying to all Her providence, steers wisely and governs Her subjects.

Rejoice you also, fathers of the senate, grave and venerable old

---

[22] Read τὸ μέτρον with the MSS: τὸ μέτριον Ar.

[23] An *ekphrasis* was a rhetorical description of a work of art, either in prose or in verse, often intended as a declamatory piece for a festive occasion. On this *genre*, see esp. P. Friedländer, *Johannes von Gaza und Paulus Silentiarius*, Leipzig–Berlin, 1912, pp. 83–103.

[24] Read ἀλλά μοι [ἀλλά γε Lig and Ar] πρὸς σὲ ὁ τοῦ λόγου δρόμος ... ἐπιστρεφόμενος ἰθυνέσθω [ἐπιστρέφεται Lig; ἐπιστρεφόμενος ἰθύνεται Ar].

[25] Ps. 44. 5.

men, as you renew your spirits together with the faithful and great Emperor and the worshipful Caesar, and join in celebrating the dedication of this renowned church. The sacerdotal and hierarchal body that is present is also rejoicing and joining in the happiness, for they regard the consecration of the church as their own glory and pride. Rejoice and join the choir you also, the rest of the pious congregation, seeing a second heaven, the Virgin's church, as it is dedicated on earth today. May we all enjoy her intercession and that blessed and endless happiness and joy in Jesus Christ our Lord, to Whom be praise and dominion now and for ever and ever. Amen.

NOTE ON HOMILIES XI AND XII

The following two sermons, of which the latter is found only in Cod. Athen. 2756, were both delivered on Holy Saturday, and expound the theme of Christ's death and burial. Aristarches, who was acquainted with only no. XI, postulated the existence of another homily on the same subject, which he pieced together out of excerpts taken from the *Amphilochia*, the *Letters*, and the *catena* on St. Luke.[1] In so doing, he was guided by two considerations: a) that Combefis had found in Chancellor Séguier's library (Aristarches mistakenly says it was Mazarin's) an *oratio Photii in dominicam sepulturam*, which he refrained from publishing because its beginning was missing; b) that the Photian scholia on Luke in the Vat. gr. 759, while they reproduce in part passages from Homily XI, contain some additional extracts not found in that Homily. These arguments are of no value, since, a) the "Seguieranus codex" mentioned by Combefis (Coislin 107) contains the truncated text of Homily XI;[2] and, b) the additional passages in the *catena* are drawn from the *Amphilochia* and the *Letters*.[3]

In Homily XI the story of the burial is given in a very simple form. In the main, it follows Mt 27. 57–66, while drawing to a smaller extent on the other Gospels. Only two extraneous elements are introduced: Joseph's speech before Pilate, and his lament over the dead body. The interview with Pilate is given a prominent place in one version of the apocryphal Gospel of Nicodemus, where every clause of Joseph's long address begins with "Give me this

[1] II. 212–219.
[2] Cf. above, p. 30.
[3] The scholion, inc. μᾶλλον δὲ ῥήγνυται, des. ὑποσαλπίζον καὶ εὐαγγελιζόμενον (Mai, *Script. vet. nova coll.*, IX, p. 716 = PG 101, col. 1225) summarizes *Amphilochia*, quaest. 212, PG 101, cols. 965–68 = *Letters*, ed. Valettas, pp. 275–76; the scholion, inc. τῆς παναγίας καὶ ἀειπαρθένου Μαρίας, des. ἐτέμνετό τε καὶ κατεμερίζετο (Mai, IX, p. 652 = PG 101, col. 1224) = *Amphil.*, quaest. 176, PG 101, cols. 877–80; the passage, inc. ἦν ποτε κρύφιος φίλος, des. θεραπείας οὐκ ἠμέλησε (Mai, IX, pp. 716–17 = PG 101, col. 1225) = *Letters*, ed. Valettas, p. 444.

stranger."[4] Joseph's lamentations are, amongst others, described in a *troparion* which still forms part of the Greek service on Good Friday.[5] For the most part, Homily XI may be traced back to older sermons, that of Gregory of Antioch,[6] that of pseudo-Epiphanius,[7] that of John of Damascus.[8] The last one includes, with some striking similarities, the themes of both our nos. XI and XII, only in the reverse order. Thus, although there is little that is original in the following two Homilies, it may be at least worth pointing out that Photius chose to exclude from the story of the burial almost all the apocryphal details, even the increasingly popular lamentations of the Holy Virgin, which had been versified by Cosmas of Maiuma,[9] and are found, greatly elaborated, in the sermons of George of Nicomedia[10] and Symeon Metaphrastes.[11]

The references to contemporary events in the following two sermons are very slight. We may note in no. XI an appeal for clemency on the part of the rulers, and orderliness on the part of the subjects;[12] while in concluding no. XII, Photius prays that his flock should not fall either into heresy or into schism,[13] meaning presumably the Iconoclast and Ignatian parties respectively.

[4] I, Recension B, ch. XI, ed. Tischendorf, *Evangelia apocrypha*², Leipzig, 1876, pp. 312–13; cf. M. R. James, *The Apocryphal New Testament*, Oxford, 1924, p. 117.
[5] Papadopoulos-Kerameus, Ἀνάλεκτα Ἱεροσολυμιτικῆς σταχυολογίας, II, St. Petersburg, 1894, p. 160; *Triodion*, ed. Saliberos, Athens, n. d., p. 432 b. See also La Piana, *Le rappresentazioni sacre*, pp. 191 sq.
[6] PG 88, esp. cols. 1849–52.
[7] PG 43, esp. cols. 444–49.
[8] PG 96, cols. 601–644.
[9] PG 98, col. 488; *Triodion*, p. 446 b (Canon of Holy Saturday, ode 9).
[10] PG 100, col. 1488.
[11] PG 114, cols. 209 sq.
[12] P. 211 below.
[13] P. 219 below.

HOMILY XI. HOLY SATURDAY

XI

OF THE SAME MOST-BLESSED PHOTIUS, ARCHBISHOP[1] OF CONSTANTINOPLE, HOMILY[2] DELIVERED ON THE BURIAL OF THE HOLY BODY OF OUR LORD JESUS CHRIST, ON HOLY SATURDAY

1. From each work and deed of Christ, our Saviour, the magnitude of His love for us is apparent, and the graces of salvation are splendidly unfolded unto us; and as the abundant sweetness of joy is distilled into men's souls, it wipes away the bitter pollution of ancestral sin. The memory and topic of the passion and the burial is, however, an awful and inexpressible matter, but inasmuch as it is the end of the Incarnation, and anchors us,[3] so to speak, in the very harbour of re-creation, and sounds forth in clear trumpet tones the Creator's providence concerning us, so the feeling it arouses is neither simple nor unmixed, but it both overwhelms us and revives us with courage; it grieves and gladdens,[4] the former by the passion and the death, the latter by the destruction of the passions and the slaying of death—which things are marvellously wrought for our resurrection in a manner surpassing words.

It is pleasant indeed to see at the wedding the water being pressed[5] into wine from jars as from a bunch of grapes for the sake of the friends. It is pleasant *to see* the raging waves of the sea as they foam over the wreck[6] being calmed and soothed by a mere command, and—what is most strange—with curving back ferrying the sailors across; and the multitude, many thousands of them, fed in the wilderness with seven loaves, and once again with five, leaving behind food for many more,[7] the remnants of their banquet. Pleasant also it is to see the blind man given eyes, harmful streams of blood stemmed, lepers scraping off the flakes of their disease and

---

[1] ἀρχιεπισκόπου codd: πατριάρχου Ar.
[2] After the word ὁμιλία Ar has added δευτέρα.
[3] Read ἡμᾶς [ὑμᾶς Ar, probably a misprint].
[4] Read δίδωσι θαρρεῖν, καὶ ἀνιᾷ καὶ ἡδύνει with the MSS: δίδωσι θαρρεῖν τε καὶ ἀνιᾶν, καὶ ἡδύνειν Ar.
[5] Read ὥσπερ ἀπὸ βοτρύων τῶν ἀγγείων εἰς οἶνον τοῖς φίλοις ἀποθλιβόμενον [ἐκ τῶν ἀγγείων ... ὑποθλιβόμενον Ar]. Cf. Diod. Sic. III. 62. 7: τὸν ἐκ τοῦ βότρυος ἀποθλιβόμενον οἶνον.
[6] Cf. Jude 13.
[7] Read with the MSS καὶ τρεφόμενος ὄχλος [τρεφόμενον ὄχλον Ar] ... πολλαὶ χιλιάδες [πολλὰς χιλιάδας Ar] καὶ πολλοῖς τροφὴν ὑπολιποῦσαι [ὑπολειπούσας Ar].

having their blood cleansed, merely by virtue of a word and of the will, the lame man leaping up, demons routed, and *God's* creature delivered from those that troubled him. Pleasant also *to see* is Lazarus called up from the grave and rising on the fourth day, and the hymn of the branch-bearing children, perfected for the King of glory. Yet not so pleasant as a passion that brings in rich measure freedom from passions, as a death blooming with the beauty of immortality; not so pleasant as Hell despoiled, as death slain, as tombs emptied out, and the Lord through His own struggles winning victory over all. Indeed, for the Maintainer and Maker of the universe to have been hanged incarnate on the cross, to have been buried in the entrails of the earth, to have visited Hell and been numbered among the dead, is terrible even to hear, frightful even for angels to conceive, and, while this is being performed, it is unbearable to the whole creation, even to that which is inanimate. But in the same measure that this has left nothing to exceed it in wonder and terror, nay, even to be conceived by one's mind, so do mercy and Providence open out for us to an unutterable degree. The veil of the temple is rent, and the sun, charioteer of the day, is plunged into deep darkness, and the earth takes fright and quakes,[8] affected by the sadness of the passion. But also tombs become pregnant and bring forth the dead, and the palaces of Hell are emptied and abolished, despoiled by the Sufferer's victory, while the human race—this was the Lord's goal, for which He endured sufferings and death—is delivered from that bitter and ancient domination.

2. Who shall tell the mighty acts of the Lord? *Who* shall cause all his praises to be heard?[9] Speech leaps with eagerness and desires with youthful ardour to attempt the unfolding of the mystery, but reason cowers and sinks to the depths of the mind, checking the impulse to speak. The ears open their doors, but the voice, restrained by the consternation of the thoughts as by bolts,[10] reduces to perplexity both those who have been emboldened to speak and those who have chosen to listen. Who shall tell the mighty acts of the Lord? *Who* shall cause all His praises to be heard? Nails are

---

[8] Mt 27. 51; Lk 23. 45.
[9] Ps. 105. 2.
[10] Read κλήθροις with Coislin. 107: λύθροις AB: λύθρος Ar.

HOMILY XI. HOLY SATURDAY

piercing the Lord's hands, and they are tearing up, roots and all, Ar II 446
the offshoots of our wickedness which had become implanted in our
members, and by which human kind was laid waste and corrupted.
A crown of thorns is bound round His head, and that encircling and
painful collar[11] of the ancient curse is cast off our neck. His side is
transfixed with a spear, and the fount of our salvation opens up and
is constantly widened, as blood and water, the cleanser of the
universal transgression, well from the wound even after death.
Who shall tell the mighty acts of the Lord? *Who* shall cause all
His praises to be heard? A disgraceful death has delivered the world
from shame, and, receiving in His face the spittle of the Jews, He
who has generated the drops of dew,[12] and counts the drops of the
sea,[13] drains the flood of sin. Who shall tell the mighty acts
of the Lord? *Who* shall cause all His praises to be heard? The Lord Ar II 447
is covered with a tomb, but the Lord's providence for all things is
not shut in with it, nor does He make the sin of His insulters *an
occasion* for universal destruction. Nay, the Creator dwells in a
tomb, yet steers the universe in goodly order. For it was not to
wreak disaster that He willingly endured the cross, death, blows,
spitting and every torment, but in order to deliver humankind
from it. The Lord is covered with a tomb, and a throng of ungrateful
slaves have made the tomb secure[14] and are sitting round. They
are astounded even as they see the Creator dead; they are astounded
indeed, but they remain unconverted in their ingratitude; for the
hardening of the mind is a terrible thing in that it does not even
distinguish what is at one's feet and most easy from what is most
difficult and obscure. They are astounded, but they do not sing
glory, and though they guard Him like a king, these wretched men
insult Him like a criminal. They have made Him secure like a
treasure, and while seeing others drawing therefrom through faith
the riches of salvation, they themselves, oppressed by extreme
poverty, miserably end their life in the ruin of unbelief. They know
the resurrection, but are hiding it; for they have betrayed truth

---

[11] κλοιός, as printed by Ar, is surely right (so Coislin. 107 and Vat. 759);
τίτλος, the reading of A and B, is, however, retained by Pg and Šest.
[12] Job 38. 28.
[13] Cf. Sir. 18. 10.
[14] Mt 27. 66.

through avarice, and they have exchanged for falsehood what they have seen with their own eyes.

Ar II 448 3. Why dost thou mislead thyself with thy deceits, O Jew? Why dost thou quibble away thy salvation? Why dost thou arm thy hands against thyself, leaving unto thyself not a drop of mercy, as much as would have been accorded for thy deed? Seest thou not the earth and the stones trembling at thy daring action? While creation is in mourning and sadness over thy lawlessness, art thou not ashamed to be more insensible than inanimate things, and dost thou rejoice dancing to thine own perdition? Hast thou not found thine outrage against the Lord and His murder, which thou wast bold enough to celebrate as a festival and make into a red-letter day, a subject of constant dejection? Those things whereby thou hadst nourished hopes of broadening the borders of thy garments,[15] and multiplying thy miracles, and being loudly proclaimed "Rabbi" on earth, and being thickened and fattened, have they not turned out contrary to thy hopes? Where is now thy celebrated great temple? Has it not been overturned from its very foundations, surviving *only* as a legend and *an object of* tears for those more inclined to sympathy? And as for the famous metropolis of thy nation, does it not now lie a topic of tragic stories, as thy plight amounts not only to an "Iliad of woes,"[16] but shows the Ilian misfortunes to have been but a small

Ar II 449 part of thine own catastrophe? Where are thy public propitiatory sacrifices, and as for thy prophetic and divine inspiration, how has it vanished away from thee? Where is the fame of thy leaders and commanders themselves, which aforetime was most glorious among the aliens, but has now been reduced to the desolation of complete leaderlessness?[17] Hast thou *not* raged against the Word? But thy oracular breastplate[18] has changed its colour not to blood, but to

---

[15] Mt 23. 5.
[16] Cf. above, p. 100, n. 19.
[17] The above rendering is tentative. The text reads: ποῦ δ' αὐτῶν σοι τῶν ἀρχόντων καὶ ἡγουμένων τὸ κλέος, εἰς ἀλλοφύλους μὲν τότε παραυτίκα [παροτρυνόντων Ar], νῦν δ' εἰς παντελοῦς [so Coislin. 107: παντελοῦς corrected from παντελῇ A: παντελῇ B, Ar] ἀναρχίας καταστραφὲν [ἀναρχίαν, καταστροφὴν Ar] ἐξερήμωσιν. Instead of παραυτίκα a neuter participle agreeing with κλέος seems to be required.
[18] Ex. 28. 15 sq. A pun on λόγος and λόγιον (i.e. λογεῖον).

HOMILY XI. HOLY SATURDAY

black, as thy misfortune penetrated[19] to its very core, and it no longer lifts up to thee a bright countenance. Hast thou *not* insulted Him who was prophesied? But thou hast lost the Urim,[20] as thine oracular letters have been reduced to the muteness of meaningless strokes. Hast thou *not* risen up against the High Priest? But thou hast been driven away from the gift of priesthood. Hast thou *not* slaughtered the Lamb? But thy sanctuary has fallen in ruins and has been corrupted into an unholy shrine. Hast thou *not* laid hands on the sacred offering? But thine altars have crumbled away. Hast thou *not* put the Heir[21] to death? But thou hast been wiped off[22] the testament. Hast thou *not* stripped bare the Lawgiver? But thou hast been denuded of thy prophetic gifts, and hast been cast down from thy boastfulness of the Law, in which thou tookest pride: for the strength and might of the laws lie in the honour and reverence to the lawgiver. Hast thou *not* parted His garments?[23] But thou hast been stripped of those many ineffable wonders, thou hast no portion or lot in the promised land, thou hast been divided up among all the gentiles and barbarians, not prospering and multiplying, but diminished and distressed and subjected to mockery. What demon has goaded thee to this frenzy? Who has inflamed thee to so much envy? Who has filled thee with such foulness?[24] Verily thou hast been proved not only to be kicking against the pricks,[25] and dashing thy face against the rock,[26] and poking the fire with a knife,[27] and bringing down the moon (which is but a small part of creation) upon thyself,[28] as the jest from old story that has become a proverb for

Ar II 450

---

[19] ἀλλ' εἰς αὐτὸ βάθος τοῦ παθήματος διαδοθέντος codd: ἀλλ' εἰς αὐτὸ τὸ βάθος ... διαδοθὲν Ar.

[20] τοὺς δήλους codd, ineptly changed to τοὺς δαλοὺς by Ar, and τὰς δέλτους by Pg.

[21] Cf. Hebr. 1. 2.

[22] ἐξηλείφης codd: ἐξηλείφθης Ar.

[23] Mt 27. 35.

[24] μύσους ἀνέπλησε codd: μίσους ἐνέπλησε Ar.

[25] Acts 9. 5; Aesch., *Agam.* 1624; Pind. *Pyth.* II. 174. Cf. Leutsch and Schneidewin, *Corpus paroem. graec.*, I. 148, 301; II, 128, 379, 628.

[26] I have been unable to find the source of this proverb (προσαράσσειν τὴν ὄψιν τῇ πέτρᾳ). Cf. K.G. Mpones (Μπόνης), Εὐθυμίου τοῦ Μαλάκη τὰ σῳζόμενα, II, Athens, 1949, p. 30_{16}.

[27] Diog. Laert. VIII. 18; Leutsch & Schneidewin, II, p. 516.

[28] Aristoph. *Clouds*, 750; Plato, *Gorg.* 513a; Leutsch & Schneidewin, I, pp. 83–84, 338; II, pp. 417–18.

the edification of the foolish *puts it*,[29] but in truth shaking down the whole world on thy head, and *the heads* of thy children and thine entire line on account of thine outrages.

4. As for the Jewish nation,[30] it is silent even against its will, and it is mute, and sighs, and is filled with dejection, as it broods over shadows, forms and empty hopes. But methinks my speech bids me turn back awhile, and fastening on to the words of the Gospel, supply therefrom what this day demands. What then do those divine words teach (for there is nothing like harkening to them)? "When," it says, "the even was come, there came a rich man of Arimathea, named Joseph, and going up to Pilate, he begged the body of Jesus."[31] Verily Joseph was rich, since he sought the treasure of life; rich he was in making provision to acquire[32] inviolate wealth; rich he was and wise in buying with inexpensive and moderate words the costly and splendid pearl,[33] and concealing with them the object of his concern. For he does not request the body like one who thinks much of himself and uses loud words, but he asks for the dead as if to give him burial out of pity and mercy. And as he approaches Pilate, putting aside all hesitation and fear, he advises him, as though imparting his counsel, to have the dead man's body taken down. For already, as the day of preparation was drawing to its close with the setting sun, the law of the Sabbath came into force with the day that was beginning, and he appeared more persuasive by indicating perchance the law according to which the bodies of the executed should not remain hanging. For while in other respects the Jews were acting unlawfully and departing barefacedly from ancestral customs, respect for the laws was cultivated by them in matters wherein they found nothing contrary to their will, and which were easy to accomplish. "Grant me," says Joseph, "if thou wilt, to bury the corpse of Jesus, whom all his inti-

---

[29] Reading βραχὺ τῆς κτίσεως μέρος, καὶ μύθου [so B and Coislin. 107; πύθου A, Lig] παίγνιον εἰς σωφρονισμὸν τοῖς ἄφροσι παροιμιαζόμενον. Ar has βραχεῖ τῆς κτίσεως μέρει, καὶ πίθου παίγνιον ... παροιμιαζόμενος. Ar's πίθου παίγνιον (? = "labour in vain"; cf. εἰς πίθον ἀντλεῖν) deserves consideration.

[30] ἀλλὰ τὸ μὲν Ἰουδαίων γένος A, B, Coislin. 107: ἀλλὰ μέντοιγε τὸ γένος νῦν τῶν Ἰουδαίων Ar after Lig (the latter, however, does not have νῦν).

[31] Mt 27. 57–58.

[32] Read τὴν κτῆσιν ἐπιμελούμενος with A, B and Lig: τὴν κτίσην Coislin. 107: τὴν κτίσιν Ar.

[33] Cf. Mt 13. 45–46.

HOMILY XI. HOLY SATURDAY

mates left and went away. Grant me to bury the corpse, to whose passion many spectators gathered, but whom none has now remained to entomb, not even among his friends. Grant me to bury the corpse of a stranger and a destitute man. Gone from thee is the apprehension of his kingship. He is dead who was accused of *wishing to* seize the might of authority, but who, from the time of the betrayal up to the very verdict, was seen to be innocent of every misdeed. It is his corpse that I seek, his, whom prophet-killing tongues, voices and hands brought under condemnation of death, whereas thou wast inclined to cast a more merciful vote. Grant me to acknowledge gratitude to thee, whereby thou doest no harm to others. Nor will the Jewish rabble be grieved when they learn that their enemy[34] is covered with earth. For they are irked even on seeing the one they hate dead, as, on the one hand, he publicly proclaims the foul murder by means of the cross, while attracting, on the other, the spectators' pity and inciting them to abominate the cruelty of those who have crucified him. Nor will they threaten thee with Caesar's friendship, saying, "Thou art not Caesar's friend,"[35] if thou givest the corpse to be buried in the ground. If only thou art willing, the fulfilment of my request is without disguise."

Soothing Pilate's soul with such words, the wise and good Joseph succeeds in his purpose, and obtains the body of Jesus after it has been taken down. How could he not have *succeeded*, coming forward as he did with great desire and a most pious love, whereby he had as helper and fulfiller of his request Him for whom he was asking? So now Joseph requests and obtains the body. Why did he not ask for Him even as He was being dragged to the cross, and prevent the murder? At that time there breathed an anger more powerful than both his resolution and his strength, and the murderers' envy cut off all hope. But as the flow of their anger subsided with the blood of the murder, and ceased (for the slaying of the envied person removes the wrath and jealousy), then he comes forward with an outspoken request, and displays the willingness which he has been concealing and cherishing for a long time; and having succeeded in his purpose, he takes up the Lord's holy body.

Ar II 453

[34] Read τὸν ἐχθρὸν [τὸν νεκρὸν Ar, probably a slip].
[35] Jn 19. 12.

HOMILIES OF PHOTIUS

Flinging himself on the recumbent *corpse*, he uttered all manner of cries, and was divided between every kind of emotion. Everything possessed him at the same time: wonder *and* dismay, gladness *and* sorrow, joy *and* tears, hatred *and* pity, fear,[36] cowardice *and* courage; his countenance was both gay and dejected. What descriptive speech could portray his condition at that time? He rejoiced at having the object of his desire; he wept to see Him dead. He pitied Him as He lay without burial. He hated the cruelty of those who had crucified Him; he wondered at the long-suffering of the One crucified. He was afraid as he touched the body; he felt courageous, strengthened by love. He was sad for the suffering; he rejoiced at his good fortune. The matter perplexed him, and he revolved his thoughts variously: "Shall I close with my hands the eyes of Him who by means of clay and speech[37] planted eyes in the blind? Shall I prepare to press together[38] His lips, at Whose word the lips of those that spoke with difficulty[39] were splendidly unfolded and their tongue became distinct? Shall I cover with a napkin this head, for which the temple rent its veil as in public mourning, baring and revealing the secrets of its inviolate sanctuary? Shall I join together the hands which have stretched out those withered arms, fettered and bound by age and sickness?[40] Shall I press together His feet on which He trod the liquid waves of the sea,[41] He by whose command the lame were set straight on their feet and were seen to run?[42] How shall I bury Him who called up a dead man from Hell, loosed him of his winding-sheet, and raised him on the fourth day?"[43] Revolving such things in his thoughts, and remaining long in doubt, yet, since the time *appointed by* the dispensation had come, he becomes himself part of the dispensation and, smearing the Lord's body with myrrh and aloes

Ar II 454

Ar II 455

---

[36] φόβος, δειλία, θάρσος A and B. Ar supplied τόλμη after φόβος. The enumeration of emotions is given somewhat differently in Coislin. 107: θάμβος· ἔκπληξις· δάκρυα· εὐφροσύνη· λύπη· χαρά· ἔλαιος (i. e. ἔλεος)· μῖσος· φόβος· δειλία· θάρσος· φαιδρότης προσώπου· καὶ κατήφεια.

[37] Jn 9. 6.

[38] Read συμπτύξαι [so Coislin. 107] or συμπῆξαι [so Lig] παρασκευάσω: συμπήξω, παρασκευάσω A, B and Ar.

[39] Mk 7. 32.

[40] Surely χρόνῳ καὶ νόσῳ πεπεδημένας [so Coislin. 107], not χρόνῳ καὶ νόμῳ [A, B, Lig and Ar].

[41] Mt 14. 25.

[42] Mt 15. 31.

[43] Jn 11. 39–44.

HOMILY XI. HOLY SATURDAY

(which among the Jews was the ultimate honour to the dead), and wrapping it up in funeral sheets, he lays it in the new sepulchre.[44] A new sepulchre was standing ready, since Joseph was seeking to honour the Lord Himself with every possible means (for a new and individual sepulchre, instead of a common one polluted by many bodies, adds funeral[45] dignity to the one that is buried), and for another twofold cause provided by the dispensation: firstly, lest, when the miracle of the resurrection takes place, the all-daring and shameless Jews should proclaim that he who arose from the dead was another one buried alongside, and not the one they had condemned to the cross, and so that every pretext for lies and godlessness be completely removed from them; and secondly, that some men might not think that only those bodies arose from the grave by whose side and in whose proximity lay the Lord's body (for one of the sainted of old had already arisen even in *the Lord's* lifetime),[46] but so that the Lord should win His victory over Hell on behalf of all men, and likewise should be clearly known to have performed through His own suffering the resurrection of all the bodies scattered over the whole earth and sea, and dispersed by fire and air. For, inasmuch as He was not buried together with other bodies, and yet many saints, who did not lie close to the Lord's sepulchre, but here and there, in different places, arose and made themselves visible to many persons, accordingly it is shown most clearly that the Lord's death and resurrection were not accomplished for some and not for others,[47]

Ar II 456

---

[44] Jn 19. 39-42.

[45] τὴν ἐν νεκροῖς ... σεμνότητα [so A and B] seems to be preferable to τὴν ὡς ἐν νεκροῖς [so Vat. 759 and Ar]: τὴν ἐν νεκρῷ Lig: τὴν ὡς νεκροῖς Coislin. 107.

[46] The MSS read ὅ καί τινος τῶν ἁγίων πάλαι καὶ ζῶντος ἔτι διεπέπρακτο. τινος should probably be corrected to τινι. Literally translated, this would be, "which had already been accomplished to one of the saints, even when He was still alive." The reference is probably to Lazarus. Ar, following Mai, adds on the authority of Vat. gr. 759 καὶ αὖ τελευτήσαντος ("and again after He was dead") after διεπέπρακτο, but that is not supported by the principal MSS, and makes little sense, unless one changed τινος to τισι, in which case the reference would be to Lazarus, the daughter of Jairus and the widow's son on the one hand, and to the dead men who arose when Christ died on the cross, on the other.

[47] This whole sentence has been radically altered by Ar. Read: οἷς [ὧν Ar] γάρ τινων μὲν οὐ συνετέθαπτο σώμασι ... διὰ τούτων [so Coislin. 107 and Vat. 759: διὰ τοῦτο AB: τούτοις Ar] μᾶλλον τρανῶς ἐπιδείκνυται μὴ τῶν μέν, τῶν δὲ μή [μὴ τοῖς μέν, τοῖς δὲ μή Ar], ἀλλ' ὑπὲρ πάντων τῷ δεσπότῃ ὅ τε θάνατος διηγωνισμένος [γεγενημένος Vat. 759] καὶ ἡ ἀνάστασις.

but for the sake of all. For such and similar reasons Joseph had a new sepulchre hewn out for the Lord, perchance not perceiving everything himself, but having in view one object only—reverence—while divine foreknowledge arranged and disposed in advance those other matters also.

5. Now the honourable Joseph,[48] having deposited in the new sepulchre the newly dead body of Him who makes empty the tombs, inaugurates the new chamber of our resurrection, and having blocked the mouth of the tomb with a big stone, goes off mourning and lamenting, while the murderous impulse of the Jews is provoked to another outrage against the Saviour, and inflamed to another insult. In the case of other men it may be observed that as soon as they have exacted as great a penalty as they desire from those who have fallen under their wrath, their anger is calmed, as their passion is dissipated by the fulfilment of their will, and often they turn to pity. But the Jewish nation, inflamed by the blood of prophets and saints, know not how to be sated in their wrath, not even when they are allowed to carry out the ultimate manner of retribution,[49] the foul deed of murder. For now once more is to be seen the excess of their depravity and cruelty. After the derision, the mockery, after the blows, the spitting, after the buffeting, the piercing of the hands and the transfixing of the feet, after the cross and death, and, as they thought, the Saviour's extermination from among men, after all these, they revert to another kind of insanity, and kindle another war against the Lord, and instead of making peace with Him who is lying low for their sake, they go up to Pilate, and they rage against the dead One, and utter cries worthy of their impious mind and tongue. Who *did* that? The scribes and the pharisees, the flower of the Jewish mercy and sagacity. For it says, "The next day that followed the day of preparation, the chief priests and Pharisees came together unto Pilate, saying, We remember that that deceiver said while he was yet alive, After three days I will rise again. Command therefore that the sepulchre be made sure until the third day, lest his disciples come and steal him away, and say unto the people, He is risen from the dead."[50]

---
[48] Mk 15. 43.
[49] Surely τῆς ἀντιλυπήσεως [τοῖς ἀντιλυπήσεως Ar, probably a misprint].
[50] Mt 27. 62–64.

HOMILY XI. HOLY SATURDAY

What could be fouler than such utterances? What could be more godless than such a resolve? What could be more insane than their shamelessness? Dost thou call a deceiver, O Jew, the unerring guide of salvation? Him who has come to deliver thee, the insulter, from deceit, and to snatch thee away from the condemnation of deceit? Is He a deceiver because He broke men away from idolatrous worship? Because He snatched them away from the demons' domination? Because He changed the heavy harness of the Law into the mild and light yoke of the Gospel?[51] Because He was outspoken in reproving thy hypocrisy?[52] Because He threatened with the lash those who dared make His Father's house a house of merchandise,[53] not actually striking them, but showing them liable to the punishment of senseless beasts? I leave aside for the present the signs and the wonders, and those ineffable and unspeakable benefits, whereby He who was merciful to everybody benefited your ungrateful race. Still, was He a deceiver? He is dead. What concern hast thou for one who no longer is, and cannot induce others into deception? Was that man a deceiver? Then let His utterances lie cast down and neglected. For nothing of what He has said shall be. So why art thou a busybody, and sayest thou rememberest Him to have said He would rise after three days? Dost thou yet fear and dread lest His words come to pass? How then art thou not afraid to call Him a deceiver? How is it that, whereas thou oughtst to sigh and weep blood and by repenting of thy daring deeds make thy condemnation more bearable, thou, as if taking pride in not leaving any excess of wantonness and shamelessness to others, strivest to exceed preceding evils with new ones? Verily, when one is entirely possessed by envy and murder, one's thoughts do not rise even for a moment from that frenzied ebriety and madness; wherefore even now these men talk nonsense in their insanity, saying, "We remember that he said, After three days I will rise," and, "Command that the sepulchre be made sure, lest his disciples steal him away."[54] Thou oughtst then to have accused the disciples of theft, instead of charging the Teacher with being a deceiver. Why, am I a deceiver

Ar II 459

[51] Mt 11. 30.
[52] Mt 23. 28.
[53] Jn 2. 16.
[54] Mt 27. 63–64.

if another man digs up my grave, and takes pleasure in dishonouring and insulting my body? It was needful in that case to ask for soldiers against those men, instead of insulting with another guard Him who was guarded by a tomb;[55] to restrain those men from their violence, instead of slandering Him who had done no harm. But what dost thou do? The ones thou incitest to theft thou leavest unwatched, but Him whom earth and a stone hold thou again ragest against, planting snares and ambuscades? Besides, why fearest thou the theft? "Lest," it says, "his disciples steal him away, and say that he is risen from the dead." When was there a dead man seen working his own resurrection so it should be easy for his disciples to invent this thing that had not happened? Or how was it reasonable that men who had dared to commit a theft should then run to the people and proclaim the resurrection, incredible as it was even when it had happened?[56] That would have meant accusing themselves of theft, instead of avoiding the charge; for by inventing an unlikely apology, they would have made the accusation certain, since a man who commits an unlawful act and seeks to escape suspicion provides himself with a plausible and likely refuge. But to have stolen a dead body and fabricated the tale that it had risen would not have been *an act* of the disciples, but the obvious mockery of enemies who took unstinting pleasure in insulting the stolen one. Thou wast not therefore afraid of their stealing it, nor that having stolen it they would invent a resurrection. Nay, the words of the crucified One distracted and harassed thy soul, and caused thee to see the resurrection, as it were, before thine eyes, and for this reason thou didst not cease from enacting its drama, not a tragic, nor a comic one, but verily a Jewish drama, a Pharisaean drama, worthy of thy prophet-killing stage; setting soldiers and locks and seals and guards round the body where it lay, so that, by secreting[57] thyself, thou mightest not appear to have devised the theft, of which thou wast thyself the author.

It is either a friend or an enemy who steals a dead body. If it is

---

[55] Read φρουρούμενον τάφῳ with the MSS [τάφον Ar].
[56] Reading ἢ πῶς ἀκόλουθον ἦν κλοπὴν ἐξεργασαμένους [so Coislin. 107 and Ar: ἐξεργασαμένου AB], πρᾶγμα τολμηρόν, ἐπὶ τὸ [ἐπὶ τὸ omitted by Ar] φημίσαι τὴν ἀνάστασιν, ἄπιστον ἔργον καὶ τετελεσμένον, ἀνθρώποις δραμεῖν;
[57] Read σαυτὸν ἐκκλέπτων with the MSS [ἐκκλέπτειν Ar].

HOMILY XI. HOLY SATURDAY

an enemy, then thou admittest that it is thy deed, and the daring action of thy hand.[58] Why then stealest thou? Is it so that the disciples should say that He is risen from the dead? But if it is a friend, then why a naked *body*? Why should he have insulted the dead one by baring him and doing unseemly things to him, over whom, even if he did him no other honour, he should at least have performed the funeral rites, and respected the law common among all men, and by no means have uncovered a body which had just been consigned to earth? Besides, for what purpose does one steal? So that, it says, His disciples should say that He is risen from the dead. It appears therefore that resurrection was a very likely thing, and very easy to accomplish, and had formerly been done by many men, so that in stealing they should have had recourse to such an acceptable and indisputable excuse. It would have been much simpler for the thieves to say, if they were going to invent a reason, that His body had been swallowed up by the earth, instead of having recourse to a resurrection that had not happened. Nay, thou hadst no fear lest they stole it and said that He was risen from the dead, but thou wast afraid of the prophets' words which, willfully and drunk with murder, thou didst neglect to thy detriment, words which both clearly foretold thy foul murder and prophesied the Saviour's resurrection. Thou wast afraid of these things.[59] Thou knewest that the whole creation mourned the Lord's passion and that the earth quaked. These things frightened and troubled thee, Ar II 462 even if thou didst strive to be unfeeling and insensible. As these things occurred to thee and crowded upon thee when thou hadst time to remember them, they caused thee, even against thy will, to suspect the resurrection. For this reason thou dost anticipate, and work wickedness, and announce the theft in advance, in order that, when the resurrection takes place, thou shouldst have a wretched refuge in the theft which thou didst seize upon beforehand.

6. Was He stolen? Then why dost thou not arrest the robbers red-handed and bring them before Pilate? For thou didst have guard of the tomb with a company of soldiers. Besides, thou wast

---

[58] τῆς σῆς παλάμης τόλμημα [so Coislin. 107] seems to be preferable to τῆς σῆς πλάνης τόλμημα [A, B, Ar].
[59] Read ἐδεδίεις ταῦτα· εἶδες, etc. [ἐδεδίεις ταύτας, ἰδὼν Ar].

not ignorant that the theft itself was going to take place, as even thou foretellest. Who are the disciples who committed the robbery? Where did they convey the stolen *body*? Why, granted they were stealing it, were they attempting to loose the grave-clothes, to remove the napkin from the head, especially as these were plastered down with myrrh and aloes? Even in solitude and quiet, with nothing terrible to suspect and no guarding soldiers to fear, one could not easily have accomplished that, or torn off the body the grave-clothes which were glued and folded together with the mixture of myrrh and aloes. Yet was He stolen? Hast thou set about to seek the thieves?[60] Dost thou punish the guards for negligence? Nay, thou doest none of these things—far from it. Nor was there anyone digging up the grave and stealing the body. But thou art thyself the thief, if there was one, thou art thyself the slanderer, thou art the one who exactest as thy reward from the more simple-minded or the most impious their incredulity of the resurrection; thou, the busybody and prattler, art in this matter the silent judge who utters not a word. For this reason dost thou keep still in this matter, and carest nothing of the laws appointed for theft, or the rest of the inquiry. Instead, having bruited about by every device

Ar II 463 and by bribery the theft of the true resurrection, which was thy purpose, thou didst content thyself with a lie, having lighted on the soldiers' corruption as on a piece of good fortune, and being thankful if no one inquired anew how and by whom the theft was committed; though it was needful to take also into account that to any sensible person it was altogether incredible either that the disciples should have committed the theft or bruited about the resurrection. For, according to thee, they would bruit about a resurrection that did not take place. How will they show the risen one? It is an incontrovertible[61] disproof of the report if the one who is bruited about has not appeared anywhere. And if they do not show Him, will they not appear to be raving, and be a laughing-stock before everybody, and make the Teacher an object of ridicule? For, by inventing[62] things which are easily disproved as non-existent, one

[60] τῶν κλεψάντων [so Coislin. 107] seems to be more appropriate than τῶν κλαπέντων [so A, B, Ar].
[61] Read ἄμαχος with Coislin. 107: ἄχαμος AB: ἄλαλος Ar.
[62] Read οἷς γάρ τις ... πλάττει with the MSS [εἰ γάρ τις Ar].

HOMILY XI. HOLY SATURDAY

foolishly deprives him on whose behalf one is acting both of his true glory and of his real deeds. For if, whereas the Saviour was seen by many men on many occasions after His resurrection from the dead, and many bodies of saints appeared unto many,[63] and the angels sat before the tomb, and so great and so many prodigies were performed, yet you strove that the lie of the theft should spread about rather than the truth (for this saying is commonly reported among the Jews until this day);[64] unless furthermore the resurrection of Christ our Saviour had been accomplished, splendid and famous and clear to all,[65] with tombs being made empty, with many dead men becoming heralds of their own resurrection, with angels Ar II 464 testifying to it, and the Lord Himself appearing to different men[66] at different times and places, unless the resurrection was confirmed and supported by all these things, how would any of the disciples have dared to say that the Teacher had risen, and not, even if other people had said it, have sunk with shame, put out of countenance by the absurdity of the report? It was indeed the unerring apprehension of things seen, the manifest and indubitable character of the resurrection, which filled the disciples with boldness and strength to become teachers and heralds of things they knew exactly. For what *explanation* could a man invent, even though he were practised in the invention of fables, or allege, though his tongue were armed in the shamelessness of falsehood, other than the unshakeable evidence of things seen by them and brought to their certain knowledge? Indeed these men, when He had been arrested and the cross[67] was being set up, abandoned their Master, and cast aside everything out of fear of what would overtake them. All the signs they had seen, all the teachings they had heard, all the miracles vouchsafed unto them by grace, all these things they forgot in their expectation of terrors.[68] How then could these men,

[63] Mt 27. 52–53.
[64] Mt 28. 15.
[65] Reading εἰ μὴ καὶ [καὶ omitted by A and Coislin. 107] λαμπρὰ καὶ περιφανὴς καὶ [ἐν Ar] πᾶσιν ἐναργής [πᾶσιν ἔργοις codd, Ar].
[66] Reading κατὰ διαφόρους καιροὺς καὶ τόπους διαφόροις [so A (?) and B: διαφόρους Coislin. 107: διαφόρως Ar] ἐπιφαινομένου.
[67] σταυρὸς ἐπήγνυτο codd: σταυρῷ ἐπήγνυτο Ar.
[68] Read ὅσα τε αὐτοῖς χορηγουμένης [so Coislin. 107 and Ar: χορηγούμενος AB] ἐκεῖθεν ἐτερατουργεῖτο τῆς χάριτος, οἱ ταῦτα πάντα φόβων ἐλπίδι λαθόμενοι [τούτων πάντων φόβῳ ἐπιλαθόμενοι Ar].

if they were convinced that He was dead and had not wrought the great mystery of His resurrection, have had strength to proclaim it instantly (not to speak of their having considered stealing Him away), or how could they,[69] all their lives long, with great joy and eagerness, have offered to die for their confession and faith in Him? Therefore those who malign the resurrection can have no resource whereby they can escape from inevitable confutation, and not appear as furious maniacs and slanderers.[70]

7. Of these things, however, a special account will be given at the proper time. As for me, I am again drawn to revert to the strangeness of the tomb and of the burial. How does He *suffer* His body to be wrapped in grave-clothes Who has spread out the vault of heaven as a much-famed wonder? How could He, the Life and Resurrection of all men, have submitted to the laws of death, even though[71] He abolished its power in His own flesh? How does He, Who before all time was jointly enthroned with the Father, become a joint-dweller with the dead? Oh, the Lord's graces for our sake! Oh, the power of Him who became dead! O tomb, *who art* the emptying out of tombs, and the destruction of Hell, and the slaying of death, and the much-sung bridal-chamber of our resurrection! The wedding-chamber of the Creation begot marriage, nourished the expectation of children, and housed the husbandmen of the human race, but it had sorrows sprouting underneath, and death installed close, by which the flower of life was spoiled, and happiness in life was made uncertain; whilst the wedding-chamber of the tomb, which houses the author Himself both of our creation and of our re-creation, does not put forth the roots of children, which quickly wither away together with their offshoot, nor does it pledge to us a life and an existence harassed by death, but it joins virginity in wedlock to human nature, giving angelic life free scope on earth, and restores to our

---

[69] Read ἢ [εἰς Ar] τὸ παραυτίκα κηρύσσειν ἐδυναμώθησαν (τί γὰρ δεῖ λέγειν ὡς κλέπτειν διενοήθησαν;) ἢ [οἳ Ar] τὸν ἅπαντα βίον ... θανάτους [so Coislin. 107 and Ar: θανάτου AB] ἐδέχοντο;

[70] This sentence has been completely perverted by Ar. Read οὕτως οὐκ ἔστι τοῖς ἐπηρεάζουσι τὴν ἀνάστασιν [ἐπηρεαζομένοις τῇ ἀναστάσει Ar] ἐφ' ᾧ τῶν ἐλέγχων τὸ ἀναπόδραστον διαδράσαντες [διαδράσειεν Ar] τὸ μὴ οὐχὶ [ἐν τῷ Ar] λυσσᾶν αὐτοὺς καὶ μαίνεσθαι καὶ συκοφαντεῖν τὴν ἀναχώρησιν ἕξουσιν [ὑποχώρησιν ἔχειν Ar].

[71] Read εἰ καὶ with the MSS: ἢ καὶ Ar.

HOMILY XI. HOLY SATURDAY

ancestors, who had defaced the Lord's image by their passions, that bridal and pristine beauty. Having consecrated to the lot of men a sorrowless and untroubled life, it has made the gift of immortality above passions and corruption.

The ark of Noah, when the common deluge had poured from the heavenly founts,[72] preserved its occupants as the seed of a second world, but kept them for a second experience of sorrows,[73] the evils of life. While this world-saving ark of the Saviour's body, which has treasured up the Dispenser of life and Giver of joy, preserves human kind by lifting it above spiritual shipwreck. Having made the tombs empty of their dead,[74] it pours forth the inexhaustible grace of the resurrection, and transporting us to the kingdom of heaven, it guards and keeps us forever away from the experience of further evils. The tabernacle made unto Moses had a pot and manna and a lantern and a table and the ordinances of the Law engraved on stone tablets;[75] while this life-giving and venerable tabernacle does not pride itself on shadows and forms, the symbols of worship according to the Law, but having served the Lawgiver and common Lord Himself for a three-day burial, it has revealed Ar II 467 the divine and great mystery of grace, after extending piety, without itself moving,[76] to the ends of the world. Even if it does not hold the treasure (for He is risen as He had willed), it has not been depleted of the riches of grace, for it keeps an inexhaustible store of miracles: it cures diseases, drives away sickness, routs demons, sanctifies souls, proclaims the folly of the Jews, preaches the Lord's resurrection with visible signs, and confirms the abyss of His mercy on our behalf. Wondrous too was the manger at Bethlehem which received my Lord, wrapped in swaddling clothes after the manner of babes, as He had just emerged from a virgin's womb and entered human life. Yet a far greater miracle does the tomb exhibit: for in the former the mystery of Christ's incarnation was taking its beginning, as the Godhead was already being covered with flesh; in

---

[72] Read τοῦ κοινοῦ ῥυέντος [ῥυεῖσα Ar] .... ναυαγίου.
[73] Read εἰς ἀλγεινῶν [ἀλγεινὴν Ar] .... πεῖραν.
[74] τοὺς δὲ [so Coislin. 107: δὲ omitted by A, B and Lig] νεκροὺς τῶν τάφων κενώσασα: τῶν νεκρῶν δὲ τοὺς τάφους Ar.
[75] Cf. Hebr. 9. 1–4.
[76] Cf. Aristotle, *Metaphysica*, 1072a 25.

the latter, however, is accomplished the end, and the purpose of God's advent—our perfection and re-creation[77]—is completed, gleaming brilliantly and illuminating everything with the flash of the resurrection. At the former, the magi from the East offer gifts to the new-born; at the latter, the peoples of East and West and the other ends of the world, nations and tongues and every generation, bring unto Him who has risen from the dead not myrrh and frankincense and gold,[78] the produce of inanimate earth, but they hand over to Him, inasmuch as He is the universal King and Creator of all, their very bodies and souls, exhaling the fragrance of faith and bedecked with the gold of piety. The songs of angels sounded over the manger, while by the tomb, too, angels were present and caused amazement. At the former, as if hinting at the condescension of the new-born, they struck up songs of "Glory to God in the highest and on earth peace, and good will toward men";[79] while at the latter, without any veil or riddle, they sound forth the power of the risen One in a loud and clear voice, crying out and saying, "He is not here: for he is risen as He said. Tell His disciples[80] that He is risen from the dead,"[81] and, "Be not affrighted: ye seek Jesus the Nazarene, which was crucified; He is risen; He is not here; behold the place where they laid Him,"[82] and, "Why seek ye the living among the dead? He is not here, but is risen."[83] Later, the Lord Himself and Author of the resurrection *saith*: "Woman, why weepest thou? Whom seekest thou?[84] Go to my brethren, and say unto them, I ascend unto my Father and your Father, and to my God and your God";[85] and, "All power is given unto me in heaven and on earth."[86]

[77] Read ἡ ἐμὴ τελείωσις καὶ ἀνάπλασις with the MSS: εἰς ἐμὴν τελείωσιν καὶ ἀνάπλασιν Ar.
[78] Mt 2. 11.
[79] Lk 2. 14.
[80] So Coislin. 107: ἠγέρθη γὰρ καθὼς καὶ εἶπεν· καὶ εἴπατε τοῖς μαθηταῖς αὐτοῦ ὅτι ἠγέρθη ἀπὸ τῶν νεκρῶν. A and B have ἠγέρθη γὰρ καθὼς εἶπε τοῖς μαθηταῖς αὐτοῦ, etc. Ar supplies from the text of Mt ἠγέρθη γὰρ καθὼς εἶπε ⟨καὶ ταχὺ πορευθεῖσαι εἴπατε⟩ τοῖς μαθηταῖς αὐτοῦ, etc.
[81] Mt 28. 6–7.
[82] Mk 16. 6.
[83] Lk 24. 5–6.
[84] Jn 20. 15.
[85] Jn 20. 17.
[86] Mt 28. 18.

HOMILY XI. HOLY SATURDAY

8. Let us, too, willingly bring the gifts of victory to Him who became man for us, and suffered and[87] was buried for our sake, and delivered us from the ancient domination of Hell, as He is rising from the dead and winning victory over all. Ye who pride yourselves on your wealth *offer* the care and consolation of the poor; ye who are oppressed by poverty, patience and gratitude; those in power and authority, the sparing of the goods of others, protecting the wronged, and governing your subjects mildly as fellow-countrymen, instead of being haughtily arrogant towards them as to aliens, that you may yourselves show that this *power and authority* was in truth appointed and granted to you by God, and that you may not, through deeds that lead you into iniquity, arm the tongues of the many against their Creator who has appointed your authority. Those who are numbered as subjects, *offer ye* the striving to be properly and humanely governed, instead of the desire to exhaust by continuous disorder the patience of the rulers, foolishly making their clemency an excuse for negligence. Ar II 470 Those who still draw the yoke of wedlock, *offer ye* concord in good will and modesty; for thus may wedlock preserve its honour. Those who have divorced themselves from this libidinous need, freed as from some painful bondage, direct yourselves towards the path of temperance. Those who have overcome these things, *offer ye* virginity as your oil, and that with a humble heart, that you may not be disappointed of being called wise, and your lamp be not dimmed by the spirit of conceit.[88] The priests and shepherds, *offer ye* the watchful care of your flock, the exhibiting of yourselves as models to those you tend, and drawing them to virtue by example rather than by verbal exhortations. The flock, obedience and ready compliance with Paul, who testifies saying, "Obey them that have the rule over you, and submit yourselves; for they watch (I dare not say, 'We watch'[89]) over your souls."[90] And all of us by all means let us bear fruit in mutual love and unhesitating faith in Him and piety, without which we would not be able to be enrolled not only

---

[87] καὶ ὑπὲρ ἡμῶν παθόντι καὶ ταφέντι Coislin. 107: καὶ ὑπὲρ ἡμῶν ταφέντι A, B, Ar.
[88] Cf. Mt 25. 1 sq.
[89] A note of modesty on the part of Photius.
[90] Hebr. 13. 17.

among the disciples, but not even among the servants or the attendants.

9. Let Christ our God, who has despoiled Hell and slain death, and raised us along with Himself, adorn all the more with piety and the other virtues him to whom He has granted to reign on earth in His stead, and show him worthy of the heavenly kingdom, and along with him all of us, by the intercessions of our most holy Lady, the Mother of God, and of all the saints. Amen.

XII

Homily Delivered on the Holy and Great Saturday[1]

1. Oh, the awesome and great mystery! For it is fitting to begin our discourse with a miracle at a time of strange and wondrous things. Oh, the unutterable providence on our behalf of our Lord and Creator! Oh, unfathomable depth of judgments, and wealth of goodness, and founts of mercy flowing with copious streams, watering the whole world in an other-worldly manner, and gushing with an inexhaustible flow! Oh, the Lord's passion, burial and death that abolish passions, death and hell! Who is there that does not laud and glorify His sufferings, and is not amazed thereat? Who is there that does not shudder and tremble and grow dizzy at the blows? Who is not filled with wonder and astonishment at the spitting, the scoffing, the jeering, the flagellation, on seeing intact feet pierced through, and stainless hands being transfixed, and the side being wounded with a spear, and, wonder upon wonder, the body being stained red with blood therefrom, and that after death? Whose *sufferings* are these? Oh, the endurance and long-suffering of the Maker and Creator of everything, Who by a word alone governs the universe! Why does He suffer? So that He may bestow freedom from passions unto that *human* race, at whose hands he undergoes this passion and mockery; so that He may free us, at whose hands He is scourged, crucified and wounded, from our scourges and wounds, us, whose nature, after being abducted and enslaved by

---

[1] The words θείῳ καί have been left out of the title by the editors, although given by them on p. 178.

HOMILY XII. HOLY SATURDAY

our transgression of the commandment, has been cruelly tormented by our passions; so that He may mould again in His image that which we have defaced and beclouded with the iniquity of our deeds, and may restore to us our ancient nobility.

2. For this reason He is crucified, and dies and is buried, so that, having snatched human kind away from the Serpent's domination, and drawn it up from the pits of death, He may raise it up along with Himself, and make it worthy again of its portion in paradise, from which it had been banished for wilful wrong-doing.[2] This is the purpose of the voluntary crucifixion, incomprehensible even to angels before its accomplishment, this is the goal of the Lord's sufferings, this is the sum of the humiliation of the Logos,[3] this is the end of Christ's incarnation—our deliverance from captivity, our setting up from the lapse, our salvation and perfection—for the sake of which *were wrought* the wondrous birth of the Logos from a virgin, the manger and the swaddling clothes, the flight to Egypt, the reversal of the withdrawal and the return, the Forerunner harvesting repentance from desolate hearts and the baptism that perfects the Baptist but not the Baptized, the tempter and the tempted, the treacherous disciple and the betrayed Teacher, agonized and bedewed with drops of sweat, the haughty mind of the rulers, and the envy of the high priests flaring up, the custody[4] and flagellation, and thereafter the cross, and death and sojourn in a tomb.

3. And yet, let no gloomy or melancholy thought fall upon thee. For indeed it is *all* for thy sake—the emptying of the tomb, and the killing of death, and the destruction of hell, and the resurrection in three days which confirms in visible deeds and inaugurates in godlike fashion the universal resurrection. All this is for us, that it may save us, disobedient ones, who have foolishly departed from the first injunction. For God, having with a wealth of goodness and wisdom of mind moulded man with His own hands, and contrived the creature's side for the formation of woman, and allotted them

---

[2] Read ἐθελοκακῆσαν (sc. τὸ ἀνθρώπειον): ἐθελοκακήσας editors.

[3] Phil. 2. 7. For a definition of the *kenosis*, or "outpouring" of the Logos, cf., amongst others, Greg. Naz., *Or.* XXXVII, § 3, PG 36, col. 285.

[4] In the N. T. the word κουστωδία occurs only in Mt 27. 65–66 and 28. 11 with reference to the watch set over the sepulchre.

to dwell without hardship in paradise, gave out an injunction as a test, so that the first citizen of paradise should not live an idle and inert life unworthy of his rational nature. Having linked His injunction with a tree, fair to see with the eyes and fair to taste (for something that is displeasing is repulsive in itself, and neither needs an extraneous guard nor is suitable to be proferred as a touchstone of disposition and a test[5]), He clearly and manifestly proclaimed what would be the prize for keeping the injunction and what the penalty for disregarding it. The latter, namely transgression, He declared to be conducive to death, while the former He showed to be the compacting and confirmation of immortality, so that deathlessness should not be merely a gift, but also the prize for striving. These things having been accomplished in such godlike manner and too excellently to be inquired into, Adam and Eve throve with all kinds of good things in an untilled and fruitful garden. But the crooked and malicious Serpent, who could not bear to see them enjoying the blessedness from which he had been banished, instead of repenting for his fall, and not making the rebellion for which he had crashed down worse through envy, nor adding evil to evil, he, I say, disregarded this (since envy is unable to keep sin within boundaries), and having cast an avid eye on our ancestors and captured their mind with deceitful words, and, alas,[6] made them a prey to transgression, forthwith stripped them of immortality and alienated them from the joyous life in paradise, and thereby having, so to speak, elbowed[7] their offspring away from their original and rightful freedom, and mischievously bound them to the *pursuit of pleasure*, he rose up as a tyrant to breathe scorn at the whole human race.

KL 190

4. But what of Logos the artificer and our Creator? Did He overlook His creature, *that He had made*[8] with a love of beauty

---

[5] Read εἰς βάσανον ἕξεως καὶ δοκιμασίαν with Chalc. 64: δοκιμασίας editors.

[6] οἴμοι would be much more appropriate than οἶμαι, as printed by the editors.

[7] The editors give the meaningless παραγκυησάμενος, which must surely be corrected to παραγκωνισάμενος.

[8] The MS has here a short lacuna which may be supplied in some such way as this: ἄρ⟨α ἔπλασε μὲν φιλο⟩κάλως καὶ ἐπιμελῶς, παρεῖδε δὲ τυραννούμενον τὸ πλασθέν, etc. Cf. above, p. 173 = Ar II. 346, and John of Damascus, *Hom. in Sabb. S.*, § 11, PG 96, col. 612: τί οὖν; ὁ φύσει συμπαθής, ὁ τὸ εἶναι δούς, καὶ τὸ εὖ εἶναι ἡμῖν χαρισάμενος, παρεῖδε τὸ οἰκεῖον πλάσμα τὸ τιμιώτατον, τὸ προσφιλέστατον, οὕτω δεινῶς τυραννούμενον; οὐδαμῶς.

HOMILY XII. HOLY SATURDAY

and with care, as it was held under tyrannical sway, or did He provide for it,[9] yet not all-wisely? Or, if all-wisely, yet not mercifully? And what excess of mercy or wisdom or providence is not shown especially in this respect? For starting from the transgression itself, He *strove* by many and various treatments to raise up the fallen,[10] by word and the Law and the prophets, by wondrous bounties and equally wondrous misfortunes. Finally, since our nature, having once and for all fallen away from the good and become subservient to the tyrant, was driven headlong to more monstrous and unutterable deeds, it needed greater help corresponding to its daring actions. And what *help was there* other than re-creation? Oh, the mercy surpassing understanding! That is what *human nature* obtains. For the jointly-throning and co-eternal Son and Word of the eternal Father, the Author of the worlds[11] and Creator of the incorporeal hosts, our Maker, Who holds together the whole creation and steers everything in good order with a mere nod, makes unto Himself a flesh from virginal blood that He may re-create us, and He is born and baptized and crucified and dies and is buried, so that we may leap over the nets of sin, which our negligence and indolence have woven and spread out, and so place ourselves above the passions and death. Seest thou the ocean of His mercy, seest thou the depth of His compassion, seest thou the unfathomable decrees of His providence and wisdom, seest thou the height of His condescension? Our Lord is struck for our sake, and He is crucified, and dies, and is buried, that He may wipe off from us the stains of servitude, that He may grant us freedom, resurrection and immortality. He is crucified and dies and is buried, and the earth quakes in fear, and the curtain of the temple is rent, and stones are torn apart, and the sun is covered with much darkness, not because the moon intercepts and stands in the way of its rays according to the inherent law of nature, but wondrously and supernaturally, as if at the farthest end of distance the moon too was grieved and darkened and sorrowful at the Creator's passion, these works of creation all but emitting a cry, and bewailing the

---

[9] Reading ἢ προὐνοήσατο μέν, οὐ πανσόφως δέ [ἢ οὐ προὐνοήσατο editors].
[10] Read τὸ πεπτωκὸς [τὸ πεπτωκὼς editors]. Delete colon after ἀνορθοῦν, and place it after συμφοραῖς.
[11] Hebr. I. 2; II. 3.

affront to the common Lord, and vividly expressing by their condition the enormity of the crime.

5. As for thee, what sayest thou, O Jew? Do not even the sufferings of inanimate things put thee to shame? Dost thou not respect even their reproof? But while the earth quakes and trembles, does thy heart, grown thick with callousness, harden all the more? While stones are rent asunder and their natural solidity is shattered, dost thou become in thy mind stiffened into the nature of a stone, mollified as thou art by no manner of *mercy*?[12] While the sun in fear withdraws its lustre, dost thou unlawfully stretch out thy murderous arms? While the moon is sorrowful, dost thou arm the fury of thy mind? Thou hast trampled the Law underfoot, thou hast slain the prophets, and now thou thrustest thy spear against the Lawgiver, and thou subjectest Him Who has been prophesied to the death of criminals. *This thou*, the slave, *doest* unto thy master, the clay unto the potter, the creature unto the Creator;[13] yea verily, ye the ungrateful unto your benefactor, the prisoners unto the deliverer, the captives unto Him Who has come to free you of your bonds, the condemned unto the judge, and that because He has given light to the blind, because He has nerved and strengthened arms that had been paralysed, because He has straightened and made firm the legs of the lame, because He has cleansed lepers of their disease, because He has braced and made fast the paralytic, because He has dried the streams of blood of the woman that touched Him, because with a few loaves He has fed many thousands, tended by the hands of His disciples, because He has set to flight and destroyed every infirmity and, having summoned up Lazarus, raised him on the fourth day.

6. Have these things caused thee to breathe murder and fury at the Lord? Instead of being thankful for these things, as it behoved thee to be, thou wast prompted by them to be ungrateful; instead of honouring Him with hymns, thou showerest Him with insults; instead of lauding Him, thou blasphemest against Him. These things were illuminated by the splendour of divinity which testified by deeds that He Who wrought manifest miracles by His preaching

[12] A short lacuna: ⟨φιλανθρωπ⟩ίας is probably to be supplied.
[13] Cf. Is. 45. 9.

HOMILY XII. HOLY SATURDAY

was the true God; *and yet*, because of these very things[14] thou didst darken thy face, and didst not at all abate thy murderous spirit in devising death by the cross against the common Saviour and Creator. "The ox at the manger knew his Master as He lay, and the ass his Lord Who rode on him, but Israel did not know me who have come for its salvation with signs and miracles, and the people whom I have come to deliver has not regarded me.[15] For this people's heart is waxed gross, and their ears are dull of hearing, and their eyes they have closed; lest at any time they should see with their eyes, and hear with their ears, and should understand with their heart, and should be converted, and I should heal them,"[16] saith the Lord Almighty.

KL 192

7. We, however, O Lord, who, from not being a people are considered the peculiar people, and from not being pitied nor loved (for our acts drove us far off from such great affection of our Lord) have been pitied and loved only through the goodness and mercy of Him Who has loved us even unto blood, let us bewail the callousness of our[17] hearts. We who have dared *to have* (?) an ungrateful mind that overcame every feeling of gratitude, *let us wipe off* (?) that incurable disease, and *make*[18] our conscience pure of every sin, having sprinkled ourselves with hyssop,[19] and cleansed it by means of repentance, and made it wholly pure; and let us draw nigh to the body of Christ our Lord, not stealthily approaching now, like that nightly friend, not enveloping our eagerness with fear, and shadowing our zeal with the timidity of our soul, not burying the treasure in earth and tomb after the general law of the departed, but with a universal cry escorting and magnifying Him, along with the Cherubic host, and with unwavering faith and zeal eagerly paying divine honours to the Lord's body; not begging it from Pilate through Joseph, but as it is mercifully granted now to all the

[14] Read δι' ἐκεῖνα [δι' ἐκεῖνον editors].
[15] Cf. Is. 1. 3.
[16] Mt 13. 15; Acts 28. 27.
[17] Read αὐτῶν [αὑτῶν editors].
[18] Three gaps in the MS. The following insertions might tentatively be suggested: καὶ τὴν ἀγνώμονα γνώμην, πᾶσαν ἐκνικήσασαν εὐγνωμοσύνην τολμήσαντες ⟨ἐπιδείξασθαι⟩, τὸ ἀνίατον ἀρρώστημα ⟨τοῦτο ἀποσμηξάμεν⟩οι, ⟨ἁγνὰς δὲ⟩ καὶ καθαρὰς πάσης ἁμαρτάδος ⟨ἐργασάμενοι⟩, διὰ τῆς μετανοίας, etc.
[19] Ps. 50. 9.

faithful by Him who once was begged for, Who cries out saying, "Take, eat, this is my body which is broken for you for the remission of sins,[20] for you on whose behalf I am become flesh, on whose behalf I am crucified, on whose behalf even now I am sacrificed every day on the mystical table, so that, being deemed worthy of the sacrifice, you may become sharers of my body and partners of my glory, you on whose behalf I have dwelled in a tomb, and the brazen gates have been broken, and the locks and iron bars have been shattered, and the empire which dominated you has been destroyed." For the Lord is covered with a tomb, but to us He holds out immortality, His face is wrapped with a napkin, but He clothes those who have believed in Him with the garment of incorruptibility, He is enveloped in funeral swathing bands, but severs the tangled chains of our sin, He becomes a fellow-dweller of the dead, but He prepares the heavenly tabernacles for the complement of them that arise from the dead, He is covered with a tomb, and the might of Hell is despoiled, the pricks of death are broken, and the choir of the dead as it rises up cries out with us in a loud voice, "O death, where is thy sting? O Hell, where is thy victory?" For verily, when Christ became flesh, was death swallowed up in victory.[21]

8. O tomb, *who art* the emptying of the tombs of ages and the filling up of the heavenly tabernacles! O tomb, out of which the death of our sin has sprouted up, and the joy of the deliverance has bloomed! O tomb, in which the condemnation of our transgressions lies buried, and the plea of salvation has been brought forth, whereby we have been delivered from the wrinkles of corruption, and have adorned ourselves with the hope of incorruption, in which[22] the mortal part of our nature has wasted away, and the dignity of immortality has been re-created! O tomb, through which the might of the demons has fallen, and the horn of men[23] has been raised, through which the impious belief of the pagans has been made dead, and the holy veneration of the faithful has been strengthened! O tomb, jeered at by the Jews yet attended by

---

[20] Mt 26. 26–28; 1 Cor. 11. 24.
[21] 1 Cor. 15. 54–55.
[22] There is a lacuna after ἐν ᾧ, but the sentence seems to be complete as it stands.
[23] Cf. Lk 1. 69.

HOMILY XII. HOLY SATURDAY

angels, guarded by a watch of soldiers yet worshipped by the whole creation!

9. But Thou Who hast dwelled for us in a tomb, and become numbered among the dead, and hast of Thyself wrought unto us our resurrection, Christ our God, mayest Thou join in tending this Thy great and numerous flock which, I know not how, Thou hast appointed me to tend, and lead it to life-giving and spiritual fields, driving it away, as from a deadly pollution, from the heretical and schismatic pasture, through which the poison of the Serpent, instigator of evil, stealthily creeps in; but gathering everyone into Thy flock and fold, and guarding with Thy hand, as Thou dost, our pious and faithful Emperor, show him all the more terrible to the foes, kindly to his subjects, and make him worthy, along with us, of Thy kingdom. For we all take refuge with Thee, and on Thee we have pinned all our hopes, and to Thee we send up our worship and praise, together with the eternal Father and the co-eternal and life-giving Spirit, now and for ever and ever. Amen.

NOTE ON HOMILIES XIII AND XIV

The following two sermons are closely linked both by virtue of their content and of their occasion. According to their titles, they were delivered on Wednesday and Friday of the first week of Lent, while in Cod. Athen. 2756, no. XIV appears under the following heading: "Sermon spoken on the Friday of *the same* first week of Lent" (τῆς αὐτῆς πρώτης ἑβδομάδος τῶν νηστειῶν). This may mean that the two sermons were preached in the same year, at merely two days' interval, which would account for their similarity both in tone and subject-matter. If, moreover, our chronological hypothesis is correct, both must date from the year 867.[1]

The duration and rites of Lent were already firmly established by the time of Photius.[2] The usage, as summarised by St. John Damascene, prescribed one preparatory week, that of Tyrophagy or "cheese-eating," when abstinence from only meat was recommended. It was followed by six weeks of abstinence from meat, eggs and cheese, and marked by the celebration of the terce, sext and none, and the liturgy of the Presanctified, and finally by Holy Week when only dry food (*xerophagia*) was permitted.[3]

As we have said, our two Homilies are ascribed to the first week of Lent. We have, however, as with Homily I, some reason to doubt the accuracy of the titles. At the end of no. XIII, after exhorting his audience to refrain from envy and slander, Photius goes on to say, "If you live in this wise ... you will enable me to converse with you more often, sometimes with addresses, sometimes by reading the Holy Writ, and the time of the coming week will provide the proof thereof."[4] The bishop's duties to preach and officiate were, of course, particularly heavy during Lent; yet we have no indication that there was any marked contrast between

---

[1] See above, p. 23.
[2] See F. X. Funk, *Die Entwickelung des Osterfastens* in *Kirchengeschichtliche Abhandlungen und Untersuchungen*, I, Paderborn, 1897, pp. 270-75.
[3] *De jejuniis*, PG 95, col. 69.
[4] P. 229 below.

NOTE ON HOMILY XIII AND XIV

the first and second week, such as would account for the words of Photius. In fact, one of the accusations that Photius made against the Latin missionaries in Bulgaria was that they had allowed a less strict observance of the first week, thus setting it apart from the other weeks of Lent.[5] Homily XIV opens with the words, "I am come to you anticipating the appointed time and striving to pay down my debt beforehand ... It is good, to be sure, that a father should not appear unpunctual to his children, but better still it is for him to discharge his debt by paying it in advance as a mark of favour."[6] If Photius was speaking on Friday of the first week of Lent, he would hardly be anticipating the time set for exhorting his flock. We suggest, therefore, that the two sermons were preached not in the first week of Lent, but in the preceding week of Tyrophagy. The Wednesday and Friday of Tyrophagy week were especially marked out as days of fasting,[7] and served as a prefiguration of Lent. On those two days the patriarch celebrated the liturgy of the Presanctified, and it was ordained that "the prophets' utterances concerning the fast and the sermons of St. Basil on the same subject should be read."[8]

With regard to its moral lesson, Homily XIII may be compared to a brief *scholion* on the Heavenly Ladder of John Climacus. This *scholion* is attributed to Photius in Rader's edition (reprinted by Migne), and is presumably derived from the Monac. gr. 297.[9] It reads as follows:

"*Scholion* of Photius, Patriarch of Constantinople.

Thus, for example, fasting is a remedy that purges away passions, when it is practised privately and by itself. But in assemblies and public gatherings it becomes a poison that destroys in many ways him that practises it, in that he is made a stumbling block either to

---

[5] *Epistola synodica*, ed. Valettas, p. 169 = PG 102, col. 724 D.
[6] P. 230 below.
[7] Cf. Theodore Studites, *Catechesis chronica*, PG 99, col. 1700.
[8] Symeon of Thessalonica, *Responsa*, PG 155, cols. 904–05.
[9] Formerly Herzogliche Bibliothek, no. LXXXVII. See Rader's preface, PG 88, cols. 617–622; the *scholion* itself is on col. 1041 A. Reprinted by Papadopoulos-Kerameus in Правосл. Палест. Сборникъ, XI 1 (1892), pp. 22–23 (where, however, the key word νηστεία has been changed to μνηστεία). On the Monac. gr. 297, see Hardt, *Catalogus codd. mss. bibl. reg. Bavaricae, codd. graec.*, III, Munich, 1806, pp. 229–31.

others or to himself, as he prides himself *on his fasting*, and puffs himself up and raves (καὶ διαπριομένῳ)." The authenticity of this and other *scholia* on the *Heavenly Ladder*, which are attributed to Photius, has, however, been contested. This question can only be settled through an extensive investigation of unpublished manuscript material; yet it appears that the argument against the authenticity of the Photian scholia may be based on a misunderstanding.[10]

Both Homilies deal especially with the evil of calumny. This topic, apart from its general moral bearing, was one of personal concern to Photius. In Homily XIII he assails directly his detractors, men of worthless character, who sought to oppose him by all available means, and thereby render his authority ineffectual.[11] The vehement tone of this passage stands in contrast to the confident offer addressed to the Ignatian opposition in Homily VI.[12] If our dating is correct, we may conclude that the Patriarch's popularity had begun to decline by 867. The same observation has already been made by Bury,[13] who argues that Basil I, irrespective of his personal feelings towards Photius, needed all the popular support he could muster in order to cover up the irregularity of his own accession; if, therefore, the first public act of Basil's reign was to oust Photius, he must have reckoned to gain thereby a large segment of public opinion. For surely Basil could ill afford to alienate the people of the capital if the majority of them supported Photius. We may add that Photius was very closely identified with Michael's government, so that the Patriarch's popularity probably

---

[10] The authenticity of the Photian *scholia* has been denied by Fabricius (*Bibl. graeca*, ed. Harles, IX, p. 525 and XI, p. 24), Oikonomos (Φωτίου τὰ Ἀμφιλόχια, Athens, 1858, pp. ξα' and 330, n. 2) and Valettas (Φωτίου ἐπιστολαί, p. 96) for the reason that the *scholia* on the *Heavenly Ladder* placed under the name of Photius in the Coislin. 87 (on which see Devreesse, *Le fonds Coislin*, pp. 76–77) are really by Elias of Crete. Yet no evidence has been offered to show that the *scholia* published by Rader after the Monac. gr. 297 are the same as those in the Coislin. 87. The question must remain in suspense until the lengthy exegetical work of Elias is examined. Hergenröther (*Photius*, III, p. 256) is undecided. Cf. also Papadopoulos-Kerameus, *op. cit.*, pp. vi–vii.

[11] Pp. 225–26 below. The same topic is picked up in Homilies XV and XVI, pp. 258 sq. and 276–77.

[12] See above, pp. 134–36.

[13] *History of the Eastern Roman Empire*, p. 204.

HOMILY XIII. TYROPHAGY WEEK

declined simultaneously with that of the once brilliant Emperor. Indeed, it may be that some of the malicious chatter which Photius decries in these two homilies was directed specifically against Michael's evil life (cf. esp. p. 233 below).

XIII

HOMILY DELIVERED FROM THE AMBO OF THE GREAT CHURCH ON KL 193
THE WEDNESDAY OF THE FIRST WEEK OF LENT

1. All ye who by your baptism unto salvation have been, as it were, born of one womb and enrolled as brothers one of another, and ye whom the judgment of the children in the Lord has assigned to the clergy, let us make the beginning of the fast a beginning of virtue,[1] so that we may confirm in works our sharing in spiritual travail, and preserve unadulterated the dignity of the adoption, and so that we may reap the fruit of our cultivation at the time of the recompense, and not, while we deprive the body of food, fill the soul with incurable passions, nor contrive to treat a disease with a disease, taking license of evil practice at our own expense, nor hide sin with sin, covering up our blindness with foul tatters, but let us wipe off illness with health, and wash off our trespasses with righteousness.

2. For there are, yea, there are some who, while they practise fasting, *destroy*[2] its grace by man-pleasing, and miserably scatter KL 194 the profit of their toils which they ought to keep, acting like some insane merchants who, after traversing the immense deep of sea and ocean and escaping unharmed the storms and tempests of the passage, yet, when they put in at the very edge of the shore, sink all their merchandise at the landing pier, no differently than *if they had done it* in the sea itself. Such is the plight of those who look up to human esteem while undergoing the toil of the fast. Some again, while they emaciate their appearance through lack of food, swell and inflame it with the puffing of vainglory, having fattened themselves thoroughly on this evil regimen and striven to

---

[1] Read ἀρχὴν ποιησώμεθα τὴν [τῆς editors] τῶν ἀρετῶν.
[2] Short lacuna in the MS. A verb like ⟨ἀφανίζ⟩ουσι is required.

hide the first passion, that of gluttony, with a worse passion, that of conceit. Others again ennoble their body with abstention from food, while they grievously devour the flesh of their neighbours with their tongue and ridicule. It would be better for them to be possessed of the devil and gnaw on their own limbs, rather than consume the lives of their neighbours with slanders, and be for ever meddling and fault-finding at their expense. For *madness*, being as it is an involuntary and grievous plight, is, I believe, capable of moving to pity those that encounter it, and it does not bar divine favour at the time when our lives are examined; whereas the man who willingly commits an insane, devilish and inhuman act draws upon himself with good reason the stigma and hatred of his fellow-countrymen, and makes divine judgment implacable and terrible for himself.

3. Why dost thou leave aside thine own affairs, O man, and examinest thy neighbour? Why, while bearing the beam that is in the pupil of thine eye, dost thou consider the motes of thy brother?, Why dost thou not hearken to the law of the Lords which enjoins, "Judge not, and ye shall not be judged,"[4] but having, as it weret enrolled thyself as a subject of some other lawgiver, thou declarese thy opposition to us, not by thy writ, but by thy life? Perchanct thou judgest thy neighbour and takest delight in calumnies against him at the cry and bidding of thy lawgiver. Nay, for ours does no' say such things as these, "Judge that thou mayest not be judged,'[3] and, "Strike and wound others with abuse that befits thyself, that thou mayest avoid the appearance of being such an one, and hide thy wickedness with calumnies and accusations of others." Our Lawgiver and God asserts, on the contrary, "Judge not, and ye shall not be judged." "Who art thou that judgest another man's servant?"[5] He speaks again in reproof through the divine Paul, "for," quoth He, "wherein thou judgest another, thou condemnest thyself."[6] What force impels thee to such a pitch of sin? What expectation of gain from this madness urges thee on to such

[3] Mt 7. 3; Lk 6. 41.
[4] Lk 6. 37.
[5] Rom. 14. 4. ἱκέτην, as given by the editors, should of course be corrected to οἰκέτην.
[6] Rom. 2. 1.

HOMILY XIII. TYROPHAGY WEEK

shamelessness, so as to disregard the injunctions of an evil-hating Lord, while bowing down to the command of a man-hating tyrant? Or rather, what penalty does not ensue for them that labour at such vain toil?

4. For, whereas we ought to mourn for our own transgressions, and repent, and punish sin with fasting, and, by not judging our neighbour, anticipate beforehand the goodwill of the common Judge, and obtain His mercy, we pay to all this no sort of attention; we leave our own sores unattended, but set ourselves up as severe investigators into those of others, which are no concern of ours; we pry into their talking and walking and smiling (need I say that our habit of malice, exercised by daily practice, most easily and convincingly forges for them actions which they have never committed, and, fostering *these forgeries* by our ingenuity, brings pain and injustice into human life?); and this we do as though a righteous judge, presiding according to divine decrees, had given license to the flow of our tongue, and we do not blush at acting thus shamefully all day long. If this is the study of our life, if this is what we dwell on, how can we but draw upon ourselves the misery of the ultimate punishment, from which there is no release? For, by lying in ambush with our shameless words against other men's lives[7] with the purpose of destroying them, we have maltreated our own life with various evils by having degraded it to the depravity of slanderers, and, lifted up to judge others, we fall ourselves into the pit of the condemned. And then, who are they *that do these things*? The worthless *condemn* the good, the wicked *condemn* the gentle, not to mention other matters more preposterous still. Do you wish me to tell you my plight as well? The sheep *condemn* the shepherd, and the passengers the captain; and they, for whose salvation he watches, slumber on, *indifferent* to his guarding; and would that they were asleep, instead of moving limb and hand and every stone[8] in order to distress him at any cost, and thereby, having made him who presides over their care more negligent, as can well be understood, they may embark without hindrance on any deed directed

---

[7] Read ταῖς γὰρ ἑτέρων πολιτείαις [πολιτείας editors].

[8] A proverb (πάντα λίθον κινεῖν). Cf. Leutsch and Schneidewin, *Corpus paroem. graec.*, I, pp. 146, 293.

towards insanity, just as their impulsive will, which has rejected the laws of obedience, ordains them, and as if there were no one to lead them by the rein and attend to them. Thus fasting results in no benefit, *when*[9] the incontinence of judging and condemning others is not punished.

5. This is the foul deed of the Evil one's craft. This is the artifice of that envious and malicious nature. This is the device of the man-hating Devil: to blunt virtue with evil, to trouble the calm of the fast with the tempests of envy, and, on the storm of garrulousness, to blow man into a sea of passions, and sink him together with his helmsman, the mind. What is the benefit of fasting when calumny acts wantonly[10] in thy lips? What is the emaciation of thy body, when thy tongue is fattened and takes delight in reviling thy neighbour? Why need thou keep a face clear of the *intoxication*[11] of
KL 196 wine, when thy thoughts are drunk with slanders of others, and infuse the red dye of murder into the very depth of thy soul? Jezebel too set up once a fast as a veil for an abomination, as she enacted the death of the righteous Naboth. For Scripture says of her: "And she sent the letter *to the elders* and to the freemen who dwelt with Naboth. And it was written in the letters *saying*, Keep a fast, and set Naboth in a chief place among the people. And set two men, sons of transgressors, before him, and let them testify against him ... and let them lead him forth, and stone him, and let him die."[12] ... Thereafter it says, "And she[13] proclaimed a fast, and they set Naboth in a chief place among the people ... and the men of the defection from Naboth[14] bore witness against him, and they led him forth out of the city, and stoned him with stones, and he died."[15] Seest thou how this fast, when greed and calumny were combined with it, not only was of no benefit, but

[9] Short lacuna. ⟨ἐπειδάν⟩ may be suggested.
[10] Cf. Amos 6. 4.
[11] Word missing. Supply μέθης or κραιπάλης.
[12] 3 Kings 20. 8–10.
[13] "They proclaimed" (ἐκάλεσαν) in the Septuagint.
[14] The words ἄνδρες τῆς ἀποστασίας τοῦ Ναβουθέ, which are absent from the standard text of the Septuagint, belong to the recension of the Cod. Alexandrinus.
[15] 3 Kings 20. 12–13. It is not made clear by the editors whether the three spaces marked by dots are lacunae in the MS, or whether they merely denote the omission of a few words from the scriptural quotation.

HOMILY XIII. TYROPHAGY WEEK

became the veil behind which the murder of the righteous man was enacted? How then could a man, while pursuing sinful actions, think that fasting will be reckoned unto him for righteousness? For considering, as it is plain to see, that when greed met calumny, the fast permitted their secret union to be accomplished, and to beget so great an abomination, it is *indeed* a zealous admirer of that wicked and wretched woman, or rather an executor of her command, who, without the other virtues and righteous deeds, hides under the mask of fasting. For he too proclaims the fast on his face until the secret drama of wickedness, which he has in mind, reaches the climax of lawlessness. "I have not chosen this fast,"[16] saith the Lord Almighty. To them who masquerade with such a fast, He crieth out in wrath, "Your fasting and rest from work, your new moons also, and your feasts my soul hateth."[17]

6. Fasting is acceptable to God when abstention from food is accompanied by refraining from sins, from envy, from hatred, from calumny, from vainglory, from wordiness, from other evils. He who is fasting the true fast *that is agreeable*[18] to God ought to shun all these things with all his strength and zeal, and remain impregnable and unshakeable against all the attacks of the Evil one that are planned from that quarter. On the other hand, he who practises abstention from food, but does not keep self-control in the face of the aforesaid passions, is like unto one who lays down splendid foundations for a house, yet takes serpents and scorpions and vipers as fellow-dwellers therein. For just as the establishment of goodly foundations for that house becomes a deadly trap to those that come nigh, as the lurking reptiles fall upon them unawares with their poison, so also that person who has established his fame among men by means of fasting, while fostering within him the beastlike heads of the passions, is fatal to those that meet him. For his neighbour approaches him as he fawns sweetly in the reputation of his fasting; but he hides within him his vainglory and hatred of his brother and calumny and creeping envy, and covertly expels his poison, and then, especially if his heart be overflowing with the

---

[16] Is. 58. 5–6.
[17] Is. 1. 13–14.
[18] Short lacuna: καὶ ἀποδεκτὴν is perhaps to be supplied.

malice of the plot, bites shrewdly with his words, and injects with all his force into his innocent and perhaps friendly neighbour the ten thousand stings of the wound; but if that *neighbour* be immune to the attacks, if he refuse to suffer or to imitate his assailant, then *his assailant* shall see him crowned victor according to the Lord's decrees, while he himself wastes and destroys himself yet worse, as the destructive passions *within him*[19] rend him body and soul at the sight of the immunity and fair repute of him whom he has envied and assailed. Thus virtue knows how to save him who fortifies himself with her, even if a thousand assailants strike him from without, while evil destroys its possessor, and, even unwilling, submits to what is contrary to his designs, so conferring on him a double tyranny, by showing him the failure of his intended insults and plots, and by filling him with its own perversity and wretchedness.

7. Dost thou abstain from food? Thou doest well. For this is a weapon against the passions for those who use it rightly. Abstain also from envy, so that thy fasting may be considered as fasting by God too, and not be a mask, hiding the other evils as with a veil behind the feigned abstinence from food; but that it should take root in the folds of thy soul like a flourishing and many-branched stock, and should propagate the other virtues, and show them, along with itself, fructified with that blessed and truly immortalizing joy of paradise. Abstain, O man, from envy. Envy is the delight of the devil, the crop raised by that evil nature. Dost thou abstain from the food proper to men?[20]. Much rather shouldst thou refrain from the diet of demons. It is good for man to eat the bread of angels,[21] but the bread of demons is fatal. For that proved to be the first and last surfeit, drunkenness, inebriation and ruin of him who had been allotted the first place in heaven; since, having inebriated himself with the pale draught of envy, and cast an envious glance at man, Lucifer wretchedly fell down from the orb of heaven, and dwelt in Hell, and from that time breathes murder at our kind. For

---

[19] Lacuna: τῶν ... φθοροποιῶν παθῶν. A word like ἐμφωλευόντων would give the required meaning.

[20] Place full stop after τρυφήν, and punctuate: νήστευσον, ἄνθρωπε, φθόνου. φθόνος ἐστὶ τὸ τοῦ διαβόλου ἐντρύφημα, τῆς πονηρᾶς ἐκείνης φύσεως τὸ γεώργιον. τῆς ἀνθρώποις προσηκούσης νηστεύεις τροφῆς; πολλῷ μᾶλλον, etc.

[21] Cf. Ps. 77. 25.

HOMILY XIII. TYROPHAGY WEEK

murder is the offspring of envy, and it is most difficult for those who have once inebriated themselves with it to return to sobriety. Dost thou abstain from food? Abstain from vainglory. She is the mother of envy, having taken folly to husband. For indeed the envious one is moved to envy those who excel him; while he who imagines about himself vain[22] and great things which do not at all become him strives to outstrip everyone else, and being foolishly lifted up by such *thoughts*, he falls into the pit of the envious, and when he is surpassed he wastes away, having wretchedly given himself up to folly and vainglory. Abstain from slander and calumny; for they too are the offspring of envy and the firstborn sisters of murder. Since envy, as a rule, first begets those out of us, and thereafter is born murder as a last and fatal offspring both for its begetter and for the ones who are envied. Let us avoid, beloved ones, their plague, let us abominate their evil, let us not wish to draw near even to the experience thereof. But let us offer God a pure fast that embellishes the soul with brotherly love, that adorns the body with humility, that sanctifies the mind with proper praise-giving, that makes the lips fragrant through decorous speech about one another, and that, by means of an attentive practice of these things, leads us to freedom from passion.

8. If you live in this wise and show in actions that you are keeping my exhortations, you will enable me to converse with you more often, sometimes with addresses, sometimes by reading the Holy Writ, and the time of the coming week will provide the proof thereof. As for yourselves, you will win the kingdom of heaven, of which may we all be deemed worthy through the grace and mercy of our great God and Saviour Jesus Christ, to Whom is due all glory, honour and veneration, together with the eternal Father, and the co-eternal and co-everlasting Spirit, the consubstantial and life-giving Trinity, now and for ever and ever. Amen.

---

[22] κενὰ καὶ μεγάλα seems to be preferable to καινὰ καὶ μεγάλα, as given by the editors, since this refers to the κενόδοξος.

HOMILIES OF PHOTIUS

XIV

Ar I 192 OF THE SAME MOST-BLESSED PHOTIUS, ARCHBISHOP OF CONSTANTINOPLE, HOMILY DELIVERED FROM THE AMBO OF ST. SOPHIA ON THE FRIDAY OF THE FIRST WEEK OF LENT[1]

1. I am come to you anticipating the appointed time and striving to pay up my debt beforehand, since willing obligations, which are extended by those who offer them in the way of gifts, do not admit of having the courtesy spoilt by delays and postponements. It is good, to be sure, that a father should not appear unpunctual to his children, but better still it is for him to discharge his debt by paying it in advance as a mark of favour. Besides, seeing your eagerness to listen (nor is it fitting for one who exhorts his neighbours to virtue to relax the intensity of their desire by evading speech), I have given myself to you all the more willingly, and while the help of the most-holy Ghost is bestowed on me, I will not refrain my lips[2] in shaping your improvement.

2. For the husbandman too rejoices when he sees his field weighed
Ar I 193 down by ears of corn, and recalling in fairness some goodly meadow; the gardener also rejoices when he sees the boughs of the trees crowded with the seasonable crop of fruit, and the pilot when he sees his freighter leaping and cutting her way across the surface of the sea before a fair wind. Sweet also is the song that the shepherd strikes up on his reeds as he sits at ease, and, laying aside his staff, he rests humming a bucolic tune to his nurslings,[3] when he sees his flock in happy condition, undiminished by an *evil* regimen. Yea indeed, the appointed shepherd of Christ's nurslings is also filled with an ineffable joy and gladness, when his rational flock progresses in righteousness and is adorned with virtuous deeds.[4] How should I not be pleased, when I see the ugly pleasures trodden down by you and virtue observed, while vice is spat upon, envy voted down, while happiness gains its rights of citizenship, slanders

---

[1] In the Athen. 2756 the title is given as follows: "Homily delivered on the Friday of the same first week of Lent."
[2] Ps. 39. 10.
[3] Almost surely an allusion to some pastoral verse.
[4] Read ταῖς ἀρεταῖς ἐξωραϊζομένης τῶν πράξεων [τῶν ἀρετῶν ἐξωραϊζομένης πράξεσι Ar]. On this passage, cf. above, p. 23, n. 75.

HOMILY XIV. TYROPHAGY WEEK

banished while brotherly love flourishes? This, I cry out with the divine Paul, is my pride and joy.[5] This puts to sleep the sorrows which spring up at us from many directions, craftily contrived by the Evil one, rids us of those many cares, and gives us unwonted contentment. This is also able to dispel the cloud of despondency which often sweeps over our thoughts; indeed your life and conduct are adorned by the brilliance of joy when by the laws of the spirit the law, or rather the usurpation, of the flesh is put to flight, when the ancient marks of sin are blotted out of your souls, and the new commandments of Christ's law are inscribed instead.

3. Easy is Christ's yoke, and his burden light.[6] For what is lighter than to check the tongue? What is easier than to have a reverent mouth? What is milder than not to begrudge thy brethren? No need for thee to suffer toils, to undergo sleepless vigils, distressed all day and all night, or to dig a ditch, or erect a mound of earth, or to work in clay and brick-making, which the Egyptians devised against the Jews,[7] or to carry out any other toilsome act. There will be need only to contain thy tongue behind thy teeth, like a fair bride guarded in her natural chamber, wherein the Creator has enclosed her with a double rampart, safeguarding her proneness to slip and her vulnerability, and teaching thee by the example of His creation not to abuse her at random, especially in matters which do not concern thee; but if thou fulfillest the divine laws, and dost not outrage the limits of nature, thou oughtst to keep her in her natural chamber like a good virgin, uttering no dissolute and wanton song, nor behaving in an unseemly manner by abusing thy neighbour, and not allow her to commit harlotry through slanders. For she is verily a harlot who, though she could have preserved her own bridal chastity, has meretriciously yielded to the vulgar passion of slander, and is not ashamed to disgrace her own beauty.

Ar I 194

Ar I 195

4. Be thou not swept along and cast down by such monstrous actions. Use her to sing hymns to Him that gave her to thee, to define accurately religious beliefs (if it pleases thee to seek into such matters also), for the pressing services of life, and for the com-

---

[5] Phil. 2. 16–17; Thess. 2. 20.
[6] Mt 11. 30.
[7] Exod. 1. 14.

mendation of thy neighbour, and that not beyond measure, lest thou slippest into the disgrace of flattery; since moderation is the best of all things, and has won its place even in the thought of some who are alien to our religion.[8] Do not use her to insult and slander thy neighbour, but, according to the proverb, "remove from thee a forward mouth, and put far away from thee unjust lips,"[9] for the Lord pulls down the houses of scorners,[10] and a talkative man shall not prosper on the earth,[11] and a man's own lips are a snare to him, and he is caught with the words of his own mouth,[12] when the use of their utterance is not observed according to nature and divine command. Do not, therefore, liken thyself to such men, nor follow

Ar I 196 them in their footsteps. For a man inspired by God and designated to be called the Lord's brother, says that "the tongue, though it be a little member, defileth the whole body, and inflameth the course of nature," and furthermore that "it is set on fire of hell," and he shows that her wickedness is worse than that of beasts and serpents,[13] when the mind leaves her vehemence unbridled and she refuses to obey the reins of the mind.

5. Yet what are also her disguised entrances?[14] So and so is behaving badly, and I cannot help but be displeased, even against my will, and those *impulses* which enjoin me to be silent and to refrain from ridicule, are the very ones which impel me to imitate his *evil* ways.[15] Verily are the devil's devices crafty in deceiving and

---

[8] I. e. the pagans, with reference to the ancient maxim μέτρον ἄριστον. At this point there is a marginal scholion which may be rendered as follows: "He says 'has won its place' (ἐξενίκησε). The idea is not theirs [i. e. of the pagans], nor are they worthy to utter such things. But the splendour of Truth has succeeded (ἐξενίκησε) to be expressed and to appear even in the mouths of the untruthful. This sense of the figure is admirably applied to all from whom, though not themselves praiseworthy, we may desire to draw some praiseworthy evidence or use." Cf. above, p. 10.

[9] Prov. 4. 24.
[10] Prov. 15. 25.
[11] Ps. 139. 12.
[12] Prov. 6. 2.
[13] James 3. 5–7.
[14] Reading κατεσχηματισμένα προσκήνια with Pg: κατεσχημένα προσήνια codd.
[15] A most obscure passage. The MSS read: κακῶς ὁ δεῖνα πολιτεύεται, καὶ δυσαρεστεῖσθαί με συμβαίνει πάντως καὶ μὴ βουλόμενον. καὶ οἷς μέ τις σιγᾶν ἐπιτρέπει, καὶ μὴ κωμῳδεῖν ἐκεῖνα, τὰ ἐκείνου μιμεῖσθαι προστάττει [κωμῳδεῖν, ἐκείνη (sc. ἡ γλῶσσα) Ar]. The meaning of this difficult passage seems to be the following: That man's evil behaviour arouses in me a feeling of moral

HOMILY XIV. TYROPHAGY WEEK

tripping us up, and when he fails with attacks from the left, he succeeds in gaining admission unnoticed with those that seem to come from the right.[16] So and so is behaving badly? Then do thou behave thyself well, lest thou in turn be the cause of others saying the same things about thee,[17] and sinning thereby. So and so *behaves* badly? But another *behaves* well. Let the former fall and stand to his own master,[18] but the latter's conduct and actions do thou remember and emulate. Is another one incontinent in his life? Why, hast thou been appointed his judge? Wilt thou discharge his accounts? Mayest thou be able to render even thine own on that terrible day of judgment! Is he incontinent in his life? And art thou not incontinent and unbridled in thy tongue, who chatterest of other men's affairs, and takest a shameful pleasure in foul stories? Art thou not steeped in passions in thy mind (would it were only in the mind!) who art so easily convinced by the slander of thy neighbour, and whereas thou shouldst cover thy face when others are uttering it, thou appearest the first to publish it abroad? For he who in his deeds has departed from the passions is not persuaded that others fall prey to them, since by his own example he has won confidence in others. But he who readily accepts the calumny of another, does not himself abstain from such actions; for the practice of this habit is wont to drag down into association with it even the innocent. Yes, says he, but this man is also a slanderer, and rejoices in calumny, and is worthy of finding his nemesis. Why, art thou not a slanderer who sayest this of him, and dost thou not become a prey to calumny? If thou didst observe carefully thyself and thy ways, thou wouldst not have had the time to examine the defects of others, and to dwell on them.—But he too is slandering me unjustly.—Then it is fitting that thou shouldst say nothing bad of him, that thou mayest prove

Ar I 197

---

superiority, which should make me refrain from abuse, but in fact prompts me to criticise him, thus making me as bad as he is. This kind of moral superiority has, therefore, all the appearances of being right, whereas it is actually a contrivance of the devil.

[16] Read ὄντως σοφά [Pg: σοφία AB] ἐστιν εἰς τὸ ἐξαπατῆσαι καὶ ὑποσκελίσαι τοῦ πονηροῦ τὰ σοφίσματα, καὶ τῶν ἀριστερῶν ταῖς ἐπιβολαῖς ἀποτυγχάνων διὰ τῶν δοκούντων δεξιῶν λεληθότως εὐπορεῖ τὴν παρείσδυσιν [σοφή ἐστιν ... οὐχὶ δὲ καὶ ὑποσκελίσαι ... ταῖς ἐπιβουλαῖς ἀποτυγχάνουσα Ar].

[17] Read τοῦ λέγειν ταὐτά with Pg: τὸ λέγειν ταῦτα codd, Ar.

[18] Rom. 14. 4. Read ἐκεῖνον μὲν ἔα [Pg]: ἐκείνου μὲν ἔα codd, Ar.

by thy action to be unjustly slandered. Is he slandering thee unjustly? Dost thou then hasten to show thyself rightly slandered, and to be that man's imitator, whose just accuser thou considerest thyself to be?[19] Fret not thyself because of evil-doers, neither be envious of them that do iniquity.[20] Nor try to defeat the tongue with the tongue; for fire is not quenched with fire, nor is evil healed with evil. The frolics of the tongue are arrested by silence, and drops of water can quench a fiery flame; yea, virtue has always been able to defeat evil.

Ar I 198

6. Thou, therefore, if thou believest me at all, or rather if thou obeyest at all the divine injunctions, refrain from heaping abuse on thy slanderer. And whatsoever another may say against him, hoping perchance to win thy favour, do thou by thy goodness confute it, so that thou mayest teach him also to repent of his rashness, and show thyself to be truly above all blasphemy. Accept not therefore the slander of thy neighbour. For the voice of truth teaches that *in so doing* thou slanderest thyself rather than him; since he who gives ear to reports against his neighbour is led to slander himself.[21] But if thou thyself inventest them—for there is indeed among men a wicked and spiteful race, of whom may we all be delivered, who make it their especial art to calumniate and besmear their neighbours with their own abominations, so that, the accusation being common, they may with less fear fill themselves like cattle with their wantonness in all things, and by contriving to have many sharing the same name, they may appear to show their transgression lighter—if then there be such an one (not that there is one in your midst—God forbid!—for, I believe, I am not so wretched as to have such beasts in my care), alas, what punishments he will be subjected to! Not a millstone about his neck, nor the depth of the sea,[22] which are the punishment and destruction of the body only, but the outer darkness,[23] and the sleepless worm,[24] and every kind of torment which surpasses words

Ar I 199

[19] Read καὶ μιμητὴν ἐκείνου γινόμενον οὗ δίκαιον σεαυτὸν ὑπολαμβάνεις κατήγορον [μιμητὴς ἐκείνου γινόμενος οὐ δίκαιον σεαυτοῦ Ar].
[20] Ps. 36. 1.
[21] Read ταῖς εἰς αὐτὸν [αὐτὸν codd, Ar] ὑποσύρεται λοιδορίαις.
[22] Mt 18. 6; Mk 9. 42; Lk 17. 2.
[23] Mt 8. 12.
[24] Cf. Mk 9. 48.

HOMILY XIV. TYROPHAGY WEEK

and comprehension by the mind and which bitterly devours the soul, will justly await him, the calumniator amidst men, the alien amidst countrymen, the curse of human kind, the accuser of the Creation.

7. Let us, however, beloved ones, avoid the wickedness of these men, that we may not share in their punishment. Let us avoid false testimony, reviling, calumny. Let us guard ourselves against every work of the Evil one, that we may receive the heavenly kingdom in Jesus Christ our Lord, to whom is due all[25] glory, honour and veneration, together with the eternal Father and the co-eternal and everlasting Ghost, the consubstantial and life-giving Trinity, now and for ever and ever. Amen.

[25] The word πᾶσα has been omitted by Ar.

NOTE ON HOMILIES XV AND XVI

The following two sermons are part of what one might almost call a lecture course on ecclesiastical history. In a series of at least four, and probably five sermons, Photius expounded the story of the Arian heresy from its inception down to the Second Oecumenical Council (381). Of this series, the beginning and end are lost. The initial sermon (or sermons) related the personal career of Arius and his condemnation at the Council of Nicaea;[1] the concluding one (or two) carried the story from the death of the Emperor Constantius (361) down to, and including, the Second Council. This series of sermons was delivered during Lent, perhaps on five successive Sundays; because in the tenth-century MS of the Greek Patriarchate at Jerusalem Homily XV appears between two sermons pertaining to the Sunday of Orthodoxy (i. e. the first Sunday of Lent).[2]

The lost parts of the narrative can be supplemented to some extent from the *Letter to Boris*, in which Photius gives an account of the First and Second Oecumenical Councils.[3] Aristarches, in his usual manner, has reconstructed three missing sermons by combining, in addition to the appropriate passages from the *Letter to Boris*, various snippets of the *Amphilochia*, the *Bibliotheca*, the *Contra Manichaeos*, and even the *Mystagogia*. Particularly regrettable is the loss of the last sermon dealing with the Second Oecumenical Council and hence with the Macedonian doctrine of the Holy Ghost. Had we had that sermon, we might have been able to date the whole series more securely, depending on whether or not

---

[1] Cf. pp. 244, 247 below.
[2] Papadopoulos Kerameus, Ἱεροσολυμιτικὴ Βιβλιοθήκη, I, pp. 3–4. Papadopoulos Kerameus (p. 4, n. 1) believes that Homily XV occurs at that place in the MS because it was originally delivered on the Sunday of Orthodoxy. If that were so, we would have to assume that it was preached on the first Sunday of Lent, and not on the second Sunday, as we have supposed; it must be pointed out, however, that the Feast of Orthodoxy does not appear to have been officially celebrated in Photius' time, and does not even figure in the *Typicon of the Great Church* (end of the 9th century): cf. below, pp. 285–6.
[3] Ed. Valettas, pp. 204–09 = PG 102, cols. 632–37.

NOTE ON HOMILIES XV AND XVI

Photius took that opportunity of denouncing the Latin teaching of the *Filioque*.[4]

In Homilies XV and XVI the story of Arianism is not told in strict chronological order. No. XV covers the death of Arius (336), the deposition of Eustathius, bishop of Antioch (330), the Council of Tyre (335), the banishment of Athanasius to Gaul (336), and, by anticipation of events described in the next sermon, the shameful plot against Stephen of Antioch (344). No. XVI reverts to the accession of Constantius (337), and proceeds to describe the Dedication Council at Antioch (341), the Macrostich Creed (344), the installation of Macedonius as Bishop of Constantinople, the Councils of Sardica and Philippopolis (which actually occurred in 343, but were evidently regarded by Photius as having taken place in 347), and various other councils, ending up with the triumph of Arianism at the Council of Constantinople (360) and the death of the Emperor Constantius (361).

The chief interest of these two sermons resides, of course, not so much in the story of Arianism, which we know in great detail from more ancient and often contemporary sources, but in the comparison which is drawn by Photius between the heretics of the fourth century and those of the ninth century. Yet, even so, it would not be amiss for historians of Arianism to take these sermons into consideration. Photius was exceedingly well-read in fourth-century Church history, as a glance at the *Bibliotheca* will reveal. He had read all the principal narrative sources, some of which, like Gelasius and Philostorgius, he knew *in toto*; furthermore, he had at his disposal much more hagiographical, polemical and conciliar material than we have. We cannot enter here into a full discussion of his sources, which we have tried to indicate in the footnotes to our translation. Photius leans most heavily on Theodoret, Socrates and Sozomen (the latter two being quoted by name). He certainly used the writings of Athanasius, especially the *Apologia contra Arianos* and the *De synodis*. The influence of hagiographical sources, namely the *Lives* of Metrophanes and Alexander, Paul, Bishop of Byzantium, and Athanasius, is also apparent. Some particulars are drawn from Gelasius of Cyzicus. Philostorgius has also been consulted, though rather sparingly.

[4] Cf. above, p. 22.

HOMILIES OF PHOTIUS

Among the statements of Photius which deserve a closer examination, are the mention of a Council at Corduba, said to have been held by Ossius after the Council of Sardica,[5] and especially the sympathetic treatment accorded to that arch-intriguer, Acacius of Caesarea. Acacius, he says, was unjustly condemned by the Council of Sardica; he was still at that time of the right faith, "although these matters ... have been left out, not to say falsified, by Socrates and Sozomen."[6] Further down, in describing the Arian Council of Constantinople (360), Photius admits that Acacius was beginning to suffer "the perversion of his faith," but even then it was his actions and not his mind that he placed in the service of the heretics.[7] This favourable judgment can hardly be due to the fact that in the reign of the orthodox Jovian Acacius embraced the Nicene faith, for that was clearly done for reasons of expediency, and only showed that he "worshipped the purple and not the deity."[8] For the orthodox, Acacius was the enemy of *ousia* and *hypostasis*,[9] who exerted all his influence to bring the edicts of Nicaea into oblivion.[10] Photius is not, therefore, following an orthodox, nor even a semi-Arian source. We would suggest that he bases his judgment of Acacius on the ultra-Arian Philostorgius. For in the eyes of Philostorgius, the disciple of Eunomius and Aetius, anyone who was not an Anhomoean was a Nicene;[11] and it was Acacius who, though decidedly an Arian, treacherously sacrificed Aetius at the Council of Constantinople (360). Consequently, Philostorgius accuses Acacius of believing one thing and doing another,[12] and (quite unjustly) of appointing Homoousian bishops to the sees left vacant by the deposition of the semi-Arians.[13] If our supposition is correct, it may be further suspected that Philostorgius gave some additional details that have not been preserved concerning the activities of Acacius prior to the Council of Constantinople.

[5] See below, p. 271 and n. 33.
[6] P. 269 below.
[7] P. 273 below.
[8] Socrates III. 25.
[9] *Ibid.*, II. 41.
[10] Sozomen IV. 26.
[11] Cf. J. Bidez, "L'historien Philostorge," *Mélanges d'histoire offerts à H. Pirenne*, I, Brussels, 1926, p. 27.
[12] IV. 12, p. 65$_{27}$ ed. Bidez. Cf. Photius, *Biblioth.*, cod. 40.
[13] V. 1, p. 66.

NOTE ON HOMILIES XV AND XVI

But be that as it may, we have here an interesting illustration of Photius' historical method. Acacius, whom Theophanes calls "that most-evil Arian of Caesarea,"[14] is not painted a solid black. We have here a beginning of that trend towards a more balanced portrayal of character that reaches a peak in Byzantine literature of the tenth and eleventh centuries.[15] The same may be said about Photius' assessment of the semi-Arians, men like Basil of Ancyra, Eustathius of Sebaste, Silvanus of Tarsus and Eleusius of Cyzicus, who, with some reservations, are pronounced to have been "athletes of true religion"; yet those same men are treated as outright heretics by Epiphanius[16] whom Photius had read.[17] That is not to say, however, that Photius is a humanistic historian; always predominant is his conception of history as being primarily edifying. To take but one example, Constantine's baptism by an Arian is rejected without discussion;[18] to admit it would have been unthinkable.

The real purpose of the two Homilies is quite transparent. It is twofold: firstly, to liken Iconoclasm to Arianism, that prototype of all heresies, and secondly, to show that to plot against bishops, provided they are orthodox, is to be on the side of the devil. Theologically, the comparison of Arianism to Iconoclasm is somewhat forced; for, whereas the former tended to deprive Christ of His complete divinity, the latter, on the contrary, tended to deprive Him of His complete humanity. The comparison was, however, drawn by some Iconodule polemicists of the time,[19] while others preferred to liken the image-breakers to the Valentinians, Marcionites, Manichees and Montanists.[20] Photius does not, however, press the comparison on dogmatic grounds. Apart from the fact that both Arianism and Iconoclasm are an insult to Christ, it is the tactics, rather than the beliefs of the two sets of heretics that he finds so similar. Both proceeded by slow degrees: the Arians,

---

[14] Ed. De Boor, p. 54₇.
[15] Cf. R. J. H. Jenkins, "The Classical Background of the *Scriptores post Theophanem,*" *Dumbarton Oaks Papers*, 8 (1954), pp. 14–15.
[16] *Haer. LXXIII.*
[17] *Biblioth.*, cod. 122.
[18] P. 255 below.
[19] E. g. Nicephorus, PG 100, cols. 244 D, 561 A–B, 796 C.
[20] Cf. Theodore Studites, PG 99, cols. 388 D; 452 C; 461 C; 481 A; 1132 C; 1305 A; 1321 D; 1513 C; 1604 C.

HOMILIES OF PHOTIUS

starting with the seemingly innocuous objection that the word *homoousios* (of like substance) was apt to be misunderstood, ended by degrading Christ to the rank of a creature; the Iconoclasts, beginning with the contention that icons should not be placed too close to the spectator, ended up by equating icons with heathen idols. The argument that images should be moved higher up to avoid gross acts of adoration is said to have been used by Leo V before the Patriarch Nicephorus,[21] and is typical of the second, rather than the first Iconoclastic period.[22]

The comparison of Arianism to Iconoclasm is also applied by Photius to the respective leaders of the two heresies, Arius on the one hand, John the Grammarian on the other.[23] We are given in this connection some highly interesting information concerning John, Patriarch of Constantinople from 837 to 843,[24] and surely one of the outstanding intellectual figures of his time. John, says Photius, began as an iconodule, and was even a professional painter. Later he joined the heretics, but repented of it, and was received back into the Church by the Patriarch Nicephorus. When, however, John had lapsed again and actually aspired to become the leader of the Iconoclasts, Nicephorus categorically refused to admit him into the Church, even were he to present a second recantation.

Our information concerning John's origin and early career is both meagre and contradictory.[25] He was of Armenian extraction, son

---

[21] Script. incert. de Leone Bardae f., Bonn ed. (along with Leo Grammaticus), p. 352.

[22] Cf. Theodore Studites, *Antirrheticus* II, PG 99, col. 352 C–D; *Letter of Michael II to Lewis the Pious* (A. D. 824), MGH Leges, sect. III, Concilia, vol. 2, pt. 2, p. 479$_{15}$. The old Latin translation of the *Vita S. Stephani Iunioris* (cf. Baronius, *Annales eccles.* ad ann. 726, § 5) is responsible for the view that at the very outbreak of Iconoclasm Leo III ordered all images to be moved up to a higher position. Cf. E. J. Martin, *A History of the Iconoclastic Controversy*, London, 1930, p. 31. The Latin version of the *Vita* is, however, defended by Bréhier, "Sur un texte relatif au début de la querelle iconoclaste," *Échos d'Orient*, XXXVII (1938), pp. 17–22.

[23] Pp. 246–47 below.

[24] On the dates, see Grumel, "Chronologie des patriarches iconoclastes du IXe siècle," *Échos d'Orient*, XXXIV (1935), pp. 162–66 and 506.

[25] See, amongst others, Th. Uspenskij, "Патріархъ Іоаннъ VII Грамматикъ и Русь-дромиты у Симеона Магистра," Журн. Мин. Нар. Просв., 267 (Jan. 1890), pp. 1–34; *id.*, Очерки по исторіи византійской образованности, St. Petersburg, 1891, pp. 61–65; L. Bréhier, "Un patriarche sorcier à Constantinople," *Revue de l'Orient chrétien*, IX (1904), pp. 261–68.

NOTE ON HOMILIES XV AND XVI

of one Pankratios, described as a *skiastes*,[26] but, whereas some sources claim him to have been of lowly origin,[27] others say that he belonged to the noble family of the Morocharzamioi.[28] Later on we hear of John's brother, the patrician Arsaber, who owned estates on the Bosphorus;[29] this is not, however, proof that John's family was wealthy, since Arsaber's elevation to the patriciate occurred in the reign of Theophilus and may have been due to John's influence at court. John himself is said to have been a lector (*anagnostes*) at the monastery of the Virgin Hodegetria during the reign of Michael I (811–813).[30] He was also known as the Grammarian, perhaps because he had composed a treatise on grammar.[31] His learning won him the recognition of Leo V (813–820), and at Pentecost 814 he was instructed to collect ancient texts against the worship of images. The research was carried on in monastic libraries, John being assisted by a number of colleagues.[32] By December the work was ready. On the expulsion of the Patriarch Nicephorus (13th March 815), Leo was allegedly anxious to make John Patriarch, but the senate objected on the grounds that he was too young and too obscure (ἀφανής).[33] So Theodotus Cassiteras became Patriarch, while John was made abbot of the monastery of SS. Ser-

---

[26] The meaning of the word σκιαστής is not too clear. According to Du Cange (*Glossarium*, s. v.) it signifies "embroiderer." Cf. Constantine Porph., *Vita Basilii*, Bonn ed., p. 318₁₃. Combefis renders it as "pileorum artifex," i. e. a maker of hats called σκιάδια (which seems to be wrong). Sophocles (*Lexicon*, s. v.) and Stephanus (*Thesaurus*, s. v. σκιαστός) explain it as a servant who held a parasol. Cf. Greg. Naz., PG 37, col. 659 A. The name Pankratios seems to conceal the Armenian Bagrat. Cf. J. Laurent, *L'Arménie entre Byzance et l'Islam*, Paris, 1919, p. 195, n. 5; Saint-Martin *ap.* Lebeau, *Histoire du Bas-Empire*, XIII (1832), p. 14, n. 3.

[27] Script. incert., pp. 349, 359; *Epist. ad Theophil. imper.* (interpolated version), PG 95, col. 368 A.

[28] Theoph. Cont., p. 154 (Bonn); Cedrenus, II, p. 144 (Bonn).

[29] Theoph. Cont., pp. 156–57; Cedrenus, II, p. 146.

[30] *Epist. ad Theophil., loc. cit.*

[31] The opprobrious epithet Hylilas, "which in Hebrew means the precursor and co-adjutor of the devil" (Script. incert., p. 350), was not John's surname, as is so often stated. Hylilas may be derived from the Hebrew Heylel in Is. 14. 12, usually rendered as Lucifer.

[32] They are named in the *Vita Nicetae Mediciani*, *Acta Sanctorum*, Apr. vol. I, ad. calc., p. XXIV, § 31.

[33] Script. incert., p. 351. In the newly-published Life of St. Peter of Atroa, John is made responsible for the persecution under Leo V. This is surely an exaggeration. See V. Laurent, *La Vie merveilleuse de Saint Pierre d'Atroa* (= *Subsidia hagiographica*, 29), Brussels, 1956, p. 187.

gius and Bacchus near the palace. His advancement, as pointed out by Uspenskij,[34] was not especially rapid. We need not follow in detail John's subsequent career. It is not until the reign of Michael II (820–829) that he comes to the fore, as Syncellus and preceptor of the young Theophilus. It was probably in 829–30 that his famous embassy to Baghdad took place.[35] John was made Patriarch in 837 and deposed on March 4th, 843. He lived on, proud and unrepenting, until after 850.[36]

It has been suggested that there were two Johns, one a simple lector, who was appointed to collect in libraries texts favourable to Iconoclasm, the other a noble and famous dialectician, who later became Patriarch.[37] The information given by Photius (which, strangely enough, has never been noticed) tends to disprove this theory. To be a painter was not, of course, a dishonourable occupation, and more than one Byzantine emperor excelled at that art; but to use painting as a profession, εἰς βίου πρόφασιν, is not indicative of wealth.[38] Clearly, John practised painting in his youth, perhaps while he was an *anagnostes* at the Hodegetria monastery. The family of the Morocharzamioi, notwithstanding their alleged ancient lineage, may have been impoverished at the time.[39] The fact that John is said to have been the godfather (σύντεκνος)[40] of the empress Theodora (married to Theophilus in 821), who herself

---

[34] "Патріархъ Іоаннъ Грамматикъ," p. 5.
[35] On the embassy see Bury, "The Embassy of John the Grammarian," *English Hist. Review*, 24 (1909), pp. 296–99; *id.*, *Hist. of the Eastern Roman Empire*, pp. 256–59; Brooks in *BZ*, X (1901), p. 298; Vasiliev, *Byzance et les Arabes*, I, Brussels, 1935, pp. 112–3, as well as M. Canard's and H. Grégoire's notes, *ibid.*, pp. 409, 416–17.
[36] Cf. Dvornik, *Les légendes de Constantin et de Méthode*, pp. 71 sq.
[37] V. Grumel, "Jean Grammaticos et S. Théodore Studite," *Échos d'Orient*, XXXVI (1937), pp. 181–89.
[38] Cod. Palat. 129, fol. 141ᵛ, reads τὴν τῶν οἰκοδόμων [instead of ζωγράφων] τέχνην εἰς βίου πρόφασιν μεταχειριζόμενος, but this is obviously a mistake, as the context indicates.
[39] We have no other contemporary reference to this family. A man by that name appears in the 11th century (Psellus, *Scripta minora*, ed. Kurtz & Drexl, II, Milan, 1941, p. 99).
[40] Not a "relative," as Grumel (*op. cit.*, p. 182) renders it. For the use of the word, cf. Theoph. Cont., pp. 24_7, 120_{22}. That John was Theodora's godfather is given as a rumour rather than as a positive statement (Contin. of Georg. Hamart., ed. Muralt, St. Petersburg, 1859, p. 718; PG 109, col. 872 C; PG 110, col. 1032 A); it appears, moreover, that the word σύντεκνος was sometimes used rather loosely to mean "mentor" or "spiritual father."

NOTE ON HOMILIES XV AND XVI

belonged to a fairly obscure Paphlagonian family, is not an indication to the contrary.

John's lapse into heresy and recantation are, most probably, to be connected with an incident told in the interpolated version of the *Synodal Letter of the Oriental Patriarchs to Theophilus*.[41] This document, which for a long time was attributed to St. John Damascene, relates that after John the Grammarian had carried out some of his research in monastic libraries (in 814), he held a disputation with Nicephorus, and was utterly defeated. Fearing excommunication, and happening at the same time to fall ill, he asked the Patriarch's pardon, and sought refuge in monastic repentance. Note that Photius also mentions an illness (νόσῳ περιπεσόντα).

It must have been very shortly after, perhaps at the end of 814, that John again sided with the Iconoclasts, since he was Leo's candidate for patriarch in March 815. Nicephorus' refusal to pardon John on the latter's second lapse may be connected with an incident that took place at the beginning of Lent, 815. A clerical deputation, of which John may have been one, came to Nicephorus and demanded of him that he endorse a pamphlet they had brought with them. At first the Patriarch refused to let them in; upon being persuaded to receive them, however, Nicephorus, spoke to them very harshly, pronounced them deposed from the clergy, and ordered them out.[42]

The date of the two Homilies under review has already been discussed.[43] It remains to lay stress on Photius' appeal that his detractors should refrain from further plots against bishops.[44] It is to this end, he says, that he has described the Arian assaults upon Athanasius and Eustathius. If a bishop is of the right faith, he must be obeyed, while his private affairs are for God to judge. One gathers that other bishops, besides Photius, had been the object of hostility, and although the Patriarch refers to his detractors as being few in number, the general impression he conveys is that opposition to him was by no means negligible.

---

[41] PG 95, col. 372 B = Mansi XIV, col. 117 A.
[42] *Vita Nicephori*, ap. Nicephori *Opuscula historica*, ed. De Boor (1880), pp. 193–96.
[43] See above, pp. 20–23.
[44] See below, pp. 258–60 and 276–77.

HOMILIES OF PHOTIUS

XV

Ar I 254   OF THE SAME PHOTIUS, ARCHBISHOP OF CONSTANTINOPLE, HOMILY FROM THE AMBO OF THE GREAT CHURCH[1]

1. The end of the foregoing sermon, if you recall, related how Arius was deposed and expelled from the Church, how he acted shamelessly, invented fictions, simulated piety, and afterwards ended his life by a most disgraceful death, and Christ's people breathed again after those many evils and snares. Seest thou the power of prayer? Seest thou the prelate's outspokenness? "Lord, if Arius is admitted into the Church, then remove me from life; but if Thou sufferest me yet to remain in this tabernacle, then keep the gates of the Church inaccessible to Arius." Thus prayed Alexander,[2] and the spear against Arius was being forged by heavenly decree. Christ's servant was stretching out his arms to the One blasphemed, while the enemy was paying the penalty for his licentious tongue, by suffering the emptying out of his miserable entrails and bowels through his belly. He, therefore, having imitated the manner of Judas, underwent also a death similar to the latter's, as told in the Ar I 255 *Acts*, for, falling headlong, he burst asunder in the midst, and all his bowels gushed out;[3] while the state of the Church remained untroubled for some time.

Perchance it will occur to some of you to ask why Arius was

---

[1] In the MSS the title is given as follows: τοῦ αὐτοῦ Φωτίου[Φωτίου τοῦ ἁγιωτάτου Hierosol. 1] ἀρχιεπισκόπου Κωνσταντινουπόλεως ὁμιλία λεχθεῖσα ἐν τῷ ἄμβωνι τῆς μεγάλης ἐκκλησίας.

[2] St. Alexander, Bishop of Byzantium and later of Constantinople from *ca.* 313 until his death *ca.* 336. More eminent for his virtue than for his learning, Alexander was an avowed adversary of Arius. When, in 336, Arius regained the Emperor's favour, Alexander was directed to enter into communion with him or resign. He shut himself up in the church of Irene and prayed for several days and nights that the differences between Arius and himself should be resolved by the death of either one of them. Soon afterwards Arius died in a public lavatory as he was going out of the palace in great pomp. See Athanasius, *Epist. ad Serapionem de morte Arii*, PG 25, col. 688; Socrates, I. 37–38, PG 67, cols. 176–77; Sozomen, II. 29, PG 67, cols. 1017–20; Theodoret, I. 14, ed. Parmentier & Scheidweiler (1954), p. 57; Epiphanius, *Adv. haer.*, LXIX. 10, PG 42, col. 217. A life of Alexander and his predecessor Metrophanes (of dubious historical value) is summarized in Photius' *Bibliotheca*, cod. 256, pp. 469–74 in Bekker's ed.

[3] Acts 1. 18. The same quotation is given in this connection by Athanasius, *loc. cit.*, and Theodoret *loc. cit.*

HOMILY XV. THE ARIAN HERESY

deposed by the holy martyr Peter,[4] but was received by his successor, the admirable Achillas,[5] and resumed the rank of deacon, and was not only absolved from his deposition by the wondrous Alexander,[6] but even promoted to the position of presbyter. Why is it, that having been previously deposed, he was accepted, but later, although he offered a tome of repentance,[7] he remained unaccepted, neither *Alexander* of Constantinople, nor Alexander of Alexandria (for both, just as their zeal for piety was the same, so had they one and the same name) by any means allowing, as I have said previously, his reception into the Church? It is clear that both

---

[4] St. Peter, Archbishop of Alexandria, appointed in 300 and beheaded in 311 by order of Maximin Daza. It was he who ordained Arius deacon after the latter had abandoned the Meletian party; but when Peter excommunicated the followers of Meletius, Arius criticized him for his severity, for which he was expelled by Peter (Soz. I. 15, PG 67, cols. 904–5).

[5] Archbishop of Alexandria for a space of a few months (311–12 or 312–13). According to Sozomen (*loc. cit.*), one of our best sources for the beginnings of Arianism, Achillas restored Arius to the deaconship and even promoted him to the priesthood. Cf. the fragment of Ararsius in the *Synodicon vetus* (Fabricius – Harles, *Bibl. graeca*, XII, p. 369). It is to be noted that Photius is following another tradition, represented by Gelasius of Cyzicus (II. 1, ed. Loeschcke and Heinemann, Leipzig, 1918, p. 34), according to which it was Alexander who ordained Arius presbyter.

[6] St. Alexander, Archbishop of Alexandria (313– †328), at first had a high regard for Arius, who was then presbyter of the parish of Baucalis (Soz. I. 15, col. 905 A). When, however, Arius began to preach openly his heretical doctrine on the Son (*ca.* 319), Alexander was obliged to abandon his previous tolerance, and summoned a synod of one hundred Egyptian bishops who excommunicated Arius (*ca.* 321).

[7] This could not refer to the so-called "first Arian Creed," i. e. the letter that Arius wrote to Alexander from Nicomedia (given by Athan., *De Synodis* XVI, PG 26, cols. 708–12), in which he denied, though in a spirit of moderation, the co-eternity of the Son; Photius' βιβλίον [μετανοίας ἐπιδιδούς seems to be a borrowing of Socrates' βιβλίον μετανοίας δούς (I. 26, col. 149), and concerns the "second Arian Creed," that evasive statement thanks to which Arius succeeded in satisfying Constantine, and was allowed to return to Alexandria. The date of Arius' recall is usually placed *ca.* 330, while Sozomen (II. 27, cols. 1012–13) makes it contemporary with the Council of Jerusalem (335). In any case, Arius' recantation seems to have taken place after Alexander's death, and it was Athanasius, and not Alexander, who refused to admit him (Socr. I. 27, col. 152). The only serious evidence to the contrary is the famous letter of Eusebius and Theognis (re-instated in 328) begging for their recall on the grounds, amongst others, that Arius had already been pardoned (Socr. I. 14, col. 113; Soz. II. 16, col. 976). This letter, however, has been considered spurious by most historians since Tillemont. Photius is probably following the *Life of Metrophanes and Alexander* and the *Life of Athanasius* (*Biblioth.*, cod. 256, pp. 472–3; cod. 258, p. 478), in both of which it is stated that Arius returned to Alexandria while Alexander was still Bishop.

measures were wise, just and holy: for to have rejected a person who had erred once and repented would have been altogether inhuman, would have appeared harsh to excess, and would have been equivalent to annulling and excluding the conversion and repentance of sinners, which is the only way to salvation left to those who have erred; whilst to accept a person, who, not once, nor twice had abjured piety, but many times had thus easily gambled it away like a player, and was again simulating piety, would have been to disdain piety, and to establish no distinction between being impious and being pious. For those who account

Ar I 256 changing positions for so little prove that they consider neither belief to be right. For this reason, therefore, the law of pardon[8] gladly received Arius when he abandoned his former error, but when he had drifted many times into the same folly, even though he simulated a recantation by a tract of repentance, the Church, foreseeing his deceitful and sly character, and providing in advance that piety should not be held in contempt, did not consent in any wise to open him the gates of mercy, which he had wretchedly shut in his own face. This *attitude* also our contemporary, the fitly-named Nicephorus,[9] has imitated with divine wisdom: for, as the blessed Alexander received Arius, so the great Nicephorus received John[10] (who was awarded this throne as a prize for his impiety), a pious person at first (for he too had been a worshipper of the venerable images, and actually exercised the art of the painter as his life's profession), but who later, because of times and change of circumstances, had stepped over to impiety, and fallen sick, and had offered a tract of repentance. But when he went astray again and aspired to be proclaimed the leader of a heresy, just as neither the blessed Alexander nor God's Church shed a single drop of mercy on Arius, feigning repentance, so also the wondrous Nicephorus with a prophetic eye barred the entrance into the Church to John and the fellow-leaders of his heresy who had done similar violence to the faith, asserting that, even if they should assume the mask of

[8] Reading ἡ τῆς συγγνώμης τάξις with Hierosol. 1: τέξασα A and B: ἡ τὴν συγγνώμην τάξασα Ar.
[9] Patriarch of Constantinople (806–815).
[10] John VII the Grammarian, Iconoclast Patriarch of Constantinople (837–843). See above, pp. 240 sq.

HOMILY XV. THE ARIAN HERESY

repentance, their conversion would be unacceptable both to God and to the Church.

2. But to what extent the heresies of image-breakers and Arian madmen resemble one another, will be expounded, with God's help, in proper time.[11] As for me, having related to you the First Council, and being about to unfold the Second, I shall try to introduce in between what befell the churches in this interval by the effort and contriving of Arius' companions, since these *events* yield much edification of their own, no less so than the story of the Councils, and besides the continuity will thus make clearer the comprehension of what I am going to say.

3. So Eusebius of Nicomedia,[12] as we have said previously, and his companions, having concealed their heresy because of their desire for their own sees and their love of a bishopric, and having at first signed their names to the Council, but, on being again detected in their impiety, and having perverted the pious statements they had signed into impious notions, and spread among their fellows in impiety the monstrous tale that they had not followed the Council, but that they had pulled the Council over to themselves, offered again tomes of repentance in order to be granted pardon for having peddled away their orthodoxy, and wrongly resumed possession of the churches whereof they had been rightly deprived.[13] Thereafter, as they were eager to stir up again the heresy of Arius, but the time was not propitious (for Constantine the Great was still living, and, as he held the sceptre of royalty, made great provision for the peace of the Churches), these evil men found another course, whereby they hoped to hide the fact that they were reviving their war against piety, and to make their purpose progress according

---

[11] See below, pp. 264–66.

[12] The ablest Church politician of his time, Eusebius was, first, Bishop of Berytus, from where he was promoted first to Nicomedia (in violation of the 15th Canon of Nicaea), and then to Constantinople (*ca.* 339– †342).

[13] After registering at first some opposition to the Nicene creed, Eusebius, along with most other Arianizers, subscribed to it for reasons of expediency or, as Philostorgius says, with a deliberate mental reservation (I. 9, ed. Bidez, p. 10). Eusebius was, however, banished three months after the Council (Nov., 325) for reasons which are not altogether clear, and replaced by one Amphion. In 328, thanks to the influence of the Princess Constantia, Eusebius and his friend Theognis of Nicaea were re-instated in their bishoprics after presenting some sort of recantation (see above, n. 7).

to their wishes. And what *course* was that? They determined to shift their plot against the faith on to the defenders of the faith, and when the latter would be out of the way, they hoped to bring about easily thereafter the destruction of piety as well. Wherefore they assailed with libel the successor of Alexander, who had survived the Council by six months,[14] Athanasius (for they knew him from his outspokenness at Nicaea to be a warm champion of truth),[15] on the pretext, amongst other things, that he had occupied his see by violence and blows, and not by vote and decision of the bishops. He, however, having by his lofty carriage utterly overturned their calumnies on to his slanderers' heads, continued to tend well his own flock.[16]

4. Having for the present failed in this *purpose*, and unable to contain themselves and hold their peace, they spit out the poison of their tongues and direct their rage against the great Eustathius of Antioch;[17] for he too had manfully and courageously championed

---

[14] Actually, Alexander died on April 17, 328, and was succeeded by Athanasius on June 8, 328. Theodoret (I. 26. 1) says that Alexander died five months after the Council. Theodoret may have been misled by a statement of Athanasius (*Apol. c. Ar.*, § 59, PG 25, col. 357 A), where the period of five months refers apparently not to Alexander's death, but to the renewal of Meletian troubles. Cf. A. Robertson, *Athanasius* (*Nicene Library*, IV, Oxford, 1892), pp. xxi, lxxxi, 131 n. 4. Epiphanius also (*Haer.* 69. 11, PG 42, col. 220) says that Alexander died "in the same year" as Arius was anathematized by the Council. It appears that the chronological confusion is related to the view that the Nicene Council stretched over three years (*Biblioth.*, pp. 471–2).

[15] Athanasius was present at the Council of Nicaea not as a regular member, since he was only deacon, but in attendance on his Bishop; he took, however, according to Sozomen (I. 17), a prominent part in the discussion.

[16] The election of Athanasius was contested by the Arians and the Meletians, who put forward their own candidates, Achillas and Theonas respectively. The Arians later alleged that Athanasius had been clandestinely appointed by seven bishops (Athan., *Apol. c. Ar.*, § 6, PG 25, cols. 257–60; Soz. II. 17); or, according to another version, that he forcibly compelled two bishops to consecrate him behind closed doors, and obtained the Emperor's confirmation by representing his election as unanimous (Philost., II. 11). See discussion of sources by Gwatkin, *Studies of Arianism*[2], p. 70, n. 2.

[17] Eustathius, Bishop first of Berrhoea, and then of Antioch (*ca.* 324–330), called "the Great" by Theodoret. He took a prominent part in the Council of Nicaea, where he may have delivered the inaugural address, and on his return to Antioch used energetic measures against the Arians, thus earning the enmity of the two Eusebii. Eusebius of Caesarea, in particular, accused him of Sabellianism (Socr. I. 23; Soz. II. 18). The deposition of Eustathius was engineered by Eusebius of Nicomedia who at that time visited in great pomp Constantine's new buildings in the process of construction at Jerusalem

HOMILY XV. THE ARIAN HERESY

the dogmas of piety at the holy Council of Nicaea. Pretending to be desirous of going to Jerusalem (for already the splendid church which Constantine the Great built on the life-giving tomb of Christ,[18] our God, after dislodging from that spot the pagan shrines, was nearing completion), Eusebius of Nicomedia, taking this pretext and bringing along his fellow-heretics, hastened to the murder of Eustathius. Having bribed a certain prostitute who made traffic of her youth, they instructed her to hold a baby in her arms and cry out that the baby was Eustathius', and demand the punishment of his misdeed. On these grounds they summoned the blessed Eustathius under the pretext that he give an explanation. He, relying on his own conscience (for when a man sees something he has not even entertained in his mind being woven into an accusation, he hastens without hesitation to disprove it), both appeared willingly and declared himself ready for the inquiry. They, on their side, brought forward the woman alone as both accuser and witness and demanded penalties from the saint. God's servant, while smiling at their unlikely fiction, insisted on the necessity that witnesses for the accusation should appear. But as nobody appeared (nor was it possible to find witnesses of what had not happened), the "unbiased" judges put the prostitute to the oath, having long beforehand trained her to be ready for every transgression. And although divine law ordains that every word should be established before two or three witnesses,[19] and the wondrous Paul cries out, "Receive not an accusation, but before two or three witnesses,"[20] these men, having set at nought the divine words, after the harlot had sworn

Ar I 259

(the Church of the Calvary was dedicated in 335). On his way back from Jerusalem, Eusebius entered Antioch with a party of Arian bishops who constituted themselves into a tribunal and condemned Eustathius on charges of immorality. The Bishop's deposition was accompanied by riots. Constantine, who received a biased version of the incident, had Eustathius banished to Thrace, where he died *ca.* 337. Photius takes the story of the trial from Theodoret I. 21. The accusation of Sabellianism at the trial is, on the other hand, mentioned only by Socr. I. 24, col. 144 B. See F. Cavallera, *Le schisme d'Antioche*, Paris, 1905, pp. 57–64; R. V. Sellers, *Eustathius of Antioch*, Cambridge, 1928, pp. 39–59.

[18] Reading ἐπὶ τῷ τοῦ Χριστοῦ καὶ Θεοῦ ἡμῶν ζωηφόρῳ τάφῳ with Hierosol. 1: ἐπὶ τῷ τοῦ Χριστοῦ ὀνόματι ἡμῶν ζωηφόρῳ τάφῳ A and B: Χριστοῦ καὶ Θεοῦ ἡμῶν ὀνόματι ἐπὶ τοῦ ζωηφόρου τάφου Ar.

[19] Deut. 19. 15.
[20] 1 Tim. 5. 19.

HOMILIES OF PHOTIUS

Ar I 260 the false oath in the way they had taught her, drove the champion away from his flock, charging him in addition with Sabellianism. Having thus bereaved[21] the Church of her own bridegroom, they condemned him to exile at Philippi in Thrace,[22] although, even in distress, he slackened in no way in his fight for the true faith, and in edifying the body of the faithful by his actions and teaching.

5. When their fraud had thus progressed according to their wishes, and as, with time, these evil men gathered boldness as well as experience in accusations, shortly they revert again to the great Athanasius, and having contrived a multitude of calumnies against him, request the Emperor to put him to trial.[23] The latter, judging others by his own character, and unable to disbelieve them since they were bishops (for, as I have said several times, they still concealed their heresy), and being besides somewhat incensed at Athanasius (for passions sometimes affect the best of men) because he absolutely refused to receive Arius, although the latter promised to repent[24]—for these reasons, at the insistence of the accusers, he ordered Athanasius to be tried on the charges at Antioch, entrusting the examination to his nephew Delmatius, who held the office of

---

[21] Reading χηρώσαντες with all the MSS: χειρώσαντες Ar.

[22] Philippi is, of course, in Macedonia. Eustathius was probably exiled to Trajanopolis in Thrace (so Jerome, *De viris illustr.*, 85), while St. John Chrysostom merely says it was in Thrace (PG 50, col. 600). Further down (p. 257) Photius refers to the place of exile as "the city of the Illyrians," following Theodoret I. 22. 1. The tradition that Eustathius was banished to Philippi is found in Theod. Lector (PG 86, col. 184 B) and Theophanes (p. 133, De Boor). See Delehaye, "Saints de Thrace et de Mésie," *Analecta Bollandiana*, XXXI (1912), p. 254; P. Lemerle, *Philippes et la Macédoine orientale*, Paris, 1945, p. 84 n. 1. The account of Eustathius illustrates very well Photius' compilative method.

[23] The charges brought against Athanasius were, a) that he had imposed a special tax to provide linen vestments for the Church; b) that he had given a sum of gold to a rebel named Philumenus; c) that he had committed sacrilege in the Mareotis; and d) that he had murdered Arsenius, a Meletian bishop, and cut off his hand for purposes of magic. Photius' account is here very succinct, and he does not mention the fact that Athanasius was summoned to Nicomedia, where he exculpated himself before the Emperor (331).

[24] Upon the recall of Arius (330 ?), Eusebius of Nicomedia wrote to Athanasius requesting him to admit Arius to communion. When Athanasius refused, another letter, this time from the Emperor himself, ordered him to admit into his Church all who should desire it. Athanasius, however, persisted in his refusal. Athan. *Apol. c. Ar.* § 59, PG 25, col. 357; Socr. I. 23; Soz. II. 18; II. 22.

HOMILY XV. THE ARIAN HERESY

Censor.[25] But, after a short time, Caesarea in Palestine was set as the second place of this trial, for it was decreed that the council should convene there. Knowing, however, that the Bishop of that city was an Arian (it was Eusebius, whom the Iconoclasts recognize as their father),[26] Athanasius declined to appear.[27] The council having dissolved with nothing accomplished, the same men forgathered again at Tyre, where they were joined by Eusebius of Nicomedia.[28] For there was not one intrigue against the pious[29] of which he was not the acknowledged leader, attracting to his side his namesake and fellow-thinker, and the latter's entourage. So, when the council had assembled at Tyre, the followers of Eusebius heaped up a great mass of charges which they used as accusations

---

[25] This enquiry was intended to investigate the case of Arsenius. Delmatius (who was really Constantine's half-brother, and not his nephew, as stated by Socrates) requested Athanasius to prepare his defense. The latter organized a quest for Arsenius and, although unable to apprehend him, proved nevertheless that his supposed victim was still alive. Socr. I. 27; Athan. *Apol. c. Ar.* § 65, PG 25, col. 366.

[26] With especial reference to the famous letter that Eusebius wrote to the Princess Constantia. The latter has asked Eusebius to send her an image of Christ, which the Bishop refused to do, arguing that the Son's glory could not be portrayed on a lifeless picture. This document was used at the Iconoclast Council of 754, and extracts from it have been preserved in the Acts of the Second Nicene Council of 787 (Mansi XIII, col. 313; a more extensive version was published by Boivin in his notes on Nicephorus Gregoras, II, pp. 1300–03 in the Bonn ed). In refuting the authority of Eusebius, the Iconodules were satisfied to show that he was an Arian heretic (Mansi XIII, cols. 176–77; 312 D; 313 D sq). See G. Florovsky, "Origen, Eusebius, and the Iconoclastic Controversy," *Church History*, XIX (1950), pp. 77–96; M. V. Anastos, "The Argument for Iconoclasm as Presented by the Iconoclastic Council of 754," *Late Classical and Mediaeval Studies in Honor of A. M. Friend, Jr.*, Princeton, 1955, pp. 183–84. For Eusebius' unfavourable attitude to images, cf. also his comments on the Paneas statue, *H.E.* VII. 18. The Patriarch Nicephorus wrote a special *Antirrheticus* against Eusebius (Pitra, *Spicilegium Solesmense* I, pp. 371–503). Cf. also his *Apologeticus pro SS. imaginibus*, PG 100, cols. 561–64.

[27] The Council of Caesarea (in Palestine) was held in 334. Athanasius was summoned to it, but refused to attend because he knew that Eusebius of Caesarea, who was probably the presiding bishop, was hostile to him (this reason is given by Soz. II. 25).

[28] The unseemly Council of Tyre (August 335) was intended to resolve ecclesiastical strife preparatory to the celebration of Constantine's *Tricennalia* and the consecration of the Church of the Resurrection.

[29] Reading οὐ γὰρ ἦν εὐσεβούντων ἐπιβουλή with the MSS. For the use of ἐπιβουλή + gen. in a passive sense, cf. Stephanus, *Thesaurus*, s. v., quoting ἡ τοῦ Διὸς ἐπιβουλή (= "a plot against Zeus," Justin Martyr). So also ἐπίβουλος + gen. Papadopoulos-Kerameus corrected εὐσεβούντων to ἀσεβούντων. Ar has οὔ γὰρ ἦν ἀσεβούντων ἐπιβουλή: Pg corrects οὐ to ποῦ.

against Athanasius. They also took into their pay a harlot from the stage and prevailed upon her to accuse him. As she was carrying on shamelessly and screaming aloud according to her promise, Timothy the presbyter, who was present along with the champion of piety, exposed the plot most deftly. For while the harlot was crying out that she had been robbed of her virginity by Athanasius, Timothy, simulating the role of Athanasius, inquired where and when he had known her. She on her side was fretting and calling it a terrible thing that, whereas her seducer ought to pay damages and take cover in silence, he, in his shamelessness, was both in charge of the trial and pretended ignorance; wherefore, pointing at him with her finger, the wretched woman asserted with oaths that verily he was her seducer, thinking Timothy to be Athanasius; for the invention of the plot having been elaborated only as far as the names went, the woman made it apparent that she knew the names but not the facts.[30]

Ar I 262 6. So when this accusation was shattered to the disgrace of its joint inventors, they turn to another calumny; for wickedness is a shameless thing, and does not refrain from levelling at others[31] even such charges as no one believes. For, having brought forward an embalmed hand in a wooden chest, they asserted it belonged to Arsenius, whom Athanasius had allegedly slain for purposes of sorcery. This Arsenius was a Meletian,[32] and derived thence the

[30] The charge of fornication is mentioned by Rufinus I. 17 (PL 21, col. 489), Soz. II. 25, Thdt. I. 30 (whom Photius follows) and in the *Life of Athanasius* (*Biblioth.*, cod. 258, p. 480). It also appears in Philostorgius II. 11 with the roles reversed.

[31] Read καθ'ἑτέρων εἰσάγειν with the MSS; ἐφ'ἕτερα εἰσάγει Ar.

[32] The case of Arsenius was concocted some time before 333. Arsenius was Bishop of Hypsele in the Thebaid (the *Synod. vetus*, p. 372 calls him a deacon), and belonged to the Meletian party, i. e. the schismatic hierarchy ordained by Meletius of Lycopolis during and after the Great Persecution. Rufinus I. 17 and the *Life of Athanasius* (*loc. cit.*) call him a lector of the Church of Alexandria. The plot against Athanasius was developed by John Archaph, Bishop of Memphis and head of the Meletians. He bribed Arsenius to go into hiding, and then circulated the tale that Athanasius had murdered him and had cut off his hand for purposes of sorcery; in evidence whereof the Meletians exhibited an embalmed hand in a wooden box. When the charge came up before the Censor Delmatius (see above, n. 25), Athanasius sent a deacon in quest of Arsenius. The deacon succeeded in apprehending Pinnes, the superior of the monastery where Arsenius had been concealed, and on being interrogated Pinnes was forced to admit that Arsenius was still alive. The chronology of the ensuing events is uncertain. Arsenius went to Tyre, where he was accidentally discovered and identified by the local bishop. If the farcical scene at the Council is authentic, we must suppose that Arsenius came to

HOMILY XV. THE ARIAN HERESY

rank of deacon. Arsenius having, however, by God's providence, put in at Tyre (for he was being hidden by the Arians lest the plot be detected), it was reported to Athanasius that the "dead man" had arrived. Having chanced upon him, when the day appointed for the trial had come, he brought him in along with himself, all covered up, and enquired from those present if any had known Arsenius beforehand. When many said they knew the man, he uncovered him and proceeded to ask if that were he. Upon their agreeing (nor was it possible to deny what was there in front of everyone's eyes), he showed the right hand, then the other, and said, "Here is the right hand, here too is the left, which we men, sprung from Adam, have received from the Creator of all, so let no one demand from me Arsenius' third hand."[33]

7. Thus the slanderers who had contrived abomination upon abomination for Athanasius were awarded shame upon shame by the incorruptible Tribunal itself, and by truth. But Oh, their impious and most shameless mind! What mean epithet is it not worthy to bear? For whereas they ought to have covered themselves up and bowed down to the ground and expiated their outrageous deeds with repentance alone, they attempted to call the disprover of their accusation and deception a sorcerer and a deceiver, and did not even refrain from condemning that irreproachable man, wherein[34] lay also their most shameless deed, that they made Arsenius, who, they asserted, had been killed and had had a hand cut off by Athanasius, to sign the condemnation of Athanasius as Bishop of Hypselis;[35] thus, ridiculous to say, the dead man was exacting a penalty from

---

Tyre shortly before or during the Council (out of curiosity?) as, in fact is stated by Socr. and Soz.; yet Athanasius (*Apol. c. Ar.* § 65, col. 365) implies that his flight to Tyre and discovery occurred *ca.* 333, in which case it is not at all clear how he could have remained at Tyre for two years without his exposure becoming known to the Meletians and Arians.

[33] In his account of this ludicrous scene Photius follows Thdt. I. 30. When Arsenius was produced with both his hands intact, the Eusebians accused Athanasius of magic. Socr. I. 29, 30 and Soz. II. 25 give somewhat different versions.

[34] Reading ἐν ᾧ καὶ τὸ ἀναιδέστατου with Pg: ἐν ᾗ codd, Ar.

[35] ὑψίλεως Hierosol. 1: A and B read ὑψιπόλεως. The form Ὕψηλις for Ὑψήλη is attested (Steph. Byz., s. v.). The reading of AB is probably derived from Socr. I. 32: ὡς τῆς Ὑψηπολιτῶν πόλεως ἐπίσκοπος καθυπέγραψε. Arsenius was later reconciled to Athanasius and remained permanently in his communion.

his murderer! Now Christ's servant, after the disproof of their calumny, departed for Constantinople, fearing assassination; while they, even in his absence, condemned him by default. At Mareotis too (the village derives its name from the adjacent lake Maria) they gave judgment in default against him, charging him with breaking holy vessels, destroying an altar, burning books, and so on.[36] When, however, the Emperor summoned them back, as a result of Athanasius' arrival at the court and his petition that, upon the convocation of many bishops for this purpose, he should be able to receive justice from his slanderers in his own presence, and to prove himself innocent of their charges—when, therefore, the Emperor decided to recall them, the greater part, fearing the refutation of their plots,

Ar I 264 did not even choose to present themselves. But Eusebius and Theogonius[37] and the rest of the Arian troop who relied more than the others on the insolence and extreme wickedness of their mind—these indeed presented themselves, and whereas they did not even mention the charges on which they had based their unjust verdict, they alleged that Athanasius had threatened to hinder the usual supply of corn that is conveyed from Alexandria to Constantinople. The followers of Eusebius, having divided themselves up into spokesmen of this accusation, judges and witnesses, contrived the banishment of Athanasius to Treveri in Gaul.[38]

[36] At Tyre the opponents of Athanasius revived the old charge of the broken chalice which had been investigated and dismissed by the emperor at Nicomedia (in 331). It was alleged that when Athanasius, soon after his election, was visiting the Mareotis, his deacon Macarius burst in on a certain Ischyras who was officiating at the time, broke the chalice and upset the holy table. This occurred allegedly in a hamlet callet Secontarurus. Mareotis is not, of course, the name of the village, as would appear from Photius; while the etymological explanation is borrowed from Thdt. I. 30. 12. The notorious Mareotic commission was appointed in Sept., 335, and proceeded to make an investigation on the spot. It consisted exclusively of Arians, and came back with a falsified report. Meanwhile Athanasius had fled in a boat to Constantinople, so that judgment against him was pronounced in default. There seem to have been two verdicts: one after Athanasius' departure, and the second after the return of the commission (Socr. I. 32). Photius is wrong in saying that judgment was given in the Mareotis: the misunderstanding may have arisen from Thdt., *loc. cit.*

[37] Bishop of Nicaea (his name appears indiscriminately as Theognis, Theognius and Theogonius), and one of the chief opponents of Athanasius. He was banished after the Nicene Council along with Eusebius of Nicomedia, and re-instated in 328. See above, n. 7.

[38] Arriving unexpectedly in Constantinople on October 29, 335, Athanasius intercepted the Emperor and requested him to summon the bishops back

HOMILY XV. THE ARIAN HERESY

8. When Constantine the Great had been perfected with holy baptism by the Orthodox in Bithynia (let heretics who are anxious to ennoble their impiety with lies be allowed to weave their heretical stories),[39] and had departed to the better life, the Arians, rose to great intimacy with his son Constantius (for he was an unstable man and followed the leaders of their party), and having held up Paul the Confessor[40] as an instigator of seditions and internecine murders, they banished him from his see, and transferred Eusebius of Nicomedia (who had been previously *bishop* of Berytus, and was now unlawfully changing his see for the third time) to Constantinople. So easy was everything for the Arians, and there was no offspring of their desire or anger that was not hatched and raised by their hands and increased to great evil.

9. I now intend to link up with the foregoing story an event that is closely related to it, though it took place in later times. Great disorder, as I have often said, having swept over all the churches of the East in the reign of Constantius, Constans, the emperor of the West, in partnership with his brother, assembled a council at

from Tyre and preside over the enquiry in person. Constantine's summons overtook the bishops at Jerusalem, where, in conciliar session, they had just received Arius back into the Church. Only the leaders repaired to Constantinople and met in council early in 336. The old charges were dropped, and this time Athanasius was accused of hindering the importation of corn from Alexandria to Constantinople. Constantine, impatient of the proceedings, banished Athanasius, unheard, to Treveri. There Athanasius remained for nearly two years. See Athan. *Apol. c. Ar.*, §§ 9, 86–7, PG 25, cols. 264–5, 401–5; Thdt. I. 31; Socr. I. 35; Soz. II. 28 says, on the contrary, that the accusation of the broken chalice was repeated at Constantinople.

[39] There can be little doubt that Constantine was baptized shortly before his death (May 22nd, 337) by the Arian Eusebius of Nicomedia (Jerome, *Chron.*, a. 2353, ed. A. Schöne, *Eusebii chronicorum libri duo*, II, Berlin, 1866, p. 192; *Chron. Pasch.* p. 532, Bonn). In asserting that Constantine was baptized by the Orthodox, Photius is probably following Gelasius of Cyzicus (*Biblioth.* cod. 88, ed. Bekker, p. 67), and certainly not the Silvester legend (found in Malalas, Bonn ed., p. 317; Theophanes, De Boor's ed., pp. 17, 33). See F. J. Dölger, "Die Taufe Konstantins und ihre Probleme," *Römische Quartalschrift*, Suppl. XIX (1913), pp. 377 sq. Note that in reviewing the *Vita Constantini*, Photius censures Eusebius for not specifying who baptized Constantine (*Biblioth.*, cod. 127, p. 95b).

[40] Paul († *ca.* 351) was chosen by the Homoousians to succeed Alexander as bishop of Constantinople. His election incensed the Emperor Constantius, who had not been consulted, and in 338 or 339 Paul was deposed by a council and replaced by Eusebius of Nicomedia († 342). Athan., *Hist. Ar.*, § 7, PG 25, col. 701; Socr. II. 7; Soz. III. 4; *Life of St. Paul* in Photius, *Biblioth.*, cod. 257, p. 474.

Sardica, at which, in addition to other matters which will be expounded below,[41] was carried out the acquittal of Athanasius. Constans conveyed the verdict of this council to his brother through the Bishops Euphratas and Vicentius, attaching to them the general Salianus, who, besides being an upright man, was also adorned with piety.[42] Constantius was then residing at Antioch, and Antioch was held by Stephen, also an Arian, and appointed by the Arians to be head of that church, for which reason the council had passed condemnation on him.[43] Salianus the general having taken up separate quarters, and the prelates being lodged together, the followers of Stephen, having taken into their company a woman who sold the disgrace of her body for a price, and told her that one of the guests just arrived had need of her to share in the nocturnal and furtive deed, persuaded her (she being quite ready) to visit his chamber; already one of the priests' servants, having been bribed to help with their scheme, opened secretly the courtyard door and gave free access to the woman. So she entered and was about to approach Euphratas, for the other Bishop was resting in the inner room. The priest, however, having become aware of her entrance, asked the woman who she was and for what reason she was coming in. As she answered in her familiar female voice, Euphratas was seized by fear and astonishment, and was thinking that it was a demon tempting him in the semblance of a woman, at which point an ambush composed of fifteen men, following the leader of the plot, broke into the house, and were about to arrest both the woman and Euphratas, as having been apprehended in fornication. At the noise and uproar which naturally spread about, the other Bishop arose along with the servants who did not take part in the plot, and having closed the courtyard gate, they caught seven of the soldiers who were in the conspiracy, the leader of the deed having escaped. The latter

[41] See below, pp. 268–70.
[42] Euphratas (or Euphrates), Bishop of Cologne (343–46); Vincent, Bishop of Capua (343–59), probably the same Vincent who had been Pope Silvester's legate at the Council of Nicaea; Salianus (Flavius Salia), magister equitum, Consul ordinarius in 348, carried a forceful letter from Constans urging the re-instatement of Athanasius.
[43] Stephen, Bishop of Antioch (342–44), took part in the Council of Philippopolis (343), on which see below, pp. 269–70. He had formerly been expelled from the clergy by Eustathius.

HOMILY XV. THE ARIAN HERESY

was Onager, an associate of Stephen's, who received his name from his occupation (for he was wont to inflict with his hands and feet unbearable wounds and blows on the pious).⁴⁴ The apprehended persons having been kept under guard, as already the sun's rays were giving faint traces of dawn, the Bishops brought the prisoners to the Emperor Constantius—Salianus⁴⁵ joined them also—and they deplored the outrage, which they used as evidence of the rumours bruited about everywhere against the champions of piety, and asked for a just verdict to be passed. The Emperor, in deference to the men, and paying heed to the foulness of the deed, allowed an exact examination to be made and entrusted the inquiry to men skilled in such trials. They, having brought forward the woman, and cross-examined the prisoners, immediately disclosed the whole plot, and through Onager discovered Stephen to be the instigator of the entire misdeed. Wherefore Stephen was handed over to the bishops that were present, and for his unlawful attempts on others was deprived of his hieratic office and driven out of his see, having drawn upon himself by divine judgment condemnation for his plots against others.⁴⁶ In Stephen's place the Arians installed on the throne of Antioch a man no less, yea, even more diseased with Arianism, a certain eunuch Leontius.⁴⁷

Ar I 267

In this way is Euphratas entrapped by Stephen; in this way the divine Paul is driven out of Constantinople; in this way the wondrous Eustathius is expelled from Antioch, and is condemned to come from the East to the setting sun, and dwell in the city of the Illyrians. In this way the much-suffering Athanasius is banished from Alexandria. When these men were out of the way, which the heretics made their goal, impiety rose up to great license and power.

⁴⁴ Onager means a wild ass.
⁴⁵ Σαλούστιος codd: corr. Ar.
⁴⁶ The account of this scandalous incident, which occurred in the spring of 344, is drawn from Thdt. II. 8. 54 – 10 (who gives the fullest story). See also Athan., *Hist. Ar.* § 20 PG 25, cols. 716–17.
⁴⁷ Leontius, a moderate Arianizer, bishop of Antioch from 344 to 358. He is chiefly remembered for muttering inaudibly the controversial part of the doxology, and coming out strong with "World without end. Amen." Early in his career Leontius had mutilated himself in order to live without reproach in the same house as the virgin Eustolium, and been expelled from the clergy by Eustathius. A moderate and astute man, Leontius has been denigrated by Athanasius in the *Apologia de fuga* (which answers the charge of cowardice made against him by Leontius). See *Dict. of Christ. Biogr.*, III, p. 688.

10. Why have slanders and calumnies against priests been the subject of my narrative? Why? That you may learn, beloved ones, and keep it in mind that to devise calumnies and weave deceits against Christ's bishops is an invention of heretics, who have risen against the Son of God, our God, in drunken fury; that it is the outgrowth of men who have received in their souls so great a seed of impiety; that it is the foul deed of men who have hawked away our Christian faith; so that, when you see some of them making a show of their abuse of bishops and priests, you may remember their begetters and teachers, and recognize them for what they are, and of what stock they happen to be (for, "by their fruits," the Lord's saying proclaims, "ye shall know them");[48] that you may avoid the imitation of them whose impiety you have abominated, and lest, having severed intercourse with them but partially, you become accustomed to suck in little by little the rest of their irreverence. Is the shepherd a heretic? Then he is a wolf, and it will be needful to flee and leap away from him, and not be deceived into approaching him,[49] even if he appears to be fawning gently. Avoid communion and intercourse with him as snake's poison: for fish are caught with hook and bait, while an evil intercourse, which contains the poison of heresy concealed therein, has captured many of the more simple-minded who came close and expected to suffer no harm. Wherefore it is fitting to avoid such men with all our might. Is the shepherd orthodox, does he bear the seal of piety, does he have none of the heretical crew trailing after him? Then submit to him, since he presides in the likeness of Christ. Thou doest honour not to him, if thou doest it with all thy soul: Christ receives it. Do not meddle in other matters. God is their examiner; leave the judgment to Him. Do thou, however, show him obedience and a pure disposition in accordance with thy love of Christ. To others it is said, "Son of man, I have set thee as a watchman to the house of Israel";[50] to you it is said, "What the priests bid you observe, that observe, but do not ye do their works."[51] Oh, how sweet and pleasant is this saying to me,

---

[48] Mt 7. 16.
[49] Reading ἀπατηθῆναι προσελθεῖν with the MSS: ἀπατηθῆναι καὶ προσελθεῖν Ar.
[50] Ez. 33. 7.
[51] Mt 23. 3.

HOMILY XV. THE ARIAN HERESY

and so desirable, yet quite impossible for me now to observe! 'Tis not thy toil, He says, nor thy labour to meddle in and scrutinize the priest's works; and do not thou do his works if they do not correspond to his words; but obey his teaching, and do not meddle in his conduct. Observe thyself, watch thyself. Leave the others to the Judge, and commit the care of them to their appointed shepherd.

11. Would that I were still in your position, would that I were enrolled, as formerly, in your ranks, that I should have no need to take account of the affairs of others, that no punishment should attend me, were I to overlook the shortcomings of my flock, that I should be allowed to look only after my own matters, and that cares of other men should not weigh down on me! That was malice indeed, and for me the worst and bitterest of malice, which snatched me away from that most pleasant, gentle and carefree life, in which I did not grieve any of my neighbours, was not required to be meddlesome towards anyone else, did not show myself severe to anyone. All was friendship and kindness, and my life was free of cares. Now, alas, the law of shepherds constrains me to grieve others, to show myself severe, to appear harsh, to judge on occasion, and to condemn—me who from the beginning have avoided this rank, and have consistently shown my aversion to it, although it did not prove possible to escape it, to have escaped which could be accounted as happiness.[52]

12. But if, O God's people and beloved children in the Lord, you believe that you observe in me any such *harshness*, then, remembering the foregoing as well as my attitude, ascribe that to the necessity of tending my flock and to the rules of authority; or rather, if it ever occurs to any of you to accuse and disparage one of the shepherds, let him leave the others and keep his tongue from them, but let him be meddlesome at my expense and seek into my affairs. I shall not be vexed, you know well, nor will I be angered at the ridicule, nor imitate the irritation of God's servant Elisha at the children.[53] Only do you practise virtue in other respects, and cleave to piety, and be reverent towards the other bishops, and observe

---

[52] A similar passage in Photius' letter to Pope Nicholas I, written in 861. See above, p. 20.
[53] 4 Kings 2. 23–24.

HOMILIES OF PHOTIUS

the customary honour for them. A father, too, gladly receives the children that abuse him, and he soothes his rightful anger with his paternal affection, and is appeased. For he knows that no matter how unruly the children are towards their father, they are gathered and joined to him again, and love him, and cling fondly to him, even if they are rebellious for a while.

13. I have, however, no charge against you who are present here,[54] be it of sedition, or of insult, or abuse, or contriving a trap,[55] or calumnies based on lies, or plots which disgust the senses even of my enemies, or any other monstrous and distressing thing, except that some perhaps, and those few in number, mutter under their breath, lest, perchance, through absolute tranquillity and lack of disturbance, I may slip into the fault of negligence and carelessness or of pride, whereof I pray to be delivered rather than of the unjust rebelliousness of those that disparage me. May our true God, the most holy deity of three persons and one nature, for your kindliness and love for me, adorn you with virtues, grant you a life without sorrows, prepare you a sorrowless existence in the other world, and bestow on you as well as on me His kingdom, through the intercessions of our Most-holy Lady, the Mother of God, and of all the saints. Amen.

XVI

Ar I 279 Of the Same Most-Blessed Photius, Archbishop of Constantinople, Homily Delivered from the Ambo of the Great Church[1]

1. The champions of the Church, as I have said before, having been entrapped by the enemies of truth, and the flocks having been deprived of their own shepherds, into whose sees crept in wolves and seducers instead of pastors, the plague of heretical corruption spread all over the East, consuming some men's souls and other men's bodies. For those who were infested with the error of impiety

---

[54] Read τῶν παρόντων ὑμῶν οὐδέν [οὐδένα Ar] ... ἐγκαλεῖν ἔχω.
[55] Read λόχον συσκευαζόμενον with all the MSS: λόγον συσκευαζόμενον Ar.
[1] In the MSS the title is given as follows: Τοῦ αὐτοῦ ἁγιωτάτου Φωτίου ἀρχιεπισκόπου Κωνσταντινουπόλεως, ὁμιλία λεχθεῖσα ἐν τῷ ἄμβωνι τῆς μεγάλης ἐκκλησίας. Ar adds τρίτη κατὰ τῶν αἱρέσεων after ὁμιλία.

HOMILY XVI. THE ARIAN HERESY

suffered the destruction of their souls, while those who placed a far higher value on avoiding this *fate* and not betraying themselves than on their life had their bodies distressed with violence, lashes and other torments.

2. When Constantius succeeded to his father's rule without accepting the right faith, and, being an unstable man gradually filling himself with the Arian madness, he allowed the heretics to do fearlessly whatever they pleased. For Eutocius,[2] who had long cherished this impiety, being on terms of great familiarity with him, made him amenable to himself and to those who shared his views. This familiarity he acquired in some such way as this. When Constantine the Great was nearing the end of his life, he had the testament of his last wishes sealed up, and handed it to Eutocius, a man who bore in his breast the poison of the Arian heresy, but as yet painted his exterior with the colours of piety; for this reason he had gained ascendency over the Emperor's sister (whose name was Constantia), already bereaved of her husband Licinius,[3] and was deemed to be a well-disposed, friendly and virtuous person.[4] She made him intimate with her brother, as if bestowing a great boon on him. So then, when the ultimate day was standing by the Emperor, this man was considered to be a faithful guardian of his wishes, and was entrusted with the will. There was written in it that the eldest son (who had the same name as his father) should receive

Ar I 280

---

[2] The name of Constantia's chaplain has been preserved only by Gelasius III. 12. 2, from whom Photius borrowed it (cf. *Biblioth.*, cod. 88, p. 66b). This cleric (whom the other sources refer to merely as an Arian presbyter) is said to have convinced Constantia that the faith of Arius was perfectly orthodox. As the Princess was dying, she recommended her chaplain to Constantine, over whom the wily Arian won considerable influence. The story of Constantine's testament is wrapt in obscurity. When the Emperor died, none of his sons was present, and there was certainly scope for intrigue. See Socr. I. 39 and II. 2; Soz. III. 1; Thdt. II. 3; Ruf. I. 11. Philost. II. 16 alleges that Constantine was poisoned, and that he delivered his will, in which he requested the punishment of his murderers, to Eusebius of Nicomedia.

[3] Constantia, Constantine's step-sister, was married to Licinius in 313. After Licinius was defeated by Constantine in Sept., 324, she pleaded for her husband's life. Licinius was, however, executed a few months later at Thessalonica. In spite of this, Constantia remained on good terms with her brother. She died some time after the Council of Nicaea, *ca.* 333, according to Piganiol (*L'Empire chrétien*, Paris, 1947, p. 59).

[4] Cf. Socr. I. 25, PG 67, 148 B.

upper Gaul, which he had governed beforehand; Constans, the youngest, should rule over the whole of Italy; while Constantius he willed to have the empire of the East (would he had not done so!), which he had administered himself. Others say that different things were inscribed in the testament, and that the eldest son was assigned the first portion of the empire, but that these *provisions* were falsified by the deceit and machinations of Eutocius.[5] For, as Constantius arrived before the others after his father's death, *Eutocius* thought it expedient to make the one who had come first his own prey. And so, having bound him by oath to be of the party of Arius, at which price he would be rewarded with the foremost imperial glory, *Eutocius* changed the testament according to his own desire, and handed it *to Constantius*, declaring him to have been inscribed Emperor of the East. In this way the seed of impiety was sown in the Emperor's ears, and having by the might of authority taken root, its offshoots extended to many parts of the world. For the rulers' evil habits, like a torrent pouring from a mountain-top into the plain, are wont to gush down easily on all the subjects.

3. Five years had not passed when a synod was convened at Antioch of Syria,[6] assuming the specious pretext of an inauguration feast (for the celebrated church of Antioch, a great and most noteworthy pile, had been completed in the tenth year of its construction, the fifth year of the reign of Constantius), but in fact inaugurating the fervour against piety, and preparing the plots against its servants. The number of the assembled amounted to ninety,[7] among whom were found not a few of the orthodox (for heterodoxy and orthodoxy were not as yet clearly marked off), but the impious band had the ascendency. For it was Eusebius, formerly of Berytus, thereafter of Nicomedia, and thirdly transferred to Constantinople after the impeachment and retreat of the wondrous Paul—yea, it

---

[5] This story is derived from hagiographical sources. See the *Life of Metrophanes and Alexander*, *Biblioth.*, cod. 256, p. 473 a; *Life of Paul, ibid.*, cod. 257, p. 474 a; *Life of Athanasius, ibid.*, cod. 258, p. 479 b.

[6] The Council of Antioch *in encaeniis* was held in the summer of 341 in the presence of the Emperor Constantius. Photius is here following Socr. II. 8.

[7] Ninety according to Socr. II. 8 and Athan. *De synodis* 25, PG 26, 725 A; ninety-seven according to Sozomen III. 5 and Hilary, *De synodis* 28, PL 10, 502.

HOMILY XVI. THE ARIAN HERESY

was he—in the absence of Julius of Rome[8] and the bishop of Jerusalem (Maximus it was at that period who, in the times of the tyrant, had distinguished himself by confessing Christ),[9] neither of the said taking part, for already they suspected and avoided their heretical band — who, receiving the presidency, cast the dice to further his own wishes, having as fellow-gamesters and contenders Flacillus and Gregory. Of these the former took possession of Antioch at the death of Euphronius,[10] while Gregory[11] was wooing the throne of Athanasius, against whom the plot was directed. Favourable to them were Theodore of Perinthus (which we now call Heracleia)[12] and a few others who loved sedition more than peace. So, having held session in the presence of Constantius himself, they again repudiated Athanasius, who had just been reinstated in Alexandria by a letter of the elder brother,[13] and handed his chair over to Gregory. Proceeding from this point, they drew up

---

[8] Pope Julius I (337–52) was not represented at the Council of Antioch, which consisted exclusively of eastern bishops. Socr. II. 8; Soz. III. 6.

[9] Maximus, Bishop of Jerusalem (336–*ca.* 348), had been a confessor in one of the persecutions, that of Maximian according to Philost. III. 12, in which he lost his right eye and had the sinews of one arm severed (Theodoret II. 26). Through weakness, he subscribed to the deposition of Athanasius at the Council of Tyre, but later repented of it. Fearing that he would be carried away again, he abstained from the Council of Antioch. Socr. II. 8; Soz. III. 6. See also below, notes 34, 35.

[10] Euphronius (332–33) was succeeded by Flacillus (333–42?), who took part in the Councils of Tyre and Jerusalem, and may have presided over the Dedication Council at Antioch. His name appears in different forms: Jerome calls him Placillus (Olymp. 277), Socrates Placitus (II. 8, 9), Sozomen Placetus (III. 5, 6), Theodoret (I. 22, II. 24, etc.) and Theophanes (pp. 37, 38, 41, ed. De Boor), Flacitus. Note that Photius gives the correct form, as found in Athan., *Apol. c. Ar.* (PG 25, 281 A, 392 C, 393 D) and Eusebius (dedication of *Theol. eccles.*).

[11] In actual fact, Gregory of Cappadocia was consecrated Bishop of Alexandria at a previous council held, at Antioch in the winter of 338–39. He was installed on March 22, 339 with the help of armed force, while Athanasius made good his escape to Rome. After perpetrating various outrages, Gregory died in 345. Photius is following the erroneous accounts of Socr. II. 10–11 and Soz. III. 6, who say that Gregory was appointed at the Dedication Council.

[12] Theodore of Heracleia (in Thrace), a writer of some note, took part later in an embassy to the Emperor Constans (342), the object of which was to present the so-called Fourth Antiochene Creed, and to explain the exile of Athanasius. He was deposed at the Council of Sardica, but remained in possession of his see († *ca.* 355).

[13] Athanasius returned to Alexandria in November, 337. On the date, see Gwatkin, *Studies of Arianism*[2], pp. 140–42. The letter of Constantine II to the people of Alexandria is given by Athan., *Apol. c. Ar.*, § 87, PG 25, 405.

an apology, as it were, by way of preamble, to the effect that they had never submitted to Arius or deigned to follow him (for how could bishops follow the lead of a presbyter?), but that they had Ar I 283 weighed his faith in a true scale, and saw it to be in accordance with the tenets of the Church, wherefore they had mercifully received him in his supplication to the Church, common mother of all. Having mischievously erected such stage-setting, they put on a corresponding mask of confession, and, as it were, drew up a creed, without on the one hand, censuring explicitly anything of the Nicene Council, while, on the other, they did not even mention the essence of the Father or the epithet Homoousios, that great engine against the Arians, nay, but gave by their actions full freedom for anyone who so desired to falsify the definition of the faith, until (and that was their purpose, for which they had equipped themselves from afar) they were altogether drawn to the Arian godlessness.[14]

4. Such are the tactics of heretics; for they have the serpent for teacher, who, having mixed the poison of death with disobedience, under the guise of solicitude and kindness, filled our common ancestors with that polluted *potion*, and drove them away to slavery from life in paradise. These men, too, first simulate piety, then, little by little, disclose their irreverence, while dissembling the insolence of their blasphemy with new-fangled and ambiguous words; when they have accustomed their audience to their disguised irreverence, then they spit out into their midst the pure poison of impiety, having prepared disaster for themselves and those that submit to them. One may observe the Iconoclasts using this same device and base artifice like the Arians; for they, too, do not reveal at once or all together the goal of their intention, but devise grades of impiety, until they have reached the very summit Ar I 284 of evil. It is fitting to consider here the similarity between the *two* heresies. The Arians alleged that the word "Homoousios" was a cause of offence to most people; the Iconoclasts started by saying that the depiction of images down below, near the ground, was a cause of error to the more simple-minded. The Arians: hence,

[14] This is the encyclical of the Eusebians, known as the First Antiochene Creed. Photius is following closely Socr. II. 10 and Soz. III. 5. Cf. Athan. *De syn.*, § 24, PG 26, 724-25.

HOMILY XVI. THE ARIAN HERESY

instead of "Homoousios," this corporeal and lowly word, it is proper to say "Homoeousios" of the Son's relation to the Father, this being somehow elevated and more fitting for the incorporeal, and avoiding the division of essence. The Iconoclasts: hence, instead of depicting images down below, near the ground, they should stand in an elevated position, since this is more appropriate for images, and avoids the reproach of deceit. The Arians: "Homoeousios" is not proper either, but instead of it we must say "homoeos," having altogether excised "ousia." The Iconoclasts: it is not proper to reverence even pictures which are high up, but to let them stand only for the sake of the subject represented, adoration being altogether spat upon. The Arians: the word "Homoousios" is without scriptural authority; the Iconoclasts: the worship of images is without scriptural authority. The Arians: the Son should be called "anhomoeos," a thing created and made, while the words "Homoousios," "ousia" and "Homoeousios" should be completely banished Ar I 285 from the Church. The Iconoclasts: images should be called vain idols, and their making, representation and worship should be altogether banished from the Church. The Arians: neither the Lord's sayings in the Gospels, nor the divine apostles, nor the Old Testament give any authority at all to say "Homoousios," "Homoeousios," or "ousia" about the Father and the Son. The Iconoclasts: neither the Lord's sayings in the Gospels, nor the divine apostles, nor the Old Testament give any authority for the making, representation, or worship of images. Is it small, do you think, the resemblance and likeness which the sons bear to their fathers, the successors to their leaders, the pupils to their teachers? The former rose arrogantly against Christ; the latter have arrayed themselves against His image. The former set at nought the men with whom they had ratified the first Nicene Council, as well as the Council itself; the latter scoffed at the men with whom they had held the second Nicene Council, as well as at the Council itself. The former charged with impiety the men who had baptized them, and ordained them priests by imposition of hands, and whom they had claimed as their fathers; the latter likewise made up the monstrous tale that the men who had ordained them, and celebrated holy baptism over them were idolaters. The former, progressing by degrees of blasphemy, fell into the ultimate godless- Ar I 286 ness, having deprived the Son of the Father's essence. The latter, having distributed their blasphemy according to the degree of its wickedness, have slipped into the ultimate impiety, having, in their folly against the images, banished from the Church the honour and reverence due to Christ. But these matters have, so to speak, been said by the way; so let the discourse direct itself to the path whence it has deviated.

5. The council of Antioch having broken up in the circumstances described, they tarried awhile, and becoming, as it were, critical of their declarations (for a lie is unsupported, and can by no means remain constant), they assembled with a view to a second falsification of the creed, in which, as they believed, they indicated with greater fulness and clarity the true relationship of the Son to the Father. But the word "Homoousios," that invincible citadel of piety, they did not choose to set up here either.[15]

6. Three years having already elapsed, the partisans of Arius met again at Antioch to dictate a new creed, and with a view to passing a rightful judgment on Photinus, Marcellus and Sabellius,[16] heretics

[15] It is not quite clear whether Photius is referring here to the Second (also known as the Lucianic) or the Fourth Antiochene Creed. Photius' wording of this passage is certainly derived from Socr. II. 10 (PG 67, 201 B), who is speaking of the Second Creed; the Second was also the longest of the four Creeds propounded at the Dedication Council. It was a semi-Nicene and, at the same time, a semi-Arian document, which did not contain the word Homoousios, but said nearly as much using a different phraseology (Soz. III. 5). The Second Creed, however, far from having been drawn up *after* the Council had broken up, as Photius would have it, was the official creed adopted by the Council. The Fourth Creed, according to Athanasius (*De syn.*, § 25, PG 26, 725) was drawn up by the Eusebians a few months after the Council had dissolved; Socrates, on the other hand, whom Photius had been following in describing these events, implies that the Fourth Creed was privately concocted by the four semi-Arian bishops, who had been deputed to carry the creed of the Council (presumably the Second) to the Emperor Constans (II. 18).

[16] Sabellius was active in Rome at the beginning of the 3rd century. His name is associated with a heresy, which was part of the larger movement of Monarchianism, and taught that the Father was the Son, that the Logos was the aspect under which God acted in the Creation and Incarnation, and that there were not three persons in the Godhead, but three aspects or modalities. Marcellus, Bishop of Ancyra († 374), while he disavowed Sabellianism, taught much the same thing, viz. that the Logos, impersonal and immanent in God, was operative in the Creation and the Incarnation by a process of expansion, while He would contract again when His work was done, thus restoring the Divine Unity. Photinus, Bishop of Sirmium (*ca.* 343–51) was a disciple of Marcellus, but went beyond his master in insisting, like Paul of Samosata, that the Lord was a mere man.

HOMILY XVI. THE ARIAN HERESY

all, so that by their just verdict against them, they might lend dignity to their other acts at the council, which flaunted their illegality in no small measure. Having stripped these men of the priesthood, and set forth the confession of their faith, which they disguised with beauty and abundance of words, thinking to evade sin by prolixity, they sent it over to those in Italy, using as conveyors of their message Eudoxius of Germanicia, Martyrius and Macedonius of Mopsuestia.[17] The inhabitants of the West, however, using as an excuse the fact that they spoke another language and were not even able to understand sufficiently the portent of the document, and declaring that they were content with the decrees of Nicaea, did not accept the creed sent by those men.[18]

7. When Eusebius had departed from life, and was taken away to his judgment in the other world, those who lived in piety reinstated Paul the Confessor, still surviving, in his own chair. But after a short interval, a violent and tyrannical hand drove him away from his flock, and installed Macedonius, who fought against the Holy Spirit.[19] Paul having been again recalled, and again deprived of his see and now of his life, the enemy of the Spirit was for the second time invested with authority over the Imperial City, though he, too, did not long enjoy his rule.[20] This man had once appeared

---

[17] So Socr. II. 19, PG 67, 224 C; Soz. III. 11, *ibid.*, 1060 B; Athan., *De syn.*, § 26, PG 26, 728 A. A fourth legate, Demophilus, is mentioned in a letter of Pope Liberius (Hilary, Fragm. V § 4, PL 10, 684 B). Eudoxius later became Bishop of Antioch (358–60) and of Constantinople (360–70).

[18] The Macrostich, or Fifth Antiochene Creed, was probably drawn up by the same Council that deposed Stephen in the summer of 344 (see above, p. 257). The text of the Macrostich is given by Athanasius, *De syn.*, § 26, PG 26, 728 sq.; Socr. II. 19; summary in Soz. III. 11. The Macrostich, like the Fourth Antiochene which it followed closely, was a compromise creed; on the one hand, it disavowed Arianism, while, on the other, it made a covert attack on Athanasius by condemning Marcellus and the Sabellians.

[19] Eusebius died towards the end of 341 or early in 342, whereupon the Orthodox party brought back Paul (who had been previously elected at Alexander's death, *ca.* 337, but deposed by an Arian council), while the Arians appointed Macedonius. The Emperor Constantius sent his general Hermogenes to eject Paul, but popular riots broke out and Hermogenes was killed (342). Greatly incensed, Constantius exiled Paul, while refusing to endorse Macedonius for the part he had taken in the disturbances. Though blamed, Macedonius seems to have been left in possession of the see (Socr. II. 12–13; Soz. III. 7).

[20] There is great uncertainty about these events. According to Socrates, Sozomen and the *Life of Paul* (*Biblioth.*, cod. 257), Paul, after being expelled in 342, went to Rome, and was returned to Constantinople thanks to the

Ar I 288 to hold a fair position with regard to Christ; for, in accordance with the orthodox, he propounded the tenet that He was consubstantial with the Father. But as time went by, he denied the consubstantiality, and fell into calling Him only "like," which opinion he and his fellow-thinkers persisted in cherishing for a considerable time. As for the most-holy Spirit, they took up from the first a most wretched and impious position; for the strange distortions which the Arian madmen made about the glory of the Son, they cast at the most-holy and consubstantial Spirit.[21]

8. So then, the third council after the one at Antioch broke session in the aforementioned circumstances. Now, in the eleventh year of the reign of Constantius[22] there forgathered a most numerous synod (for three hundred and seventy[23] made ready to assemble in

---

support of Pope Julius (Socr. II. 15; Soz. III. 8). Constantius was, however, as unwilling as ever to admit him. A trap was set for Paul by Philip, prefect of the East, and the Bishop removed to Thessalonica, while Macedonius was re-instated with military help (Socr. II. 16; Soz. III. 9). Paul went again to Italy and, after the Council of Sardica, was returned to his see under threat of war by the Emperor Constans (Socr. II. 23; Soz. III. 20, 24). On the death of Constans (350), Paul was exiled to Cucusus in Cappadocia and strangled (Socr. II. 26; Soz. IV. 2 and III. 3), while Macedonius remained Bishop until 360, when he was deposed by a council at Constantinople. It would appear that Paul's two sojourns in Italy should be reduced to one, and the incident involving Philip should be connected with the last exile in 350. See discussion of sources by G. Bardy, s. v. "Macédonius et les Macédoniens," *Dict. de théol. cath.*, IX 2, 1468 sq.; W. Telfer, "Paul of Constantinople," *Harvard Theological Review*, XLIII (1950), pp. 31–92.

[21] If Macedonius was ever a Nicene (which does not appear to be stated in our other sources), it was probably in Alexander's lifetime; for we have seen that Macedonius was the candidate of the Arians on Alexander's death. Later on, he appears as a Homoean and a partisan of Basil of Ancyra, to whose party he remained attached. As for the heresy that bears his name, we are told that he began propounding it about the time of his deposition in 360 (Socr. II. 45; Soz. IV. 27); while in other sources there is no evidence for the existence of Macedonianism before 380. The doctrine of this heresy was, apparently, that the Holy Ghost held an intermediate position between God and creature; although Macedonius himself is accused of saying that the Holy Ghost was a "servant," in fact something like an angel (Soz., *loc. cit.*).

[22] ἐν δεκάτῳ δέ [Ar: ἐν ιω δέ A and B] should probably be changed to ἐνδεκάτῳ δέ, because both Socr. II. 20 (PG 67, 236 A) and Soz. III. 12 (*ibid.*, 1065 B) assert that the Council of Sardica took place in the 11th year after Constantine's death (hence in 347, after May 22nd). It is well known that this date is incorrect, and that the Council of Sardica actually took place in the summer of 343.

[23] Photius is here following Socr. II. 20 (col. 236 B) and Soz. III. 12 (col. 1065 B) who say that there were about 300 Western bishops and 76 Eastern ones. For the figure 300, Socr. quotes the authority of Athanasius who, however, does not say anything of the sort: in *Apol. c. Ar.* § 1, PG 25, 249 A,

HOMILY XVI. THE ARIAN HERESY

it), the brothers Constantius and Constans having both manifested exceptional zeal and come to an agreement that the assembly should convene at Sardica (that was a city of Illyricum).[24] It was hoped to resolve thereby the bishops' disputes about their sees, and to check innovations contrary to faith. But the wicked perversity of the heretics contrived that none of the things intended and hoped for should come about. For sixty in number, having seceded from the common body, gathered at Philippi,[25] and made it their purpose to act contrariwise to those at Sardica; nor was the latter *synod* any longer behaving with unbiased judgment and passionless intent in all matters. Wherefore, each *synod* deposed the outstanding men of the other: that of Sardica deposed Basil of Ancyra, who, in addition to living a life abounding in other good qualities, had an ardent zeal against the madness of Arius, as well as Acacius of Caesarea, neither of whom just mentioned had been detected in having deviated to alien beliefs, although these matters, like much other information more ancient than their time, have been left out, not to say falsified, by Sozomen and Socrates.[26] *The synod* also subjected to a just

---

he says, it is true, that more than 300 bishops had signed in his favour at Sardica, but that includes absentees; in *Apol. c. Ar.* § 50, PG 25, 337 sq. he lists 282 signatures, again including absentees; while in *Hist. Ar.* § 15, PG 25, 709 B, he reckons there were about 170 both from East and West. Theodoret II. 7 places the total at 250.

[24] Read: Κωνσταντίου [omit δὲ, added by Ar] καὶ Κώνσταντος τῶν ἀδελφῶν σπουδὴν οὐ τὴν τυχοῦσαν συνεισαγαγόντων καὶ συμψήφων γενομένων ἐν Σαρδῷ [Σαρδικῇ Ar] ... τὸν σύλλογον [omit φασιν, added by Ar] ἁλισθῆναι.

[25] εἰς Φιλίππους codd: εἰς Φιλίππου πόλιν Ar. The Council met at Philippopolis in Thrace (modern Plovdiv), not at Philippi in Macedonia. It is not unlikely, however, that Photius wrote "Philippi," being perhaps misled by the *Life of Paul* (*Biblioth.*, cod. 257, p. 476a) which says τὴν ἐν Μακεδονίᾳ Φιλίππου. Confusion between the two cities is very frequent.

[26] The deposition of Basil of Ancyra (336–343, 350–360) and Acacius of Caesarea (340–366) is briefly mentioned by Socr. II. 20, col. 237 B and II. 23, col. 257 A; Soz. III. 12, col. 1064. For Photius' censure of Socr., cf. *Biblioth.*, cod. 28, p. 6a. It is not perhaps so strange that Photius should vindicate the orthodoxy of Basil, leader of the Homoeousian or Semi-Arian party, since even Athanasius took a fairly favourable view of him (*De syn.*, § 41, PG 26, 765; a severer judgment in *Epist. ad. episc. Aeg.*, § 7, PG 25, 553 B), while Philost. IV. 9, p. 62 (ed. Bidez) treats him as a Nicene. Basil was a learned and respected prelate, whose subsequent opposition to the extreme Arianizers, like Aetius and Acacius, was to his credit. More puzzling is the vindication of Acacius, the shifty leader of the Homoeans, unless it has something to do with his refutation of Marcellus (Epiph. *Haer.* 72. 5–10). Note that in Soz. III. 14, col. 1081 C both Basil and Acacius are singled out among the distinguished churchmen of the time.

deposition Gregory, who unlawfully ruled Alexandria, Menophantus of Ephesus, Theodore of Heracleia, and along with them many others.[27] It vindicated Athanasius and Paul, the champions, yea, along with Marcellus, Lucius and Asclepas, men of little sanctity.[28] In addition, it unnecessarily extended to an inordinate length the Nicene definition of faith, thereby restricting altogether the glory of its own reputation.[29] The *synod* of Philippi,[30] on the other hand, most of whose members came forward in rebellion against the very word "Homoousios," passed deposition in default on Julius of Rome for having received those who had been deposed by it, as well as on Hosius, celebrated and venerable among priests, I mean the one of Corduba,[31] and on Protogenes and Gaudentius.[32] It also confirmed the deposition of the wondrous Athanasius and Paul, as well as of Marcellus and Asclepas, whom I have mentioned.

9. Thus, instead of the settlement and peace of the churches, the whole world was filled with confusion and disorder. The evil attacked

---

[27] Gregory, the Arian Bishop of Alexandria, who superseded Athanasius in 339 (see above, n. 11); Menophantus of Ephesus took part in the Councils of Nicaea (to which he subscibed, though being an Arian), Philippopolis and subsequently that of Antioch (356) which intruded George into the see of Alexandria. On Theodore, see above, n. 12.

[28] On Marcellus, see above, n. 16. Lucius, Bishop of Adrianople, was a victim of Arian persecution, against which he appealed to Pope Julius. Having been pronounced innocent at Sardica, he was returned to his see, but soon banished again; he died in prison. The Roman Church celebrates his memory on Feb. 11th (*Acta Sanctorum*, Feb. II, pp. 519–20). Asclepas, bishop of Gaza, was deposed by the Arians some time after the Council of Nicaea; he also appealed to Pope Julius, and was rehabilitated both at the Roman Council of 340 and at Sardica, though, apparently, he was never able to return to his see. It is not clear on what grounds Photius disapproves of Lucius and Asclepas. The Arians at Philippopolis charged Asclepas with having thrown the eucharistic elements to the dogs, and Lucius with having broken an altar and instigated riots (Mansi III, 130 B–C).

[29] The creed in question is the one preserved by Thdt. II. 8. 39–52 and mentioned by Soz. III. 12, col. 1065 A, which was probably drafted by Hosius and Protogenes. It was not, however, officially adopted by the Council.

[30] ἐν Φιλίπποις codd: ἐν Φιλίππου πόλει Ar. See above, n. 25.

[31] Hosius († ca. 358) was the most venerable bishop of his time. A confessor under Maximian, he was Constantine's chief religious counsellor up to the time of the Nicene Council, over which he is said to have presided. He likewise presided at Sardica, being then nearly ninety years old. In 357 he was compelled by force to communicate with the Arians at Sirmium, and died shortly afterwards.

[32] Cf. Soz. III. 11, col. 1061 C. Protogenes had been Bishop of Sardica from before 316, and had taken part in the Council of Nicaea. Gaudentius was Bishop of Naissus (Niš).

HOMILY XVI. THE ARIAN HERESY

everyone and did not halt anywhere. Every day some were deposed by others and acquitted by others, and whom some vindicated others again, or the very same, condemned; great and variable was the mutual conflict and the war against the churches, and until the Second Oecumenical Council no remedy was found for this most distressing illness. Hosius convened again a synod at Corduba, which proclaimed the same tenets as the one of Sardica, and, as he had hoped, confirmed the latter, but no account of either of them was taken at all by the opposing party.[33] Maximus of Jerusalem, a man outstanding in confessing Christ, whose right eye had been gouged out in the times of the tyrant, convened forthwith another synod at Jerusalem, vindicated Athanasius, and joined in upholding previous *councils*, insofar as they were in accordance.[34] But the other side not only made these null and void, but, casting accusations at Maximus himself, which they had made up on their own, subjected him to deposition, replacing him in the church of Jerusalem by Cyril, a man who at that time had not as yet been purified of the error of Arius, but who later manifested great ardour on behalf of piety, and edified many a man with his catechetical speeches; because of this practice, he is known in the Church by the name Catechete.[35]

Ar I 291

10. Thereafter, that I may not weary your ears by relating all the particulars severally, another council was assembled at Sir-

---

[33] This Council is known only through the *Synodicon Vetus*, an anti-Photian document of the late 9th century (Mansi III, cols. 177–8; Fabricius – Harles, *Bibl. graeca*, XII, p. 377). Cf. V. C. De Clercq, *Ossius of Cordova* (The Catholic Univ. of America Studies in Christ. Ant., 13), Washington, D.C., 1954, pp. 407–8. It cannot, therefore, be ascertained what source Photius is using here.

[34] This gathering of bishops was assembled by Maximus (on whom see above, n. 9) in 346 to welcome Athanasius when the latter was passing through Jerusalem on his way to resume his seat at Alexandria. See Socr. II. 24; Soz. III. 21, 22; Athan. *Apol. c. Ar.*, § 57, PG 25, 352; *Hist. Ar.*, § 25, *ibid.*, 721; *Life of Athanasius, Biblioth.*, cod. 258, p. 482 b.

[35] Photius is here following Socr. II. 38, col. 324 B, Soz. IV. 20, col. 1173 A, and the *Life of Athanasius, loc. cit.*, in saying that Maximus was expelled by Acacius of Caesarea, his metropolitan, and replaced by Cyril; as against Thdt. II. 26. 6 and Jerome, *Olymp.* 282, who report that Cyril was appointed on the death of Maximus. Cyril (348–386) was at first a Homoeousian (Soz. IV. 25) of the party of Basil of Ancyra (Epiphan., *Haer.* 73. 23, 27), and did not embrace the Nicene faith until the time of the Second Oecumenical Council, according to Socr. V. 8 and Soz. VII. 7.

mium,³⁶ then at Ariminum,³⁷ yea, and another one at Nike of Thrace,³⁸ and later at Seleucia again,³⁹ then at Constantinople,⁴⁰ by *all of* which the word "Homoousios" was altogether banished. At Constantinople, internecine strife, breaking forth from Seleucia and from those whose profession it was to govern others in peace, burst upon the defenders of "Homoousios" themselves, and caused total confusion.⁴¹ By the efforts of Acacius of Caesarea, Basil,

Ar I 292

---

³⁶ Four Councils appear to have taken place at Sirmium between the years 350–360, and each of them produced a creed of its own. The First (351) is a repetition of the Fourth Antiochene, followed by 27 anathemas (text in Athan., *De syn.*, § 27, PG 26, 736–40 and Socr. II. 30); the Second (357) is the Anhomoean manifesto, rejecting both the words *homoousios* and *homoeousios*, and proclaiming the Son to be inferior to the Father (text in Athan. *De syn.*, § 28; Socr. II. 30); the Third (358) was the homoeousian reaction to the Second, due to Basil of Ancyra (Soz. IV. 15); the Fourth, or Dated Creed (359) was thoroughly Arian, and represented a partial return to the Second (Athan. *De syn.*, §§ 8, 29; Socr. II. 37).

³⁷ The Council of Ariminum (Rimini) met in the summer of 359. The Catholics were in the majority, and they ratified the Nicene formula, while the Arians met separately and adopted the Dated Creed. Each party sent a deputation to the Emperor, who was then busied with the renewal of hostilities with Persia. See Socr. II. 37; Soz. IV. 17–19; Thdt. II. 18–20; Athan. *De syn.*, §§ 8–11.

³⁸ Constantius refused to see the envoys of the Council of Rimini. They were instructed to await his leisure, first at Adrianople, and then at Nike (in Thrace), where, under pressure of violence, they were obliged to sign a revised version of the Dated Creed (Oct. 10, 359). See Thdt. II. 21; Socr. II. 37, cols. 321–24; Soz. IV. 19; Athan. *De syn.*, § 30.

³⁹ The Council of Seleucia (in Isauria) met in Sept.–Oct., 359, and was composed predominently of Homoeousians. In spite of the opposition of Acacius, who led the Arianizing minority, the Dedication Creed of Antioch was adopted. See Socr. II. 39–40; Soz. IV. 22; Thdt. II. 26. 4–11; Athan. *De syn.* § 12.

⁴⁰ The Council of Constantinople (January 360) marked the victory of the Arians in the East. It ratified the creed of Nike and destituted the more prominent Homoeousian bishops, who were replaced by Homoeans and even Anhomoeans. See Socr. II. 41; Soz. IV. 24; Thdt. II. 28–29.

⁴¹ It would be more accurate to say that the strife that had come into the open at Seleucia broke upon the Homoeousian leaders at Constantinople; Photius, however, treats Basil and his party as being practically orthodox, so there is no need to change the reading. The Acacian deputation from Seleucia reached the Emperor first. When the ten Homoeousian delegates (Basil, Eustathius, Eleusius, Silvanus and others) arrived at Constantinople, they had an unfavourable reception. They did, it is true, succeed in having Aetius, that extreme Anhomoean, exposed and banished; but as Silvanus and Eleusius persisted in defending *homoeousios* in preference to *homoeos*, the Emperor ordered them to be deposed, while the rest of the delegation was constrained, on the night of Dec. 31, 359, to sign the Arian creed of Rimini. See Thdt. II. 27; Soz. IV. 23–24.

HOMILY XVI. THE ARIAN HERESY

Eustathius and Silvanus of Tarsus[42] were deposed, men whom Constantius punished with exile abroad because of their splendid struggle for piety at that time, even though they were inspired with Novatianism;[43] just as others are attracted to the opinions of those they have denounced, so these men were attracted towards the opponents against whom they had proved their valour. Nor—although some of them, as they say, were known later to have changed their position with readiness—is there reason to show that what had happened had not happened. Deposed also was Cyril of Jerusalem, whom we have mentioned. On his account[44] Acacius was inflamed with a smouldering enmity against those men, and the perversion of his faith was taking shape; his tongue, but not his mind, he misused for the heretics, as both his previous and his subsequent

---

[42] On Basil see above, n. 26. Eustathius, Bishop of Sebaste in Armenia (*ca.* 356–*ca.* 377), is the famous ascetic and friend of St. Basil's, who later broke with him on dogmatic grounds. Silvanus of Tarsus, one of the most creditable figures in the semi-Arian party, stood out against Acacius both by befriending Cyril of Jerusalem and by his opposition at Seleucia. The deposition of these Bishops at the Council of Constantinople was based not on questions of faith, but on alleged infringements of ecclesiastical discipline.

[43] εἰ καὶ τοῖς τὰ Ναυάτου ὑποθειάζουσι [εἰ καὶ τὰ Ναυάτου ὑποθειάζοντας Ar]. Unless this phrase is used in some special idiomatic sense (cf. τὰ Ναυάτου φυσᾶν, a proverb = "to be arrogant," discussed by R. Strömberg, *Greek Proverbs*, Göteborg, 1954, p. 18), it is not at all clear how these semi-Arian Bishops could be said to have been tainted with Novatianism. The Novatians professed the consubstantiality of the Son just as the Orthodox did, while differing from the latter in matters of discipline and ethics. The Novatians were in fact severely persecuted by Macedonius, a member of the semi-Arian party (Socr. II. 38). As regards the dogmatic vacillations of the semi-Arian bishops, Basil was among those who, under pressure from Constantius, signed the Arian Creed of Rimini-Nike, although he is later represented, along with Silvanus, as proclaiming his adherence to the Nicene Creed (Socr. III. 25); while Eustathius, though he subscribed to the Catholic doctrine on several occasions, ended up in the Macedonian camp.

[44] The text should certainly be emended to read δι' ὅν [διὸ codd: δι' ὅ Ar], since the hostility of Acacius towards the semi-Arian leaders was due to his personal dislike of Cyril. It was Acacius who, as metropolitan of Caesarea, had consecrated Cyril to the see of Jerusalem, but the two fell out over the question of their respective precedence. In 358 Cyril was deposed by the efforts of Acacius; he was restored at Seleucia, but banished again by the Council of Constantinople (Socr. II. 42; Soz. IV. 25; Thdt. II. 26). Philostorgius, whom Photius is using in this connection, likewise says that Acacius was revenging himself on the followers of Basil, because they held Cyril in esteem, διότι κἀκεῖνοι Κύριλλον, τῶν Ἱεροσολύμων ὑπ' αὐτοῦ παυθέντα τοῦ ἱερᾶσθαι, διὰ τιμῆς ἔφερον (IV. 12, p. 64). The reading διὸ (="for which reason") would imply that the hostility of Acacius was inflamed by Cyril's deposition, which is contrary to the known facts.

actions, starting from this point, demonstrate. At his instigation, Aetius[45] was also deprived of the deaconship, the successor to Arius' impiety, the teacher of Eunomius and Eudoxius, who pushed beyond all impiety, together with whom and on whose account *were* also *deposed* Serras, Stephen and Heliodorus, who had attained the rank of bishops, but were ardent supporters of the error of Aetius;[46] yea, also that famous Theophilus,[47] whom the bold tongue of heretics proclaims to be the author of miracles, no less than *what* the Acts proclaim concerning the apostles.[48] Yet all these men, along with Aetius, were each stripped of his office, Eudoxius being, even against his will, one of the judges who condemned the impiety of Aetius, of which he, no less than they, was a notorious lover. For he was easily pressed into doing even what he did not believe in, so as not to lose the see of Constantinople; for already he ruled over Constantinople, having beforehand seized Antioch from Germanicia.[49] Cyzicus was unlawfully assigned[50] to Eunomius, as a

---

[45] Aetius carried the teaching of Arius to its logical conclusion by maintaining that the Son was utterly unlike the Father. A man of humble birth and a chequered past, successively a tinker, a goldsmith, a physician and a theologian, Aetius was ordained deacon at Antioch by the bishop Leontius. At the Council of Constantinople the Acacians sacrificed him as a scapegoat in the following circumstances. When the Homoeousian delegation came before the Emperor, Eustathius produced a clearly Anhomean statement of faith which he attributed to Eudoxius (on whom see n. 49). Its contents incensed Constantius, whereupon Eudoxius immediately disowned it and designated Aetius as its author. On being summoned to the palace, Aetius, who was unaware of what had occurred, readily acknowledged his profession of faith. He was forthwith banished and stripped of the deaconship. Pressing his advantage, Eustathius demanded a formal repudiation of Aetius' views, which Eudoxius, though sharing them, was obliged to make (Thdt. II. 27. 5–16).

[46] Thdt. II. 28. 3. Serras, Stephan and Heliodorus were all three Bishops from Libya, of whom very little is known. They were excommunicated for refusing to sign the condemnation of Aetius.

[47] Theophilus the Indian is known chiefly through Philost. (II. 6; III. 4–6; IV. 1, 7, 8; V. 4; VII. 6; VIII. 2; IX. 1, 3, 18). A native of Ceylon, he came as a hostage in the days of Constantine, and was educated as an Arian by Eusebius of Nicomedia, who ordained him deacon. Later he was made a bishop, and sent as a missionary to the Himyaritic kingdom. He is said to have worked miracles among the Sabaeans, to have raised a dead woman at Antioch (Suidas, s. v. Θεόφιλος, Θ 197) and to have cured the Empress Eusebia of a malady. Cf. Photius, *Biblioth.*, cod. 40, p. 8b).

[48] The reading of the MSS, ἣ τοὺς ἀποστόλους αἱ πράξεις ... ἀνακηρύττουσιν may be kept [τῶν ἀποστόλων Ar].

[49] Eudoxius, the "worst of the Arians" and friend of Aetius, was first Bishop of Germanicia (*ca.* 350–358). On the death of Leontius, he succeeded

HOMILY XVI. THE ARIAN HERESY

prize for his impiety, its previous pastor Eleusius having undergone condemnation along with the aforementioned athletes of true religion.[51] Macedonius, the enemy of the Spirit, was banished even earlier, as being responsible for many murders, and paying the penalty for the transportation of the Emperor's body, which he had carried out in spite of the opposition of many persons and without the reigning son's approval.[52]

11. Constantius having survived but for a short time after these events, was taken away from among men at Mopsucrenae, as he was preparing to oppose Julian who was already in full rebellion.[53] Thus the fluctuating opinion of the ruler and the precariousness of his beliefs confounded everything. Thus, little by little, did the contingent of the impious progress. Thus mutual discord and wrangles upset life, and rent the faith asunder. For discord in an animal's body results in dissolution and death, while in the Church *it results* in the scattering of her members, and the dissolution of the harmony which attends piety, and the rending and disaster of the soul.

12. Those things were thus badly and confusedly carried out at that time, and the Church was borne along in a great storm and turmoil. As for us, beloved ones, worshipping with our heart and lips the Father, Son and Holy Ghost in one essence, glory, kingdom and divinity, let us neither blaspheme *by saying that* the Son

---

in making himself Bishop of Antioch (358–360). Deposed by the Council of Seleucia, he sought shelter at Constantinople, and was made, in spite of his notorious profanities, Bishop of that city (Jan. 27, 360– †370).

[50] Read Εὐνομίῳ ... ἡ Κύζικος καταδικάζεται with Pg instead of the meaningless καταδύεται.

[51] Eleusius, a prominent and upright semi-Arian, who had done much to stamp out paganism and Novatianism at Cyzicus, was deposed by the Council of Constantinople, and replaced by Eunomius, the disciple and secretary of Aetius. Eunomius was soon, however, driven out by popular opposition, and founded a sect of his own that taught the complete comprehensibility of God by all men. Photius was acquainted with several works of Eunomius, upon which, in the words of Venables, he "exhausts a whole vocabulary of vituperation" (*Biblioth.*, codd. 137–38, pp. 97–8).

[52] The Emperor's hostility towards Macedonius is partly attributed to the fact that the latter had transported without authorisation the body of Constantine the Great from the church of the Holy Apostles to that of St. Acacius, an act that had caused popular riots and much bloodshed (Socr. II. 28; Soz. IV. 21).

[53] Constantius died at Mopsucrenae, in Cilicia, on Nov. 3, 361 (Socr. II. 47; Soz. V. 1).

is different in kind from the Father, thus insulting the Begetter, nor banish the Holy Ghost from dominion and equipollent authority to the maiming, debasement and amputation of the stainless and complete Godhead, by including a thing created, made and subservient in the suprasubstantial and almighty Trinity. But piously professing the Trinity to be consubstantial, jointly throning and of the same nature to itself, let us maintain in correct faith the identity of Father, Son and Holy Ghost unmingled, believing the Father to be unbegotten, the Son begotten, and the Holy Ghost emanated, and proclaiming them to be not jointly without beginning as to cause (for the Father is the beginning and cause of the Son, as begetter; for the latter is begotten, One out of One; and as producer, He is the cause of the Holy Ghost; for that, too, is produced, One out of One), but jointly without beginning in time: for the One gave birth, the Other was born, and the Third has proceeded beyond time and age, and beyond comprehension, neither the Spirit being included in the birth of the Son, nor the Son having a share in the procession of the Ghost,[54] but each preserving His identity pure and unmingled, inasmuch as the diversity of identity and of name does not introduce a diversity of essence but shows the difference of persons, and silences the blasphemy of Sabellius.[55]

13. Thinking and believing in this wise, let us spit upon all heretical company, and abominate every schismatic wickedness. Let us hate mutual dissensions, remembering the foregoing, and how great a harvest of evils internal seditions begat. Let none among you say, "I am of Paul, and I of Cephas,[56] and I of this man or of that." Christ hath redeemed us from the curse of the law[57] by His own blood: of Christ we both are and bear the name. Christ was crucified for us, suffered death, was buried and arose, that He may unite them that stand wide and far apart, having divinely established one baptism, one faith, and one Catholic and Apostolic Church. This is the core of Christ's coming among men. This is the achievement of that extreme and ineffable humiliation.[58] He who

---

[54] See above, p. 21.
[55] Cf. above, n. 16.
[56] 1 Cor. 1. 12.
[57] Galat. 3. 13.
[58] Read κενώσεως with A and B (cf. Phil. 2. 7): καινώσεως Ar.

HOMILY XVI. THE ARIAN HERESY

attempts to tear asunder or cut to pieces any one of these things, either by the love of a most impious heresy, or the pride of schismatic madness, such a man arrays himself against Christ's incarnation, arms himself against the common salvation, opposes His deed, and, broken off from union with Him, and torn away from the Lord's body, the Church, enrolls himself on the side of the enemy. Having rent his members away from the Bride Church, he makes them members of the harlot conventicle. The latter, sitting high on the tribune of sin, crowned with unchaste flowers, and besmeared with artificial paints, addresses them that walk the road of life in a loud, shameless and alluring voice: "Whoso of you is foolish, let him turn aside to me, and ye that lack understanding,[59] approach and rest on my bosom. Life with me is relaxed and unbridled. Luxury, drunkenness and pleasure are my struggles, toils and rewards. Here the slave of pleasure is not afraid, the detected perjurer is not condemned, he who sharpens his tongue against his neighbour and hides the asp's poison under his lips[60] is not convicted of having committed any wrong; for such are the common deeds of my lovers. A splendid table of rich meats and delicacies is set before you. You should fill and glut yourselves, and arm your tongue against those who pity you for being miserable. You should do everything that desire suggests to you. For the meddlesome and severe rulings of the apostles and the councils do not look in here, nor do the verdicts and gatherings of bishops correct the sinners, and, suffocating, so to speak, their wishes, make life grievous; for that, too, I promised you from the start, while tearing you away from thence, and embracing you in my arms. Nay, nor is it our custom to steer life by the canons, or to punish the desire of our heart with fortitude of reason; those are the commandments of the Church, unnecessary, hard to bear, and hard to achieve. Hers it is to do nothing without reason, mine to grant everything to passion and desire; hers to conduct those who obey her through the strait gate, mine to drag my lovers after me through the wide and broad;[61] hers to disregard the present and reach out for the future, mine to neglect none of the pleasures of

Ar I 297

---

[59] Prov. 9. 4.
[60] Cf. Ps. 139. 4.
[61] Mt 7. 13.

life, nor to be deprived of the enjoyment of what we see by the expectation of the future."

Ar I 298 14. Such and the like things has the harlot conventicle been crying out and doing⁶² for a long time, and many until now has she drawn to the pit of perdition. Let us all, however, flee as far from her as possible, and be guarded and cherished continuously by the most-pure arms of the Church, Christ's bride; so that through her we may walk a straight course and be guided to the heavenly path, in Jesus Christ our Lord, to whom be glory and power, together with the eternal Father and the consubstantial and life-giving Ghost, now and for ever and ever. Amen.

⁶² Read ἐμβοῶσα καὶ πράττουσα with the MSS: πλάττουσα Ar.

NOTE ON HOMILY XVII

This Homily is the only one out of the whole collection that can be dated with absolute accuracy. It was delivered on Holy Saturday, before the Emperors Michael III and Basil I, hence on the 29th of March, 867. The occasion was the unveiling or inauguration of the image of the Virgin and Child in the cathedral of St. Sophia.

After the exordium, the Homily opens with a digression intended to show the gains that were being made by Orthodoxy. A band of former heretics, dressed in white raiment, were being admitted that day into the Church and would soon join the congregation. The previous day (Good Friday) they had doubtless received their final catechism and abjured their errors. These heretics were Tessareskaidekatitai (Quartodecimans), and their presence at this date is very interesting.[1] Inasmuch as the Homily was delivered on Holy Saturday, and the converts were dressed in white, one might at first suppose that they were baptized on that day; a canon, however, ascribed to the Second Oecumenical Council,[2] and re-iterated by the Council *in Trullo*,[3] decreed that Quartodecimans, along with Arians, Macedonians, Novatians and Apollinarians should not be re-baptized, but merely anointed with holy oil and required to give statements of abjuration. This ceremony was probably performed in the baptistery.[4]

The sect of the Quartodecimans was of very ancient origin, and was particularly prevalent in Asia Minor. Alleging the authority of St. John, they held that Easter should be celebrated according to Jewish custom on the 14th of the first lunar month (Nisan), regard-

---

[1] Aristarches (II. 290) does not seem to have understood the actual presence of these heretics, since he says that Photius is "comparing" the Quartodecimans to the Iconoclasts.

[2] Can. 7, Mansi III, col. 564. On the probable date of this canon (*ca.* 460), see Hefele – Leclercq, *Histoire des Conciles*, II, 1, p. 39; P. de Labriolle, *Les sources de l'histoire du Montanisme*, Freiburg – Paris, 1913, p. 219.

[3] Can. 95, Mansi XI, col. 984.

[4] The "Patriarchal Euchology" prescribed that it should take place "in front of the holy font" (PG 100, col. 1320 A).

less of the day of the week. This doctrine played a large part in the paschal controversies of the second century. By the time of the First Nicene Council (325), the Quartodecimans appear to have lost much of their importance, since the resolutions adopted on that occasion concerning the date of Easter were directed not against the original usage of the Quartodecimans, but against the observance of the Sunday following the Jewish feast, which was then prevalent in Syria, Cilicia and Mesopotamia.[5] Although the regulations made at Nicaea were thus not aimed directly at the Quartodecimans, they were certainly incompatible with the observance of the 14th of the month of Nisan. The Council of Antioch *in encaeniis* (341) condemned those who celebrated Easter together with the Jews.[6] The Quartodecimans are specifically mentioned in the Acts of the so-called Council of Laodicea (towards the end of the fourth century);[7] while, as we have seen, a canon (probably spurious) of the Second Oecumenical Council (381), repeated by the Council *in Trullo* (692), contained instructions on how they should be admitted into the Church. The Council of Ephesus (431) in its sixth session (known as the *actio Charisii*) dealt with the case of several former Quartodecimans and a few Novatians, mostly from Philadelphia in Lydia, who, desirous of espousing Orthodoxy, were deceived into subscribing to the Nestorian creed.[8]

From the little we know, it would seem that the Quartodecimans were divided into regional groups, and gradually absorbed certain tenets of kindred heresies. This partial fusion was probably facilitated by the fact that other sects prevalent in Asia Minor, such as the Montanists and the Sabbatians (an offshoot of the Novatians) followed a similar usage with regard to the date of Easter. Epiphanius tells us that the Quartodecimans in Cappadocia celebrated Easter on the 25th of March on the evidence of the *Acta Pilati*.[9]

---

[5] This was shown by Duchesne, "La question de la Pâque au concile de Nicée," *Revue des questions historiques*, XXVIII (1880), pp. 5–42. See also Joseph Schmid, *Die Osterfestfrage auf dem ersten allgemeinen Konzil von Nicäa*, Vienna, 1905; F. Daunoy, "La question pascale au concile de Nicée," *Échos d'Orient*, XXIV (1925), pp. 424–444.
[6] Can. 1, Mansi II, col. 1308.
[7] Can. 7, *ibid.*, col. 566.
[8] Mansi IV, cols. 1352–61; Schwartz, *Acta conc. oecum.*, I. 1. 7, pp. 100–105.
[9] PG 41, col. 885.

NOTE ON HOMILY XVII

Theodoret says that they used the apocryphal Acts of the Apostles, and that, along with the Novatians, they rejected the efficacy of penitence.[10] The same statement is repeated by the canonist Aristenus.[11] All this tends to show that they were a puritan sect; so Photius is right in saying that they prided themselves on having preserved the apostolic teaching in all its purity.[12]

We have seen that the Quartodecimans were concentrated in Asia Minor. St. John Chrysostom (398–404) is said to have taken away their churches in the province of Asia and in Lydia.[13] Theodoret, writing in the second half of the fifth century, says that they remained only in a few parts of Asia and Pontus.[14] It is a well-known fact that Asia Minor was favourable to the continued survival of old heretical, and even pagan communities. With regard to the Quartodecimans, our information becomes exceedingly meagre after the fifth century. We can, however, adduce certain scattered allusions referring to the ninth century. Thus, the Emperor Michael II, a Phrygian by birth, is said to have been a Sabbatian,[15] and to have held Jewish views regarding the date of Easter.[16] We have, in addition, several references to the Tetraditai, who were apparently synonymous with the Quartodecimans,[17] and were so called because "when they celebrate the Pasch, instead of breaking the fast, they fast, as we (i. e. the Orthodox) do on Wednesday (τὰς τετράδας); this too they observe after the manner of the Jews."[18] A canon

---

[10] *Haer. fabul. comp.*, PG 83, col. 405; cf. Timotheus, *De recept. haer.*, PG 86 1, cols. 33–36.
[11] Ralles & Potles, Σύνταγμα τῶν ἱερῶν κανόνων, III, p. 177.
[12] See p. 288 below.
[13] Socrates VI. 19.
[14] *Haer. fabul. comp.*, PG 83, col. 409.
[15] *Vita Ignatii*, PG 105, col. 493 C. The Quartodecimans are identified with the Sabbatians in one version of the *De recept. haer.* by Timotheus (PG 86 1, col. 33, n. 42).
[16] Theoph. Cont., p. 49 (Bonn); Cedrenus, II, p. 74 (Bonn).
[17] So the supposed 7th canon of the Second General Council, and the 95th of the Trullan, quoted above, notes 2–3. Cf. PG 86 1, col. 72 A; PG 100, col. 1317 D, etc. Timotheus, on the other hand, applies the name Tetraditai to certain branches of the Severians because they were accused of worshipping not a Trinity, but a Quaternity (PG 86 1, cols. 60 B, D; 61 B). Presumably in the same sense, the epithet Tetraditai was given to a 6th-century Origenist sect in Palestine (Cyril of Scythopolis, *Life of Sabas*, § 89, ed. E. Schwartz, *Texte und Untersuchungen*, 49 2 [1939], p. 197).
[18] Balsamon's commentary on Can. 7 of the Second General Council in Ralles & Potles, *op. cit.*, II, p. 190.

attributed to the Patriarch Nicephorus (806–815), which also figures with some slight changes in the *Catechesis chronica* of St. Theodore the Studite,[19] allows the use of cheese and eggs on Wednesday and Friday of Tyrophagy week, and adds: "this canon refutes the doctrine of Jacob and the heresy of the Tetraditai."[20] The latter apparently regarded the week of Tyrophagy as an important fast.[21] Theophanes, in deploring the Bulgarian successes in 812, lays the blame on the toleration of heretics within the Empire, viz. the Tetraditai, Paulicians, Athingans and Iconoclasts.[22]

It may be assumed that the Quartodecimans converted in 867 came from Asia Minor. The decisive Byzantine victory over the Emir of Melitene in 863 ensured a relative quiet on the eastern front until the end of Michael's reign. That doubtless provided a suitable opportunity for stamping out heretical sects. The efforts of the imperial government in that direction are known to us chiefly with reference to the cruel persecution of the Paulicians; we can now add that other heretics were also affected, and treated less harshly. Photius may be exaggerating when he says that the converted Quartodecimans were "a numberless throng of men"; in any case, we have here a hitherto unknown instance of the proselytizing activity of Photius.

We now come to the main topic of the sermon, which is the restoration of images in St. Sophia. It would not be an exaggeration to say that no other text expresses the re-establishment of "Orthodoxy" with equal authority and eloquence. The underlying theory is given in almost Platonic terms. In the eyes of Photius, painting is the most direct form of instruction, for a picture that is in agreement with religious truth contains the *eidos*, or essence, of the prototype, which is in turn apprehended by the faculty of sight and indelibly imprinted upon the mind. A painter is guided by divine inspiration, so that his work is not merely mimetic, but contains an actual share of the prototype.[23] One would look in vain for a better

[19] PG 99, col. 1700.
[20] PG 100, col. 852. Cf. Grumel, *Les régestes des actes du patriarcat de Constantinople*, I 2 (1936), no. 406, p. 37.
[21] Balsamon on Can. Apost. 69 in Ralles & Potles, *op. cit.*, II, p. 89.
[22] Ed. De Boor, p. 496.
[23] Cf. A. Grabar, "Plotin et les origines de l'esthétique médiévale," *Cahiers archéologiques*, I (1945), pp. 15 sq.

NOTE ON HOMILY XVII

expression of Byzantine art theory. As for St. Sophia, we learn with some surprise that until that time, i. e. for over twenty years after the restoration of Orthodoxy in 843, the cathedral had remained bare of sacred pictures, as the Iconoclasts had left it. This delay has been quite plausibly explained by the strength of the Iconoclast opposition and the policy of conciliation that Theodora's government tried to follow.[24] Specific details concerning the redecoration of buildings with sacred images are very meagre for the period concerned. It is perhaps not entirely coincidental that all the earliest instances should have been in the imperial palace, and therefore inaccessible to the general public: the image of Christ over the Chalke gate, before 847; Our Lady of the Pharos, 864; the Chrysotriklinos, between 856 and 867; another hall in the palace, before 867.[25] A further important factor must have been the scarcity of competent artists, due to the interruption in the tradition of monumental sacred painting. Only one contemporary painter is known to us by name; it is the monk Lazarus, whose hands had been mutilated in the reign of Theophilus, and who, after 843, seems to have taken a more active part in Church politics than in painting.

The redecoration of a church as big as St. Sophia was naturally an undertaking that required many years of labour and a whole team of artists. To what extent it had been adorned with sacred images between the two periods of Iconoclasm (787–814) we are unable to say. Photius attributes the "scars" of the church to Isaurian impiety;[26] if that is to be taken literally, it would be an indication that some, at least, of the mural pictures obliterated by the Isaurian emperors had not been restored by Irene and her immediate successors. We are further told that the images had been *scraped* (or *pecked*) *off* (τὰ τῆς ὁράσεως ἐκκεκολαμμένος μυστήρια), which is in itself interesting, as in many cases it was deemed sufficient to cover them over with plaster or whitewash.[27]

[24] Cf. F. Dvornık, "Lettre à M. Henri Grégoire," *Byzantion*, X (1935), p. 6; id., "The Patriarch Photius and Iconoclasm," *Dumbarton Oaks Papers*, 7 (1953), pp. 69–97.
[25] Cf. Jenkins and Mango, "The Date and Significance of the Tenth Homily of Photius," *Dumbarton Oaks Papers*, 9–10 (1956), pp. 139–140.
[26] See below, p. 291.
[27] Cf. *Vita Nicephori*, ap. Nicephori *Opuscula historica*, ed. De Boor, p. 205.

HOMILIES OF PHOTIUS

It is apparent from the whole tenor of the sermon that the image of the Virgin was the first important picture to have been unveiled, while the rest of the church still bore the marks of the Iconoclasts' fury. In concluding his sermon, Photius expresses the wish that the emperors should "consecrate the remainder of the church, too, with holy images."[28] That is not to say that certain other pictures, placed in less crucial positions, may not have been executed at about the same time. Photius says that the Theotokos was resurrecting, along with herself, the likenesses of the saints (συνανιστώσης ἑαυτῇ τὰ τῶν ἁγίων μορφώματα),[29] which may be construed to mean that certain images of saints had been set up simultaneously. It is more than likely that the image of the Virgin was in the apse, and not on the western arch, as Aristarches supposed;[30] it was not, however, in all probability the image that we see there today. In his description, Photius indicates that the Theotokos was erect (ἕστηκε), and that the Christ Child was reclining in her arms (ἀνακλινόμενον), neither of which particulars fits the mosaic that is extant.[31]

Further difficulties were raised by Šestakov,[32] who contended that the image described by Photius was not a mosaic but a painting, and not a new one, at that, but a restored one. With regard to the first point, it must be admitted that Photius speaks of "colours" (τοῖς χρώμασιν),[33] and the "art of painting" (ἡ ζωγράφος τέχνη),[34] yet such terms are not incompatible with a mosaic. We have, furthermore, a remnant of the redecoration undertaken in 867, the commemorative inscription on the vertical surface between the barrel-vault and the semi-dome of the apse. Originally it ran:

---

[28] See below, p. 296.
[29] See below, p. 293.
[30] II. 287. This is chronologically impossible, since the Virgin in the soffit of the western arch was made in the reign of Basil I, after the earthquake of Jan. 9, 869.
[31] Cf. C. Mango, "Documentary Evidence on the Apse Mosaics of St. Sophia," *BZ*, XLVII (1954), pp. 395–402. The mosaic of the Virgin has been reproduced by Th. Whittemore in the *Amer. Journal of Archaeol.*, XLVI, 2 (1942), pls. II–III; *Mosaics of Haghia Sophia at Istanbul* (album), 1950, pls. 24–26, and elsewhere.
[32] *Vizant. Vrem.*, IX (1902), pp. 537–38.
[33] See p. 290 below.
[34] *Ibid.*

NOTE ON HOMILY XVII

"Ἃς οἱ πλάνοι καθεῖλον ἐνθάδ' εἰκόνας
ἄνακτες ἐστήλωσαν εὐσεβεῖς πάλιν.

"The images which the impostors had formerly cast down here, pious emperors have again set up."[35] There can be little doubt now that this inscription refers to Michael III and Basil I, and not to Theodora and Michael as has commonly been supposed. The inscription was, moreover, in mosaic,[36] so it is highly unlikely that the adjoining image of the Virgin was in a different medium. Šestakov's second contention deserves more serious consideration, though it cannot be supported on the grounds he alleges. The mention of "scars" and "wounds" in paragraphs 3 and 4 does not refer to the image of the Virgin, as Šestakov thought, but to the whole cathedral of St. Sophia and figuratively to the Orthodox Church. The statement, however, that the Virgin was rising up from the depths of oblivion[37] may indicate that the image of 867 was replacing an older one that had been effaced by the Iconoclasts. The word ἀνεκαλύφθη ("uncovered") in the title is also suggestive, though its precise meaning in this context is not altogether clear. Could it simply mean "unveiled"? Or does it imply that the remains of an older image were uncovered and restored?

It remains to draw attention to Photius' proud statement: "If one called this day the beginning and day of Orthodoxy (lest I say something excessive), one would not be far wrong."[38] If, as has always been thought, the feast of Orthodoxy was established on the 11th of March 843, and observed thenceforward every year on the first Sunday of Lent,[39] such a statement would have been rather surprising. Evidently, in the eyes of Photius the real triumph over Iconoclasm occurred not in 843, but in 867, at the moment when the images were set up in St. Sophia. This suggests that the Sunday of Orthodoxy was not observed at the time; nor, for that matter,

---

[35] *Anthol. Palatina*, I. 1. See S. G. Mercati, "Sulle iscrizioni di Santa Sofia," *Bessarione*, XXVI (1922), pp. 204–5.
[36] Its beginning and end have been preserved. Reproduced by Whittemore, *Mosaics of Hagia Sophia*, pl. 29.
[37] See p. 293 below.
[38] See p. 291 below.
[39] Cf. *De Theophili imp. absolutione* in Regel, *Analecta byzantino-russica*, St. Petersburg, 1891, p. 39.

HOMILIES OF PHOTIUS

is it commemorated in the *Typikon of the Great Church* which dates from the end of the century.[40]

XVII

Ar II 294 OF THE SAME MOST-BLESSED PHOTIUS, PATRIARCH OF CONSTANTINOPLE, HOMILY DELIVERED FROM THE AMBO OF THE GREAT CHURCH, ON HOLY SATURDAY, IN THE PRESENCE OF THE CHRIST-LOVING EMPERORS, WHEN THE FORM OF THE THEOTOKOS HAD BEEN DEPICTED AND UNCOVERED.[1]

1. Even if a man practised silence all his life long, he would now,
Ar II 295 above all else, strive to be loquacious and exercise his tongue in the arts of rhetoric. Or rather, he will be emboldened to ask, what he did not dare heretofore, for his lips to be parted with the tongs of the prophet,[2] and for his mouth to speak out with the voice of fiery tongues,[3] being, methinks, unable to bear the joy in silence, or with still tongue to take pride in this feast. For in truth this *feast* pours forth the inexhaustible graces of joy and all manner of gladness, drives out sorrow, and charms away all dejection from every face. Indeed, the three greatest things that have happened under the witnessing sun[4] (except what directly appertains to the divine working of the Logos)[5] shine out in this *festival*: the invincible power

---

[40] Dmitrievskij, Описаніе литургическихъ рукописей, I (1895), pp. 115–16. Cf. Krasnosel'cev, "Типикъ церкви св. Софіи," Лѣтопись Истор.-филол. Общ. при Имп. Новоросс. Унив., Виз. Отдѣл. I, Odessa, 1892, pp. 223–26; *id.*, "Къ изученію Типика Великой Церкви," *ibid.*, III (1896), pp. 340–44.

[1] The complete title, preserved in A, B and Lig, is as follows: τοῦ αὐτοῦ ἁγιωτάτου Φωτίου πατριάρχου Κωνσταντινουπόλεως, ὁμιλία λεχθεῖσα ἐν τῷ ἄμβωνι τῆς μεγάλης ἐκκλησίας τῷ μεγάλῳ σαββάτῳ, ἐπὶ παρουσίᾳ τοῦ φιλοχρίστου βασιλέως [τῶν φιλοχρίστων βασιλέων Ar], ὅτε τῆς [ἡ τῆς Cod. Athen. 2756, Ar] θεοτόκου ἐξεικονίσθη καὶ ἀνεκαλύφθη [ἀπεκαλύφθη Ar] μορφή. Ar's correction τῶν φιλοχρίστων βασιλέων should probably be retained, as the presence of two emperors is made perfectly clear by the text of the Homily. Cod. Athen. 2756 has not preserved the complete title. In Cod. Palat. 129 the title is ἐπὶ τῇ στηλογραφίᾳ τῆς ὀρθοδοξίας.

[2] Cf. Is. 6. 6.

[3] Cf. Acts 2. 3.

[4] Read τῶν ὑφ' ἡλίῳ [ὑφ' ἥλιον Ar] πεπραγμένων μάρτυρι.

[5] πλὴν ὅσα μὴ θεουργικὸς ἐξαιρεῖται λόγος, literally "save for those things which the divinely-working Word sets apart for Himself." In other words, the three lessons contained in the festival represent the most significant things that have ever happened on earth, except for events such as the Incarnation, which are direct manifestations of God's workings. This passage is an important illustration of Photius' view of history as a didactic process.

HOMILY XVII. IMAGE OF THE VIRGIN

of piety which towers above the vault of heaven, the senseless insolence of impiety which is dragged down to ultimate ruin and the depths of hell, yea, and the monument of folly and ineffaceable disgrace of those who have ended their life in impiety, though deeming to be lifted up thereby[6] to great glory and domination (*witness* the unerring eye[7] of the prophets!), transmitted as a forceful lesson to posterity.[8] For indeed it is to be seen in many cases that the memory of those men who have used the brief time-span at their disposal for innovations is forever kept fresh by the Eye of Justice for the censure of their crimes. Also, if you will, the godly zeal of the Emperors (and, before the tribunal of Truth, time gone by has none more pious for its adornment),[9] through whom the wise teachings of theology blossom and shoot forth, growing out of their reflective soul[10] as from some noble and fair root; whence we too have often to our great joy plucked many a ripe fruit which distilled the honey of spiritual salvation. For even if it is we that have sown and first ploughed with much toil the fallow land, yet that too was not independent of imperial zeal and co-operation.[11]

---

[6] Read ἐξ ἧς [sc. ἀσεβείας: ἐξ ἧς που Pg: ἐξ ὅτου Ar] ἔδοξαν ἐπὶ μέγα δόξης καὶ δυναστείας ἐπαίρεσθαι. The men who had hoped to attain glory and power by impiety were, of course, the Iconoclasts. This remark is especially apt in the case of Leo V who, after pondering on the glorious careers of the Isaurian emperors and the unhappy reigns of their Iconodule successors, came to the conclusion that Iconoclasm was indeed the road to victory and happiness (Script. incert. de Leone Bardae filio, Bonn ed. [along with Leo Grammaticus], p. 349).

[7] Read ὄμμα with the MSS: στόμα Ar.

[8] τῷ μακρῷ αἰῶνι σὺν ἀκμῇ παραπεμπόμενα [παραπεμπόμενον Ar], a curious phrase. Cod. Palat. 129 (fol. 141ʳ) has τῷ μακρῷ αἰῶνι σὺν ἀκμῇ παραπεμπόμενα τὰ κακά. The meaning seems to be that the memorial of the Iconoclasts' wickedness will be remembered for all eternity without loss of forcefulness. ἀκμή is probably used in the sense of "vigour." It is defined as ὀξύτης or δύναμις in Photius' *Lexicon* (Reitzenstein, *Der Anfang des Lexikons des Photios* [1907], p. 61; so also Suidas, s. v.) ἀκμή was also a rhetorical term denoting a climax or elevated forcefulness of speech. Cf. Hermogenes, Περὶ Ἰδεῶν, I. 10.

[9] Reading ὧν ὁ παρελθὼν οὐκ ἔχει [so Pg: ὁ παρελθὼν οὐχὶ codd: ὁ παρελθὼν οὐκ ἦν Ar] χρόνος ὑπ' ἀληθείᾳ [ἐπ'ἀληθείᾳ Ar] δικαζούσῃ [δικάζων Ar] εὐσεβεστέροις ἐγκαλλωπίζεσθαι [so B: ἐγκαλλωπίσμασι A, Lig: εὐσεβέστερα ἐγκαλλωπίσματα Ar].

[10] φιλοθεάμονος ψυχῆς, a Platonic term (literally "spectacle-loving"). In *Rep.* 475e Plato uses τῆς ἀληθείας φιλοθεάμονες of the philosophers who loved the contemplation of truth. Quoted by Clement of Alexandria, *Strom.*, I. xix. 93. 3; II. v. 24. 3; V. iii. 16. 2.

[11] A significant passage. While congratulating the Emperor on his religious zeal, Photius plainly ascribes to himself the initiative in propagating orthodoxy, which in this context refers specifically to the suppression of Iconoclasm.

HOMILIES OF PHOTIUS

The white-clad choir of yesterday, which will soon be present, is part of the fruit being borne, and will suffice as evident testimony to everybody. A choir which today are resplendent in white raiment, and radiate the purity of their souls, were for many years past buried in the darkness of error, and were not even conscious of all this murk that submerged them. A numberless throng of men, who in other respects did not appear to have deviated from the true faith as regards divine worship, yet who, from the time when the Nicene edifice of holy dogma was found sufficient[12] for the holy Fathers (wherein they set up the pillars of Orthodoxy, and from which not a single holy man was absent, not even of those who inhabited the ends of the world), instead of coming to union thereby, rather segregated themselves into a hostile party, and remained from that time until now uncorrected by the rulings of subsequent councils and unwilling to be amended by the pronouncements of the Fathers. Accusing us of introducing daring innovations into apostolic teaching, they prided themselves on being, of all men under the sun, the only ones who had not deviated from it. Thus did the disease of superstitious prejudice inflame them, and the sickness came nigh to being altogether incurable. In these matters they were puffed up and arrogant towards men of all countries who were adorned with the Christian creed, though themselves confined by Jewish customs, and led by the hand of those whose blindness they themselves did not hesitate to scorn. For they, too, determined the Pasch by the time when the orb of the moon regained its full light and lay diametrically opposite the sun, on the fourteenth day after it was *first* observed to reflect the sun's rays to our eyes, subsequent to the spring equinox.[13] Hence they were called *Tessareskaidekatitai*

Ar II 297

---

[12] The MSS read: ἐξότου [i. e. ἐξ ὅτου] δὲ Νίκαια πατράσιν ἱερεῖς [i. e. ἱεροῖς] ἱερῶν δογμάτων ἐξήρκεσε τέμενος. Ar's correction ἐξήρτυσε for ἐξήρκεσε is not without merit.

[13] A very confused sentence: ᾑροῦντο γὰρ καὶ αὐτοὶ τὸ πάσχα κατ' ἐκεῖνο καιροῦ καθ' ὃν ὁ τῆς σελήνης πλησιφαὴς ἀποκαθίσταται [ἀποκαθίστατο Cod. Palat. 129, fol. 122ʳ] δίσκος τῷ ἡλίῳ διαμετρούμενος, τεσσαρεσκαιδεκάτην ἀγούσης μετ' ἰσημερίαν τοῦ ἔαρος ἀφ' ἧς [sc. ἡμέρας understood] ὕπαυγος ταῖς ἡλιακαῖς ἀκτίσι πρὸς τὴν ἡμετέραν ὄψιν ἐκρίνετο. The phrase μετ' ἰσημερίαν τοῦ ἔαρος is somewhat awkwardly placed, since the full moon of Nisan is not 14 days after the spring equinox, as Photius appears on first sight to be saying. The spring equinox was, of course, a fixed date in the solar calendar, and did not, therefore, bear any determined relation to the first lunar month. The

HOMILY XVII. IMAGE OF THE VIRGIN

by the truthful judgment of yore. But their error did not stop at that point; once the evil momentum had seized them and torn them away from the teaching of the Fathers, it induced them into bizarre and puerile notions. They used interpolated books, fell into monstrous fables and confounded[14] the laws of ecclesiastical primacy. They *alleged* that baptizands should not be sanctified by the application of holy oil, and they were frenzied with other similar drunken ravings. But having been raised from this absurd depravity, and having escaped the darkness, they have returned in splendid fashion to the paternal fold, increasing to no small extent the body of the Catholic Church.

2. But perhaps we have been drawn into too lengthy a digression, unwilling as we were to pass over in silence a matter cognate to the one before us,[15] and through which the light of truth shines no less brightly. But the cause of the celebration, whereby today's feast is conspicuously adorned, is, as we have already said, the following: splendid piety erecting trophies against belief hostile to Christ; impiety lying low, stripped of her very last hopes; and the ungodly ideas of those half-barbarous and bastard clans which had crept into the Roman government[16] (who were an insult and a disgrace to the emperors) being exposed to everyone as an object of hatred[17] and aversion. Yea, and as for us, beloved pair of pious Emperors, shining forth from the purple, connected with the dearest names of father and son,[18] and not allowing the name to belie the relation-

Ar II 298

---

ancient Jewish Pasch had always to be after the spring equinox, but owing to a calendar revision *ca.* the 2nd century A.D., the observance of the equinox was abandoned, with the result that there could be two Paschs within one solar year. This situation existed at the time of the First Nicene Council, and probably applied to the Quartodecimans as well. As described by Photius, however, the usage of the Quartodecimans took the spring equinox into account. Photius was well acquainted with the subject, having perused several works on Paschal computations which dealt directly with the Quartodecimans (*Bibliotheca*, codd. 115, 116).

[14] Reading ἀρχιεροσύνης τε συγχέοντες [συνέχοντες codd, Ar] νόμους. This correction is due to Mr. G. L. Kustas.

[15] Reading οὐκ ἀνασχομένους [so Pg: ἀνασχομένου codd, Ar] πρᾶξιν ἀδελφὴν τῆς προκειμένης [τοῖς προκειμένοις Ar] σιγῇ παρελθεῖν.

[16] Iconoclasm did in fact draw most of its support from the non-Hellenic elements of Asia Minor. Photius is probably referring to the Isaurian dynasty (cf. below, p. 291), while conveniently forgetting that the Amorian ancestry of Michael III could have been described in the same disparaging terms.

[17] Read μῖσος with the MSS: μύσος Ar. Cf. below, n. 22.

[18] Basil was Michael's adopted son (Theoph. Cont., p. 238).

ship, but striving to set in all other respects also an example of superhuman love, whose preoccupation is Orthodoxy rather than pride in the imperial diadem,—it is in these things that the deed which is before our eyes instigates us to take pride. With such a welcome does the representation of the Virgin's form cheer us, inviting us to draw not from a bowl of wine, but from a fair spec-
Ar II 299 tacle, by which the rational part of our soul, being watered through our bodily eyes, and given eyesight in its growth towards the divine love of Orthodoxy, puts forth in the way of fruit the most exact vision of truth. Thus, even in her images does the Virgin's grace delight, comfort and strengthen us! A virgin mother carrying in her pure arms, for the common salvation of our kind, the common Creator reclining as an infant—that great and ineffable mystery of the Dispensation! A virgin mother, with a virgin's and a mother's gaze, dividing in indivisible form her temperament between both capacities, yet belittling neither by its incompleteness. With such exactitude has the art of painting, which is a reflection of inspiration from above, set up a lifelike imitation.[19] For, as it were, she fondly turns her eyes on her begotten Child in the affection of her heart, yet assumes the expression of a detached and imperturbable mood at the passionless and wondrous nature of her offspring, and composes her gaze accordingly. You might think her not incapable of speaking, even if one were to ask her, "How didst thou give birth and remainest a virgin?" To such an extent have the lips been made flesh by the colours, that they appear merely to be pressed together and stilled as in the mysteries,[20] yet their silence is not at all inert neither is the fairness of her form derivatory, but rather is it the real archetype.

Ar II 300 3. Seest thou of what beauty was the face of the Church bereft? Of what splendour was it deprived? Over what graces did gloomy dejection prevail? That was the daring deed of a wretched Jewish hand, lacking in no insolence. This is a most conspicuous token of a heart seized by God and of the Lord's love, whereby the initiated

---

[19] ὑπόκρισις ἄρα τῆς ἄνωθεν ἐπιπνοίας ἡ ζωγράφος [ζωγράφου Uspenskij, Ar] τέχνη, οὕτως ἀκριβῶς εἰς φύσιν τὴν μίμησιν ἔστησεν [so Cod. Chalc. 64, fol. 301ʳ and Pg: ἕστηκε A, Ar: ἕστηκε B].

[20] ὡς ἐν μυστηρίοις codd: μυστηρίῳ Uspenskij, Ar.

HOMILY XVII. IMAGE OF THE VIRGIN

band of the apostles were led to perfection, through which the martyrs' winged course sped to the crowns of victory, and the prophets, God's tongues,[21] with knowledge of future things and truthful foretelling, came unto men *bringing* undoubting belief. For verily are these things the prizes and gifts of a most sincere and divine love, from which depends likewise the veneration of holy images, just as their destruction *comes* from an irrepressible and most foul hatred.[22] Those men, after stripping the Church, Christ's bride, of her own ornaments, and wantonly inflicting bitter wounds on her, wherewith her face was scarred, sought in their insolence to submerge her in deep oblivion, naked as she was, so to speak, and unsightly, and afflicted with those many wounds—herein too emulating Jewish folly. Still bearing on her body the scars of those wounds, in reproof of their Isaurian and godless belief, and wiping them off, and in their stead putting on the splendour of her own glory, she now regains the ancient dignity of her comeliness, and sheds the rude mockery of those who have insulted her, pitying their truly absurd madness. If one called this day the beginning and day of Orthodoxy (lest I say something excessive), one would not be far wrong. For though the time is short since the pride of the iconoclastic heresy has been reduced to ashes, and true religion has spread its light to the ends of the world, fired like a beacon by imperial and divine command, this too is our ornament; for it is the achievement of the same God-loving reign.

4. And so, as the eye of the universe, this celebrated and sacred church, looked sad with its visual mysteries scraped off, as it were (for it had not yet received the privilege of pictorial restoration),[23] it shed but faint rays from its face to visitors, and in this respect the countenance of Orthodoxy appeared gloomy. Now, casting off this sadness also, and beautifying herself with all her own conspicuous ornaments, and displaying her rich dowry, gladly and joyously she hearkens to the Bridegroom's voice, Who cries out saying, "All fair is my companion, and there is no spot in her. Fair is

---

[21] Reading προφῆται, θεοῦ γλῶσσαι: προφητῶν Ar.
[22] Reading μίσους with the MSS: μύσους Ar. Cf. above, n. 17.
[23] The very important clause τῆς γὰρ εἰκονουργικῆς ἀναστηλώσεως οὔπω ἀπείληφει τὸ δικαίωμα has been excised from the text by Ar who, no doubt, considered it a gloss.

my companion."²⁴ For, having mingled the bloom of colours with religious truth, and by means of both having in holy manner fashioned unto herself a holy beauty, and bearing, so to speak, a complete and perfect image of piety, she is seen not only to be fair in beauty surpassing the sons of men,²⁵ but elevated to an inexpressible fairness of dignity beyond any comparison beside.²⁶ All fair is my companion. She has escaped the blows, has been freed of her wounds, has wiped off all blemish, has cast down her detractors into Hell, has raised up those who sang her praises. And there is no spot in her. She has overcome the blemishes wherewith a foul foreign hand had aimed and spotted her whole body. She has wiped off all those stains, and taking up again her former bridal raiment, she has put it on. The daughters saw her, and they will bless her; yea, the queens, and they will praise her. Who is she that looketh forth as the morning, fair as the moon, choice as the sun?²⁷ This then is the dignity and royal raiment which David was describing from of old, when he sang hymns to the Lord and King of all: "The queen stood by on thy right hand, clothed in vesture wrought with gold, and arrayed in divers colours."²⁸ Verily are her "steps beautiful."²⁹ Awake, O Sion, as in the early time, as the ancient generation,³⁰ for up on thy head shall come exultation and praise and joy.³¹ "I, even I, am he that comforts thee," saith the Lord.³² "Behold, I have painted thy walls on my hands, and thou art continually before me."³³ This is her joyousness she herself foresaw

²⁴ Cf. Solomon's Song 4. 7.
²⁵ Ps. 44. 3.
²⁶ The precise meaning of this sentence is not altogether clear. The MSS read: οὐ παρὰ τοὺς υἱοὺς τῶν ἀνθρώπων ὡραία κάλλει γνωρίζεται, ἀλλὰ καὶ τὰς [τὰς corrected to τὴν Lig: τὰς omitted by Uspenskij and Ar] παρ' οὕστινας οὖν ἑτέρους εἰς ἄφραστον εὐπρεπείας ἐξήρτηται [ἐξήρτυται Uspenskij, Ar] ὡραιότητα. The sense seems to require the insertion of μόνον after οὐ. Uspenskij's corrections have some merit, though he himself completely misunderstood the meaning, witness his translation (p. 35): "she is acknowledged beautiful not only by the sons of mankind, but is also praised by God-inspired men (?) for her ineffable beauty."
²⁷ Song 6. 9–10.
²⁸ Ps. 44. 10.
²⁹ Song 7. 2.
³⁰ Cf. Is. 51. 9.
³¹ Is. 51. 11.
³² Is. 51. 12.
³³ Is. 49. 16.

HOMILY XVII. IMAGE OF THE VIRGIN

when she exclaimed prophetically through Isaiah, saying, "Let my soul rejoice in the Lord; for He has clothed me in the robe of salvation, and the garment of joy, and has put a mitre on me as on a bridegroom, and adorned me with ornaments as a bride.[34] And no longer shall I be as a city forsaken, but as one sought out,[35] and as a crown of beauty in the hand of the Lord, and a royal diadem in the hand of God."[36]

5. We too, with gladness and joy in our the souls, join the choir of this festival, and sharing today in the celebration of this restoration, we exclaim those prophetic words,[37] saying, "Rejoice greatly, O daughter of Sion; cry aloud, O daughter of Jerusalem. The Lord has taken away thine injuries; He has delivered thee from the hand of thine enemies.[38] Lift up thine eyes round about, and see thy children gathered. For behold, all thy sons have come from far, yea and thy daughters,[39] bearing unto thee not gold and frankincense[40] and stones, all begotten of the earth and by human custom adorning what is precious, but purer than all gold, and more precious than all stones, the ancestral faith unadulterated. Rejoice and delight thyself with all thine heart,[41] for behold, the Lord is coming, and He shall fix His tabernacle in thy midst."[42] What could be more agreeable than this day? What could be more explicit than this feast to give expression to gladness and joy? This is another shaft being driven today right through the heart of Death, not as the Saviour is engulfed by the tomb of mortality for the common resurrection of our kind, but as the image of the Mother rises up from the very depths of oblivion, and raises along with herself the likenesses of the saints. Christ came to us in the flesh, and was borne in the arms of His Mother. This is seen and confirmed and proclaimed in pictures, the teaching made manifest by means of personal eye-witness, and impelling the spectators to unhesitating assent. Does

Ar II 304

---

[34] Is. 61. 10.
[35] Cf. Is. 62. 12.
[36] Is. 62. 3.
[37] The word φωνὰς has been supplied by Pg.
[38] Zeph. 3. 14–15.
[39] Is. 60. 4.
[40] Is. 60. 6.
[41] Zeph. 3. 14.
[42] Zeph. 3. 15.

a man hate the teaching by means of pictures? Then how could he not have previously rejected and hated the message of the Gospels? Just as speech *is transmitted* by hearing, so a form through sight is imprinted upon the tablets of the soul, giving to those whose apprehension is not soiled by wicked doctrines a representation of knowledge concordant with piety. Martyrs have suffered for their love of God, showing with their blood the ardour of their desire,[43] and their memory is contained in books. These *deeds* they are also seen performing in pictures,[44] as painting presents the martyrdom of those blessed men more vividly to our knowledge.[45] Others have been burnt alive, a sacrifice sanctified by their prayer, fasting and other labours. These things are conveyed both by stories and by pictures, but it is the spectators rather than the hearers who are drawn to emulation. The Virgin is holding the Creator in her arms as an infant. Who is there who would not marvel, more from the sight of it than from the report, at the magnitude of the mystery, and would not rise up to laud the ineffable condescension that surpasses all words? For even if the one introduces the other, yet the comprehension that comes about through sight is shown in very fact to be far superior to the learning that penetrates through the ears. Has a man lent his ear to a story? Has his intelligence visualized and drawn to itself what he has heard? Then, after judging it with sober attention, he deposits it in his memory. No less—indeed much greater—is the power of sight. For surely, having somehow through the outpouring and effluence of the optical rays touched and encompassed the object, it too sends the essence of the thing seen on to the mind, letting it be conveyed from there to the memory for the concentration of unfailing knowledge.[46] Has the mind seen?[47] Has it grasped? Has it visualized? Then it has effortlessly transmitted the forms to the memory.

6. Is there one who rejects the holy writings on these matters and, in spite of the fact that all lies are dispelled by them, considers them

---

[43] Read τὸ φίλτρον τοῦ πόθου with the MSS: τὸ φίλτερον Ar.
[44] Reading διαπραττόμενοι (sc. μάρτυρες) with the MSS: διαπραττόμενα Ar.
[45] Reading ἐναργεστέραν τῆς γραφῆς παρεχομένης with the MSS: παρεχομέναις Ar.
[46] πρὸς ἐπιστήμην ἀπλανεστάτην συνάθροισιν codd: πρὸς ἐπιστήμης ἀπλανεστάτην συνάθροισιν Ar. I would prefer πρὸς ἐπιστήμης ἀπλανεστάτης συνάθροισιν.
[47] Read εἶδεν ὁ νοῦς with the MSS: οἶδεν Ar.

HOMILY XVII. IMAGE OF THE VIRGIN

to be not above dispute? Then this man has long since transgressed by scorning the veneration of holy images. Does he, on the contrary, reverence the latter, and honour them with proper respect? Then he will be disposed likewise towards the writings. If he treats either one with reverence or with contempt, he necessarily bestows the same on the other, unless, in addition to being impious, he has also abandoned reason, and is not only irreverent, but also preaches things which are in conflict with his own position. Those, therefore, who have slipped into assailing the holy images are proved not to have kept the correctness of doctrine either, but with the one they abjure the other. They do not dare confess what they believe, chary, not of being impious, but of appearing so; and they avoid the name whereof they willingly pursue the actions. Abominable in their misdeeds, they are more abominable in their impiety. Their whole offshoot has perished, branches, roots and all, even as the wondrous David in his canticles sings of the memorial of the impious being destroyed with a noise,[48] and it is He Whom they have set at nought through His picture Who has passed righteous judgment on them. But before our eyes stands motionless the Virgin carrying the Creator in her arms as an infant, *depicted* in painting as she is in Ar II 307 writings and visions, an interceder for our salvation and a teacher of reverence to God, a grace of the eyes and a grace of the mind, carried by which the divine love in us is uplifted to the intelligible beauty of truth.[49]

7. But what is to become of me, driven as I am at the same time to speak and to be silent? For such is the charm of the subject before me that I prefer to continue speaking without ever being sated by speech. But time, which flows on and knows no delay, urges me to conclude my speech with silence and turn to another compelling duty.[50] Yet, since time can no longer be grasped once it is passed,[51] and as for the topic, even if we talked all our life about it, no one would succeed in expressing it worthily, so, as it is ill to

---

[48] Ps. 9. 7.
[49] Read with the MSS: αἷς [sc. χάρισι understood] εἰς τὸ νοητὸν τῆς ἀληθείας κάλλος ὁ ἐν ἡμῖν θεῖος ἔρως ὀχούμενος ἀναφέρεται [ἧς for αἷς … ἀναφύρεται Ar].
[50] I. e. the celebration of the liturgy.
[51] Reading τὸν μὲν οὐκ ἔστι [so Pg: οὐκ ἔτι A, Lig: οὐκέτι B, Ar] λαβεῖν παρελθόντα.

HOMILIES OF PHOTIUS

fail in both respects, *I shall do* what I can and ought, and at the bidding of time consent to be silent. But O Word and Bridegroom and substantiated Wisdom of the Father, Whose name this sacred and holy temple bears, grant us forgiveness for what has been inadequately said. For it is Thine wont to look not at the deficiencies but at the intention, and to make that the standard for the gift, instead of weighing the words according to their worth. Grant those also who have received it through Thee to reign on earth to consecrate the remainder of the church too with holy images; and as they have been made by Thee to be the eyes of the universe,[52] so guard them like the pupil of the eye, place them above any bad influence, showing them terrible and irresistible to the foes, gracious and salutary to their subjects, and render them, together with us, worthy of Thine endless and blessed kingdom. For Thine is the power and the honour and the veneration, of the consubstantial, life-giving and all-powerful Trinity, now and for ever and ever. Amen.

---

[52] The MSS read καὶ οἷά περ [so B: οἷαπερ A, Lig] τῆς οἰκουμένης ὑπὸ σοῦ τεχθέντας [ταχθέντας Ar] ὀφθαλμούς.

NOTE ON HOMILY XVIII

Porfirij Uspenskij, who first published this Homily, believed it to have been delivered at the inauguration by the Emperors Michael and Basil of a commemorative pillar bearing a condemnation of all the heresies.[1] This interpretation was accepted by Aristarches,[2] who furthermore connected this Homily with the victory over the Manichaeans, dated by him in the spring of 867, whereas in fact the triumph over the Manichaeans was not celebrated until the autumn of 872. It is hardly worth while discussing the views advanced by other scholars. Thus, Hergenröther who, it is true, was only acquainted with the title and *incipit*, suggested that this Homily was given either in September 863 or in 866–67.[3] K.K.Müller put forward the year 866,[4] while Ivantsov-Platonov thought that the Homily referred to the establishment of the feast of Orthodoxy.[5]

It is not of primary importance whether the *stele*, to which Photius constantly refers, was in fact a monumental inscription, as modern commentators have supposed.[6] I would be more inclined

---

[1] Четыре бесѣды Фотія, pp. 81 sq.

[2] II. 309 sq.

[3] *Photius, Patriarch von Constantinopel*, I, pp. 468–69; II, p. 236.

[4] *Zeitschrift für Kirchengeschichte*, IV (1880), p. 136.

[5] Къ изслѣдованіямъ о Фотіѣ, St. Petersburg, 1892, pp. 24–25.

[6] F. Uspenskij (Очерки по исторіи византійской образованности, St. Petersburg, 1891, p. 4) asserts that the *Synodicon of Orthodoxy* "was carved in stone and kept in St. Sophia," and that "three marble plaques, each of them three fathoms long and two fathoms wide, remained in position until the 16th century, when the Sultans took advantage of them to adorn their mausolea." Uspenskij gives no authority for this statement. His source may be Dositheus of Jerusalem ('Ιστορία περὶ τῶν ἐν 'Ιεροσολύμοις πατριαρχευσάντων, VIII. 9. 1), who reports that four marble slabs, each of them three fathoms long and not as wide, which were inscribed with the edicts of the Council of 1166 (cf. Nicetas Choniates, p. 278, Bonn ed.), were removed from the north side of St. Sophia by Selim II. By order of the Sultan three of the slabs were destroyed, while the fourth, which bore the pompous titles of Manuel I, was set up in the tomb of Suleiman the Magnificent. Cf. Skarlatos Byzantios, 'Η Κωνσταντινούπολις, I, Athens, 1851, pp. 512–13. This story is confirmed by an eyewitness, Marco Antonio Pigafetta, who writes as follows concerning Suleiman's mausoleum: "Tra molte pietre, et marmi, che quivi erano per compimento di detta fabrica, io vidi quatro lastre di marmo, longhe circa nove et più piedi l'una, antiche molto, et intagliate tutte di

to think that the verb στηλογραφέω⁷ was used here metaphorically, much as we would say "to placard,"⁸ and that the Homily did not concern the setting up of any memorial. What we are interested in determining is the occasion on which the Homily was delivered, and to do so we have only to read its text. It was an occasion of great solemnity, attended by both Emperors, the higher clergy and the senate. The victory over all the heresies was not a military one, and was not accompanied by loss of life. It was achieved by the pen, not the sword.⁹ The "monument" inaugurated on that day was a confession of faith, a document signed by the Emperors, and towards which the senators had also contributed their help. The only such occasion during the joint reign of Michael III and Basil I was the Council of 867. Photius himself makes it quite clear when he says that each previous Synod, even the one of Nicaea, had drawn on older conciliar decisions, while the "holy deed" of the Emperor Michael was inspired directly by the Almighty.¹⁰ The participation of the senators as signatories of the Acts was admitted at the Council of 869–70 by the Emperor's spokesman Baanes,¹¹ and is confirmed by anti-Photian sources.¹²

---

lettere greche, et queste furono levate di S. Sophia il 8 mese d'agosto 1567... In questi marmi si leggono alcuni decreti, et constitutioni di un concilio, celebrato in Constantinopoli a tempi d'un Emanuelo imperatore, et altre cose pertinenti alla nostra religione." See P. Matković, "Putopis Marka Antuna Pigafette u Carigrad od god. 1567," *Starine*, XXII, Zagreb, 1890, p. 109. This inscription, if indeed it is the one alluded to by Uspenskij, had therefore no bearing on the 9th century.

[7] ἐστηλογραφήθη θρίαμβος in the title and Ar II. 322₅. Cf. II. 318₁₂ τὸ θεοστυγὲς τῶν αἱρέσεων στηλιτεύεται. II. 325₁₄: στήλην ὀρθοδοξίας .... ἀναστήσασα.

[8] Cf., for example, *Vita Nicephori* (*Nicephori opuscula historica*, ed. De Boor, Leipzig, 1880), p. 161, concerning that Patriarch's profession of faith: στηλίτευμα μὲν τῶν ἑτεροδόξων οὖσαν αἱρέσεων, στήλην δὲ τῆς ὀρθοδόξου ὑπάρχουσαν πίστεως. Or again the *Synodicon* for the Sunday of Orthodoxy (Montfaucon, *Bibliotheca Coisliniana*, Paris, 1715, p. 98): οἷα στήλη τινὶ ἐκ μεγίστων λίθων συνηρμοσμένη καὶ πρὸς ὑποδοχὴν γραφῆς διευθετισμένη ταῖς τῶν ἀδελφῶν καρδίαις τάς τε εὐλογίας αἳ ὀφείλονται τοῖς νομοφυλακοῦσι, καὶ τὰς ἀρὰς δὲ αἷς καὶ ἑαυτοὺς ὑποβάλλουσιν οἱ παρανομοῦντες, δίκαιόν τε καὶ ὀφειλόμενον δεῖν ᾠήθημεν ἀναγράψαι.

[9] Pp. 311, 313 below.
[10] P. 312 below.
[11] Mansi XVI, col. 384 A.
[12] *Vita Ignatii*, PG 105, col. 537 C; Metrophanes of Smyrna in Mansi, XVI, col. 417 C; *Synodicon vetus* in Fabricius and Harless, *Biblioth. graeca*, XII, p. 419.

NOTE ON HOMILY XVIII

Once the occasion is understood, the Homily under consideration becomes a historical document of the greatest importance, being as it is the only official piece that has come down to us from the Council of 867.

We know with what systematic care the Acts of the Council were destroyed. The copy found in Photius' archives, sumptuously bound in silk and precious metals, was confiscated by Basil's emissaries and burned before the eighth session of the Council of 869–70.[13] The other official copy was conveyed to Rome by an imperial embassy and solemnly burned in 869 in front of St. Peter's church.[14] Moreover, Pope Hadrian II decreed that whoever concealed and refused to surrender the writings of the condemned Council would be excommunicated.[15] Such drastic measures were required not so much because the Acts of the Council were considered to be impious, but because they were highly embarrassing; for they contained a condemnation of Pope Nicholas I, probably based on some well-documented evidence, and, what is more, bore the signatures of Basil I, a great part of the Greek clergy and the senatorial class. To screen Basil, the Synod of 869 had to resort to barefaced fraud. It alleged that the signatures had been forged by Photius; that in order to swell the number of subscriptions, he had called in shoemakers, fishmongers and other menial persons; that the legates of the Oriental Patriarchs were false; and finally that there had been no Council at all.[16] The same inept allegations are found in other anti-Photian sources. Thus, Anastasius says that one thousand signatures had been forged by Photius.[17] Basil's envoy to Pope Hadrian II alleged that Michael was made to sign the Acts when he was drunk; that Basil's signature was false; and that Photius had bribed a number of stray laymen to simulate the bishops' signatures with both fine and coarse pens in order to diversify the handwriting.[18]

Before discussing the new evidence afforded by Homily XVIII

---

[13] *Vita Ignatii*, cols. 540–41; Mansi, XVI, col. 384 B–C.
[14] *Liber Pontificalis*, ed. Duchesne, II, p. 179.
[15] Mansi, XVI, cols. 129–30, 380 B.
[16] Mansi, XVI, col. 384.
[17] *Ibid.*, col. 5 C.
[18] *Lib. Pont.*, II, p. 179.

we should summarize what has previously been known about the Council of 867.[19] Some of its aims are expressed in Photius' famous Encyclical Letter to the Oriental Patriarchs,[20] and it may be assumed that they were in fact carried out. From this letter, written in the early part of 867, we learn that the teachings of the Latin missionaries in Bulgaria had just been condemned by a local synod at Constantinople. In requesting the three Oriental Patriarchs to despatch their legates without delay, Photius indicates the agenda of the Council as follows: 1) to extirpate the innovations introduced by the Latin missionaries (viz. the Sabbath fast, the taking of milk and cheese in the first week of Lent, the enforced celibacy of the clergy, the invalidation of the chrism conferred by priests, and the procession of the Holy Ghost from the Son); 2) to consider the grievances of the Western clergy against the Pope; and 3) to rule that the Seventh Oecumenical Council (of 787) should be numbered and honoured with the other six, which some Eastern Churches had neglected to do.[21]

It can be stated with some assurance that the Council met in late summer 867. On the one hand, the Encyclical Letter could not have been sent before the early part of the year, so that the emissaries of the Oriental Patriarchs could hardly have arrived at Constantinople before the summer.[22] On the other hand, we know that Zacharias of Chalcedon, who was deputed to carry the Acts of the Council

---

[19] For a discussion of the Council, see Ivantsov-Platonov, *op. cit.*, pp. 108–111; Rossejkin, "Константинопольскій соборъ 867 года," Богословскій Вѣстникъ, 1915, I, pp. 365–394; Bury, *History of the Eastern Roman Empire*, pp. 201–203; Dvornik, *The Photian Schism*, pp. 120–129; F. Dölger, *Byzanz und die Europäische Staatenwelt*, Speyer am Rhein, 1953, pp. 311–12, n. 54.

[20] Ed. Valettas, pp. 165–181 = PG 102, cols. 721–741.

[21] On the Encyclical Letter, see esp. Rossejkin, "Окружное посланіе Фотія," Богосл. Вѣстникъ, 1915, I, pp. 122–157.

[22] Rossejkin in Богосл. Вѣстникъ, 1915, I, pp. 370–75 has shown at some length that the Oriental Patriarchs were in full communion with Photius and had no valid reason not to send their legates. It is true that the presence of genuine legates was denied at the Council of 869–70, but it is altogether incredible that Photius, at the height of his power, should have resorted, as claimed, to picking up three impostors in the streets and making them pose as legates. Both at the Council of 869–70 and at the one of 879–80 the emissaries of the Oriental Patriarchs did nothing but follow the dictates of imperial policy. There is no reason to doubt that in 867 they acted in the same way. Cf. Dvornik, *The Photian Schism*, p. 151, n. 2.

NOTE ON HOMILY XVIII

to Italy, was intercepted on his journey as a result of Michael's murder on September 24th, and brought back to Constantinople.[23] It follows that Zacharias embarked only a few days before the murder, so that the concluding sessions of the Council probably took place in the early part of September. The fact that our Homily was delivered in that fateful month of September lends to it a dramatic touch. Two or three weeks later, Basil, the Emperor's "beloved son," was to assassinate his adoptive father, and Photius himself, who might well have considered the "triumph over all the heresies" as the high point of his career, was to be deposed and banished.

The Council met, therefore, in the summer of 867, and was attended by the two Emperors, the legates of the three Oriental Patriarchs and most of the Byzantine higher clergy, probably numbering in all upward of 300 members.[24] Everything tends to show that it was an occasion of the greatest importance and solemnity. At this point we have to fall back, unfortunately, on the anti-Photian sources. The latter, while differing among themselves on points of detail, are unanimous in saying that Nicholas I was condemned and excommunicated by the Council.[25] This condemnation applied, of course, solely to the person of Nicholas, and was not a general measure against the Papacy. It is further alleged that at the instigation of Photius the Council conferred the title of Emperor on Lewis II in the hope that the latter would drive Pope Nicholas out of Rome.[26] The existence of secret negotiations between Constantinople and Lewis has been supposed by several historians, and we are further told that Photius wrote a letter to Lewis' wife Engelberta,[27] which, however, does not imply that Photius, and not the imperial Foreign Office, was the instigator of the whole manoeuvre. But be that as it may, we can hardly believe that a Church Council conferred the imperial title on a foreign prince, since such an action could have been taken only by the emperor.

[23] *Vita Ignatii*, cols. 540, 541.
[24] According to Rossejkin's calculations, *op. cit.*, p. 384.
[25] Mansi XVI, cols. 174 C, 405 C; *Vita Ignatii*, col. 541; etc.
[26] Metrophanes of Smyrna in Mansi XVI, col. 417 E; *Vita Ignatii*, col. 537. Cf. Dölger, *loc. cit.*
[27] Cf. Grumel, *Les régestes des Actes du Patriarcat de Constantinople*, I 2 (1936), nos. 479, 484. Great caution should, however, be observed regarding the scope of these negotiations.

HOMILIES OF PHOTIUS

When we turn to our Homily, we are at once struck by the absence of any polemical topic. The Papacy, the *Filioque*, the Latin missionaries in Bulgaria are not even mentioned. At first, one may even doubt whether the Homily belongs to the Council of 867 at all. Yet, would it have been proper to engage in controversy and invective in an official panegyric? The Council of 867 was clearly meant to be oecumenical, and for a Council to be oecumenical, it had to rule on matters of doctrine. The positive achievements of the Council which are extolled in the Homily were not the disciplinary measures, but the refutation of every heresy and the preservation of the faith in all its purity. The evaluation of this claim, to paraphrase Bury's very apt remark,[28] depends largely on the religious affiliations of the critic. In other words, was the "triumph over all the heresies" a mere formality, designed to give the Council the garb of oecumenicity, while the real objective was directed against the Papacy?[29] To anyone well acquainted with the writings of Photius it is clear that confounding the Pope was neither the sole nor the principal preoccupation of the Patriarch. The thoughts expressed in the Homily are so genuinely characteristic of the age, that we must try to accept them at their face value.

What the Homily says in effect is that the Council assembled by the Emperor Michael has put a final check to the resurgence of every heresy: "no manner of impiety shall henceforth speak freely."[30] This claim may seem somewhat exaggerated in view of the fact that the Council merely ratified previous conciliar condemnations; to understand it, we must remember the contemporary belief that with the defeat of Iconoclasm true faith had reached its final perfection. Iconoclasm had, of course, been condemned at the Council of 787, but that Council had not been generally accepted either in the East or in the West, and furthermore Iconoclasm had since enjoyed a second period of supremacy. The renewed ratification of the Second Nicene Council (even if that had already been done by an ecclesi-

[28] *Op. cit.*, p. 203.
[29] Such a view has been expressed regarding the two last [sessions of the Council of 879–80. Cf., for example, Jugie, "Les actes du synode photien de Ste-Sophie," *Échos d'Orient*, XXXVII (1938), p. 93.
[30] P. 311 below.

NOTE ON HOMILY XVIII

astical gathering in 843,[31] and doubtless also by the Synod of 861) was a subject that remained constantly in Photius' mind.[32] Thus, while each of the Seven Oecumenical Councils had refuted some particular heresy, there was need for a summation, for a final definition of Christian dogma. This is what, in the words of Photius, the Council of 867 accomplished.

Things, of course, turned out otherwise. After the assassination of Michael III, the very reality of the Council was denied. Even Photius himself refrained from bringing up the subject again, probably for reasons of expediency: for to revive the issue would have been extremely embarrassing for the Emperor Basil, and would have made a settlement with Rome impossible. It is, however, instructive, with our Homily in mind, to turn to the Photian Council of 879–80. It is well known that at the sixth session of that Council was issued the famous prohibition against altering in any way the symbol of faith.[33] We need not enquire whether this measure represented an essential departure from the practice of previous councils, as claimed by Grumel;[34] it certainly, however, implied a complete attainment of religious truth, a belief that underlies contemporary Byzantine thinking and art.[35] In this respect the Council of 879–80 was acting in the same spirit as the one of 867. Both Councils likewise ratified anew the Seventh Oecumenical. To carry the comparison even further, we may quote the following title

---

[31] According to the *Synodicon vetus* (Fabricius – Harless, *Bibl. graeca*, XII, p. 416), the re-establishment of Orthodoxy in 843 was carried out by a local synod (held ἐν τοῖς Κανικλείου) which ratified the Seven Oecumenical Councils. Great caution, however, should be observed regarding the religious events of 843. Some of the discrepancies between our sources have been pointed out by F. Uspenskij, Очерки, pp. 3–88, but a new study of the Feast of Orthodoxy is needed.

[32] Cf. Dvornik, "The Patriarch Photius and Iconoclasm," *Dumbarton Oaks Papers*, 7 (1953), pp. 92 sq.

[33] The authenticity of the last two sessions of that Council has been quite gratuitously contested. See Dvornik, *The Photian Schism*, p. 196; Amann, *Dict. de théol. cath.*, s. v. Photius, cols. 1589–90.

[34] "Le décret du synode photien de 879–80 sur le Symbole de la foi," *Échos d'Orient*, XXXVII (1938), pp. 357–72. The novelty of this decree has, however, been contested by Jugie, "Origine de la controverse sur l'addition du *Filioque* au Symbole," *Rev. des sciences philos. et théol.*, XXVIII (1939), pp. 379 sq.

[35] A. Grabar, "L'art religieux et l'empire byzantin à l'époque des Macédoniens," École prat. des Hautes Études, *Annuaire*, 1939–40, esp. pp. 8 sq.

which heads a summary of the canons of 879–80: "Canons formulated by the Holy Synod that convened in the Renowned Church named after the Wisdom of God, the Logos, that confirmed the Seventh Oecumenical Synod, and repulsed every schismatic and heretical error" (πᾶσαν δὲ σχισματικὴν καὶ αἱρετικὴν πλάνην ἀπελασάσης).[36] An echo of the "triumph over all the heresies" certainly lingers in the final clause of this title. Essentially the same idea was later embodied in the *Synodicon of Orthodoxy*, which in one important manuscript (Escor. y.–III.–10) is entitled τὸ συνοδικὸν κατὰ πασῶν τῶν αἱρέσεων.[37]

There remains to explain why our Homily makes no mention of a doctrinal matter like the double procession of the Holy Ghost. This omission may seem strange to us in the light of the immense disputes that the *Filioque* clause provoked for several centuries. But we may well ask this question: did Photius in 867 consider the Western addition to be on a par with the major Trinitarian heresies of the past? The answer seems to be in the negative. In the first place, Photius had no grounds for imputing the doctrine to Rome, since Rome had not yet officially accepted it. As far as the Council was concerned, the *Filioque* was an aberration introduced, along with other errors, by the "so-called" bishops in Bulgaria;[38] an aberration, moreover, which carried its own inherent contradictions and which was reducible to the teaching of older heretics such as Sabellius and Macedonius, and even to the tales of Greek mythology.[39] There was, therefore, no compelling reason why the *Filioque* doctrine should have been explicitly mentioned in the Homily; the general condemnation of every heresy sufficed.

[36] Mansi, XVI, col. 549 A. This title is found in Cod. Chalc. 175, f. 215^v, claimed to be of the year 883 (Tsakopoulos, Περιγραφικὸς κατάλογος τῶν χειρογράφων τῆς βιβλ. τοῦ Οἰκουμενικοῦ Πατριαρχείου, Istanbul, 1953, p. 258). On the probable date of this manuscript (11th century?) see, however, Laurent in *Rev. des ét. byz.*, XIV (1956), pp. 222–23; V. N. Beneševič, Каноническій сборникъ XIV титуловъ, St. Petersburg, 1905, p. 118.

[37] E. Miller, *Catalogue des manuscrits grecs de la Bibl. de l'Escurial*, Paris, 1848, p. 285. On the history of the *Synodicon*, a subject that is still greatly in need of elucidation, see F. Uspenskij, Очерки, pp. 89–145; *id.*, Синодикъ въ недѣлю [православія, Odessa, 1893; Anton Michel, *Humbert und Kerullarios*, II, Paderborn, 1930, pp. 1–21.

[38] Cf. Dvornik, *The Photian Schism*, p. 122.

[39] Cf. *De Spiritus S. mystagogia*, ed. Hergenröther (1857), pp. 14, 15, 36, 37, 109.

NOTE ON HOMILY XVIII

Thus, although Homily no. XVIII does not give us any fresh factual information on the proceedings of the Council, it certainly places the Council in an entirely new light. In a wider sense, the Homily is one of the most important documents for the intellectual history of ninth-century Byzantium. Nowhere else is the idea of a renascence more clearly stated. Attention should be drawn especially to the opening sentence: Time, says Photius, had long ceased to produce anything new or noble, but merely went round and round, carrying the self-same load of its ancient achievements. Now, at last, Time has been rejuvenated and has given birth to new and noble deeds. The repetitive cyclic motion has given way to a new flowering. A new era is beginning, and all it lacks is an orator who can rise to the grandeur of the occasion.[40]

Students of Byzantine literature should not, for their part, fail to note paragraph 2 of the Homily. Here, while disclaiming the role of a panegyrist, Photius traces a brief encomium of the emperor in due classical form: deeds of war and deeds of peace, the construction of cities, liberality, mercy, religious zeal, in fact the very opposite of the same Emperor's odious portrait which the Macedonian apologists of the tenth century have imposed upon posterity.[41] After introducing the various elements of a panegyric, Photius adroitly excuses himself from the task, which he leaves to others (τὰ μὲν γὰρ ἄλλοις παρεῖται).[42] The rebirth of the secular encomium, of which Leo VI's *Funeral Oration* and the *Vita Basilii* are the

---

[40] This passage is far from implying a cyclic recurrence of history, the Stoic doctrine whose incompatibility with Christianity was already pointed out by Origen (*De princ.*, II. 3. 4; *Contra Celsum*, IV. 67–68; V. 20–21). In the fourth *Oration against the Arians* of Athanasius, which was used widely by Photius in Homilies XV and XVI, the absurdity of Marcellianism is demonstrated by the fact that it leads to an eternal cycle of creations (PG 26, col. 484). The parallel has been drawn by G. L. Kustas in an unpublished dissertation entitled *Photius' Idea of History* (Harvard Univ., 1953), pp. 196 sq. What Photius is saying is that history is made up of periods of fecundity followed by periods of fruitless repetition; cyclic movement belongs not to history as a whole, but to time, and even that may be nothing more than a classical reminiscence. Cf. Aristotle, *Metaph.* 1071 b, 7–11.

[41] Note that the denigration of Michael III also draws heavily on classical sources. This has been pointed out by R. J. H. Jenkins, "Constantine VII's Portrait of Michael III," Acad. Roy. de Belgique, *Bull. de la Cl. des Lettres*, XXXIV (1948), pp. 71–77.

[42] P. 308 below = Ar II. 317_{14}.

HOMILIES OF PHOTIUS

earliest extant instances, has attracted the attention of scholars,[43] and it has been pointed out with some credibility that the *genre* may have been cultivated at the University of the Caesar Bardas.[44] We may now say with complete assurance that Michael III had been the recipient of such encomia, so that the renascence of the tenth century can hardly be credited with any originality in this respect.

XVIII

Ar II 314 OF THE SAME,[1] HOMILY DELIVERED FROM THE AMBO OF ST. SOPHIA, WHEN THE TRIUMPH OVER ALL THE HERESIES WAS PROCLAIMED BY OUR ORTHODOX AND GREAT EMPERORS MICHAEL AND BASIL[2]

1. Time, it seems, has long since grown old, and brought forth no more the offspring of his youthful confidence and pride; but only brooded over those antique children of his and, being no longer able to renew his youth in any brilliant or noble generation, revolved about bearing the self-same things, and glorying only in the bringing forth of them whose birth[3] past years had recorded, who gave him
Ar II 315 no return to youthful grace and bloom. Now, however, thanks to one man,[4] the champion of pious, new and noble deeds, he is glorified with the birth-pangs of youth, and puts off old age with its reproaches, as if he had succeeded in showing everyone in the light of truth a well-born and excellent offspring blooming with the grace of all good things. Had he also borne a generation of orators, who knew how to make words commensurate with the facts, and to elevate the power of their tongue to the magnitude of the deeds,

---

[43] Cf. Paul J. Alexander, "Secular Biography at Byzantium," *Speculum*, XV (1940), pp. 194–209.
[44] R. J. H. Jenkins, "The Classical Background of the *Scriptores post Theophanem*," *Dumbarton Oaks Papers*, 8 (1954), pp. 20–21.
[1] After τοῦ αὐτοῦ Ar has added ἁγιωτάτου Φωτίου, πατριάρχου Κωνσταντίνου πόλεως.
[2] Basil's name is missing in the principal MSS. A, B and Lig read ἡνίκα τοῖς ὀρθοδόξοις καὶ μεγάλοις ἡμῶν Μιχαὴλ καὶ *** ὁ κατὰ πάσης αἱρέσεως ἐστηλογραφήθη θρίαμβος. In A Βασιλείου has been added by a later hand. *Athen.* 2756 has ἡνίκα τοῖς ὀρθοδόξοις καὶ μεγάλοις ἡμῶν βασιλεῦσι κατὰ πάσης etc. The full title in *Palat.* 129 is εἰς τοὺς βασιλεῖς Μιχαὴλ καὶ Βασίλειον.
[3] Read ὧν [ὃν Ar] ὁ φθάσας ἐμέτρει τὴν γένεσιν with the MSS.
[4] The Emperor Michael III. Read ἑνὸς ἀνδρὸς εὐσεβῶν [εὐσεβοῦς Ar] καὶ καινῶν καὶ γενναίων ἔργων ἀθλητοῦ.

HOMILY XVIII. THE COUNCIL OF 867

then his prime and renovation would have been altogether confirmed. At the moment, though losing not a little, he can none the less, thanks to the offspring of his prime, display his perfection to those who are here to see it,[5] even though no orator be present. But to those who shall emerge in later ages of life he will not be able to bestow the memory in words, and will, I presume, be charged again with senility, sickness and the like. For words are wont to flow freely before deeds of moderate dignity,[6] but hide away with cowardice and shrinking when they see a mass of events bearing down on them, or a vast expanse of accomplishments set before them. Wherefore I for my part intended to be silent, and not to insult with the feebleness of the speaker the magnitude of the deeds which surpass words, putting forward in self-defence, before being worsted, my fear of defeat. But since the deeds themselves are present with us, and the splendour of the actions is before everybody's eyes, there will be, methinks, no great loss[7] if the narrative falls below the mark. The visible facts will supply its deficiencies, and the shortcomings of the speech will only trumpet forth the pre-eminence of what has been done.[8]

Ar II 316

2. Splendid to behold are *the emperor's* feats in war, his victories, his trophies, whereof no moment of time since he has acceeded[9] to the kingly office has remained barren. It is not my intention to enumerate any of those; for it has often and on many occasions been proved that they are not due to strength or even to intelligence, nay, to neither of these, but rather to an unknown cause. Nay, not indeed the capture and depopulation of hostile cities and the construction and restoration of friendly ones; nor the fact that he converses with those he meets with a joyful and smiling countenance, and has removed all dejection from every face by changing

---

[5] The reading of A and *Palat.* 129, ταῖς γοναῖς ἐνακμάζων, seems preferable to γεγονὼς ἐνακμάζων which Ar has adopted on the authority of B.

[6] Read πράξεων μὲν γὰρ μετριαζούσῃ σεμνότητι [μετριάζουσαν σεμνότητα Ar].

[7] Read οὐκ ἐν μεγάλῳ τὰ τῆς ζημίας οἶμαι πεσεῖσθαι [πεπεῖσθαι Ar, probably a misprint].

[8] Read τὴν ὑπεροχὴν [ἡ ὑπεροχὴ Ar] σαλπίσει τῆς πράξεως.

[9] ἐξ οὗ τῆς βασιλείας οὗτος διέκυψεν, literally "since he has peered out of the kingship." This curious phrase may refer to Michael's assumption of sole power (A. D. 856), as contrasted to the time when he was Emperor only in name under his mother's tutelage.

THE HOMILIES OF PHOTIUS

Ar II 317

the tyranny of fear into a spontaneous love, taking pride in being called the father rather than the master of his country, not assuming the titles prior to the deeds,[10] after the manner of those men of yore, Cyrus and Augustus, the former ruler of the Persians, the latter of the Romans, who left to the populace a reputation for gentleness and mercy,[11] but, as proper reason ordains, glorying in the actions prior to the titles; not even that he has extended to the citizens a hand flowing with gold, having driven poverty out of the body politic as no man has driven it out of his own home, and that the queenly City, which lords it in wealth, has spread the gifts of prosperity to all subjects thanks to one imperial gesture; it is not my concern and purpose to enumerate any of these things, though they have truth herself standing by as witness. Nay, nor am I a showman artfully working to accord his hearers delectation out of words, for which those things I pass over would be fitting material;[12] nor indeed do I train my tongue in laudations to draw the applause of a theatre with my speeches, since both the manner of my life and the office of priesthood are incapable of assuming these roles, even if churches[13] and the holy care of holy buildings have, thanks to him, reached an unhoped-for attainment and matchless beauty; *the laudations* I have left to others, while *his care of churches* forms the subject of another speech on another festival.[14] Those *themes* only do I abstract from all the rest for my present narrative which

---

[10] The right reading is surely πρὸ τῶν ἔργων τὰς κλήσεις ἀρνύμενος. The MSS have ἀρνούμενος: ἀρυσάμενοι Ar: αἱρησάμενος or αἱρετισάμενος Pg.

[11] According to Themistius (*Or.* XXXIV, pp. 467–68 in Dindorf's ed.), Cyrus, Alexander and Augustus did not possess genuine *philanthropia*, because they loved only their respective countries, and not the whole of mankind. Cf. V. Valdenberg, "Discours politiques de Thémistius dans leur rapport avec l'antiquité," *Byzantion*, I (1924), p. 565.

[12] Reading: οὐδὲ γὰρ [οὐδὲ πομπικός [πομπτικός A] τις ἐγὼ καὶ τέρψιν [or τέρψεις with Ar: τέρψις AB] ἐκ λόγων τοῖς ἀκροαταῖς τεχνάζων χαρίζεσθαι, ὧνπερ [ὥσπερ codd, Ar] ὕλη [ὕλην Ar] μᾶλλον ἃ παρέρχομαι.

[13] It would be interesting to know whether Photius is referring specifically to St. Sophia or to other churches which had been either built or restored by Michael. Unfortunately, the text seems to be faulty: οὐδ' ὅτι [ὅτε Ar, without good reason] νεὼς αὐτῷ καὶ οἰκοδομημάτων ἱερῶν ἱεραὶ φροντίδες εἰς ἀνέλπιστον προελθεῖν πρᾶξιν ... ἐξενίκησαν. If several churches are meant, νεὼς should be changed to νεῴ: if only St. Sophia, a demonstrative adjective, like οὗτος, is called for.

[14] Probably referring to Homily XVII. Keep here the reading of the MSS: τὰ δὲ λόγος ἄλλος ὑπόθεσιν ἄλλης ἔχει [ἔχει om B] πανηγύρεως [λόγῳ ἄλλῳ ... ἔχοντι Ar].

HOMILY XVIII. THE COUNCIL OF 867

bring out straightaway the purity of his faith and his extraordinarily great zeal.

3. But from where shall I start? What shall I narrate first? Shall I announce the good tidings of the Church, or exhibit the triumph over the heresies? Or shall I make a preamble about the spiritual courage and struggles on behalf of piety of the one who has won this triumph and erected these splendid trophies? For each of the said *themes* leaps forward in my thoughts, and striving to occupy the first place, makes the beginning of my story undecided. And just as in a fair meadow of many blooms, each beautiful flower and fruit, by drawing and attracting all eyes to itself, makes it impossible for the spectators *to decide* which one of the things they see should be adjudged the winner; so also these noble and beautiful spectacles before us, by dazzling the beholders with the splendour of piety through each of the aforesaid *themes* alike, make choice undiscriminating. Since, however, in the joyful gladness of the Church both the heresies abhorred of God are put to disgrace and the victor's achievements shine forth, I shall in some way make this the beginning and foundation of my speech, and call out with the prophet the *tidings* of joy to Christ's bride, the Church: "Rejoice greatly, O daughter of Sion; cry aloud, O daughter of Jerusalem; the Lord hath taken away thine iniquities; He hath delivered thee from the hand of thine enemies."[15] Seest thou thy beloved son, whom thou hast adopted from the very cradle and made Emperor, and after breeding him in piety and rearing him to manhood in reverence,[16] hast led him up to the measure of Christ's years?[17] Seest thou him, what novel and gay rewards he has offered thee with great interest for his rearing, and with how many and how great trophies he has filled this holy and august church? For he does not bring thee Arius in chains, or Macedonius a captive, or Nestorius a prisoner,

Ar II 318

Ar II 319

---

[15] Zeph. 3. 14–15.

[16] A and B read εὐσεβείᾳ μὲν συνεκθρέψασα, εὐσεβείᾳ δὲ συνανθρώσασα (sic). Ar has emended the apodosis to εὐλαβείᾳ δὲ συνανδρώσασα. Attention should, however, be drawn to Lig's συναρθρώσασα.

[17] Michael was born most probably in 836, not in 839, as has commonly been supposed. See *Vita S. Theodorae* in Regel, *Analecta byzantino-russica*, St. Petersburg, 1891, p. 11₁₀; E. Stein, "Post-consulat et αὐτοκρατορία," *Ann. de l'Inst. de phil. et d'hist. orient.*, II (Mélanges Bidez), 1934, p. 899, n. 2. Thus Michael was 30 or 31 in 867.

or the children of Dioscorus who barbarized the whole universe with a multitude of unnatural offspring, or this or that enemy and foe of the Church, or the leader of one or several heresies, but all the contingents of the enemy at once, with their leaders, their devices and their designs, he has laid dead and stripped bare with one and the same blow of his imperial right hand. Lift up thine eyes round about, and behold thy children gathered,[18] whom the bacchantes and harpies of the heresies and schisms had formerly snatched away, and having filled them with corybantic frenzy and goaded them on, scattered them on the mountains and cliffs of perdition. Rejoice and delight thyself with all thine heart:[19] the Son is proclaimed consubstantial with the Father;[20] the Spirit is included into the same Godhead with them;[21] the Word which took on flesh from a virgin for the common salvation and renovation of our kind is not separated from the Godhead;[22] the natures in Him remain unmingled,[23] and each volition[24] is seen to act after its own nature;[25] all error and tedious nonsense[26] are driven away, no transmigration of souls is vainly imagined, nor does a throng of demons, borne on myths, leap back into the sphere whence they have fallen through wilful wrongdoing.[27] Nay, nor is Christ Himself under the pretext of due reverence bitterly insulted and taunted:[28] this is another inanity,[29] and a strange

Ar II 320

---

[18] Is. 60. 4.
[19] Zeph. 3. 14.
[20] As against the heresy of Arius, condemned by the First Oecumenical Council.
[21] As against the heresy of Macedonius, condemned by the Second Oecumenical Council.
[22] As against the heresy of Nestorius, condemned by the Third Oecumenical Council.
[23] As against Monophysitism, the doctrine of Eutyches and Dioscorus, condemned by the Fourth Oecumenical Council.
[24] A and B clearly present a lacuna here: αἱ φύσεις ἐπ' αὐτοῦ φυλάττουσι τὸ ἀσύγχυτον *** τῇ οἰκείᾳ φύσει συναναφαίνεται ἐνεργούμενον. Ar supplies ὃ after ἀσύγχυτον. The missing words appear to be καὶ τῶν θελημάτων ἑκάτερον, and are said to be present in Cod. Athen. 2756.
[25] As against the Monothelites, condemned by the Sixth Oecumenical Council.
[26] The MSS read λῆρος μακρὸς ἀπελήλαται [μακρὰν Uspenskij, Ar].
[27] As against the Origenistic doctrines of the 6th century, condemned by the Fifth Oecumenical Council. These doctrines taught the pre-existence and transmigration of souls, and the ultimate restitution of demons to grace. Cf. *Letter to Boris*, ed. Valettas, p. 213 = PG 102, col. 645.
[28] As against Iconoclasm, condemned by the Seventh Oecumenical Council.
[29] Reading κενολόγημα with the MSS [καινολόγημα Ar].

HOMILY XVIII. THE COUNCIL OF 867

kind of contumely devised by the Evil one, to inveigh against the image, while monstrously pretending to be tearing it apart in honour of the One represented, thus raging with a double frenzy. No manner of impiety shall henceforth speak freely. For our victorious protagonist, using the writing pen like a spear forged by God, has struck the plague right through the vitals. Now every kind of irreverence is lying prostrate, stripped of its very last hopes, and not even revived by dreams of a rebirth. This is by far more splendid and loftier than all the other trophies which long ages past have recorded, and the pious hands of pious emperors have set up; for what all of them scarcely accomplished in part and at different times, each one of those and all together, by one cast of the hand, have been mightily won by our faithful and great Emperor.[30] These are the military plans, the preoccupations, and the successes of the one who is truly God's general. This delivers from every harassment and elevates above every disaster the whole universe that is encircled and crowned by the Christian creed, and opens up the streams of every kind of joy and happiness to gush *and mingle* with one another, on seeing[31] one concord, and one confession of faith, and one Catholic Church extending to the ends of the world.

4. Let the mountains drop sweet wine and the hills gladness,[32] because the Lord has looked upon His people and His inheritance with merciful eyes, in setting up and raising the truly imperial majesty of the state[33]—His beloved son Basil. For it is clear that those things which the father[34] has succeeded in achieving, and which words leap with joy to narrate, he is inheriting as his own portion and pride. It was the grace of the most-holy Ghost that assembled the Councils which at different times cleansed the world of tares; but they too derived their wisdom from others. The First

---

[30] On the title πιστὸς καὶ μέγας βασιλεύς, see above, p. 188, n. 21.
[31] The MSS read τοῦτο ... πάσης δὲ χαρᾶς καὶ εὐφροσύνης ἀναστομοῖ δι' ἀλλήλων [ἐξ ἀλλήλων Ar] πηγάζειν τὰ νάματα, μίαν ὁρᾶν συμφωνίαν καὶ μίαν ὁμολογίαν πίστεως καὶ καθολικὴν ἐκκλησίαν μίαν εἰς πάντα διαπλουμένην τὰ πέρατα. Since ὁρᾶν cannot be governed by ἀναστομοῖ, we should either change it to ὁρῶν (to agree with τοῦτο), or supply a missing word, perhaps a participle like παρεχόμενον.
[32] Cf. Is. 45. 8; Joel 3. 18.
[33] A pun on the name of Basil: τὴν βασίλειον ὄντως τοῦ κράτους δυναστείαν, Βασίλειον τὸν ἠγαπημένον υἱὸν αὐτοῦ.
[34] I. e. Michael III.

Council had the acts of many previous ones to imitate in part; the Second adopted the First as a pattern and model, while for the Third the Second in addition to the First served as exemplars, yea, and the Fourth was enriched by imitating them,[35] and the previous ones were the teachers of the ones following. As for thee, champion of piety,[36] what example hast thou taken in mind, in coming forward as the novel creator of this holy deed? What teacher hast thou found? To what leader hast thou referred thyself? What guide hast thou followed? Indeed it is evident that the common Lord and Creator of all has been thy initiator in this mystery also, Who Himself[37] proclaims in holy Scripture, crying out loud: "Whoever shall confess me before men, him will I confess also before my father which is in heaven."[38] For not only in the presence of men and of the angelic choirs, but also, methinks, with the Lord's very nature looking on from above and awarding the victory, has the triumph over all the heresies been proclaimed with a bold mind, tongue and hand, and the mystery of piety, strengthened as never before, has been confessed again. Yea, he was also thy adviser, the keybearer of the heavenly gates, proclaimed by Truth to be the rock and foundation of the faith,[39] Peter, the chief of the disciples, who whispered some such inspired and holy words in the ears of thy heart, saying that thou shouldst be ready to give an answer to every man that asketh the reason for thy most-pure and unadulterated faith.[40] Thou tookest the advice to heart after the throes of study. Thou didst not await anyone to ask thee, but as soon as this work had reached maturity, thou didst know it,[41] and didst bring it forth into the light, *a work* truly agreeable to God, having shown to all that the fruit was worthy of the seed, in that thou didst proclaim and set down the faith correctly, and didst hurl all the heresies into

---

[35] All the MSS read ναὶ δὴ καὶ τετάρτην ταύταις ἐπλούτει μιμήσασθαι. One might conjecture instead ναὶ δὴ καὶ τετάρτη ⟨τῷ⟩ ταύτας ἐπλούτει μιμήσασθαι.
[36] Turning again to Michael III.
[37] Read ὃς [ὡς Ar] ἐν τοῖς ἱεροῖς λογίοις ἀποθεσπίζει with all the MSS.
[38] Mt 10. 32.
[39] The words ὁ τῶν οὐρανίων κλειδοῦχος πυλῶν καὶ τῆς πίστεως πέτρα καὶ θεμέλιος ὑπὸ τῆς ἀληθείας ἀναρρηθεὶς (cf. Mt 16. 18–19) have been omitted by Ar, as being, no doubt, too redolent of Papal claims. Ar is further mistaken in saying that these words are crossed out in A. Cf. above, p. 40 and n. 11.
[40] Cf. 1 Pet. 3. 15.
[41] Read τελεσφορηθεῖσαν ἔγνως with the MSS [τελεσφορηθεὶς ἀνέγνως Ar].

HOMILY XVIII. THE COUNCIL OF 867

the snare of hell.[42] This takes the prize over all those matters that are administered for the body politic by the emperor's cares with a view to the peaceful condition of land and sea and an untroubled life, in the same measure[43] that the soul surpasses the body, and the sun surpasses the moon, and spiritual contemplation surpasses the apprehension of the senses. Thus, by a most splendid and novel exercise of piety, thou hast worked thy will in pious deeds, and every tongue is now busy with stories of thee.

That great Moses, God's servant, who lashed Egypt with unheard-of[44] blows (for he turned the elements into scourges), who made passable the waves of the sea, who with his prayer and tongue tilled the clouds like furrows and reaped therefrom abundant food for those who were distressed in the desert, that very man, on seeing the people he guided, and on whose account everything was being done, a-whoring after idolatry, did not suffer the plight meekly, but straightaway roused himself, and, wishing to check the prevalence of evil, he dyed his sword in no small measure *of blood*, and after diminishing the throng, he delivered the remainder from error;[45] so that the salvation which he accomplished for the remnant depended on the destruction of his fellow-countrymen, whose massacre begat the conversion of the former. But Christ's disciple has not destroyed fellow-men to deliver the remainder of the plague, nay, he saves the sum total of his subjects by defeating evil itself, and while thrusting against the latter the spear of his pen, he has showed all the people under his rule untouched by the stain of evil. That famous Phinees, too, checked the plague which was ravaging his whole people by transfixing the Israelite together with the Medianitish woman;[46] but not even he was innocent of a fellow-man's blood, nor did he deliver from bodily destruction those whose

---

[42] Prov. 9. 18.
[43] The reading of the MSS should be kept: τοῦτο (i. e. the true profession of faith and defeat of the heresies) τῶν ὁπόσα ... βασιλικαὶ φροντίδες τῇ πολιτείᾳ χρηματίζουσιν, ὅσῳ ψυχὴ σώματος ... προανέστηκεν, ἐπὶ τοσούτῳ μέτρῳ ... φέρει τὰ νικητήρια [τοιγάρτοι ὁπόσα ... καὶ ὅσῳ ψυχὴ Ar: τούτων ὁπόσα ... ὑπερανέστηκεν ... φέρῃ τὰ νικητήρια Pg].
[44] There appears to be no reason for changing ἀπίστοις to ἀποίστοις (so Ar). Cf. above, p. 88, n. 38. Besides, the word ἄποιστος (supposed to mean "unbearable") does not seem ever to have existed in the Greek language.
[45] Ex. 32. 27 sq.
[46] Num. 25. 7–8.

champion he was. But our Phinees, not allowing the plague to prevail, nor drenching his right hand in kindred blood, but transfixing most courageously and royally the pestilence, not of the bodies, but of the souls, has made the whole commonwealth to rise above every error and plague. David rather, in that he was King, is closer by his example: for by slaying one foreigner, he snatched away his whole people from servitude, wounds and the enemies' sword (yet here too he was caring about their bodies only); but in that he struck one only, and left behind many of the gentiles, who were engaged in an implacable war against the Israelites, he let the splendour of his victory be overshadowed by the expectation of another battle, so that the present joy of triumph did not gladden[47] the victorious camp any more than the fear of the future frightened and disturbed it. But the Emperor's hand did not draw the sword of the Cross against one alien heresy, nor did it make the joy of the achievement incomplete, nor did it leave the enemy even the shadow of a hope to retrieve their defeat, but after breaking up all their ranks at once, and splendidly exhibiting its strategic feats against them all, it bestows on the whole body of the Church a profound and undisturbed peace, and secures for the whole commonwealth a similar and like concord,[48] having set up an eternal monument of the orthodoxy of our truly pious and victorious Emperors Michael and Basil for all generations to come.

5. Happy, therefore, and thrice-blessed are you also, choir of patricians, honorable and reverend old men, who were picked to share the command of such great generals and captains against so great and so many heresies, and have taken part in bearing these sacred and holy labours. As for you, O holy gathering of priests and bishops, why stand you so silent, and resemble, as it were, in the effusion of your excessive pleasure and joy, men who are amazed and in ecstasy, fixing your eyes and your mind itself on nothing else but the very joyfulness of the deeds? For great joy, like sorrow, though the two are diametrically opposed, are wont to produce the same disposition in those they come upon. Nay, but utter a sound

---

[47] Read καὶ πλέον οὐκ εἶχε τέρπειν [οὐκ omitted by Ar].
[48] παραπλησίαν δὲ τὴν ὁμοφροσύνην καὶ ὁμοίαν is read by all the MSS. Ar has changed ὁμοίαν to ὁμόνοιαν.

worthy of the festival, and setting David, the ancestor of God, at the head of your choir, cry out clear and loud, "Bend *the bow*, prosper and reign, O admirable pair, in whom the grace of the Trinity dwells. Bend *the bow* and prosper and reign, because of truth and meekness and righteousness."[49] Amen.

[49] Ps. 44. 5.

Addendum

A microfilm of the Buchar. 595, pp. 73–87 (Homily IX), procured through the kind offices of the Institutul Romîn pentru Relațile Culturale cu Străinătatea, reached me too late to be used for the textual notes. The Buchar. 595 belongs to the same recension as the Monac. 443, Vat. Reg. gr. 15 and Chalc. 1, being closest to the Chalc. 1. For the purposes of our translation, the variants of the Buchar. 595 are of no consequence. For the sake of completeness, the following may be noted:

p. 166, n. 4: ἧς γὰρ νηδὺς ἄγονος
p. 166, n. 5: δι' ὧν τερατουργεῖται
p. 169, n. 21: τὰ μὲν παρὰ φύσιν καὶ ἃ μηδοστισοῦν (sic) τρόποις (sic) συγκροτήσειεν, ταῦτα τιμᾶν καὶ θαυμάζειν· ἃ δὲ πολλῷ κρεῖσσον καὶ λόγου καὶ φύσεως καὶ ἀνέσεως, etc.
p. 169, n. 22: νεότης οὕτω (sic) ἡβάσκουσα
p. 170, n. 25: καὶ τοῦ καιροῦ μήπω παραστάντος, καὶ χειρόνων ὄντων, etc.
p. 171, n. 33: ὕμνει σου
p. 176, n. 50: καὶ εἰ καὶ ἀ⟨χ⟩ρήστῳ.

INDEX

Abbreviations

A	= Iviron 684.
Ar	= S. Aristarches, Τοῦ ἐν ἁγίοις πατρὸς ἡμῶν Φωτίου .... λόγοι καὶ ὁμιλίαι ὀγδοήκοντα τρεῖς, 2 vols., Constantinople, 1900.
B	= Metochion Panagiou Taphou 529.
BZ	= *Byzantinische Zeitschrift* (1892–).
KL	= G. P. Kournoutos and B. Laourdas in Θεολογία, XXV 2 (1954), pp. 177–99.
Lig	= Excerpts of Paisios Ligarides, Paris, Suppl. gr. 286.
Mansi	= Mansi, *Sacrorum Conciliorum nova et amplissima collectio*, Florence, Venice, 1759–98.
MGH	= *Monumenta Germaniae historica* (1826–).
Müller	= C. Müller, *Fragmenta historicorum graecorum*, V, Paris, 1883.
Nauck	= A. Nauck, *Lexicon Vindobonense*, St. Petersburg, 1867.
Uspenskij	= P. Uspenskij, Четыре бесѣды Фотія. St. Petersburg, 1864.
Pg	= P. N. Papageorgiou, ῾Υπόμνημα εἰς Φωτίου τοῦ πατριάρχου ὁμιλίας κριτικόν, I–II, Leipzig, 1901.
PG	= Migne, *Patrologia graeca*, Paris, 1857–66.
PL	= Migne, *Patrologia latina*, Paris, 1844–55.
Šest.	= Review of Ar by S. Šestakov in *Viz. Vrem.*, IX (1902), pp. 512–45.
Theoph. Cont.	= Theophanes Continuatus, ed. Bekker, Bonn, 1838.
Viz. Vrem.	= Византійскій Временникъ (1893–).

Index

Aaron, 49, 119
Abiron, 49
Abiud, 49
Abraham, 62, 92–94
Acacius, Bishop of Caesarea, 238–39, 269, 271 n. 35, 272–73
Acathistos Hymn, 82, 112
Achillas, Bishop of Alexandria, 245
Acta Pilati, 280
Adam, 115, 121, 142, 160, 167, 171–73, 214, 253
Aeacus, 168 n. 19
Aetius, heretic, 238, 269 n. 26, 272 n. 41, 274, 275 n. 51
Alexander, Byzantine emperor, 179
Alexander, Bishop of Alexandria, 245–46, 248
Alexander, Bishop of Constantinople, 244–45, 255 n. 40, 267 n. 19, 268 n. 21
Alexandria, 254, 257, 263; parish of Baucalis, 245 n. 6
Alexis, Czar, 14–16
Amphion, Bishop of Nicomedia, 247 n. 13
Amyclas, 170 n. 27
Ananias, 50
Anastasius Bibliothecarius, 299
Anastasius Sinaita, 152
Ancyra, 179; church of St. Clement, 182
Andrew of Crete, St., 111–12
anhomoeos, 265
Anna, 166–67, 175
Antioch, 250, 256–57, 274; cathedral, 262
Antiochene Creeds: First, 264 n. 14; Second (Dedication Creed), 266 n. 15, 272 n. 39; Fourth, 263 n. 12, 266 n. 15, 267 n. 18, 272 n. 36; Fifth (Macrostich), 237, 267
Anzen, battle of, 79
Apollinarians, 279

Apollo, 170 n. 27, 28, 30
Apollodorus, 163 n. 14
Arabs, 4, 76, 78 n. 16, 79, 80, 81 n. 27, 89 n. 42, 179, 180; raid on Proconnesus, 81 n. 27
Arethas of Caesarea, 10, 162 n. 9, 164
Arianism, 236 sq., 279, 310 n. 20
Arion, 170 n. 32
Aristarches, S., 6, 7, 18, 20, 21, 25, 26, 36, 40, 111, 191, 236, 284, 297
Aristenus, canonist, 281
Aristotle, 163
Arius, 236–37, 240, 244–46, 248 n. 14, 250, 254 n. 38, 264, 274, 309
Arsaber, patrician, 241
Arsenius, Bishop of Hypsele, 250 n. 23, 251 n. 25, 252–53
Artemis, 170 n. 28
Ascension, lost homily on, 5, 33
Asclepas, Bishop of Gaza, 270
Asia, 91
Askold and Dir, Russian princes, 91 n. 59
Athanasius, St., 237, 243, 245 n. 7, 248, 250–54, 256–57, 263, 267 n. 18, 269 n. 26, 270–71; *Apologia contra Arianos*, 237; *Apologia de fuga*, 257 n. 47; *De synodis*, 237; *Oratio IV contra Arianos*, 305 n. 40; *Life of*, 237
Athingani, 152, 282
Augustus, 308
Avar raid in 619, 80 n. 23, 81 n. 27

Baanes, minister of Basil I, 298
Baghdad, 242
Balaam, 139, 188
Bardas, Caesar, 4, 5 n. 4, 20, 163, 179–80, 189–90, 306
Barvoetius, 33–34
Basil I, emperor, 4, 5, 9, 19, 152, 178–80, 183, 222, 279, 284 n. 30,

INDEX

285, 289 n. 18, 297–99, 301, 303, 306, 311, 314
Basil, Bishop of Ancyra, 239, 268 n. 21, 269, 271 n. 35, 272, 273 n. 43, 44
Basil, St., 221, 273 n. 42
Basil of Neopatrae, 152
Basil of Seleucia, 112
Berytus, 255, 262
Bethany, 153
Bethlehem, 209
Bigot, Emeric, 17
Bithynia, 255
Boris, King of Bulgaria, 4, 180
Brussels Chronicle, 75, 76, 78, 79
Bulgaria, 4, 21, 22, 150–51, 179, 221, 300, 302, 304; Bulgarians, 282
Bury, J. B., 222, 302
Busbecq, Augier Ghislain de, 11

Cadmus, 168 n. 15
Caesar, rank of, 179
Caesarea in Palestine, 251
Cain, 48
Cantacuzenus, Constantine, 16
catechism (*catechesis*), 38–40, 41, 55, 123
catenae, 6, 7
Cedrenus, Georgius, 12 n. 31, 76, 79
Cephas, 276
Ceyx, 170 n. 31
chairetismoi, 82, 111–12
Cherubim, 72, 116, 217
Chios, 13; Nea Moni, 182
Christ, relics of, 183; Pantocrator, iconographic type, 182
Classical revival in the ninth century, 161–64
Combefis, F., 12, 17, 30, 191
Constans I, emperor, 255–56, 262, 263 n. 12, 266 n. 15, 267 n. 20, 269
Constantia, wife of Licinius, 247 n. 13, 251 n. 26, 261
Constantine I, emperor, 245 n. 7, 247, 249–50, 251 n. 28, 270 n. 31; baptism and death, 239, 255; testament of, 261–62; body moved from church of Apostles, 275
Constantine II, emperor, 261, 263 n. 13

Constantine V, emperor, 180 n. 23, 181
Constantine VII, emperor: *Book of Ceremonies*, 38, 138
Constantine, pupil of Leo the Mathematician, 162 n. 5
Constantine, son of Basil I, 179–80, 183 n. 38
Constantine and Methodius, saints, 4, 152
Constantine of Tius, 112
Constantine Rhodius, 162 n. 9
Constantinople, *passim*; attacked by the Avars in 619, *see* Avar raid; attacked by the Russians in 860 and 941, *see* Russians; besieged by the Turks in 1422, 10, 82. Churches: St. Acacius, 275 n. 52; H. Apostles, 275 n. 52; St. Irene, 4, 38, 39, 41, 55, 124, 244 n. 2; St. Mary of the Blachernae, 76, 81 n. 27, 102 n. 29; St. Mary Chalkoprateia, 138; St. Mary of the Pharos, 177–190; mosaics, 182–83, 187–88, 283; Nea (New Church), 177–78, 183; St. Sophia (Great Church), 92, 138, 139 n. 4, 140 n. 6, 183, 185 n. 7, 230, 244, 260, 286 sq., 304, 306, 308 n. 13; image of the Virgin, 279, 282 sq.; inscriptions, 284–85, 297 n. 6; *metatorion*, 138. Deuteron quarter, 5 n. 4. Monasteries: St. Mary Hodegetria, 241–42; St. Mary of the Source, 183 n. 38; Monastery of Kauleas, 183; SS. Sergius and Bacchus, 241–42; Monastery of Stylianus Zaoutzes, 182. Great Palace, 177, 180, 184–85; Chalke gate, 283; Chrysotriklinos, 183, 283. University, 161–62, 306
Constantius II, emperor, 236–37, 255–57, 261–63, 267 n. 19, 20, 268–69, 272 n. 37, 38, 273, 274 n. 45, 275
Cosmas of Maiuma, 192
Councils: Antioch (338–39), 263 n. 11; Antioch *in encaeniis* (341), 237, 262–64, 266, 280; Antioch

320

INDEX

(356), 270 n. 27; Ariminum (Rimini, 359), 272; Caesarea (334), 251; Chalcedon, IV Oecum. (451), 310 n. 23, 312; Constantinople (336), 254 n. 38; Constantinople (360), 237–38, 267 n. 20, 272, 273 n. 42, 44, 274 n. 45, 275 n. 51; Constantinople, II Oecum. (381), 22, 24 n. 76, 236, 247, 271, 279–80, 310 n. 21, 312; Constantinople, V Oecum. (553), 310 n. 27; Constantinople, VI Oecum. (680), 310 n. 25; Constantinople, *in Trullo* (692), 279–80; Constantinople (843), 303; Constantinople, at St. Irene (859), 4; Constantinople, at H. Apostles (859), 4; Constantinople (861), 4, 19–20, 22–23, 25, 28, 81, 124, 303; Constantinople, local (867), 4, 300; Constantinople (867), 4–5, 9, 22, 298 sq.; Constantinople (869–70), 5 n. 5, 179 n. 10, 298–99, 300 n. 22; Constantinople (879–80), 179 n. 11, 180, 300 n. 22, 303–04; Constantinople (1166), 297 n. 6; Corduba (after 343), 238, 271; Ephesus, III Oecum. (431), 280, 310 n. 22, 312; Hiereia (754), 251 n. 26; Jerusalem (335), 245 n. 7, 254 n. 38, 263 n. 10; Jerusalem (346), 271; Laodicea, 38, 280; Nicaea, I Oecum. (325), 236, 247–49, 254 n. 37, 256 n. 42, 264–65, 270 n. 27, 28, 31, 32, 280, 288, 310 n. 20, 311–12; Nicaea, VII Oecum. (787), 265, 300, 302–04, 310 n. 28; Nike (359), 272; Philippopolis (343), 237–38, 256 n. 43, 269–70; Rimini, *see* Ariminum; Rome (340), 270 n. 28; Rome (863), 4; Sardica (343), 237–38, 255–56, 263 n. 9, 10, 12, 267 n. 20, 268–71; Seleucia (359), 272, 273 n. 44, 275 n. 49; Sirmium (351–359), 270 n. 31, 271–72; Tyre (335), 237, 251–54, 263 n. 10
Cramer, J. A., 6
Croesus, 53
Crusius, Martin, 11
Cycnus, 170 n. 30
Cyril of Jerusalem, St., 271, 273
Cyrus, 308
Cyzicus, 274, 275 n. 51

Daphne, nymph, 170 n. 27
Dathan, 49
David, prophet, 47, 50, 51, 58, 71, 88, 113, 119, 139, 142, 143, 155, 182, 188, 292, 295, 314–15
Delmatius, censor, 250, 251 n. 25, 252 n. 32
Delos, 170 n. 28
Democritus, 187
Demophilus, bishop of Berea, 267 n. 17
Deucalion and Pyrrha, 168 n. 18
Dionysius IV, Patriarch of Constantinople, 25
Dioscorus, heretic, 310
Dorotheus, Metropolitan of Mitylene, 10, 82
Dositheus, Patriarch of Jerusalem, 297 n. 6
Dousa, George, 11

Earthquakes: in 862–865, 5 n. 4; on Jan. 9, 869, 284 n. 30
Easter, date of, 279–81, 288
Egypt, Egyptians, 49, 108, 213, 231, 313
ekphrasis, 189
Eleusius, Bishop of Cyzicus, 239, 272 n. 41, 275
Elias of Crete, exegete, 222 n. 10
Elijah, prophet, 178
Elisha, 259
Elizabeth, 120
Elzevier, 17
Enalos, 170 n. 32
encomium, secular, 305–06
Engelberta, wife of Lewis II, 301
Epiphanius, St., 239, 280; pseudo-Epiphanius, 192
Eudoxius, Bishop of Germanicia, 267, 274
Eunomius, Bishop of Cyzicus, 238, 274, 275 n. 51
Euphemia, St., 112

INDEX

Euphratas, Bishop of Cologne, 256–57
Euphronius, Bishop of Antioch, 263
Europa, 171 n. 35
Europe, 91
Eusebia, empress, 274 n. 47
Eusebius, Bishop of Caesarea, 248 n. 17, 251
Eusebius, Bishop of Nicomedia, 245 n. 7, 247, 248 n. 17, 249, 250 n. 24, 251, 254–55, 261 n. 2, 262–63, 267, 274 n. 47
Eustathius, Bishop of Antioch, 237, 243, 248–50, 256 n. 43, 257
Eustathius, Bishop of Sebaste, 239, 272 n. 41, 273, 274 n. 45
Euthymius, Patriarch of Constantinople, 9
Eutocius, Constantia's chaplain, 261–62
Eutyches, heretic, 310 n. 23
Eve, 112, 142, 144, 167, 171–73, 214

Filioque, doctrine of, 21–23, 237, 302, 304
Flacillus, Bishop of Antioch, 263
Forty-two martyrs of Amorium, 151

Gabriel, archangel, 111, 113, 121, 141, 143, 146, 178
Galilee, 113
Gaudentius, Bishop of Naissus, 270
Gaul, 262
Gelasius of Cyzicus, 237
Genesius, chronicler, 79
George, Bishop of Nicomedia, 8, 81–82, 111, 163, 192
Gerlach, Stephan, 11
Germanicia, 274
Germanus, Patriarch of Constantinople, 111
Graevius, J., 14–15, 17 n. 48
Greeks, 129
Grégoire, Henri, 79
Gregory Asbestas, 152
Gregory of Antioch, 192
Gregory of Cappadocia, Bishop of Alexandria, 263, 270
Gregory the Wonderworker, St., 111
Grumel, V., 303

Hadrian II, Pope, 299
Halcyone, 170 n. 31
Hase, C. B., 17
Heinsius, Nicholas, 14–17
Heliades, 170 n. 26
Heliodorus, Libyan bishop, 274
Hera, 170 n. 31, 171 n. 34
Heracleia, 263
Hergenröther, J., 6, 297
Hermogenes, general, 267 n. 19
Hesychius of Jerusalem, 111 n. 6
Hezekiah, 59
Hierax, Alexander Constantine, 11–12, 25–26
Hierax, Constantine, 11, 12 n. 31
Hoeschel, David, 12
Homeric students, 68
homoeos, 265, 272 n. 41
homoeousios, 265, 272 n. 36, 41
homoousios, 240, 264–66, 270, 272
Hosius, *see* Ossius
Hylilas, epithet of John the Grammarian, 241 n. 31
Hypselis (Hypsele) in the Thebaid, 253

Iconoclasm, Iconoclasts, 3, 20, 22, 139 n. 4, 152, 192, 239–40, 242–43, 247, 264–66, 282–85, 287, 289–91, 294–95, 302, 310 n. 28
Icons, restoration of, 138, 139 n. 4, 283–84
Ierotheus, metropolitan of Monembasia, 26 n. 86
Ignatius, Patriarch of Constantinople, 3–5, 9, 19–20, 76, 123–24; Ignatians, 19, 123–24, 192, 222
Illyrians, 257; Illyricum, 269
Immaculate Conception, doctrine of, 112
Irene, empress, 283
Isaac, 167
Isaiah, prophet, 46, 48, 103, 117, 156, 293
Isaurian dynasty, 283, 287 n. 6, 289 n. 16, 291
Ischyras, priest, 254 n. 36
Israel, Israelites, 49, 106, 108–09, 139, 258, 313–14. *See also* Jews

INDEX

Italy, 262, 267
Ivantsov-Platonov, A. M., 297
Iviron monastery, *see* Mount Athos

Jacob, 84, 139, 182, 188
Jacob, heretic, 282
Jacob Kokkinobaphos, 173 n. 44
Jacob of Vatopedi, monk, 25
Jason, 168 n. 15
Jeremiah, 84, 94
Jernstedt, V. K., 28
Jerusalem, 13, 16, 21, 84, 90, 92, 109; temple, 188, 196; Holy Sepulchre, 209, 249, 251 n. 28
Jews, 43, 49 n. 81, 87, 103, 153, 155, 159, 164–68, 195–99, 201–07, 209, 216–18, 231, 280–81, 288, 290–91; anti-Jewish polemics, 151–53; Jews in Bulgaria and South Russia, 151 n. 6
Jezebel, 226
Joachim, 166, 175
Job, 48
John the Baptist, St., 213
John the Evangelist, St., 279
John VIII, Pope, 179 n. 12
John VII the Grammarian, Patriarch of Constantinople, 162, 240–43, 246
John Archaph, Bishop of Memphis, 252 n. 32
John Climacus, St., 221
John Chrysostom, St., 14, 281
John of Damascus, St., 192, 243
Joseph, 113
Joseph of Arimathea, 191–92, 198–202, 217
Jovian, emperor, 238
Judas, 244
Jugie, M., 21
Julian, emperor, 164, 275
Julius I, Pope, 263, 267 n. 20, 270

Katefaros, Antonios, 31
kenosis, 213 n. 3
Kiev, 15–16; monastery of the Brotherhood, 15, 17; St. Sophia, 182
Koiranos, 170 n. 32
Kournoutos, G. P., 36
Kunik, A. A., 17

Ladon, 170 n. 27
Lamanskij, V., 79
Lambeck, Peter, 12, 32, 177
Laourdas, B., 36
Latona, 170 n. 28
Lazarus, 59, 153, 157, 165, 194, 216
Lazarus, beggar, 61, 130–31
Lazarus, painter, 283
Lent, rites of, 220–21
Leo I, emperor, 102 n. 29
Leo III, emperor, 240 n. 22
Leo V, emperor, 240–41, 243, 287 n. 6
Leo VI, emperor, 8, 75 n. 3, 179, 182; *Funeral Oration*, 305
Leo Choirosphactes, 24, 162, 164
Leo the Mathematician, Bishop of Thessalonica, 5 n. 4, 161–62
Leontius, Bishop of Antioch, 257, 274 n. 45, 49
Lewis II, western emperor, 301
Liberius, Pope, 267 n. 17
Libya, 91
Licinius, emperor, 261
Ligarides, Paisios, 12–17, 28
Lindanus, Guill., 32, 34
Lucifer, 228
Lucius, bishop of Adrianople, 270
Lydia, 281

Macarius, deacon of Athanasius, 254 n. 36
Macarius, Patriarch of Antioch, 14
Macedonius, Bishop of Constantinople, 22, 237, 267–68, 273 n. 43, 275, 304, 309; Macedonian heresy, 236, 268 n. 21, 279, 310 n. 21
Macedonius, Bishop of Mopsuestia, 267
Macrostich Creed, *see* Antiochene Creeds
Mai, A., 32
Malachi, prophet, 44
Manichaeans, 239, 297
Manuel I, emperor, 297 n. 6
Manuscripts of the Homilies: *Athen. 2449*, 31; *Athen. 2756*, 18, 23 n. 75, 27–28, 191, 220; *Bucharest gr. 595*, 31, 316; *Chalki, Camariot. 1*, 9, 31, 316; *Chalki, Camariot. 64*, 30;

21*   323

INDEX

Escorial MS (lost), 5, 32–34; *Heidelberg, Palat. gr. 129*, 29; *Jerusalem, Gr. Patr. 1*, 30, 236; *Metochion Panagiou Taphou 529*, 11, 13 n. 34, 18, 26–27; *Moscow MS* (lost), 15–18; *Mount Athos, Iviron 684*, 10—11, 16, 18, 24–26; *Munich, gr. 443*, 9, 31, 316; *Naples, gr. III. A. A. 6*, 31–32, 177; *Paris, Coisl. 107*, 9, 30, 191; *Paris, Suppl. gr. 286*, 28–29; *Rome, Vat. gr. 759*, 32, 191; *Rome, Vat. Reg. gr. 15*, 30–31, 316; *Suprasliensis*, 32, 150–51. Other manuscripts: *Athen. 1474*, 11 n. 29; *Brussels 19 (14870)*, 11 n. 29, 12; *Chalki, Camariot. 175*, 304 n. 36; *Dresden D. a 43. E*, 27 n. 88; *Escor. y.–III.–10*, 304; *Jerusalem, Sabait. 232*, 7; *Metochion 252*, 26 n. 86; *Metochion 339*, 11 n. 29; *Metochion 363, ibid.*; *Metochion 415, ibid.*; *Metochion 520, ibid.*; *Mount Athos, Esphigmenou 2277. 264, ibid.*; *Mount Athos, Vatopedi 869*, 39; *Munich, gr. 297*, 221, 222 n. 10; *Nürnberg* (Chronicle of Cedrenus, unnumbered), 12 n. 31; *Oxford, Barocc. gr. 217*, 10; *Paris, gr. 2420 and 2424*, 162 n. 6; *Paris, Coisl. 87*, 222 n. 10; *Paris, Suppl. gr. 471*, 12 n. 31; *Rome, Barb. gr. 336*, 39, 40, 123; *Sinait. 959*, 39

Marcellus, Bishop of Ancyra, 266, 267 n. 18, 269 n. 26, 270; Marcellianism, 305 n. 40

Marcionites, 239

Mareotis, 250 n. 23, 254

Maria, lake, 254

Margounios, Maximos, 12

Martha, sister of Lazarus, 59

Martyrius, bishop, 267

Mary, sister of Lazarus, 59

Mavropotamon, river, 76, 80

Maximian, emperor, 263 n. 9

Maximin Daza, 245 n. 4

Maximus IV, Patriarch of Constantinople, 11

Maximus, Bishop of Jerusalem, 263, 271

Mazarin, cardinal, 30, 191

Medianitish woman, 313

Meletius of Lycopolis, 252 n. 32; Meletians, 245 n. 4, 248 n. 14, 16, 252

Melitene, Emir of, 282

Mendoza, Diego Hurtado de, 32

Menophantus, Bishop of Ephesus, 270

Mesarites, Nicholas, 183

Methodius, St., apostle of the Slavs, *see* Constantine and Methodius

Metochites, Theodore, 31 n. 104

Metrophanes and Alexander, *Life* of, 237

Michael I, emperor, 152, 241

Michael II, emperor, 152, 242, 281

Michael III, emperor, 4–5, 9, 19, 76–77, 79–80, 86 n. 22, 124, 138, 179, 181, 183–85, 188 n. 21, 189, 222, 279, 282, 285, 289 n. 18, 297–99, 301–03, 305–09, 311–14; date of birth, 309 n. 17

Michael Syncellus, St., 21–22

Miller, E., 17

Monarchianism, 266 n. 16

Monophysitism, 310 n. 23

Monothelites, 310 n. 25

Montanists, 239, 280

Montfaucon, Bernard de, 17

Mopsucrenae, 275

Morocharzamioi, family, 241–42

Moscow, 14–16; Simonovskij monastery, 15, 17; Synodal Library, 17; Voskresenskij monastery, 16

Moses, 49, 92–94, 108, 188, 209, 313

Mount Athos, Iviron monastery, 16–17, 25

Müller, K. K., 29, 297

mythological fables, 161, 168, 170–71

Naboth, 226

Nadab, 49

Nauck, A., 18

Nazareth, 113

Nectarius, Patriarch of Jerusalem, 14

Neoplatonism, 163

Nestorius, heretic, 309; Nestorianism, 280, 310 n. 22

Nicaea, 161 n. 2, 179

INDEX

Nicephorus, Patriarch of Constantinople, 152, 240–41, 243, 246, 251 n. 26, 282
Nicephorus Blemmydes, 25, 26 n. 86
Nicetas Paphlagon, 75–76
Nicholas I, Pope, 4–5, 9, 20, 40, 78 n. 16, 299, 301
Nicodemus, Gospel of, 191
Nikon, Patriarch of Moscow, 14
Ninevites, 50
Noah, 148, 209
Nomocanon, 13
Normans, 78 n. 16
Novatianism, Novatians, 273, 275 n. 51, 279–81

Olympus, 171
Onager, associate of Stephen of Antioch, 257
Oriental Patriarchs at Council of 867, 299–301; Letter of to Theophilus, 243
Origenist heresy, 281 n. 17, 310 n. 27
Orion, 44
Orpheus, 186
Orthodoxy, Feast of, 236, 285–86, 297
Oryphas, prefect, 76, 80
Ossius (Hosius), Bishop of Cordova, 238, 270–71
ousia, 238, 265

Paisios, Patriarch of Jerusalem, 13
Paneas, statue of Christ at, 251 n. 26
Pankratios, father of John the Grammarian, 241
Papadopoulos-Kerameus, A., 7, 11, 25–26, 30, 81
Papageorgiou, P. N., 29, 36
Paris, Bibliothèque Nationale, 17; Saint-Germain-des-Prés, 17
Parrhasius, 187
Parthenius, monk, see Petraşcu
Paul, Bishop of Constantinople, 255, 257, 262, 267, 270; *Life* of, 237
Paul of Alexandria, astrologer, 162 n. 6
Paul of Samosata, 266 n. 16
Paul, St., 41–42, 133–35, 154, 163, 211, 224, 231, 249, 276

Paulicians, 282
Peneus, river-god, 170 n. 27
Peter, Bishop of Alexandria, 245
Peter, St., 40, 50, 59, 163, 312
Peter Cercel, Prince of Wallachia, 26, 27 n. 88
Peter of Laodicea, commentator, 7
Petraşcu, son of Peter Cercel, 26–27
Pharaoh, 49, 58, 108
Pharisees, 202
Pheidias, 187
Philadelphia in Lydia, 280
Philip, prefect of the East, 267 n. 20
Philippi, 250, 269
Philostorgius, 237–38
Philumenus, rebel, 250 n. 23
Phinees, 50, 313–14
Photinus, Bishop of Sirmium, 266
Photius, *passim*; summary of first patriarchate, 3–5; *Amphilochia*, 6, 26, 28, 40, 191, 236; *Bibliotheca*, 6, 7, 12, 163, 236–37; *Catena* on Luke, 191; Commentaries on Bible, 7–8; *Contra Manichaeos*, 6, 236; Encomium of St. Thekla, 6; Fragment on Last Judgment, 6; Letters, 6, 10, 14, 25–28, 30, 40, 191; Letter to archbishop of Aquileia, 22; Letter to Syncellus of Antioch, 25, 28; Letter to Bardas, 20; Letter to Boris of Bulgaria, 236; Letter to archbishop of Kerch, 152; Letters to Pope Nicholas I, 20, 23 n. 75, 25, 28, 259 n. 52; Encyclical Letter to Oriental Patriarchs, 4, 22, 74 n. 2, 300; *Mystagogia*, 21–22, 236; Scholia on St. John Climacus (dubious), 221–22
Pigafetta, Marco Antonio, traveller, 297 n. 6
Pilate, 191, 198–99, 202, 205, 217
Pinnes, Egyptian abbot, 252 n. 32
Planudes, Maximus, 29
Plato, 163, 282
Porphyry, philosopher, 164
Praxiteles, 187
Princes' Islands, 76
Procne and Philomela, 170 n. 29
Proconnesus, 81 n. 27

INDEX

Protoevangelium of James, 111
Protogenes, Bishop of Sardica, 270

Quartodecimans, *see* Tessareskaidekatitai

Rader, M., 221
Radoald, Papal legate, 4
Rhaedestus, 11 n. 27
Rhos' (Russians), 74, 98 n. 13
Romans (= Byzantines), 97
Romanus Melodus, 112
Rome, Greek College, 13; St. Peter's 299
Russians, 4; Russian embassy to Constantinople in 838, 98 n. 13; alleged Russian raids before 842, 74 n. 2, 98 n. 13; Russian attack on Constantinople in 860, 74 sq.; Russian attack on Constantinople in 941, 81 n. 27

Sabbatians, 280–81
Sabellius, heretic, 22, 266, 276; Sabellianism, Sabellians, 248 n. 17, 250, 267 n. 18, 304
Salianus (Flavius Salia), general, 256–57
Sangarius, river, 80
Sapphira, 50
Saracens, *see* Arabs
Sarah, 167
Scythians, 89
Secontarurus, village, 254 n. 36
Séguier, chancellor, 191
Selymbria, 179 n. 17
Serras, Libyan bishop, 274
Serres, monastery of St. John, 31
Šestakov, S., 27, 36, 284–85
Sevast'janov, P. I., 18
Severians, 281 n. 17
Silvanus, Bishop of Tarsus, 239, 272 n. 41, 273
Silvester, Pope, 256 n. 42
Sins, seven deadly, 50 n. 93
Socrates, Church historian, 237–38, 269
Sodom, Sodomites, 19, 40, 49, 87
Solomon, 188

Sophronius of Damascus, 112
soughîthâ, 111
Sozomen, 237–38, 269
Spatharios, Nicholas, dragoman, 15–16
Stephen, Bishop of Antioch, 237, 256–57, 267 n. 18
Stephen, Libyan bishop, 274
Stephen Petriceicu, Prince of Moldavia, 26
Sthenelos, 170 n. 30
Studite monks, 123–24
Stylianus Zaoutzes, 182
Suchanov, Arsenij, 13, 16
Sun (Helios), 170 n. 26
Symeon, King of Bulgaria, 151
Symeon Logothete, chronicler, 76, 78, 80, 180
Symeon Metaphrastes, 192
Symeon (pseudo-), chronicler, 5 n. 4, 81 n. 27, 178
Synaxarium of Constantinople, 81 n. 27
Synodicon of Orthodoxy, 297 n. 6, 304
Synodicon Vetus, 271 n. 33
Syracuse, 180

Tabari, Arab historian, 79
Tarasius, Patriarch of Constantinople, 8
Tereus, 170 n. 29
Tessareskaidekatitai, heretics, 279–82, 288–89
Tetraditai, heretics, 281–82
Theodora, empress, wife of Theophilus, 242, 283, 285
Theodore and Theophanes Grapti, saints, 21
Theodore of Edessa, St., *Life* of, 152
Theodore, bishop of Perinthus, 263, 270
Theodore Studite, St., 24; *Catechesis chronica*, 282
Theodoret, 237, 281
Theodotus Cassiteras, Patriarch of Constantinople, 241
Theognis, Bishop of Nicaea, 245 n. 7, 247 n. 13, 254

INDEX

Theognostus, abbot, 124
Theophanes, chronicler, 239, 282
Theophanes Continuatus, 75–76, 78–79
Theophilus, emperor, 98 n. 13, 161, 241–42, 283
Theophilus the Indian, 274
Thrace, 250
Timothy, presbyter, 252
Tiresias, 171
Treveri (Trier), 254
Two souls, doctrine of, 5
Tyche, statue of, 163
Typicon of St. Sophia, 38, 236 n. 2, 286
Tyrophagy week, 220–21, 282

Urim, 197
Uspenskij, F., 242, 297 n. 6
Uspenskij, Porfirij, 18, 25, 292 n. 26, 297

Valentinians, 239
Valverde, 33–34
Vasiliev, A. A., 74, 78 n. 16, 80 n. 24
Vicentius (Vincent), Bishop of Capua, 256
Virgin's robe (*maphorion*), 75, 77, 80 n. 23, 102, 109
Vita Basilii, 178, 305

Xylander, G. (Holzmann), 12 n. 31

Zachary, papal legate, 4
Zachary of Chalcedon, 300–01
Zechariah, 156
Zeus, 168 n. 18, 19, 170 n. 31, 171 n. 34, 35
Zeuxis, 187
Zonaras, 76, 79

www.ingramcontent.com/pod-product-compliance
Lightning Source LLC
Chambersburg PA
CBHW060507300426
44112CB00017B/2577